To Marilou, Anne and Kent

PREFACE

THE GENESIS of a book is rarely of interest to anyone except its author. If this book is an exception, the explanation lies in the fact that by reference to its origin one can best understand its purposes, methodology and limitations. These words are being written after the main body of the book is completed. In reviewing the initial stirring of interest, the development of working hypotheses, the hopes and the disappointments of investigation, I have the opportunity—or perhaps more appropriately, I fulfill the obligation—to assess my efforts before turning to new tasks ahead.

American legal scholarship has only recently discovered Africa. While doubtless sustained in part by the interest and excitement of that discovery, this study grew, not out of a specialized area interest in Africa, but out of a primary concern with some of the perennial problems of legal philosophy. What is law or, more appropriately, what do we mean when we talk about law? Does it imply a necessary value content? If not, what is the source or sources of the value acceptances discernible in various legal orders? How does a particular value acceptance achieve such a degree of articulation and strength that it can call upon the technique of law for support and implementation? And what role has law to play in altering critical value perceptions so that it can be an instrument of planned social change?

My concern with these questions has not prompted an effort to construct a new general theory of law. On the contrary, the existing literature has nurtured a conviction that what is needed is not new theory but a closer study of the law-society interplay, guided by an effort to treat values only as social facts and not as standards of criticism. The philosophical position implicit in such a study is somewhat more fully stated in Chapter VIII. It will suffice here to say that I accept a positivist position on the nature of law; but from that starting position, I want to press certain inquiries that have infrequently at best claimed the interest of the legal positivist. Like the positivist, I am concerned with the description and analysis of existing law. Instead of the common positivistic preoccupation with conceptual analysis and rationalization, however, the focus here is on the pattern of claims or the demands in a particular society that have shaped the positive law and, insofar as this can be determined, the reciprocal effect of that law on the structure, processes and values of the society.

This study deals with the evolution of the legal order in Ghana. Two factors guided this choice. The first was a hope that in the so-called emergent nations some of the critical processes of value choice, which determined the basic orientation of the legal order, would be more easily visible and amenable to study than in the more mature and complex societies. Similarly, since these countries had experienced within relatively recent years radical changes in the elite groups, I also hoped that significant insights could be developed into the use of law as an instrument of planned social change under the guidance of different elites.

Secondly, legal research in the almost virgin systems of the emergent nations seemed to offer the prospect that scholarship could make an immediate, practical contribution to solving pressing problems and meeting urgent needs. Such utility, while surely not the hallmark of valid scholarship, should not be rejected as unworthy of scholarly concern.

Originally I had hoped to find sufficient existing description and analysis of customary legal institutions and colonial innovations in the Gold Coast to establish a base line from which developments under an African government since 1951 could be examined in detail. Unfortunately, this did not prove to be the case. Even older works on traditional government and law reflect changes in customary patterns attributable to the colonial experience. These studies were done largely by anthropologists and sociologists; for legal analysis, the data are usually painfully inadequate. I was not able to undertake new research in an effort to eliminate these deficiencies. Consequently, customary institutions are considered here, in the light of research done by others, only as part of a background survey, with the gaps in the available knowledge noted.

Legal experience under the colonial administration has not been adequately treated in the existing literature. Most of the relevant formal sources are available, however, and these can be supplemented by a number of helpful studies by special commissions of the actual operation of parts of the legal system. The latter lack the sophistication of contemporary empirical research, but they are very useful in revealing the gap between the formal law and actual events. The emphasis of this book is not on the colonial experience, however; that again is summarized in order to establish the 1951 base line.

Legal developments under a responsible African government in the Gold Coast and Ghana since 1951 are the primary subject of this study. During this period, important developments have occurred throughout the spectrum of public and private law. All of these deserve careful analysis within the theoretical framework suggested earlier. The present book is more limited, however, for it deals with those aspects of public law that structure, channel, allocate and control public power and define the role of the citizen in relation to the power structure. Thus, I will deal mainly with constitutional law and the various legal tools that shape the political role of the citizen.

The basic data of the study are constitutions, statutes, judicial decisions, delegated legislation and executive actions. At best, however, these data give a partial picture. They need to be supplemented by systematic factual inquiry to enable one to discern more fully the motive forces behind the making of law and the effects of formal enactments on official actors and on the social group. During two preliminary visits to Ghana, each of a few weeks' duration, and a year and a half of residence there, I sought to meet this need. The result is not totally satisfactory. For several years, Ghana has not been an open society, and the outside investigator is dealt with at arm's length. This is in part attributable to the apologists' concern to avoid unfavorable impressions, in part to the fear of the consequences of candid disclosure of facts or opinions, and, in part at least, to the engaging desire of many Africans to please, to say what the hearer is believed to want to hear. Despite a rigorous effort to achieve objectivity, therefore, I would claim for my own observations no scientific validity. They are impressionistic and at best partial. For general background beyond my own inquiries I have relied on the better newspapers and journals, both in this country and abroad, checking their accuracy as fully as possible.

Anyone writing about Africa today must be content to write history. The pace of change is so rapid that currency may not survive the period required for publication. In these circumstances the only expedient is to choose an arbitrary cutoff date. In this study that date falls in mid-May, 1964. The somewhat erratic flow of material to me since my departure from Ghana on February 12, 1964, creates the risk however that in the final period before the cutoff date some development of significance has been overlooked.

For financial assistance during periods of travel and residence in West Africa I am grateful to the Rockefeller Foundation, the Ford Foundation and the University of Michigan. To the University, and particularly to Dean Allan F. Smith, of the Law School, I am indebted for time free from teaching and committee assignments, without which this book could not have been written.

The entire manuscript was read by Professor Richard A. Falk of Princeton University and Professor Thomas

M. Franck of New York University who made many valuable suggestions. Chapter VII was corrected on a number of vital points as a result of criticisms by Mr. Gordon R. Woodman, my former colleague in the Faculty of Law of the University of Ghana. The thoughtful comments and shrewd questions of my colleagues, Professors Luke K. Cooperrider and Spencer L. Kimball, of the University of Michigan, about parts of the manuscript increase my long-standing indebtedness to them. This is a better book because of this help; its residual defects and inadequacies are however entirely my own.

To many persons in Ghana who have contributed to this book, an acknowledgment of my gratitude would now be only an embarrassment. I am sure they will accept my private thanks, sharing the hope that this study will contribute to an understanding of the problems and the promise of their troubled country.

To Miss Gail Frank, who typed the manuscript and checked all the citations, and to Mrs. Juanita Grundman, who typed and checked the final revisions, go my special thanks.

My wife and son shared with me the unforgettable experience of living and working in Ghana from September, 1962, until my deportation in February, 1964. During that period, thought and discussion about the developments covered by this book were a part of the fabric of our daily lives. My own gratitude to them for their calm judgment and unfailing good cheer is matched only by our joint indebtedness to the people of Ghana who invariably showed us their friendliness and good will.

CONTENTS

xiii

LAW AND
SOCIAL
CHANGE IN
GHANA

INTRODUCTION

THE LAND AND ITS PEOPLE

THROUGHOUT THE post-World War II period of de-
colonization, Ghana has claimed a substantial share of
world attention. The first of the dependent territories
in sub-Saharan Africa to achieve independence, it was
a focus for the hopes and expectations of many who
sought to justify colonialism by the foundations it laid
for orderly, democratic development. Once independent, Ghana has had stable and aggressive political leadership; its image, particularly as projected by Dr.
Nkrumah himself, has become familiar on the international stage. As a consequence, there is a considerable degree of popular awareness of Ghana, even among
those who do not follow developments in Africa with
care. The country, therefore, requires less preliminary
attention than would be appropriate for many of the
new African states.

The only purpose of this brief chapter is to elaborate
slightly an introduction to the land and its people, to
emphasize the special social setting in which the legal
order has developed. For those unfamiliar with the
Gold Coast or Ghana, it will provide a summary historical and geographic outline and a synoptic view of
the economic life of the people.

Ghana, known as the Gold Coast before independence, is situated on the Gulf of Guinea under the western bulge of the continent. Its coastline from west to
east extends between latitude 4½° and 6½° North. The
northern border lies near latitude 11° North, giving the
country a north-south extension of about 420 miles.
The greatest distance from east to west is approximately 334 miles, between longitude 1½° East and
3½° West. The total area of the country is 91,843
square miles, approximately the size of the state of
Oregon. Ghana is bounded on the west by the Ivory
Coast, on the north by Upper Volta, and on the east

3

by the Republic of Togo. Thus, it is surrounded entirely by areas previously under French control, countries in which the imported cultural features are markedly different from Britain's legacy to Ghana.

Most of the coastline of Ghana presents a picture of boiling surf, a few promontories and large sand-filled bays. In the extreme west, and more prominently in the vicinity of Ada and Keta on the delta of the Volta River in the east, large lagoons have been formed. None of the land is particularly high, the maximum elevation of near 3,000 feet being found in the Togo-Akwapim hills which extend from the Togo border in the east in a southwesterly direction to a point about 20 miles north of Accra. The other principal physical feature of the country is the Kwahu Scarp which runs for 180 miles from northwest to southeast, terminating on its connection with the Akwapim hills, about 40 miles north of Accra.

The principal vegetation types of Ghana are the high forest, the savannah-woodland and the coastal scrub and grassland. The coastal scrub and grassland is limited to a narrow strip beginning near Takoradi in the west and extending to the vicinity of Keta in the east. Its maximum width of about 20 miles is found near the eastern extremity. In this coastal strip the rainfall is very low, averaging 33 inches per year and only about 28 inches near Accra.

The high forest, in total area about 25,000 square miles, is in part rain forest, but most is of the moist semi-deciduous type. The rain forest area lies in the southwestern corner of the country, behind a very narrow coastal belt of strand and mangrove—except around Cape Three Points where it reaches the sea. Here, annual rainfall averages between 70 and 86 inches. The moist semi-deciduous forest reaches a point almost 200 miles north of the coast in the west and follows a northwest to southeast line along the Kwahu Scarp to the Togo-Akwapim hills in the east. In this forest area the average annual rainfall varies between 50 and 70 inches.

To the north of the Kwahu Scarp and in the south-eastern part of the country down to the margin of the coastal scrub and grassland is the savannah-woodland, covering an area of about 65,000 square miles. Short, widely spaced trees are scattered across a more or less continuous grass carpet. Throughout most of the area, almost all of the average annual rainfall (between 40 and 50 inches) occurs during a heavy rainy season in August and September. The dry season, lasting most of the year, is intense, and the soil becomes so baked that there is a substantial run-off of the rains, particularly at the beginning of the rainy season.

Almost all of the people of Ghana are Negroes; the significant diversity is ethnic. The Akans, occupying most of the former Colony and Ashanti areas, are the principal linguistic group. They may be subdivided into the Fanti- and Twi-speaking groups. The grassy plains around Accra are the home of the Ga people. East of the Volta River in the southeast corner of the country are the Ewe-speaking people, who also make up a large part of the population of Togo and Dahomey. The greater part of the savannah lands of the north are occupied by people speaking various forms of the Moshi-Dagomba language. In a large crescent-shaped area between the Moshi-Dagomba regions and Ashanti, on the Afram plains to the east of Ashanti and along the range of Togo-Akwapim hills as far west as Winneba (25 miles to the west of Accra), the Guan language is now spoken or is known to have been spoken. It appears, however, that the Guan language is tending to die out in the intercourse with those who speak Twi, Fanti or Ewe. Certain other ethnic diversities are considered more fully in later chapters.

European contact with the Guinea coast began early in the fifteenth century. The first to arrive were the Portuguese, and in the centuries that followed, the English, French, Dutch, Swedes, Danes and Brandenburgers competed for footholds on the Guinea coast from which to pursue their trading activities. The pattern of contact and exploitation was fairly uniform. The European traders established coastal fortified posts, many of which remain today, and developed working relations with the chiefs and people of the surrounding area. European guns, cloth and spirits were traded for slaves, gold, ivory and pepper. Trade was not limited to the people in the immediate environs of the forts, however. Native traders from far in the interior brought their human, or other, cargoes to the coast to trade with the Europeans. As the region's early name indicated, gold was an important export, as it is today. Through the dark period of the slave trade, however, enormous numbers of Africans were sold at the forts and loaded aboard ships bound for the new world.

Missionary activity was long a prominent feature of the European contact with the Gold Coast. The early explorer-traders saw themselves as the bearers of Christianity and civilization to the pagan people. Organized missionary activity, distinct from that of the early explorer-traders, began around the middle of the eighteenth century with the arrival of representatives of the Society for the Propagation of the Gospel. The Basel missionaries arrived in 1827, the Methodists in 1833, the Breman group in 1847 and in 1881, the first Catholic missionaries since the fifteenth-century Portuguese. Beyond their religious instruction, the missionaries for many years carried on almost all educational activity in the Gold Coast. Even though government support of education has increased over the years, particularly since independence, church-connected schools continue to represent a major segment of the educational establishment of Ghana. Despite the long activity of mission groups, as of 1964, of the population aged 15 and over, only about 42.8 per cent of the population are Christian; the remainder are Muslims (12 per cent) or animists (38.2 per cent).

By the middle of the nineteenth century, the English

had succeeded in excluding their European rivals from the Gold Coast. English attitudes toward the assumption of responsibilities on the Coast remained ambivalent, and until the Gold Coast Colony was established in 1874, responsibility for British interests vacillated between governmental and private hands. The pattern of contact remained fairly consistent, however. Effective control was exercised only over the coastal forts and the immediately surrounding areas. Various associations of the native states in the Colony area gradually developed patterns of reliance upon British supervision or influence over wider areas. In the interior, however, British influence was minimal. In the latter half of the nineteenth century, several wars were fought by the British and their native allies in the Colony to restrain the incursions of the Ashantis. In 1901, after the last Ashanti war, Ashanti became a British protectorate; that same year, after the conclusion of agreements with a number of the chiefs, the area to the north of Ashanti also became a protectorate. The remainder of the territory of modern Ghana, lying east of the Volta River, was included in the independent country after a plebiscite conducted in 1956 under United Nations auspices. This area had been administered by the British under a League of Nations mandate and later a UN trusteeship.

Nationalistic movements in the Gold Coast were relatively moderate until the period of rapid political awakening which followed World War II. Postwar dissatisfactions led to a new constitution for the Gold Coast in 1946, another in 1950 and further modifications in 1954, with the final grant of independence in 1957. Acceleration of the drive toward independence was stimulated by the return of the young Kwame Nkrumah to the Gold Coast in December, 1947. He was brought back after ten years of study in the United States and England by the leaders of the United Gold Coast Convention to serve as secretary of the Convention; however, his differences with the older and more conservative leaders on the methods and the objectives of the movement led to a parting of the ways and to Nkrumah's organization of the Convention People's Party in 1949. After the elections under the Coussey Constitution of 1950, Nkrumah was released from prison, where he was serving a sentence imposed by the British authorities for sedition, to become Leader of Government Business in the first semi-responsible African government of the Gold Coast. The uninterrupted aggressive leadership by Dr. Nkrumah since 1950 has unquestionably been one of the major reasons for the prominence Ghana has achieved.

According to the 1960 census, Ghana had a population of 6,690,730, with almost 3 million concentrated in the southern areas formerly included in the old Gold Coast Colony.[1] Somewhat over 1½ million were in the Ashanti Region, including Brong-Ahafo. The Volta Region, representing a substantial part of the trusteeship area of Togoland, had a 1960 population of slightly under 800,000. The more sparsely settled north claimed a population of somewhat over 1,282,000. Urban centers are growing rapidly. Accra, the capital city, had a 1960 population of 388,231. Kumasi, the capital of Ashanti, ranked second in size with 220,922 people, and Sekondi-Takoradi was third with a population of 120,793. Other significant urban centers are Tamale, the administrative center of the Northern Region, and Tema, the new industrial town about 18 miles east of Accra.

Agriculture is the principal occupation of the people of Ghana. A wide variety of crops is produced, with the diversities depending upon the climate and soil in the main agricultural divisions. In the forest zone the principal crop is cocoa, which is produced on small private holdings. Other crops grown for local consumption are yams, plantains, bananas, cocoayams, cassava,

[1] The 1965 census statistics released by the Ghana Government give the current population as 7.5 million, an increase of 800,000 since 1960.

8

maize, rice, peppers, eggplant, okra, onions, tomatoes, avocado pears, oranges and pineapples. The coastal savannahs have important coconut plantations; while most of the nuts are consumed locally, the basis for an export industry in copra is formed especially in the extreme southeast. The largest crop on the coastal savannahs is cassava, but okra, peppers, tomatoes and eggplant are also grown. Poultry, pigs, goats and sheep are kept throughout the coastal plains for local consumption, but in the more open area between Accra and the Shai hills there are extensive pastures for cattle. In the dry northern savannahs, cattle raising is important, and a substantial amount of livestock and poultry is exported from here to other regions. There is little besides subsistence farming in the north, with common crops including peppers, tomatoes, okra, eggplant, cotton, guinea corn, millets, pulses, maize, rice and ground nuts. The cultivation of yams and cassava is also widespread.

Fishing is probably the second most common occupation in Ghana, salt-water fishing being most important. The best fishing season extends from June to September. Herring, the most plentiful fish, is then taken in large quantities, but there are several other good species including the large sea bream. Typically, the fishermen use dugout canoes, propelled by paddles and on occasion by sails, and cast their nets into the sea in a large crescent, with the two ends attached to ropes on the shore. A typical sight on the shoreline is the men, women and children pulling in the nets until the center bag reaches the shore with the catch. Other types of nets are also used, and hooks and lines are used for some varieties of fish. Fishing also takes place in the coastal lagoons and in the rivers throughout the country. In recent years, the government has assisted in the introduction of trawlers and encouraged the use of outboard motors for propelling fishing canoes, in order to increase the sea catch. Distribution of fish remains a problem, however. Some fish canning is done in Accra, but limited facilities for cold storage and quick transportation make it necessary for most of the fish to be smoke-cured before reaching the customer.

Cocoa, the most important agricultural product of Ghana is grown in the high forest regions. Ghana is the world's largest producer of cocoa, with revenue from it accounting for approximately 70 per cent of her total export earnings. Cocoa requires little attention between the planting of the trees and the first harvest five to seven years later; thus, farmers are able to produce their subsistence crops at the same time they cultivate the trees. In recent years, a major problem of the cocoa industry has been swollen shoot disease, which can be controlled only by cutting out the affected trees. The farmers have resisted the Government's cutting program, and it has never been prosecuted with the vigor required. The privately produced cocoa is purchased by a government corporation for international marketing. The difference between the price assured to the farmers and the international market price, together with export duty on cocoa, provides the largest source of foreign exchange available to the Ghana Government.

Second in importance among the exports are minerals —gold, diamonds, manganese and bauxite. Together they comprise more than 20 per cent of total exports. Another important export is timber from the forest zone, primarily mahogany but also odum, wawa and sapele.

The Ghanaian Government is committed to economic development along socialistic lines. Implementation of a socialistic program has been only partial at best, however, and important areas of activity have been left for the private sector, both domestic and foreign. Thus far, the principal governmental activities have been in the development of infrastructure. The road system has been greatly improved with the completion of arterial highways east and west along the coast, as well as north-south arteries converging at Kumasi and continuing to Tamale in the north. Harbor facilities have been greatly extended and improved with the completion of the modern artificial harbor at Tema and the abandonment of the colorful but wasteful surf harbor at Accra. University facilities have been developed at Legon (Accra), Kumasi and Cape Coast. Considerable progress has also been made in the development of elementary schools and there are now enough schools for a program of compulsory primary education. The principal shortage of educational facilities is at the secondary level. Health facilities have been improved and substantial housing programs undertaken. The Volta River dam, which is nearing completion, is by far the most ambitious project. The hydroelectric output of the dam will be committed to meeting the general consumer demand in the southern area of the country, the needs of the mines and, most importantly, the needs of an aluminum smelter to be established at Tema by the Volta Aluminium Company (VALCO). A private corporation sponsored by Kaiser Aluminum and Reynolds Metals, VALCO operates mainly on capital borrowed from the United States Government.

The successful implementation of the present Seven Year Development Plan (1963-1970) depends upon a large influx of foreign private capital (£G 100 million), foreign grants and credits (£G 145 million) and resident private investment of greatly enlarged proportions (£G 400 million). A favorable Capital Investments Act has been enacted to attract foreign investors, but its effects have been prejudiced by political tensions and the general image projected by spokesmen of the Government and the dominant Convention People's Party.

Industry, other than the extractive segment, makes a relatively small contribution to the national income of Ghana. Most of the industrial establishments are still little more than small service enterprises—bakers, tailors, brewers, carpenters—employing family labor almost entirely and using little capital. Manufacturing on a somewhat larger scale first developed in beverages, tobacco, wood processing and motor vehicle assembly, but in more recent years, medium-sized industries have been established for the manufacture of alcoholic beverages, clothing, soap, footwear and furniture.

Tema, with its modern harbor facilities, is developing into a significant manufacturing center. An oil refinery, owned jointly by the Government and a foreign company has been opened there, and a small plant for the manufacture of steel from scrap is under construction. The Volta Aluminium Company plans to construct an aluminum smelter, probably the most ambitious single industrial project in Ghana.

While Ghana's economic position seems well advanced when contrasted with many African countries, there are complex and difficult problems to be solved. Relying for its foreign exchange income primarily on the production of raw materials, Ghana faces the perennial problem of primary producers—stable or declining income from its products and increasing costs of the manufactures it imports, including the capital goods required for its own development. For several years, Ghana has experienced an unfavorable balance of trade, a situation that has persisted despite limited efforts to restrict imports to essentials and to increase exports. Ghana has cooperated in the establishment of an organization of producing countries designed to restrict the flow of cocoa to the international market in order to assure a minimum fair price. Experience thus far raises substantial doubt, however, that this device will succeed in sufficiently controlling the flow of cocoa to the markets to achieve a major impact on prices.

The people of Ghana possess a rich and varied culture. Their pride in that heritage, and their determination to preserve its integrity, are coupled with an insistent demand for rapid development. Legal institutions can aid or deter economic progress in many ways, and it is to the most fundamental of these institutions that we now turn.

CHAPTER I

ALLOCATION AND CONTROL
OF PUBLIC POWER

IDENTIFICATION of the persons who are critical to the manipulation of the legal technique is in the first instance made by reference to a set of institutionalized roles. In traditional terms, certain roles involve the function of creating law and thus determining its value content (legislative power); others involve the interpretation and application of law to actual controversies or disputes (judicial power); another set of roles relates to the function of executing or administering the scheme whereby the public force is actually brought to bear on the social group and its members (executive power). Thus, as a first step toward understanding any regime of law, its value content and its social impact, it is essential to study the institutional pattern within which these roles are defined and related to each other; it is also necessary to determine how these roles come to be assigned to members of the social group.

Analysis in the traditional language of separation of powers, applied to a formal scheme of role allocation, is useful as a first step. If a simplistic distortion of view is to be avoided, however, it is essential to bear in mind constantly two cautionary comments.

The first relates to the concept of separation of function within the basic legal order. One must avoid what might be called the absolutist fallacy. While perhaps conceptually discrete, the functions of making, interpreting, applying and executing the law have in actual operation a tendency to become imprecise at their borders and to merge. A judicial decision, for example, that a statute imposing criminal sanctions on the interstate transportation of "motor vehicles" does not apply to flying airplanes across state lines is in a real sense legislative; the interpretation of law differs from law-making mainly in the range of the creative choices available to the actor. For further illustration, consider the application of a penal statute simply prohibiting games of chance. If, as would often be the case, a police department (executive) refuses to apply the prohibition to the penny-ante poker at the businessmen's luncheon club, does this decision represent the introduction of an exception not specified in the statute (legislation) or an interpretation and application of the legislative will (judiciary)? Surely it involves more than straightforward execution of the legal norm by the police, an executive agency.

Any legal order provides innumerable illustrations of this kind of overlapping or merger of functions and power, and this is not a recent development. Another kind, however, is largely a reflection of the increasing complexity of the law in an advanced society. This has led to the proliferation of specialized executive agencies to which legislative or judicial powers, or both, may be assigned. Thus, under general policy guidelines established by the legislature, an executive agency may be authorized to legislate on a wide range of detail. Similarly, the same or another specialized agency may be granted power to interpret statutes and subordinate legislation and to apply these to the settlement of disputes, with access to the ordinary courts being foreclosed or limited to a narrow range of appellate review.

The second caution to be applied in considering the scheme of formal allocation relates to what might be called the positivistic fallacy. This involves the assumption that critical roles in manipulating the legal technique are adequately revealed by an examination of formal sources such as constitutions and statutes. While of obvious relevance and importance, these are limited by two categories of factors. The first is normative, arising from the politico-legal philosophy that expressly or tacitly underlies the system or motivates the particular actor to whom a law job is formally assigned.

For example, the legislator will to some extent be affected by his democratic or autocratic value acceptances and, even the democratic legislator, by the extent to which he insists on making his role directly representative. The second category of factors, rarely if ever reflected in formal sources, includes the innumerable influences from which no human conduct is fully immune —self-interest, individual and group pressures, religious persuasions, etc. To avoid the positivistic fallacy, one must fully recognize the limited perspective provided by the analysis of formal sources and, insofar as possible, utilize data supplied by research in related social sciences to locate the fulcrum points of choice in the performance of law jobs.

This chapter will consider the evolution of the formal structure of legal power from the Gold Coast Constitution of 1954 (the Nkrumah Constitution) to the present. While utilizing the traditional language of separation of powers, it will emphasize the extent to which the walls of separation have been eroded. Avoidance of the positivistic fallacy will largely depend, however, on a recognition of the limited basis of the discussion. While I have attempted to supplement the formal sources through discussions and observations in Ghana, I cannot claim any scientific validity for the data so acquired. Empirical research into the legal institutions of Ghana is still substantially limited to a fairly primitive impressionism. Finally, it should be noted that treatment of the judiciary is reserved for a separate chapter.

PHILOSOPHICAL BASIS

During the colonial period, the legal structure of the Gold Coast was not encumbered by expressed concern for its philosophical underpinning. From the colonial experience, however, one may infer certain premises suggesting a philosophical schizophrenia. The policy of indirect rule, it could be argued, was not merely a reflection of the limited resources and governmental staff that the metropolitan power was able or willing to commit to the Gold Coast, but also of a democratic philosophy of government and law. So regarded, indirect rule rested on the premise that the power to choose their rulers should rest with the people themselves and that the law should reflect the group judgment as crystallized in actual practice.

Without denying that this premise affected British policy, one may fairly insist that it did not control it fully. The extension of British governmental power, some basic English ideas of justice and, ultimately, English law beyond the coastal settlements and throughout the area comprising modern Ghana cannot in any sense be related to a democratic theory of government and law. The Foreign Jurisdiction Act of 1843, which regularized the jurisdiction already exercised by Captain George Maclean outside the coastal settlements, its successor of 1890 and the various exercises of prerogative power to extend the application of English law in the Gold Coast can be sustained philosophically only on an autocratic basis. This conclusion is not affected by the advent of local legislative bodies as long as these preserved an official majority. The Legislative Council in the Gold Coast did not acquire a clear African majority until 1946. It is irrelevant at the moment to inquire into the extent of the benevolence motivating the autocracy. Doubtless the advancement of the African people was always an important objective of the colonial power. Nevertheless, the significant fact in this context is the attribution to an alien elite of the dominant power to manipulate the legal technique through the higher organs of government. As Lord Milner once declared, "the only justification for keeping an official majority in any colony is that we are convinced that we are better judges, for the time being, of the interests of the native population than they are themselves."[1]

The progressive implementation of democratic values

[1] Quoted in Taylor, *The Political Development of Tanganyika* (1963).

as the Gold Coast moved rapidly toward independence in the years after World War II will be considered in the following sections. The formal articulation of the philosophical basis for this development did not come until the Republican Constitution of 1960 which declares (Article I) that "the powers of the State derive from the people,[2] by whom certain of those powers are now conferred on the institutions established by this Constitution and who shall have the right to exercise the remainder of those powers. . . ."

SURVEY OF CONSTITUTIONAL CHANGE

Not surprisingly, constitutional orders have been highly transient in the Gold Coast and Ghana since the end of World War II. As background to a detailed consideration of the evolving institutions, a brief survey of the principal steps will be useful.

The Burns Constitution of 1946,[3] while providing for the representation of both the Colony and Ashanti in a Legislative Council which for the first time had an African majority, did not provide a satisfactory answer to the increasing demands for self-government. Economic difficulties, the unrest of demobilized servicemen and burgeoning nationalism produced riots in Accra and other towns in 1948. In late 1947, Kwame Nkrumah returned to the Gold Coast after ten years of study and political agitation in the United States and England to become General Secretary of the United Gold Coast Convention. The U.G.C.C., a relatively conservative nationalist group, dominated by the upper-middle class—intellectuals, lawyers and merchants—was soon overshadowed by Nkrumah's Convention People's Party which he formed on breaking with the

[2] The Constitution (Amendment) Act, 1964, Act 224, Sec. 1, inserts at this point the phrase "as the source of power and the guardians of the State." This amendment does not seem to alter the juridical effect of Article 1.

[3] The Gold Coast Colony and Ashanti (Legislative Council) Order in Council [1946], 1 STAT. RULES & ORDERS 640 (No. 353), 9 STAT. RULES & ORDERS & STAT. INSTR. Rev. to Dec. 31, 1948, at 673.

17

U.G.C.C. in mid-1949. Building and manipulating with consummate skill the first mass political party in black Africa, Nkrumah dominated the progression toward independence eight years later.

In October, 1949, a committee appointed by the Gold Coast Government under the chairmanship of Sir Henley Coussey, an African judge, reported its recommendations for changes in the structure of central, regional and local governments.[4] The main proposals were accepted by the British Government and incorporated in the Constitution of 1950.[5] While Nkrumah denounced the Coussey Constitution as "bogus and fraudulent," he decided to cooperate under it while pressing toward the objective of full self-government. Elected to the Legislative Assembly while still in prison, Nkrumah was released and accepted designation as Leader of Government Business. This title was changed to Prime Minister in March, 1952, but the powers of the office were not increased. The Coussey Constitution was significant not only because it provided for an African government directly responsible to the legislative body but also because, with the inclusion of the Northern Territories, the Legislative Assembly was for the first time representative of all parts of pre-independence Ghana, with the exception of the area of Togoland under British mandate.

The relation developed between Nkrumah and the Governor, Sir Charles N. Arden-Clarke, was cordial and cooperative.[6] With this support, and with the maturing responsibilities of governing, Nkrumah moved toward the goal of full independence at a more deliberate pace. In 1952, he initiated procedures to consult a wide range of opinion on possible changes in the constitutional structure. From these came new proposals

[4] Report to His Excellency The Governor by the Committee on Constitutional Reform, Colonial No. 248 (1949).

[5] The Gold Coast (Constitution) Order in Council, 1950 [1950], I STAT. INSTR. 831 (No. 2094).

[6] See Nkrumah's own testimonial in *Autobiography*, 137, 204, 281-82 (1957).

for constitutional development which were implemented in the so-called Nkrumah Constitution of 1954.[7] This forms the base line for the detailed analysis in the following sections.

Constitutional developments between 1954 and 1957 need only be sketched here. The central issue during this period, a federal or a unitary governmental structure, will be fully discussed in a later chapter. It was primarily an issue between the new mass political organization led by Nkrumah and the sectional groups representing a traditional orientation. The latter were organized in the National Liberation Movement (N.L.M.) which emerged in Ashanti in September, 1954. After extended negotiations and consultations and the election of a new National Assembly in July, 1956, in which Nkrumah's C.P.P. retained its dominant position, the federalism issue was resolved (see Chapter III) and the pace toward independence quickened. On August 3, 1956, the National Assembly passed a motion asking the United Kingdom Government to introduce independence legislation. In a dispatch dated September 15, 1956, the British Government declared its intention to proceed with the appropriate steps for the grant of independence on March 6, 1957, the 113th anniversary of the Fante Bond.[8] Subsequently, the Independence Constitution was issued as the Ghana (Constitution) Order in Council, 1957.[9]

[7] The Gold Coast (Constitution) Order in Council [1954], 2 STAT. INSTR. 2788 (No. 551). This instrument came into operation on May 5, 1954, except for Part II (secs. 4-21) dealing with the executive, section 56 on the Public Service, section 63 on the Judiciary and section 70 on the Powers of the Governor in Council (L.N. 170/54). Part II and section 70 become operative on June 18, 1954 (L.N. 242/54), and sections 56 and 63 on July 31, 1955 (L.N. 1/55). The Order in Council will be cited hereafter as 1954 Constitution.

[8] Dispatch from the Secretary of State for the Colonies to the Governor of the Gold Coast, printed as Appendix 1 to *The Making of Ghana* (H.M.S.O., 1957).

[9] [1957], 1 STAT. INSTR. 1036 (No. 277) hereafter cited as 1957 Constitution. Other constitutional instruments were Letters Patent Constituting the Office of Governor General of Ghana, Royal Instructions to the Governor General and the Ghana Independ-

The compromises imposed on the Nkrumah Government to achieve independence in 1957 did not long survive the political pressures of Ghana. Regional and traditional loyalties, and fear of a powerful central government, had led to the imposition of substantial restraints on constitutional revision and certain basic kinds of legislation. These will be considered fully in the following section. The organs relied upon to restrain the central government were the Regional Assemblies which, though contemplated by the Independence. Constitution, were not established until later—under the Regional Assemblies Act of 1958.[10] When elections for these assemblies were scheduled, the opposition groups decided to boycott them—with the result that the Convention People's Party, already firmly in control of the central government, acquired control of all the Regional Assemblies as well. This power was promptly exercised to eliminate the chaffing restraints of the Independence Constitution and in December of 1958, Parliament enacted the Constitution (Repeal of Restrictions) Act.[11] Since this legislation was subject to the restraints, the Speaker of the Assembly duly certified that it was passed by not less than two-thirds of the entire membership, that it had been referred to all Regional Assemblies and Houses of Chiefs and that it had been approved by all Regional Assemblies.

With the power of constitutional revision[12] in the hands of the parliamentary majority, other changes were made in 1959. These amendments, which related to the judiciary, the regional organizations and

---

ence Act (5 & 6 Eliz. 2, c. 6). The significance of these instruments and the reasons for their taking the particular form used are discussed in D. Smith, "The Independence of Ghana," 20 Mod. L. Rev. 847 (1957).

[10] Act No. 25 of 1958.   [11] Act No. 38 of 1958.

[12] As restrictions on parliamentary power were reduced or eliminated, the distinction between constitutional and other enactments became less significant. The term "constitution" or "constitutional enactment" will be used, however, to designate that legislation which determined basic governmental structures and powers.

the public service[13] and provided special representation for women in the National Assembly,[14] will be analyzed in the appropriate sections.

The next phase in Ghana's constitutional development centered on the establishment of a republic. This had been forecast by Dr. Nkrumah even prior to the independence of the Gold Coast.[15] In April, 1959, Minister of Information Kofi Baako announced that the necessary constitutional changes would be made after a projected visit to Ghana in November by Queen Elizabeth.[16] There were discussions and some concern about the form required to eliminate any doubts of the legal validity of the Republic.[17] It seems sufficiently clear, however, that the simplification of constitutional amendment by the 1958 legislation would have permitted the change to a republican form of government by an Act of Parliament passed by a majority vote. A more complex procedure was adopted, probably less because of legalistic reservations than from a desire to dramatize the change and root it in a renewed mandate for the Nkrumah Government. By the Constituent Assembly and Plebiscite Act (1960),[18] the National Assembly was authorized to resolve itself, from time to time, into a constituent assembly with full power to make constitutional changes, including the establishment of a republic. The Constituent Assembly was also authorized to hold a plebiscite before adopting the new constitution, in order "to inform itself as to the wishes of the people on the form of the Constitution, or the person who is to become the new Head of the State or any other matter."

In preparation for the plebiscite, the Government

---

[13] The Constitution (Amendment) Act, 1959, Act No. 7 of 1959.

[14] The Representation of the People (Women Members) Act, 1959, Act No. 72 of 1959, and Representation of the People (Women Members) Act, 1960, Act No. 8 of 1960.

[15] *New York Times*, April 15, 1955, p. 9, col. 1.

[16] *New York Times*, April 5, 1959, p. 17, cols. 1-2.

[17] The possible bases of such doubts are discussed in Bennion, *Constitutional Law of Ghana*, 74-80 (1962).

[18] Act No. 1 of 1960.

published a White Paper, containing a draft constitution and an extended though reasonably clear explanation of it.[19] The process of constitutional revision outlined in the White Paper is noteworthy. The draft constitution was, of course, prepared entirely within the Government. Explanation of it to the people, and the debate concerning its provisions, were to occupy the period between the White Paper's publication on March 7, 1960, and the plebiscite held between April 19 and April 26. The White Paper announced an intention to have the draft constitution endorsed by the National Assembly immediately, but neither this step nor approval by the people in the plebiscite would amount to adoption of the draft as a constitution. The people would be asked only "whether they approve the main provisions of the draft Constitution." The Government candidly declared that popular approval would not commit it to the introduction of a constitution bill identical with the draft. It pointed out that during the period of discussion of the draft, "it may well be that changes of detail, arrangement and emphasis will be found desirable." Such changes were in fact made, as were changes of substance which will be discussed later.

While not committing itself to the details of the draft constitution, the Government did make it clear that approval by the people would be deemed assent to certain fundamental principles which it committed itself to urge upon the Constituent Assembly. These fundamental principles held to be implicit in the draft were as follows:

1. That Ghana should be a sovereign unitary Republic with power to surrender any part of her sovereignty to a Union of African States.

2. That the Head of State and holder of the ex-

---

[19] Government Proposals for a Republican Constitution, W.P. 1/60 (1960). The Ghana Information Services on behalf of the Ministry of Education and Information also published a booklet in question-answer format entitled *Ghana as a Republic.*

ecutive power should be an elected President responsible to the people.

3. That Parliament should be the Sovereign legislature and should consist of the President and the National Assembly, and that the President should have a power to veto legislation and to dissolve Parliament.

4. That a President should be elected whenever there is a general election by a method which insures that he will normally be the leader of the party which is successful in the General Election.

5. That there should be a Cabinet appointed by the President from among Members of Parliament to assist the President in the exercise of his executive functions.

6. That the system of Courts and the security of tenure of Judges should continue on present lines.

7. That the control of the armed forces and the civil service should be vested in the President.

In the later discussion of the republican constitutional structure, these guiding principles should be kept in mind.

The presidential campaign, held in conjunction with the plebiscite, opposed Dr. Nkrumah, as candidate of the ruling Convention People's Party, and Dr. J. B. Danquah, lawyer, politician and leader of the old, conservative and traditionally oriented Gold Coast independence movements. Danquah's principal policy statement for the opposition United Party was made in an address delivered at the Palladium in Accra on March 28, 1960. He referred to the Government's draft constitution as "a Constitution aimed at destroying Parliamentary democracy in Ghana," an "evil draft constitution," but only two of his fifteen specific policy proposals related clearly to the proposed constitution or the procedure for constitutional change adopted by the Government. The first of these (Point 2) proposed the establishment of a constitutional reform commission "to make enquiries and report on a constitution truly desired by the people and to call upon a truly representative constituent assembly to enact such a constitution. The emphasis in the new constitution will be to secure the rights of the individual against the great powers of the State, and the motto of the new Ghana will be Right, Freedom and Justice." Danquah severely criticized the Government for submitting to a people 80 per cent illiterate a constitution of 56 Articles and asking for a "yes" or "no" vote. He favored the preparation of a draft by a special commission (set up in an unspecified manner) which, after public hearings, would submit the draft directly to a constituent assembly. In the political address preceding his fifteen points, Danquah seemed to favor a bicameral legislature, but this was not included as a specific constitutional proposal.[20]

Dr. Danquah and his supporters were unable to avoid a peculiar ambivalence. They urged a "no" vote in the constitutional plebiscite, preferring revision through a special commission. At the same time, Danquah campaigned vigorously for election as the first President, an office which would be available only if the new constitution were approved. A truly anomalous situation would have resulted if the United Party had been successful in both aspects of its campaign. Rejection of the new constitution by the people would not, of course, have foreclosed constitutional revision, which could have been accomplished by a simply majority vote in Parliament where Nkrumah's C.P.P. had an absolute majority. At the same time, a popular preference for

[20] In August, 1960, I discussed with Dr. Danquah his ideas on a second legislative chamber. My notes on these conversations indicate that he did not conceive of the second chamber as a body equal to the lower house, but rather as an assembly of representatives of various special groups, e.g., the chiefs, the university, churches, labor unions and business groups, together with a certain number of government nominees. The functions of this upper house would be to advise the President in such areas as the appointment of judges and ambassadors and perhaps to delay legislation, although not necessarily to prevent its ultimate enactment.

Dr. Danquah would have embarrassed such a course of action as well as undermined confidence in the existing National Assembly as a currently representative body.

The published plebiscite results were decisive. The draft constitution was approved by a vote of 1,008,740 to 131,425; in the presidential election, Nkrumah had 1,016,076 votes to 124,623 for Danquah.[21] That the plebiscite did not occur under ideal conditions seems clear. When I was in Ghana, shortly after the plebiscite, reports of police obstruction in United Party campaigning, intimidation by organized gangs of toughs not only of those at rallies but even voters at the polls, and ballot-box stuffing came to me from prominent public figures as well as from nonpartisan observers. It was impossible, however, to determine the extent of such action or its initiators. It was apparent that each side had resorted to violence, though the extent to which each initiated or merely used violence in legitimate defense cannot be determined. Despite some assertions to the contrary, I find no real reason to conclude that the published plebiscite results did not reflect the popular will with substantial accuracy.

Later discussion will focus on the final provisions of the Republican Constitution,[22] though significant departures from the draft appended to the White Paper or the constitution bills as introduced in the Constituent Assembly will be noted. The constitution itself was relatively brief, consisting of 55 Articles. Much more detail was provided, however, in 11 other acts passed by the Constituent Assembly which came into operation simultaneously with the constitution.[23]

[21] Keesing's Contemporary Archives, June 18-25, 1960, 17480 A.

[22] The constitution was formally enacted on June 29, 1960, and came into operation on July 1, 1960. Hereafter it will be cited as "Republican Constitution."

[23] These acts were as follows: 1) Presidential Affairs Act, 1960, C.A. 2; Cabinet and Ministers Act, 1960, C.A. 3; Interpretation Act, 1960, C.A. 4; Civil Service Act, 1960, C.A. 5; State Property and Contracts Act, 1960, C.A. 6; Acts of Parliament Act, 1960, C.A. 7; Constitution (Consequential Provisions) Act,

The Republican Constitution was amended for the first time in January, 1964, though numerous amendments were required earlier in the basic acts passed by the Constituent Assembly.

THE LEGISLATIVE POWER

Since the governmental institutions with which the Gold Coast approached independence were clearly patterned on Westminister, it is appropriate to begin detailed analysis of the 1954 Constitution by considering the structure of legislative power. The Legislative Assembly comprised a Speaker and 104 members, elected in 97 rural and 7 municipal electoral districts; elections were required every four years, or oftener—in the event of dissolution of the Assembly.[24] The formation of a government out of the Assembly was subject to the constitutional convention applicable in the United Kingdom, with the Governor performing the functions of the Queen. Within the Cabinet, the allocation of responsibilities for departments or subjects was assigned to the Prime Minister.[25]

Three affirmative qualifications were specified for election to the Legislative Assembly:

1. status as a British subject or British protected person;
2. attainment of the age of twenty-five years; and
3. sufficient competence in the English language to permit active participation in the proceedings of the Assembly.[26]

These affirmative criteria were supplemented by eleven reasons for disqualification:

1. acknowledging allegiance to a foreign power;

1960, C.A. 8; Courts Act, 1960, C.A. 9; Judicial Service Act, 1960, C.A. 10; Regions of Ghana Act, 1960, C.A. 11; and Oaths Act, 1960, C.A. 12.

[24] 1954 Constitution, sec. 24; sec. 28; secs. 50-51.
[25] *Id.*, sec. 7; sec. 16.   [26] *Id.*, sec. 29.

2. holding or acting in any public office or the office of Speaker of the Assembly;
3. having certain business relations with the Government, unless these were properly publicized;
4. being an undischarged bankrupt;
5. disqualification in any part of Her Majesty's dominions from practicing a profession for which qualification had existed;
6. being adjudged of unsound mind or a criminal lunatic;
7. being sentenced to death or imprisonment for a term exceeding twelve months or being convicted of an offense involving dishonesty, and not having been pardoned;
8. not being qualified for registration as an elector;
9. disqualification under any law by reason of functioning as an election official; and
10. disqualification under any law relating to election offenses.[27]

Finally, the tenure of a properly elected member could be terminated by the factors causing initial disqualification as well as by absence from two consecutive meetings of the Assembly without the permission of the Speaker.[28]

On the Assembly thus constituted, a wide range of legislative power was expressly conferred,[29] and convention made the tenure of the Cabinet depend on the continuing support of a majority in the Assembly. Thus in the shaping of the law, the Assembly played the most significant role, but its powers were restricted in a number of respects. One such restriction affected the introduction of bills and motions.[30] In general, any member of the Assembly could initiate such action. If the Speaker or member presiding in the Assembly should be of the opinion, however, that a bill or motion would "dispose of or charge any public revenue or public funds of the Gold Coast, or revoke or alter any

[27] *Id.*, sec. 30.   [28] *Id.*, sec. 31.   [29] *Id.*, sec. 36.   [30] *Id.*, sec. 43.

disposition thereof or charge thereon, or impose, alter or repeal any rate, tax or duty," the Assembly could not proceed except upon the recommendation or consent of the Governor. Since resort was not expressly made to the Governor's discretion, and he was not required to act on the advice or recommendation of any authority other than the Cabinet, the substantive supervisory control over proposed legislation of the specified types was vested in the Cabinet itself.[31]

A further range of controls on legislation was reserved to the metropolitan power itself. If the Speaker or the Attorney General should be of the opinion that any bill or motion would change the salary, perquisites or conditions of service of any public officer, the Assembly could not proceed except with the recommendation or consent of the Governor, acting at his discretion. If the Governor, acting at his discretion, should consider that any change effected by any such bill would prejudicially affect a public officer, he was required to reserve the bill for the signification of Her Majesty's pleasure. Similar controls applied to any bill or motion which in the opinion of the Speaker or Attorney General related to or affected any subject for which responsibility was vested in the Governor.[32] The opinion concerning the nature of the bill or motion which might initiate the restraint on proceedings in the Assembly might be that of the Speaker or Attorney General. To be sure, the Speaker was elected by—and to some limited extent might be controlled by—the Assembly itself.[33] The Attorney General, however, was appointed by the Governor, in his discretion until July 31, 1955, and thereafter, after consultation with the Prime Minister.[34]

The sharing of legislative power between the African Government and the metropolitan power was

[31] *Id.*, sec. 6(1)(a).
[32] The principal categories of subjects so reserved were defense and external affairs. 1954 Constitution, sec. 17 and Second Schedule.
[33] *Id.*, sec. 25. [34] *Id.*, sec. 52; sec. 53 and Third Schedule.

further illustrated by the provisions relating to the reserved powers of the Governor. He was authorized, if he considered that it was in the interests of public order, public faith or good government, to declare any bill or motion introduced in the Assembly effective, without passage in the Assembly.[35] Before making any such declaration, however, he was required to submit it in the first instance to the Cabinet. If the Cabinet approved it, the declaration could then be made; if the Cabinet declined to approve, the Governor was empowered to issue the declaration only with the prior authorization of a Secretary of State, except when "in the Governor's opinion urgent necessity requires that the declaration be made" without such prior authorization.[36] Power to revoke a declaration, other than one relating to a bill, was conferred on a Secretary of State.[37] Why declarations relating to bills were excluded from this power is not immediately apparent.

Further illustration of the continuing supervision of the Governor is found in the provisions requiring his assent to bills. When a bill was presented to the Governor, he had three alternatives: to assent, to refuse to assent or to reserve the bill for the signification of the pleasure of the metropole.[38] Two specific types of bills were required to be treated in the third manner unless prior authority to give assent had been conferred by a Secretary of State: 1) any bill revoking or amending or being in any way repugnant to or inconsistent with the constitutional Order in Council, and 2) any bill determining or regulating the privileges, immunities and powers of the Assembly or its members. If the Governor

[35] Introduction in the Assembly was no limitation on the Governor's power in this respect since he was authorized at his discretion to send draft legislation to the Assembly and to require that it be introduced. 1954 Constitution, sec. 43(7); sec. 44(1).

[36] *Id.*, sec. 44(2)(b).

[37] *Id.*, sec. 44(5).

[38] *Id.*, sec. 45(2). The Instructions to the Governor listed a number of kinds of legislation to which the Governor was not to assent without instructions. L.N. 217/54, cl. 8, 1 Laws of the Gold Coast 793 at 796 (1954).

had assented to a bill, however, it might later be disallowed by the metropolitan government.[39]

Another illustration of shared legislative power was provided by the provisions relating to the making of laws for Togoland under United Kingdom trusteeship. In general, this area was administered as a part of the Gold Coast, and the legislative power of the Assembly extended to it. The Order in Council made clear, however, that any legislation repugnant to any provision of the Trusteeship Agreement, as approved by the General Assembly of the United Nations, should be void to the extent of the repugnancy.[40]

In addition to the foregoing areas where legislative powers were shared between the African Government and the metropolitan power, two broadly defined areas —defense (including police) and external affairs—were totally reserved to the British Government.[41] Also reserved were the full power to amend or revoke the Order in Council, the basic constitutive document itself, and the ultimate power of Her Majesty in Council to make laws for the peace, order and good government of the Gold Coast.[42]

In addition to the substantive definitions of legislative power, the 1954 Constitution established a number of procedural safeguards around its exercise. While these did not ultimately limit or control the manipulation of the legal order, nevertheless, by subjecting the exercise of legislative power to certain procedural requirements, its use could be delayed and other techniques for controlling it could be brought to bear. For example, a requirement of multiple readings of a bill in a legislative assembly, with stipulated minimum times between readings, at least slows the legislative process and provides opportunities for other controlling factors (e.g., political opposition) to be mobilized and brought to bear.

The 1954 Constitution made the exercise of the

---

[39] 1954 Constitution, sec. 46(1).　　[40] *Id.*, sec. 36(1).
[41] *Id.*, sec. 17 and Second Schedule.　　[42] *Id.*, sec. 73.

legislative power subject to directions to the Governor contained in any Instructions under Her Majesty's Sign Manual and Signet.[43] Instructions issued in 1954[44] provided a number of requirements concerning the form of enactments as well as a requirement of annual publication of all ordinances. Other extremely important procedural safeguards surrounded the Governor's power to legislate: before declaring any bill or motion effective, he was required to submit to the Cabinet the question whether the declaration should be made; if the Governor made the declaration without Cabinet approval, he was required to inform the Cabinet in writing of his reasons for so doing.[45]

The cardinal feature of the 1954 Constitution was the careful division of power between the metropolitan government and the indigenous leaders who were pressing to take the reins fully into their own hands. The institutional framework was parliamentary democracy qualified by the tutelary reservations of the United Kingdom Government. Since both the indigenous elite and the metropolitan power desired the early completion of the transfer process, the accommodation between them was generally harmonious. The Nkrumah Government, in fact, sufficiently controlled the organs of government that it could justify the claim to responsibility and to full independence at an early date.

The institutional forms of parliamentary democracy were preserved in the Independence Constitution of 1957, although the constitutional document itself incorporates more detail and in a few situations departs from the British model.[46] Discussion properly focuses, therefore, on the constitutional provisions relating to the composition and functioning of the National Assembly. The size of the Assembly remained at 104, but

---

[43] *Id.*, sec. 37.   [44] Instructions, supra note 38, at 793-99.
[45] 1954 Constitution, sec. 44.
[46] For example, sec. 8(1) provides that the offices of all Ministers shall become vacant whenever the office of the Prime Minister has become vacant and a new Prime Minister has been appointed.

there was provision for an increase in the number of members to a maximum of 130.[47] Qualifications for election to Parliament were altered somewhat as a consequence of severing the British ties.[48] The first criterion for qualification under the 1954 Constitution, status as a British subject or a British protected person, was changed to Ghana citizenship. The bases for determining such citizenship were spelled out in the Ghana Nationality and Citizenship Act (1957).[49] While these bases were not unduly restrictive, they did tighten the first qualification for election to Parliament by factors which rendered somewhat more intimate the relation between the member and the new nation. The bases for disqualification remained the same, except that in fixing the locus of disqualifying acts, the geographical limitation "in Ghana" was substituted for the earlier and broader "in any part of Her Majesty's dominion."[50]

Power was conferred on "Parliament, to make laws for the peace, order and good government of Ghana."[51] No longer was this power restricted with respect to Togoland which by plebiscite, held in May, 1956 under the auspices of the United Nations, had elected to join an independent Gold Coast. The metropolitan reservation of power over defense (including police) and external affairs was also eliminated. Yet there still existed certain limitations on the power of Parliament which foreclosed a claim to full legal sovereignty. Three of these limitations were of substance. The first, retained from Section 36(2) of the 1954 Constitution, provided that "no law shall make persons of any racial community liable to disabilities to which persons of other such communities are not made liable."[52] The second limitation provided that "Subject to such restrictions as may be imposed for the purposes of preserving public order, morality or health, no law shall deprive any person of his freedom of conscience or the

[47] 1957 Constitution, sec. 20.   [48] Id., sec. 24.
[49] Act No. 1 of 1957.   [50] 1957 Constitution, sec. 25.
[51] Id., sec. 31(1).
[52] 1957 Constitution, sec. 31(2).

right freely to profess, practice or propagate any religion."[53] The third guaranteed adequate compensation on the compulsory acquisition of property, the amount to be judicially determined.[54] While both the 1954 and 1957 constitutions declared laws in contravention of their substantive limitations on legislative power to be void to the extent of the contravention, the latter vested in the Supreme Court original jurisdiction in all proceedings in which the validity of a law was questioned.[55] This grant of judicial power seemingly extended to all claims of invalidity and not merely those grounded on the three preceding restraints. It represented the first articulation in the evolution of the Ghanaian constitutional structure of a resort to judicial review of the constitutional validity of laws which is so familiar in the United States.

In addition to the foregoing substantive restraints on legislative power, three sets of procedural safeguards were included in the Independence Constitution. Two of these, relating to the alteration of regional boundaries and names of regions and to bills affecting chiefs, will be discussed in subsequent chapters.[56] Of interest here is the special procedure for passing bills relating to the constitution itself and to certain other highly important matters.[57] For the purpose of determining the applicability of this procedure, a "constitutional provision" included the various Orders in Council from 1954 to 1956 relating to the Gold Coast, the 1957 Constitutional Order in Council and any act amending, modifying or re-enacting any of these. Any bill relating to these constitutional provisions could not be presented for the Royal Assent unless the Speaker of

[53] Id., sec. 31(3).
[54] Id., sec. 34. Such a guarantee did not appear in the 1954 Constitution but was added by the Gold Coast (Constitution) (Amendment) Order in Council, 1955 [1955], 2 STAT. INSTR. 3150 (No. 1218).
[55] 1957 Constitution, sec. 31(5).
[56] On regional organization, see ch. III; on chieftaincy, see ch. II.
[57] 1957 Constitution, sec. 32.

the National Assembly certified that at the third reading the bill was passed by at least the vote of two-thirds of the entire membership.[58]

A bill modifying, repealing or re-enacting a listed group of entrenched provisions, or one abolishing, suspending or diminishing the powers or functions of any Regional Assembly, required an additional certification of reference to all the Regional Assemblies, and in some instances to all Houses of Chiefs, and approval by at least two-thirds of the Regional Assemblies including any Regional Assembly affected by the bill. Bills affecting any Regional Assembly required reference to all Regional Assemblies only, but bills affecting the entrenched provisions of the constitution had to be referred to all Houses of Chiefs as well. Where the reference included Houses of Chiefs, the House in each region was to communicate its views on the bill to the Regional Assembly, to be considered by the Assembly in reaching its decision. Approval in the Regional Assembly required a majority vote of those present and voting. If the Speaker of the National Assembly was not informed of the action taken on a bill within three months of the reference, it was to be deemed approved by the Regional Assembly. If a bill affecting the existence, powers or functions of a Regional Assembly was not approved by that Assembly, the Governor General was authorized to submit the bill to a referendum of the registered electors in that region. Majority approval in such a referendum would suffice as a substitute for approval by the Regional Assembly.

The complex provisions of the 1954 Constitution which restricted the introduction of bills in the Assembly, with much of the restraining control reserved for the metropolitan government, were of course not retained. Subject to the constitution and the Standing Orders of the Assembly, any Member could initiate

[58] The Gold Coast Government's original proposals for the independence constitution provided only for a two-thirds majority of those present and voting. Constitutional Proposals for Gold Coast Independence (1956), para. 35.

34

legislative action by bill, motion or petition. The Assembly was not authorized to proceed, however, if in the opinion of the Speaker or presiding member, the bill, motion or petition would "dispose of or charge the Consolidated Fund or other public funds of Ghana, or revoke or alter any disposition thereof or charge thereon, or impose, alter or repeal any rate, tax or duty," except with the recommendation or consent of the Governor General.[59] Thus, the Cabinet, on whose instruction the Governor General acted in this regard, retained at least negative control in these important areas. Similar Cabinet control was assured by the provision requiring assent by the Governor General before any bill could become law.[60] The Assembly, which was required to meet at least once a year, had a maximum life of five years[61] as compared with four years for the previous Assembly.

The safeguards on constitutional revision requiring reference of proposed changes to the Houses of Chiefs and Regional Assemblies and approval by two-thirds of the latter before parliamentary adoption could be valid were eliminated in 1958. The Convention People's Party, having gained control of all Regional Assemblies in elections boycotted by the opposition, acted promptly in securing passage of the Constitution (Repeal of Restrictions) Act.[62] The Speaker certified that the bill was passed by not less than two-thirds of the entire membership of the National Assembly, that it had been referred to all Regional Assemblies and all Houses of Chiefs and had been approved by all Regional Assemblies. The act was simple and direct. It repealed those sections of the 1957 Constitution[63] and the Ghana Independence Act[63a] which had required special pro-

[59] 1957 Constitution, sec. 41.
[60] *Id.*, sec. 42. On reservation, disallowance or other restriction on legislative autonomy in other Commonwealth countries, see 5 Halsbury's Laws of England, 448-52 (3rd ed. 1952).
[61] 1957 Constitution, sec. 46; *id.*, sec. 47(3).
[62] Act No. 38 of 1958.
[63] Secs. 32, 33, 35 and 47(2) and the Third Schedule.
[63a] 5 & 6 Eliz. 2, c. 6, para. 6 of the First Schedule.

cedures for constitutional revision and for bills altering the boundaries of a region or affecting the traditional functions or privileges of a chief. Parliament thus moved substantially toward full sovereignty. While the provisions of the 1957 Constitution that prohibited discriminatory disabilities of racial communities and restrictions on freedom of conscience and religion, and guaranteed adequate compensation for the compulsory acquisition of property, were not changed, they were reduced to statutory level, fully subject to revision or elimination by majority action in Parliament.

In 1959, the Nkrumah Government took steps to alter significantly the composition of Parliament. The Assembly had, since the 1954 Constitution, comprised 104 members who were elected on the basis of adult suffrage. No sex qualification applied to registration as an elector or to election to the Assembly; there had, however, been no women members. The termination of this male monopoly was the objective of the Representation of the People (Women Members) Act (1959).[64] The act made provision for the election in each region of a Women's Electoral College, to be chosen by the registered female electors either in a special election or contemporaneously with any general election. In addition to her vote for a candidate to the Electoral College, each woman elector also retained her franchise in the regular parliamentary elections. When in existence, each Electoral College was to elect a specified number of women members of Parliament who would hold office as if they had been elected in the basic constitutional manner. The total number of women members so provided for was ten. Thus, the membership of the Assembly was increased to 114, and the women of Ghana were assured a special representation.[65] Although enacted, this legislation was

[64] Act No. 72 of 1959.
[65] The legal basis for the composition, organization, proceedings and privileges of the National Assembly, as well as the definition of certain offenses against the Assembly, were revised and restated in the National Assembly Act, No. 78 of 1959.

never brought into operation by the necessary order of the Minister for Local Government. New legislation was enacted in 1960,[66] however, repealing the 1959 act and providing a different method of election for the new women members. They were to be nominated and elected for each region by the members representing that region in the National Assembly. The most significant provision of the 1960 act was that the new seats for women members were not to be permanent. When a vacancy occurred, it was not to be filled. The governing elite had apparently concluded that women needed the *entré* of special representation for a term but thereafter would have to contest regular seats in general parliamentary elections.[67]

Legislative power under the Republican Constitution of 1960 was vested in a Parliament which consists of the President and the National Assembly.[68] The Assembly, composed of a minimum of 104 members, has a maximum life of five years but is subject to dissolution by the President at any time.[69] The last general election in Ghana occurred in 1956. In the formulation of plans for the creation of the Republic, the Government announced that it would regard an endorsement of the draft constitution and an expressed preference for Dr. Nkrumah as President as a renewal of the mandate of the existing Assembly, thus avoiding the inconvenience and expense of another national election. The life of the 1956 Assembly was extended in this way until 1965. Dr. Nkrumah has never found it necessary to dissolve the Assembly.

The provisions of the draft constitution, relating to the legislative powers of Parliament, that were submitted to the people, were extensively revised before

[66] Representation of the People (Women Members) Act, No. 8 of 1960.
[67] Elections were held for the special women's seats on June 27, 1960, and the names of the new members published in *Ghana Gazette*, July 8, 1960, p. 19.
[68] Republican Constitution, art. 20(1).
[69] *Id.*, art. 21(1); art. 23.

enactment by the Constituent Assembly. A number of revisions, however, were designed to clarify the operation of one cardinal feature of the power structure, i.e., the limitation of parliamentary power by the entrenchment of a number of provisions of the constitution. Action to repeal or alter these is, in the constitutional language, "reserved to the people."[70] The entire group of entrenched provisions is summarized in the following list:

1. The declaration of popular sovereignty and the one-man one-vote principle (Article 1).
2. The authorization to Parliament to surrender Ghanaian sovereignty to a larger African union (Article 2).
3. The declaration that Ghana is a unitary republic (Article 4).
4. The provisions conferring the executive power on a President, responsible to the people, who shall be Head of the State, Commander in Chief of the Armed Forces and Fount of Honor (Article 8).
5. The provisions of the declaration to be made by the President immediately after assuming office, except by the addition of further provisions (Article 13).
6. The provisions for the appointment by the President of Members of Parliament as Ministers of Ghana (Article 15).
7. The provisions for the appointment by the President of a Cabinet of at least eight Ministers (Article 16).
8. The provisions for a Parliament of stated powers (Article 20).

[70] The philosophical insistence that all legislative power sprang from the people was re-emphasized by the Constitution (Amendment) Act, 1964, Act 224, sec. 5, by inserting in Article 20 (2) which confers on Parliament all legislative power not reserved to the people, a phrase characterizing Parliament "as the corporate representative of the People." The significance of this addition appears to be philosophical and political, not juridical.

9. Provisions relating to the composition of and proceedings in the National Assembly (Article 21).
10. The requirement of an annual session of the National Assembly and authorization to the President to summon or prorogue it (Article 22).
11. Provisions relating to the dissolution of the National Assembly (Article 23).
12. The prohibition of the imposition of taxation except by Act of Parliament (Article 26).
13. Provisions making the public debt and interest, sinking fund payments and management costs incident thereto charges on the general revenues and assets of Ghana (Article 37).
14. Provisions for a Supreme Court and a High Court on which were conferred the judicial power of the State (Article 41).
15. Provisions relating to the appointment and tenure in office of judges (Article 45).
16. The prohibition of the raising of any armed force except under authority of an Act of Parliament (Article 53).
17. Provisions for special powers of the first President (Article 55).

Alteration of these entrenched provisions requires action of the President, the people and the National Assembly. Only the President is authorized to put an entrenched provision to referendum. Approval of repeal or alteration by the people in a referendum does not accomplish the change, however. It merely authorizes the National Assembly to enact the repealing or altering measure, the certification by the Speaker that the appropriate authority has been conferred on Parliament in a referendum being made conclusive.[71] It should be noted as well that Parliament may by simple enactment entrench additional provisions of the con-

71 *Id.*, art. 20.

stitution, and such provisions are thereafter to be treated as if they had been entrenched originally.[72]

Aside from the entrenchment device, the legislative power of Parliament is not substantively limited.[73] There is a minor procedural limitation in that any enactment to alter the constitution must be expressed to be an amending act and must be limited to provisions effecting the amendment.[74] It will be recalled that the pre-Republic Constitution contained substantive limitations in the form of guarantees against certain forms of discrimination and against the taking of property without compensation. These have been eliminated as far as formalized limits on legislative power are concerned and survive only as parts of a "solemn declaration before the people" which the President is required to make immediately after his assumption of office.[75] Among the fundamental principles to which the President must declare his adherence are these:

> That no person should suffer discrimination on grounds of sex, race, tribe, religion or political belief. . . .
>
> That subject to such restrictions as may be necessary for preserving public order, morality or health, no person should be deprived of freedom of religion or speech, of the right to move and assemble without hindrance or of the right of access to courts of law.
>
> That no person should be deprived of his property save where the public interest so requires and the law so provides.[76]

[72] Id., art. 20(3).　　[73] Id., art. 20(6).
[74] Id., art. 20(2).　　[75] Id., art. 13.
[76] The principle relating to property was more extensive in the draft constitution appended to the White Paper. It then provided: "That no person should be deprived of his property save in accordance with law, and that no law should be made by which a person is deprived of his property without adequate compensation other than a law imposing taxation or prescribing penalties for offences or giving restitution for civil wrongs or protecting health or property." In commenting on the Constitution Bill, which eliminated all reference to compensation, the Government

It seems clear that these "principles" are merely political and ceremonial and have no actual juridical effect.[77] They are "declared" by the President and not by Parliament. The provisions quoted above are somewhat similar to guarantees of basic rights that in certain other constitutions do limit the law-making power; but they are joined with others which obviously cannot be more than the postulation of political ideals—for example, "that every citizen of Ghana should receive his fair share of the produce yielded by the development of the country." Finally, Article 20 is explicit that aside from the entrenched provisions, "the power of Parliament to make laws shall be under no limitation whatsoever."

The functioning of the National Assembly is protected by a guarantee of freedom of speech, debate; its proceedings "shall not be impeached or questioned in any court or place out of the Assembly."[78] The functioning of the Assembly is qualified, however, by the presidential power to summon, prorogue and dissolve the Assembly.[79] Despite the extensive legislative powers of the President (to be discussed later), some assurance of the continuing operation of the representative Assembly is offered by the requirement of annual sessions[80] and by the requirement of an Act of Parliament for the imposition of taxation.[81] The ultimate power of the Assembly is, of course, limited by the necessity

---

merely stated that the presidential declaration had been amended to make clear "that persons should not be deprived of their property save where the public interest so requires."

[77] See below, ch. VII, pp. 285-290.
[78] Republican Constitution, art. 21(3).
[79] *Id.*, art. 22(2), 23(1).   [80] *Id.*, art. 22(1).
[81] *Id.*, art. 26(1). This latter provision as well as Article 36 relating to the raising of loans for the purposes of the Republic and Article 53(1) on the raising of any armed force expressly require an Act of Parliament. The directions of the President under Article 55, while valid legislation, clearly do not qualify as Acts of Parliament. See Interpretation Act, 1960, C.A. 4, sec. 32(1). Thus, the legislative power of the President is seemingly limited on these specific matters as well as on constitutional revision which Article 55 itself expressly forecloses.

for Presidential assent before a bill can become effective, and by the prohibition of amendments of the annual estimates (money bills).[82]

The significant role of the President, as a part of Parliament, in the legislative process has already been noted. He may summon, prorogue or dissolve the Assembly, may attend any of its sittings and may address it at any time.[83] All legislation passed in the Assembly requires the assent of the President, who may give or refuse it to a bill in its entirety or to any part thereof.[84] Executive agencies under the President prepare, for submission to the Assembly, annual estimates of expenditure for public purposes, and while the Assembly may approve or reject each head of the estimates, it totally lacks a power of amendment.[85] In addition to these powers which inhere in any President under the present Republican Constitution, Dr. Nkrumah as the first President of Ghana enjoys a special range of legislative powers.

The legislative power of the first President is provided by Article 55 of the constitution. This article was not included in the draft constitution submitted to the people before the referendum, nor was it in the Constitution Bill submitted to the Constituent Assembly[86] Article 55 provides:

[82] Republican Constitution, art. 24; art. 31(2).
[83] *Id.*, art. 21(4); art. 25(4).
[84] *Id.*, art. 24(1).   [85] *Id.*, art. 31.
[86] In interviews conducted in Ghana in August, 1960, I attempted to determine where the initiative for Article 55 came from and why it had been included when Nkrumah controlled a large and loyal majority in the Assembly. One highly placed official gave, according to my notes, a rather vague and evasive explanation, suggesting that these special powers were thought necessary in the light of such events as those in the Congo but that, of course, it was not contemplated that these special presidential powers would be used. When I raised the question with a prominent politician of the opposition United Party, he acknowledged that he did not even know Article 55 was in the constitution. Another informant whose position should have given him a close view of the processes of constitution making within the Government, indicated that the initiative on Article 55 appeared to come from a small number of C.P.P. backbenchers in Parliament, that perhaps the President and the majority in the

(1) Notwithstanding anything in Article Twenty of the Constitution, the person appointed as first President of Ghana shall have, during his initial period of office, the powers conferred on him by this Article.

(2) The first President may, whenever he considers it to be in the national interest to do so, give directions by legislative instrument.

(3) An instrument made under this Article may alter (whether expressly or by implication) any enactment other than the Constitution.

(4) Section (2) of Article Forty-two of the Constitution shall apply in relation to the powers conferred by this Article as it applies in relation to the powers conferred on Parliament.

(5) For the purposes of this Article, the first President's initial period of office shall be taken to continue until some other person assumes office as President.

(6) The power to repeal or alter this Article during the first President's initial period of office is reserved to the people.

Although the article thus confers extensive legislative powers on the first President, it is clear that his power is not fully equal to that of the National Assembly. The latter has power to amend the constitution itself, subject to referendum approval in case the affected provision is entrenched, whereas the President lacks such amending power altogether. Similarly, the imposition of taxes and the raising of public loans and armed forces require an Act of Parliament.[87] It would seem that a legislative instrument issued by the President under Article 55, though a form of primary legis-

Constituent Assembly had been receptive to the idea of special powers for Nkrumah more because of international developments, such as the revolution in Turkey and the assassination of the Prime Minister of Ceylon, than because of internal conditions in Ghana.

[87] Republican Constitution, art. 26(1); art. 36; art. 53(1).

lation, would not suffice for those purposes. The exercise of the powers of Article 55 by the President is subject to the same power of judicial review as is granted to the Supreme Court with respect to Acts of Parliament.[88] It should also be noted that these special powers of the President do not lapse at the end of the term for which Dr. Nkrumah was first elected in 1960. They last for his "initial period in office" which is defined to mean "until some other person assumes office as President." Since an incumbent President is eligible for re-election any number of times,[89] Nkrumah will enjoy the same powers in any terms for which he is elected to succeed himself. In other words, Nkrumah as President would not have these powers only if he were elected after an intervening term of another person as President.

It is difficult to assess the practical significance of the special legislative powers of the first President. Having maintained a large and pliable C.P.P. majority in the Assembly, Nkrumah has not, to the present, found it necessary or desirable to legislate directly under Article 55. It is possible, however, that the very existence of this large reserve of legislative power in the President has maintained in the Assembly itself a more compliant attitude. In any event, the makers of the Republican Constitution were not content to rely on the realities of political control over legislation that the President could exercise; they have formalized that control in the constitution itself.

EXECUTIVE POWER

The 1954 Constitution divided the executive power between the Governor and the Cabinet, but it was silent on criteria and procedures for selecting a Governor. This officer first appeared in an unrevealing definition and thereafter was a *fait accompli*. Like the

[88] *Id.*, arts. 55(4) and 42(2).
[89] *Id.*, art. 11; Presidential Elections Act, No. 1 of 1960, secs. 4-5.

metropolitan power itself, he simply *was*. Sir Charles N. Arden-Clarke, the Governor at the time the 1954 Constitution was adopted, became highly acceptable to the Nkrumah Government, with whom he worked closely in the progression toward independence. This relationship tended to augment and emphasize the Cabinet's role and de-emphasize that of the Governor.

The Cabinet was to consist of not less than eight members of the Assembly.[90] Ministers, including the Prime Minister, were appointed and subject to dismissal by the Governor, who in this respect was required to act in accordance with the constitutional convention applicable to the exercise of such functions by the Queen in the United Kingdom.[91] The assignment of responsibilities to Ministers was the function of the Prime Minister.[92] The Cabinet of Ministers was declared to be the "principal instrument of policy" and was collectively responsible to the Assembly.[93]

In carrying out his functions, the Governor was subject to Instructions issued by the metropolitan power under Her Majesty's Sign Manual and Signet.[94] Certain of his functions the Governor was authorized to exercise in his discretion, as in meeting his responsibilities for defense and foreign affairs.[95] In others, he was required to act on the advice of a designated person (for example, the Prime Minister),[96] and in such cases he was required to act in accordance with the advice. In other instances, the Governor was to act on the recommendation of a designated person or authority, e.g., to appoint public officers on the recommendation of the Public Service Commission.[97] In such cases the Governor was required to act in accordance with the recommendation received; but if he chose to do so, he could refer the recommendation back for further consideration. Where the Governor was to act on the

---

[90] 1954 Constitution, sec. 4.   [91] *Id.*, sec. 7.
[92] *Id.*, sec. 16.   [93] *Id.*, sec. 5.
[94] *Id.*, sec. 6.   [95] *Id.*, sec. 17.
[96] *Id.*, sec. 19, on the appointment of Ministerial Secretaries.
[97] *Id.*, secs. 52, 56 and Third Schedule.

advice of a person or authority, he was bound by the advice. In all cases not falling into one of the foregoing categories, the Governor was required to act on and in accordance with the advice of the Cabinet.[98] This final category of functions included all acts of the Governor not expressly qualified in one of the other manners. Thus the constitution and other laws required careful examination to determine if the grant of power to the Governor was merely formal or carried also the substantive responsibility for decision.

Control of Cabinet action was not extensively treated in the 1954 Constitution. The Cabinet, of course, could not take any action relating to defense and external affairs or to matters affecting the responsibility of the United Kingdom Government under the Togoland Trusteeship.[99] Cabinet decisions were taken by majority vote of those present and voting, and in the case of an equal division, the person presiding had a vote.[100] In general, however, control of the Cabinet depended upon the grant of legislative powers to the Assembly and upon the collective responsibility of the Cabinet to the Assembly.[101]

The general structure of parliamentary government was retained by the Independence Constitution of 1957. While the conventional language of British constitutional law was preserved in the vesting of executive power in the Queen, to "be exercised by the Queen or by the Governor-General as Her Representative,"[102] the substantive executive power was in the indigenous Cabinet. The Cabinet was charged with the general direction and control of the Government.[103] Except in a few instances where the Governor General was to act on the binding advice of some person or authority other than the Cabinet,[104] he was to function in accordance

---

[98] For example, under sec. 8(4) in declaring a Minister incapable by reason of illness of discharging his functions.

[99] *Id.*, sec. 5(1) and Second Schedule; sec. 17.

[100] *Id.*, sec. 14.   [101] *Id.*, sec. 36; sec. 5(2).

[102] 1957 Constitution, sec. 6.   [103] *Id.*, sec. 7(1).

[104] For example, under sec. 51(1) in appointing public offices on the advice of the Public Service Commission; sec. 4(2).

with the constitutional convention applicable in the United Kingdom to the Queen. All discretionary powers of the former Governor were lost, as was his exclusive responsibility for defense and external affairs. Even in the appointment of the Governor General, advice from the Ghana Government to the Queen was binding.[105]

An executive structure closely following the Westminster model continued until the creation of the Republic in 1960. At that time, the shift was toward what may be called a presidential system, though the Ghana variation is unique.[106] Executive power is conferred on the President who is also the Head of the State, Commander in Chief of the armed forces and is declared to be responsible to the people. The President thus inherited the role of the Queen as represented by the Governor General, but all doubt of the reality of his power is removed by the express provision that in the exercise of his powers and functions the "President shall act in his own discretion and shall not be obliged to follow advice tendered by any other person." The foregoing provisions of Article 8 were entrenched. The presidential term is of indefinite duration, as will be explained later, beginning with his assumption of office and ending with the assumption of office of his successor.[107] In accordance with the earlier plebiscite, Dr. Nkrumah was named first President of Ghana.[108]

[105] The 1957 Constitution, sec. 4(1), merely vests the appointing power in the Queen. The British Government expressly recognized, however, that he was to be appointed "in accordance with the conventions obtaining in other Commonwealth Countries." The Proposed Constitution of Ghana, p. 4, Cmnd. 71 (1957). The convention provides for appointment on the advice of the Ghana Government. See also 5 Halsbury's Laws of England, 448 (3rd ed. 1952).

[106] The Republican Constitution of Ghana later served as a model for the Republican Constitution of Tanganyika but with significant differences. See McAuslan, "The Republican Constitution of Tanganyika," 13 International and Comparative Law Quarterly 502-73 (Apr., 1964).

[107] Republican Constitution, art. 9.

[108] Id., art. 10.

The election of a President is intimately tied to the election of Parliament. Upon the dissolution of the National Assembly, or the death or resignation of the President, a new President is to be elected.[109] The only qualifications for office expressed in the constitution are Ghanaian citizenship and attainment of thirty-five years of age.[110] The constitutional provisions for the election of a President were not entrenched, and most of the details of the procedure appear in the legislation enacted by the republican parliament.[111]

Procedures for electing a President differ, depending upon whether the election is held by reason of the dissolution of the National Assembly (dissolution election) or by reason of the death or resignation of the President (interim election). In the former case, nomination of a constitutionally qualified person can be made by a notice signed by two or more citizens which declares that the nominee has consented and that the nominators have reason to believe that at the ensuing parliamentary election, candidates exceeding in number one-half the number of seats in the Assembly will declare their preference for the nominee.[112] In the case of an interim election, nominations may be made by a notice signed by ten or more members of Parliament.[113]

In the event of a dissolution election, each candidate for the National Assembly is required to declare his preference for President, but such a declaration requires the consent of the candidate preferred. After the successful candidates for the Assembly have been determined, they proceed to elect the President by majority vote. Each candidate's pre-election declaration of preference is automatically considered his vote on the first presidential ballot.[114] If no presidential nominee has a majority on the first ballot, further balloting takes place in which each member of the Assembly

---

[109] *Id.*, art. 11. [110] *Id.*, art. 11(2)(a).
[111] The Presidential Elections Act, No. 1 of 1960.
[112] *Id.*, sec. 4. [113] *Id.*, sec. 5.
[114] *Id.*, sec. 7.

may vote his uncommitted preference. Election results when the Chief Justice determines that the number of votes cast for one of the candidates exceeds the total votes cast for all other candidates. Thus, if absences or abstentions are considered, it is possible for a President to be elected by a mere plurality in the Assembly. If a President has not been elected on the completion of five ballots, the Assembly is deemed dissolved and the whole procedure must be repeated.[115] Interim elections differ only in the absence of the automatic first ballot cast on the basis of the declared preference by a member of the Assembly.[116]

After his election, the President is authorized to appoint his Cabinet, consisting, as under previous constitutions, of at least eight members of Parliament. The Cabinet is charged, subject to the powers of the President, "with the general direction and control of the Government of Ghana."[117] Although he is not a member of the National Assembly, the President is not merely an executive but is intimately involved in a variety of ways in the legislative process. He alone is authorized to order a referendum looking toward the modification of one of the entrenched clauses of the constitution.[118] He may at any time summon or prorogue the Assembly, attend any of its sittings and address it at any time.[119] Most significantly, the President may at any time dissolve the Assembly.[120] Thus, if differences arise between the President and the Assembly, differences which in a parliamentary system might produce a vote of no confidence or the breakdown of a really viable cooperation, the President is in a position at any time to permit the people to resolve— in a new general election—the issues thus raised. It

---

[115] Republican Constitution, art. 11(3); Presidential Elections Act, 1960, sec. 9(4).

[116] Presidential Elections Act, 1960, sec. 10. Detailed provisions for dealing with the death, withdrawal or substitution of candidates, secs. 12-14, need not be explained here.

[117] Republican Constitution, arts. 15, 16. [118] *Id.*, art. 20(2).

[119] *Id.*, art. 22(2); art. 21(4); art. 25(4). [120] *Id.*, art. 23(1).

49

should be noted, however, that restraint in dissolving the Assembly may be recommended by the fact that on dissolution, a new presidential election must also be held, the President's term depending directly on the life of the Assembly.[121] Should the President decline to dissolve the Assembly, no breakdown of cooperation, even to the extent of a direct expression of lack of confidence in the executive, can force the President out of office. This fact takes on added significance in view of the special legislative powers granted by Article 55 to the first President.

All legislation passed in the Assembly requires the assent of the President, who may give or refuse it to a bill in its entirety or to any part.[122] Expenditures from public funds are to be made only under a warrant issued by authority of the President.[123] Expenditures for "a public service" which in the opinion of the President are sufficiently urgent may be made without authorization by the Assembly.[124] If the President "thinks it expedient in the public interest so to do," he may make loans out of public funds; no limitations as to borrowers or purposes, other than the general reference to the President's opinion on "public interest," are specified.[125] The National Assembly may resolve, however, that a loan agreement made by the President for an amount in excess of that specified by the Assembly shall not be operative unless ratified by the Assembly.[126]

The constitution grants large but not plenary powers over the armed forces to the President. Not even the President can raise an armed force except by authority of an Act of Parliament.[127] The President is, however, Commander in Chief of the Armed Forces and in this capacity has power "to commission persons as officers . . . , to order any of said Forces to engage in operations

[121] *Id.*, art. 11(1)(a).   [122] *Id.*, art. 24(1).
[123] *Id.*, art. 29.   [124] *Id.*, art. 34.
[125] *Id.*, art. 35(1).
[126] *Id.*, art. 35(2). It should be noted that this limitation on the President's lending power did not appear in the draft constitution appended to the White Paper.
[127] *Id.*, art. 53.

for the defence of Ghana, for the preservation of public order, for relief in cases of emergency or for any other purpose appearing to the Commander in Chief to be expedient."[128] He may also, subject only to his determination of expediency, dismiss a member of the armed forces or order a member not to exercise any of his authority until the President as Commander in Chief permits him to do so.[129]

The constitutional provisions dealing with the exercise of presidential powers in the event of the death or incapacity of the incumbent were amended in 1964. The referendum did not cover these amendments, since the relevant provisions of the Republican Constitution (Article 18) were not entrenched.

Article 18 in its original form provided for two types of presidential commission, differently constituted and designed to perform in different circumstances:

1. A commission of three persons appointed by the Cabinet and bound to act in accordance with the advice of the Cabinet, to exercise presidential powers during the interval between the death or resignation of a President and his successor's assumption of office and when the President was adjudged incapable of acting;

2. a commission of three persons appointed by the President to exercise his powers when by reason of illness, not resulting in his being adjudged incapable of acting, or his absence from Ghana, it was inconvenient for him to act in person; in such circumstances the commission would be merely the delegee of the President, bound by his instructions and enjoying only such discretion as he should grant.

Either type of commission could act by any two of its members. Casual vacancies in a commission were to be filled by whoever had appointed the Commissioner being replaced.

---

[128] *Id.*, art. 54(1).   [129] *Id.*, art. 54(2).

The transfer of presidential powers to a commission of the first type, other than upon the death or resignation of the President, required a joint declaration by the Chief Justice and the Speaker of the National Assembly that after considering medical evidence, they were satisfied that the President was unable because of physical or mental infirmity to exercise the functions of his office. Such a declaration could be withdrawn if the President recovered his capacity, thus terminating the powers of the commission. No presidential commission of the first type was ever created; on a number of occasions when he has been absent from Ghana, Dr. Nkrumah has appointed commissions of the second kind.

Article 18 was substantially revised by the Constitution (Amendment) Act of 1964 (Act 224, Sec. 8). The former differentiation between two types of commission was abolished, and the constitution now provides simply for a presidential commission to be appointed by the President; it will act in accordance with the advice of the Cabinet in any of the circumstances previously dealt with by a commission of either type. This commission is apparently to be a continuing body whose members are not given terms of fixed duration but remain subject to removal by the President at any time.

The procedure for determining the incapacity of the President was also modified. The critical declaration must now be made by the Speaker in pursuance of a resolution of the National Assembly that, after considering medical evidence, the Assembly is satisfied that the President cannot, because of physical or mental infirmity, exercise the functions of his office. Such a declaration may be withdrawn, however, so as to revest in the President his usual powers.

The effect of the 1964 amendments was to transform presidential commissions from occasional bodies brought into being to meet special circumstances into a continuing agency immediately available to act when circumstances, possibly involving extreme emergency, remove or incapacitate the President. Thus, greatly improved legal provision was made for the orderly transfer of presidential powers to a body authorized to act until the constitutional provisions for the election of a new President can be implemented. It is also significant that the incumbent President, through his power to appoint and dismiss Commissioners, is able to determine who will exercise the powers of his office immediately after his death, resignation or incapacity. Finally, it should be noted that the important role of the Chief Justice in determining the President's incapacity to act has been terminated and the role of the Speaker has been reduced to the function of announcing the critical determination of the National Assembly. Thus, the power to judge the capacity of the President to act has been significantly dispersed and, at least in theory, democratized.

THE PUBLIC SERVICE

The effectiveness of the executive is in large measure a reflection of the competence, imagination and loyalty of the public service. Because of its importance, the public service, its recruitment and control, will be considered separately from the political executive.

When the postwar nationalistic ferment began in the Gold Coast, the great majority of senior civil service posts were occupied by expatriate officers. While the pressure for Africanization had already brought some response, it was officially asserted as late as 1951 that the "supply of Africans suitable and qualified to fill the higher posts in the Government Service will not in the foreseeable future be equal to the needs of the Gold Coast which must remain largely dependent upon the recruitment of expatriate staff."[130] The legal provisions relevant here were primarily designed for the protection of incumbent expatriate officers and the assurance of adequate expatriate recruits until full Africanization was possible.

[130] Report of the Commission on the Civil Service of the Gold Coast, 1950-51, vol. I, para. 68 (1951).

53

The 1954 Constitution contained provisions relating to the public service which became effective on May 5, 1954, as well as substitute provisions which were brought into effect on July 31, 1955. The similarities and significant differences in these two sets of provisions should be noted. Under the provisions included in the constitution for immediate effect,[131] the appointment, promotion, dismissal and disciplinary control of public officers—other than the Deputy Governor, judges of the Supreme Court, judicial officers and the Auditor General—were vested in the Governor acting in his discretion. The Governor was authorized, also in his discretion, to issue regulations providing for the delegation to any public officer of his powers relating to the public service, except the power to appoint or dismiss public officers in positions carrying an initial salary exceeding £430 per year. In making appointments or otherwise exercising these powers, the Governor was to consult with the Prime Minister in relation to the appointment or promotion to a "special post," defined to mean that of permanent secretary and posts of a corresponding or higher grade. There was provision as well for a public service commission to be appointed by the Governor after consultation with the Prime Minister. The functions of the Public Service Commission consisted of giving advice to the Governor on any question which he might in his discretion refer to it. The questions contemplated related to the appointment or termination of appointment, dismissal or other disciplinary control of public officers, or to other matters which in the opinion of the Governor affected the public service. It was expressly stipulated, however, that the Governor should not be required to act in accordance with the advice tendered by the Commission. The Governor was also empowered in his discretion to make regulations for the purpose of giving effect to the provisions regarding the Public Service Commission.

[131] 1954 Constitution, secs. 52-55, 57-59.

The substitute provisions,[132] effective a year later, were significantly different. In them, provision was also made for a public service commission appointed by the Governor after consultation with the Prime Minister, and the same procedure applied with respect to the removal of a Commissioner from his office. On the matter of appointment, promotion, transfer, dismissal and disciplinary control of public officers (other than a limited number of high-ranking officers), the new provisions vested the power in the Governor acting on the recommendation of the Public Service Commission, except in the case of appointments, promotions and transfers to the office of Attorney General or to any special post. Appointment to the office of Attorney General was to be made by the Governor after consultation with the Prime Minister, and appointment, promotion and transfer to a special post were to be made by the Governor acting in his discretion after consultation with the Prime Minister and after obtaining the advice of the Public Service Commission. Again the Governor, acting on the recommendation of the Public Service Commission, was authorized to make regulations on a variety of subjects relating to the carrying out by the Commission of its functions.

The effect of the changes in the provisions relating to public service recruitment, dismissal and disciplinary control was to diminish the discretionary power of the Governor, representing the metropolitan power, and to increase the power of the Prime Minister. The function of the Public Service Commission was also significantly changed. In the earlier provisions its function was purely advisory, and discretion rested exclusively with the Governor with respect to seeking the advice of the Commission and determining whether such advice should be followed. The later provisions gave the Public Service Commission substantial power over the recommendation of appointments to most grades or posts in the public service and recommendations concerning

132 *Id.*, sec. 56 and Third Schedule.

55

the regulations governing the carrying out of the Commission's own functions. The 1954 Constitution thus showed a continuing shift of power over the public service from metropolitan discretion to an indigenous political leader and a specialized Commission. Increased responsibility of the latter agency suggested recruitment on substantive criteria of technical competence; this suggestion was borne out by the applicable Public Service Regulations.

In negotiations for the Independence Constitution, the Gold Coast Government indicated a desire that the existing provisions relating to the Public Service be altered as little as possible.[133] While the Government suggested that the appointments of all members of the Public Service Commission would terminate at independence, it indicated also an intention to advise the re-appointment of any existing member of the Commission who desired to continue.[134] With the exception of special posts, overseas posts and the posts of Attorney General and Auditor General, who would be appointed by the Governor General on the advice of the Prime Minister or the Cabinet,[135] it was proposed that the Governor General should act on the advice of the Public Service Commission.[136]

The Independence Constitution followed these proposals. Appointments to the Public Service Commission for five-year terms were to be made by the Governor General acting on the advice of the Prime Minister; the Commissioners could be removed by a similar process.[137] Power to appoint, dismiss and discipline public service officers was vested in the Governor General acting on and in accordance with the advice of the Commission. Officers of the rank of Permanent Secretary or above ("special posts") were to be appointed on the advice of the Prime Minister after consultation

[133] Constitutional Proposals for Gold Coast Independence, para. 20 (1956).
[134] Id., para. 22.   [135] Id., para. 23.   [136] Id., para. 20.
[137] 1957 Constitution, sec. 50.

with the Commission. Overseas posts were to be filled on the advice of the Prime Minister, but without the stipulation of consultation with the Commission.[138] It should be noted that although the Attorney General, who retained responsibility over all except petty criminal prosecutions, was a public officer, his post was expressly excluded from the category of "special posts" and was therefore to be filled by the Governor General acting on and in accordance with the advice of the Public Service Commission.[139]

A number of significant changes affecting the public service were made by the Constitution (Amendment) Act of 1959.[140] Foreign service posts were entirely excluded from the control of the Public Service Commission, which retained only the function of consulting with the Prime Minister before he advised the Governor General on appointments below the level of ambassadors and heads of missions. The top-level foreign service appointments required no such consultation. A large number of positions were added to the category of "special posts," and the earlier exclusion of the Attorney General from that category was eliminated. It will be remembered that "special post" appointments were not made on the advice of the Public Service Commission but on the advice of the Prime Minister, after consultation with the Commission. Thus, the new provisions tended to increase or at least formalize an increase in political control over the appointment, dismissal and discipline of a number of senior officers, perhaps the most significant of them being the Attorney General. The movement toward making his office clearly political is further manifested by the new provision that in discharging his responsibility for criminal prosecutions for offenses against the safety of the state, the Attorney General should act on the direction of the Prime Minister.[141]

In preparation for the creation of the Republic, the

138 *Id.*, sec. 51.
139 *Id.*, sec. 15; sec. 51(4)(a); sec. 51(1).
140 Act No. 7 of 1959.   141 *Id.*, sec. 9.

Government's views on the administration of the civil service were thought sufficiently important to warrant the publication of a separate White Paper,[142] prior to the plebiscite. The views there expressed were implemented in the Republican Constitution and in the Civil Service Act passed by the Constituent Assembly to take effect immediately after the implementation of the constitution.[143]

The White Paper asserted the inappropriateness in Ghana's circumstances of the old civil service which "had loyalties and values which grew up to meet the needs of a colonial system with the seat of authority in the United Kingdom." While recognizing that Ghana's needs could be met only by the continued employment of foreign officers for a time, the Government pledged the Africanization of the civil service as early as possible. Especially interesting were the Government's views on the loyalty of the service. It commented: "As a servant of the State, a civil servant's first loyalty is to the State and, since the Government is charged, by popular choice and by the authority of Parliament, with responsibility for managing the affairs of the State, the civil servant should appropriately feel a positive and consistent loyalty to the interests of the Government as his employer. This concept will become clearer under a Republic Constitution when the focal point of the Civil Servant's loyalty becomes the President as both Head of State and Head of Government." To be sure, the Government immediately cautioned that this principle of loyalty to the State and to the Government "does not imply participation in party politics. . . . Civil Servants must, therefore, be in a position to serve all Governments of whatever complexion with equal loyalty and to obtain the confidence of Ministers irrespective of their political party." The suggested loyalties to State and Government are complex and sophisticated. The

[142] A New Charter for the Civil Service, W.P. 2/60 (Accra 1960).
[143] Civil Service Act, 1960, C.A. 5.

role of the President as both Head of State and leader of the Government of the moment increases the possibility that the two loyalties will merge, thus foreclosing a truly nonpartisan civil service.

The White Paper points out that under the 1957 Constitution, control of the civil service was placed in an independent commission. It then declared that "it is considered quite inappropriate that the control of the Civil Service machine should not be in the hands of the Government which relies on it for getting its work done." The constitution therefore vests control of the service in the President: "Subject to the provisions of the Constitution and save as is otherwise provided by law, the appointment, promotion, transfer, termination of appointment, dismissal and disciplinary control of members of the Public Services is vested in the President."[144] A statutory Civil Service Commission, appointed by the President, was retained to assist the President in the discharge of his functions. The operating allocations of responsibility for the civil service are indicated by Table I (p. 60).[145]

While extensive delegation of appointive and disciplinary powers is contemplated, the fact is entirely clear that all authority stems from and in the important cases is actually to be exercised by the President.

The enlarged powers of the President are further reflected in the constitutional provisions concerning the Attorney General. This officer may be a Minister or other person appointed by the President and is no longer categorized as a "public officer."[146] Authority is vested

[144] Republican Constitution, art. 51(2). It should be noted that this power covers the "Public Services of Ghana," which include the civil service, the judicial service, the police service, the local government service and such others as may be provided by law.

[145] The table is derived from the Civil Service Act, 1960, and the Civil Service (Interim) Regulations, 1960, issued by the President.

[146] Republican Constitution, art. 47. The Attorney General from independence to September, 1961, was Mr. Geoffrey Bing, Q.C., an English barrister and former British M.P., who prior to independence served as constitutional advisor to Dr. Nkrumah.

TABLE 1

CATEGORY OF EMPLOYEE
1. *Category A*—All permanent secretaries and other officers of paramount importance in effectuating Government policy. Posts listed in First Schedule to Regulations.

HOW APPOINTED
By the President

DISCIPLINING AUTHORITY
The President

REVIEW BY
None

2. *Category B*—Staff Grade Posts, such as Government Printer, Accountant General. Posts listed in Second Schedule to Regulations.

HOW APPOINTED
By the President who shall, "unless he considers it inexpedient to do so," consult the Civil Service Commission and the relevant Minister, if any.

DISCIPLINING AUTHORITY
Posts in or attached to a Ministry—The Minister*
Posts in the Administrative class—Secretary to the Cabinet
Posts in a special department—Head of a Department or Secretary to the Cabinet

REVIEW BY
The President in cases of major penalties

3. *Category C*—From Higher Executive officer up to Category "B" level.

HOW APPOINTED
By the Civil Service Commission under delegation from the President

DISCIPLINING AUTHORITY
Posts in the Administrative class—secretary to the Cabinet. All other posts head of the Department*

REVIEW BY
Head of Department when discipline first imposed by a delegee.

4. *Category D*—All posts not in higher category.

HOW APPOINTED
By the head of Department

DISCIPLINING AUTHORITY
Head of Department*

REVIEW BY
Head of Department when discipline first imposed by a delegee.

* Indicates that a further delegation may be authorized.

in the Attorney General, subject to the directions of the President, to initiate, conduct and discontinue civil and criminal proceedings and to defend in civil proceedings brought against the Republic. Prior to the Republic, the constitution made the functions in criminal proceedings subject to the direction of the Prime Minister only in connection with offenses against the safety of the State.[147] Thus, further control by the Head of Government was formalized in the new constitution. As a Presidential appointee, the Attorney General's appointment is of course subject to revocation.[148] Parenthetically, it should be noted that in connection with criminal offenses, the President is also granted large powers of mercy. He may pardon, grant respite of execution of any sentence, remission of any sentence, penalty or forfeiture; and in cases where he remits a death sentence, he may order imprisonment of the offender until he orders his release.[149]

Relations between the civil service, particularly at more senior levels, and the political leadership of the country have never been easy. Civil service appointment has offered the most attractive career opportunities, and these have been shielded by standards for qualification set at reasonably high levels. As a consequence, the civil service has represented a relatively cohesive segment of the better educated and economically advantaged part of the population. On the other hand, the C.P.P., gaining power as a mass movement, has attracted few of the intellectuals and has presented a practically unlimited supply of poorly trained manpower before the narrow gates of the civil service. Suspicion and hostility have therefore been the classic lot of the civil service in dealing with the dominant party.

From time to time, the Party has organized moves to intimidate the civil service and thereby alter its char-

---

[147] Constitution (Amendment) Act, Act No. 7 of 1959, sec. 9.
[148] Republican Constitution, art. 47(3).
[149] Id., art. 48.

acter. In 1961, C.P.P. sound-trucks moved through the ministries area in Accra blaring threats against the obstructionist and possibly disloyal civil servants. In December, 1963, following the acquittal of certain persons accused of treason and the consequent dismissal of the Chief Justice,[150] the Party press renewed its attack on the civil service. After alleging "a massive plot to seek the overthrow of the Government by force, in which the civil service machinery is involved," the *Evening News* continued

> Ghana is passing through a phase in which the pattern of the future is being settled and the shape of future events depends to a large extent on the interpretation that the graduates, lawyers and professional intellectuals give to the Party line. It is assumed at times that the mere presence of a Minister or a Deputy Minister alone guarantees security against anti-State activities in the Ministries.
>
> This assumption is not generally correct. It is necessary in several departments that political activists and security officers are drafted from the Party to assist the leading State functionaries, thus instead of one there will be two respectives [perspectives?] on every question—from above and below. Closer contact with the working people can also be effected in this way.
>
> Experience shows that when Ministers of State make establishment proposals, there is automatic reaction against this by anti-Party elements from the Civil Service Commission as well as other sources. This is by no means an accident, for there have been Ministers who have sky-rocketed reactionaries to top posts on basis of personal relations, nepotism, etc. The fact that Civil Servants and the old order was practising worse forms of nepotism is hardly mentioned today. One result of such practices is the disillusioning of the working people, but the Party's

[150] See below, pp. 234-37, 341-42.

campaign against corruption and nepotism led by "Party Chronicle" and "Evening News" is very useful in this connection.

The question is: "Which is better—A highly loyal personnel with little professional technique and a lot of revolutionary experience, or a highly-skilled intellectual group which continuously seeks new and overt ways of undermining State security?"

It is high time, in fact, that the Civil Service Commission recognises that political reliability is more valuable an asset than a chain of degrees from abroad in our epoch of socialist reconstruction. In fact the claim to impartiality of the Civil Service is not genuine.

The CSC has a distinct class character outlook which guides its selection of candidates for work in Government offices. There have been examples of important posts lying unfilled for years merely because of alleged lack of "qualified" personnel.[151]

The Party's solution to the problem lay in a fundamental revamping of the Civil Service Commission. As the *Evening News* declared

In order to streamline the State administration and security into new channels, it is necessary that the Civil Service Commission is stripped of all pretences to impartiality, and becomes a genuine machinery for the promotion of the Party's aims and objectives.

The State Security organs and foreign service too, need to be purged of their foreign line trappings and the formalities of a decadent colonialist epoch.

The existence of the CSC, in view of the class character of its appointments, amounts to the existence of a second party in a one-party State. Nearly 90% of officers in Government service in the higher grades appointed by the CSC, have to supply refer-

[151] Thursday, December 12, 1963, p. 3, cols. 2-6.

ences from reactionary institutions or hostile elements from time to time.

Another contradiction in the Civil Service set-up is the history behind the whole setting. It is British in character, and bourgeois British codes apply. In Foreign Affairs for example, there are three grades of people. A for graduate, B for non-graduate professionals and C for junior staff, with corresponding privileges.

The result of this class division is that a build-up of subversive lawyers, reactionaries and dark-coated intellectuals and friends of Western diplomats hold sway, and show little or no respect for the Party as custodians of State administration in a Socialist State.

THE POINT IS THAT THE CIVIL SERVICE COMMISSION, BECAUSE IT HAS NO POLITICAL PERSPECTIVE, IS TOTALLY UNRELIABLE and unfit to select candidates for foreign service and state security work.

It must prepare to consider appointments in terms of political reliability other than academic standards alone.

This can only be realised if its members are elected by the Party's executive organs.

The Civil Service Commission is a colonialist institution in the power of one class—the class of lawyer intellectuals and former privileged. It is for the interests of the anti-socialist forces in Ghana and must be overhauled. Like Establishments, it has yet to declare a conclusive role in the Socialist Revolution.

It is a refuge for subversionists and foreign agents. If it is non-political as it purports to be, then how does it justify its appointments for political work?

In order to consolidate the gains of the Revolution, it is necessary to strengthen the ideological basis of the Party, to stress the supremacy of the Party line and positively combat bourgeois ideology and all the colonialist set-ups not yet overhauled.[152]

152 Friday, December 13, 1963, p. 3, cols. 1-6.

It is clear that the British ideal of a nonpolitical civil service may find the revolutionary climate of Ghana unpropitious for taking root. This conclusion is not inevitable, however. Ghana's endowment of senior civil servants, recruited on the basis of objective qualification, is one of her greatest national resources. Despite the attacks of the Party press, it is not clear that Dr. Nkrumah is prepared to sacrifice the competence of the civil service in favor of a more fervent but clearly less qualified body of Party activists.

CHAPTER II

STATUS OF THE TRADITIONAL AUTHORITIES

CLASSIFICATION OF systems of colonial administration is often made to depend on the attitude adopted toward the traditional rulers of a subject people and the uses made of these rulers in the daily tasks of government. They may be allies and collaborators or the focal points of dissidence and active opposition. A similar classification might be made of the newly independent governments of African states. In this chapter the traditional status and role of the indigenous authorities of Ghana, who are usually described indiscriminately as chiefs, will be reviewed; and to establish the 1951 base line, the effects of colonial administration will be summarized. The prime focus of the chapter will be on the legal treatment of the traditional authorities under an African government in the pre-independence Gold Coast and modern Ghana.

The diversity of traditional societies in what is now Ghana, as well as the inadequacy of the data available, makes generalization hazardous.[1] Political organization covered a wide spectrum from the complex institutions of Ashanti to the rudimentary structures of some groups in the Northern Territories. In the middle range lay the traditional orders of the Ga towns and the loosely allied divisions of the Ewe. For present purposes, however, we will place primary emphasis on the institu-

[1] Information on the traditional authorities is drawn mainly from Busia, *The Position of the Chief in the Modern Political System of Ashanti* (1951); Casely-Hayford, *Gold Coast Native Institutions* (1903); Danquah, *Akan Laws and Customs and the Akim Abuakwa Constitution* (1928); Field, *Social Organization of the Ga People* (1940); Hailey, *Native Administration in the British African Territories*, Part III (1951); Manoukian, *The Ewe-Speaking People of Togoland and the Gold Coast* (1952); Manoukian, *Tribes of the Northern Territories of the Gold Coast* (1951); Rattray, *Ashanti Law and Constitution* (1929).

tions of the Akan people who occupied most of the Gold Coast Colony and Ashanti.

For the purpose of civil government, the major unit among the Akan was a division or state ruled by a Paramount Chief or King. In Ashanti several such states were federated largely for military purposes under the Paramount Chief of Kumasi as Asantehene or King of Ashanti. Leader of his people in war, an Akan King was also the head of the civil government. A third aspect of his office was fundamental, however. The Akan chief was sacred, being regarded as the intermediary between the living community and his own royal ancestors who were believed to watch over and protect the people. Thus, ritual functions, drawing vitality from a general system of ancestor worship, sustained the Akan chieftaincy even when its military role was ended and its civil functions subjected to serious threats. In the Northern Territories, chieftaincy was a mere secular office, religious functions being carried out by priests (*Tendanas*) who were also regarded as trustees of the tribal land.

An Akan state was a hierarchy, the basic unit being the lineage composed of people tracing their descent through the female line from a common ancestor. Several lineages, each with its own head, occupied a village. A number of villages were organized into a subdivision and these in turn formed the state or division. In Ashanti, the several divisions formed the federation whose leader, the Asantehene, as occupant of the Golden Stool, symbolized the unity and nationhood of the Ashanti people. The other Akan divisions or states outside Ashanti remained independent units loosely connected by shifting alliances, though one abortive effort at confederation was made.[2]

Despite certain aristocratic features, Akan political institutions involved a large measure of popular control in both the selection of leaders and in guiding their later conduct in office. The lineage head or elder,

[2] See ch. III, pp. 125-26.

who served as both the political head of his lineage and as intermediary between the ancestors and the living, was chosen by the adult members of the group. The heads of the several lineages occupying a village served as a council to the village head who was selected by them and who served as the representative of the village in the higher councils of the subdivision or division. At the village or town level existed another Akan institution which had great significance in the selection and control of the traditional authorities. This was the company of commoners, at least one of which existed in each village and town. Important as a military unit, it retained its structure in times of peace, and its elected leader, chosen without regard to family connections, was the recognized spokesman of the members on political and governmental questions. In some of the Akan states, representatives of the companies of commoners were members of the council of the Paramount Chief or King, along with other councilors who held their seats as heads of noble families or by appointment of the King.

Through these channels, the critical processes of selection of the traditional rulers took place. At village, subdivision or division level, the headman or chief was required to come from one particular family. Each eligible family presented a number of possible candidates, however, and the selection of the leader was ultimately determined by the preferences of other lineage groups as well as by the elected representatives of the commoners. Popular participation was not exhausted in the processes of selection of the traditional rulers. On important questions, it was contemplated that widespread consultation would take place and popular views would be transmitted through the hierarchy of lineage, village, and subdivision to the Council of the King. The injunction to the Akan chief to act only on the advice of his elders, who were themselves representatives, was given at the time of his enstoolment, and he was expected to follow it strictly. The chief of an Ewe division and the elders of a Ga town were similarly controlled. In the Northern Territories, in the most politically developed groups, acceptable lineage heads were promoted over a period of time to higher and higher offices in the hierarchy. While the Northern chief was expected to consult his council, his own authority was more nearly absolute than that of the chief in tribes of the central and southern regions.

Among the Akans, the ultimate sanction against a chief was removal from office or de-stoolment. Grounds for such action included disregard of the advice of his councilors and people, general mismanagement of affairs, unjustified disposal of stool property, certain physical disabilities and grievous breaches of traditional etiquette. Power to de-stool was distributed among the elders and councilors and the representatives of the companies of commoners. A similar though rarely used power to de-stool existed among some of the Ewe sub-tribes. In the Northern Territories, apparently no such possibility of a chief's removal existed, though the available data on this point are not adequate.

When its early reluctance to assume wide governmental responsibilities on the Gold Coast was abandoned, the British colonial administration pursued a policy that in theory should have preserved indigenous institutions in relatively pure form. Indirect rule, pioneered by Sir Frederick Lugard for governing the emirates of Northern Nigeria, was the accepted policy. Native chiefs were regarded as an integral part of the administrative structure, carrying out their assigned duties under the guidance of a small colonial staff and subject to the general restraints of British conceptions of humanity and justice. The serious distortions of indigenous institutions resulting from this policy were due in part to ignorance of tribal structures and customs. An excellent case, by way of illustration, was the acceptance of the Ga Manche, a minor priest who had certain magic functions in war but no civil authority, as the chief of the Gas and the development around him of an organization having no traditional base. Further distortion resulted from the tendency of the colonial administration to press for the election to the position of chief of persons loyal to the British administration but having little or no title under native law and custom, and to resist efforts to de-stool favored chiefs who had lost the support of their people. Inevitably, significant changes in the popular conception of the chieftaincy resulted. Closely identified with the colonial regime but having an obviously lower echelon status within it, the chief experienced a severe loss of prestige. Because his selection often was influenced by the British and the scope of his powers largely defined by them, the chief became increasingly a civil administrator. The religious aspects of his office were de-emphasized, and his more active administrative role increased the incidence of friction or conflict with his people. Consequently, the number of actual or attempted de-stoolments increased. Governmental authority was centralized on a larger territorial basis than the indigenous state. These factors inevitably distorted the traditional dispersion of authority among the indigenous rulers and disrupted the delicate processes of consultation through which, in large measure, popular sentiment had been reflected. Rather than the chief, the District Commissioner came to be regarded as the main guardian of the popular interests. Rattray has aptly summarized the effect of indirect rule on chieftaincy: "In introducing Indirect Rule into this country, we would therefore appear to be encouraging on the one hand an institution which draws its inspiration and vitality from the indigenous religious beliefs, while on the other we are systematically destroying the very foundation upon which the structure that we are striving to perpetuate stands. Its shell and outward form might remain, but it would seem too much to expect that its vital energy could survive such a process."[3]

3 Rattray, supra note 1, at viii-ix.

This result, which was far less marked in the Northern Territories than in Ashanti and the Colony, was of profound importance when a true nationalist movement later developed.

The pattern of colonial legal enactment affecting the status of the traditional rulers need only be sketched here.[4] After the establishment of the Gold Coast Colony in 1874, relations between the colonial power and the chiefs of the Colony were regulated by the Native Jurisdiction Ordinance of 1883.[5] This granted to such chiefs as were designated by Order, together with their councilors, limited legislative and judicial powers. The power to enact bylaws was little used, however, and serious abuses arose in the administration of justice in the native tribunals which were operated largely as sources of income. The Chiefs' Ordinance of 1904[6] authorized the Governor, on the application of a chief, to confirm his election and installation as in accord with native law and custom. While such confirmation was doubtless designed to buttress the position of the chief and was not a prerequisite to his exercise of the traditional powers of his office, in practice it supported the popular impression of the chief as an agent of British power.

A common cause of discontent in the native states sprang from the chiefs' handling of the revenue and property of their stools, particularly land. Concessions for the exploitation of timber and mineral resources were granted without adequate compensation and without proper accounting of the proceeds. To solve these problems, the colonial government enacted the Concessions Ordinance of 1900.[7] This granted to a division of the Supreme Court the power to determine and certify the validity of a concession, if it found that

[4] For a fuller summary see Hailey, supra note 1, at 194-278.
[5] Ord. No. 5 of 1883, as amended, Cap. 113, 2 Laws of the Gold Coast Colony 1195 (1928).
[6] Ord. No. 4 of 1904, Cap. 21, 1 Laws of the Gold Coast Colony 151 (1928).
[7] Ord. No. 14 of 1900, as amended, Cap. 27, 1 Laws of the Gold Coast Colony 260 (1928).

the concession was granted by the proper persons for an adequate valuable consideration and with sufficient protection of the customary rights of natives inhabiting the area. The Court was authorized to modify the terms of a concession and impose such conditions on it as the Court deemed just. Concession rents, payable to any native, were required to be paid to a treasurer appointed by the Governor and by him distributed to the entitled individual.

Growing tension between the chiefs and the more politically progressive elements, as well as widespread dissatisfaction with the management of stool property and the administration of justice in the native tribunals, led to limited reforms in 1927. The Native Administration (Colony) Ordinance[8] dealt with the election and deposition of chiefs, significantly vesting in the Governor final power of review and approval of action taken by the traditional authorities in contested cases. The ordinance also defined the status and powers of state and provincial councils. Authority of the chiefs and their councilors to make bylaws, subject to the approval or disallowance of the Governor, was continued. Judicial powers of the Native Tribunals were also defined and somewhat enlarged. However, aside from a prohibition of taking and receiving bribes or exacting fines or fees other than those authorized, the only control of the tribunals arose from the power of the Provincial Commissioner's Court to stop the hearing of cases and to transfer them to another Native Tribunal, a District Commissioner's Court or a division of the Supreme Court. Nothing was done to control the management or accounting of stool revenues and other property.

This chapter will focus on subsequent efforts to control the system of native administration, development of the Native Court system being treated extensively in Chapter V. A modest move toward the establishment

[8] Ord. No. 18 of 1927, Cap. 111, 2 Laws of the Gold Coast Colony 1120 (1928).

of centralized control of stool property and finances was made in 1936, when the Governor was authorized to issue regulations on the keeping of accounts of stool revenue and expenditures, the establishment of stool treasuries and the maintenance of inventories and records of property.[9] This led in turn to the Native Administration Treasuries Ordinance of 1939[10] which permitted the Governor to require the establishment of treasuries for state councils or subordinate authorities within a state and to issue relevant regulations on accounting for and expending funds. Native authorities with established treasuries were permitted, on approval of the Governor, to levy taxes to support their activities. The culmination of colonial development in this direction was the Native Authority (Colony) Ordinance of 1944.[11]

The premise underlying the 1944 legislation was profoundly significant for the chiefs of the Colony, though the practice under it was not radical. The ordinance vested local government responsibilities in Native Authorities to be created by Order of the Governor to replace the old Native Administrations. While any chief or Native Council might be designated the Native Authority for an area, the Governor was authorized, if he deemed it expedient to do so, to name any native of the area whom he thought fit. Thus, the ordinance formally articulated the position that local governmental responsibility depended entirely on the fiat of the central government and that chiefly status did not assure receipt of the governmental mandate. The appointment of a person to the post of Native Authority was fully subject to revocation by the Governor; the powers outlined in the ordinance for such Authorities, including powers and duties imposed by customary law as well as wide local government responsibilities, could be curtailed at his discretion. If, in the exercise of its order-making powers, a Native Authority failed

[9] The Native Administration (Amendment) Ord., No. 25 of 1936.
[10] Ord. No. 16 of 1939. [11] Ord. No. 21 of 1944.

73

to make an order deemed expedient by the Provincial Commissioner, the latter was authorized to issue the order himself as well as to revoke or suspend orders issued by the Authority. Central governmental control was not so extreme in the area of rule-making, though rules adopted by a Native Authority required the Governor's approval, and even approved rules could be revoked by him.

Continuing functions of the chiefs in their state councils, other than traditional ritual, were limited mainly to the handling of constitutional matters—that is, questions concerning the election and deposition of chiefs, related problems of the recovery or delivery of stool property and political relations under native customary law. Even these matters could be taken from the state councils by the Provincial Commissioner, however, and committed to a specially appointed committee of enquiry. Ultimate review of the determination of constitutional questions by either a committee of enquiry or a state council was to be made by the Governor whose decision was conclusive. Another little-used power of the state councils was in declaring the customary law or recommending its modification. Such declarations and recommendations had no force however until approved by the Governor in Council as representing existing or desirable customary law, neither repugnant to justice, equity or good conscience nor incompatible with enacted colonial law in force in the Colony.

For revenue, Native Authorities were given entitlement to all customary stool income from lands, customary tributes and levies, Native Court fees and fines, license fees and authorized taxes. Management of the financial affairs of an Authority was committed to an appointive finance committee whose members were not required to be members of the Authority. Annual estimates of revenue and expenditure required the approval of the Governor, and no unapproved expenditure could be made save on the authority of the Provincial

Commissioner. The Governor in Council was granted extensive authority to make regulations on Native Authority taxation, the keeping and auditing of accounts and the necessary records of revenue and income-producing property.

The 1944 legislation undoubtedly served to reduce the abuses, corruption and inefficiency which had characterized the scheme of native administration. Unfortunately, difficulty in staffing the new Native Authorities kept the reforms from being as effective as they might have been. The Government followed the practice of designating as the Native Authority for an area the Paramount Chief and his council. Thus, commoners and the better educated and more politically conscious elements were brought into the system only to the extent that they enjoyed membership on the traditional state councils. This occurred in a number of instances,[12] but the majority of members were divisional chiefs, subchiefs, or village headmen. The dual capacity in which most members served often made it difficult to determine whether a particular action was intended to come from the Native Authority or from the traditional state council. While the financial provisions of the new ordinance effected some improvements, not all stool revenues found their way into the established treasuries, tax collection was still haphazard and the level of services provided was poor. It is significant that local administration in the major urban centers of the Colony—Accra, Takoradi and Cape Coast—was handled under different legislation; the traditional rulers of the states in which the municipalities were located were empowered to nominate only a small minority of the members of the town council, the others being elected or nominated by the Government and business interests.[13] Education and experi-

[12] Hailey, supra note 1, at 206, estimates that almost 30 per cent of the membership of the state councils in the Colony as of 1950 were not within the several categories of traditional rulers.
[13] The Accra Town Council Ordinance, No. 26 of 1943; The

ence qualifications of the members of the town councils consequently were substantially above those of the Native Authorities.

Before examining developments in Ashanti and the Northern Territories, one further aspect of the status of the chiefs of the Colony must be noted. In the reconstitution of the Legislative Council in 1925, provincial councils in the three provinces of the Colony were also established.[14] A provincial council consisted of the head chiefs of the province, that is, those chiefs who were in the opinion of the Governor not subordinate in their ordinary jurisdiction to any other chief, and who were so recognized by the Governor. The three provincial councils were authorized to elect six members of the Legislative Council of the Colony. This development gave the chiefs closer identification with the British administration and provided settings for political and governmental activity that had no basis in the traditional order. This new role of the chiefs served further to alienate them from their own people as well as from the politically active elements then represented by the Gold Coast Aborigines Rights Protection Society.[15]

While in general, developments in Ashanti affecting the status of the chiefs paralleled those in the Colony, a number of differences merit discussion. As mentioned earlier, the typical Akan political organization of ter-

Cape Coast Town Council Ordinance, No. 18 of 1944; The Sekondi-Takoradi Town Council Ordinance, No. 29 of 1945.

[14] The Gold Coast Colony (Legislative Council) Order in Council, 1925, para. xvi [1925], STAT. RULES & ORDERS, 1740.

[15] See Apter, *The Gold Coast in Transition*, 147 (1955): "The orientational effects of the structure of indirect rule on role definition were, of course, complex. The decorated and admired chiefs had their affiliations to the members of their tribe, of course, but these links became less close and personal. Instead, the tribe was a base from which chieftainship qualified a few individuals for positions of national honor in British-inspired councils. When the nationalist movement did develop, the chiefs were identified with British imperialism. They donned traditional robes and business suits with equal dispatch, without realizing the inconsistencies in these positions."

ritorial divisions or states, each under a Paramount Chief, was further developed in Ashanti by the organization of the Confederacy. The Omanhene of the Kumasi Division, in his capacity as Asantehene and occupant of the Golden Stool (which symbolically contained the soul of the entire Ashanti people), received the sworn allegiance of the other divisional chiefs. He thus served as the focus of a substantial national sentiment. While historically the functions of the Confederacy were military, certain civil functions developed, particularly in juridical matters.

Throughout the nineteenth century, British activity in Ashanti was largely limited to the several Ashanti wars. At the conclusion of the war in 1896, in an effort to make the Ashanti more tractable, the British dissolved the Confederacy and exiled the Asantehene, Prempeh I, with a number of his head chiefs. The futile demand of Sir Frederic Hodgson in 1900—that the Ashanti deliver to him the Golden Stool so that he might sit on it[16]—precipitated the last Ashanti war and the formal annexation of Ashanti in 1901. In the succeeding years, the Governor legislated for Ashanti, and administrative functions within the region were carried out by commissioners in conjunction with the more cooperative chiefs under the general theory of indirect rule. The unifying structures of the Confederation were in disarray, however. At the divisional level the subservience of the chiefs to the British authorities lowered their prestige and stimulated popular distrust; it also undermined traditional lines of allegiance from subordinate to Paramount Chiefs. The chiefly prerogative of holding court provided an attractive source of income and stimulated bribery and other corrupt practices in the election and de-stoolment of chiefs.[17]

16 On the significance of this event for traditional institutions in Ashanti see Rattray, supra note 1, at 291-93.

17 A special study committee, reporting to the 1938 session of the Confederacy Council, was of the opinion that offering and accepting bribes in connection with enstoolments and de-stool-

In the 1920's, British policy turned toward an attempt to revitalize indigenous institutions in Ashanti. Claims to possession of the Golden Stool were renounced in 1921, and five years later, Nana Prempeh was returned from exile and re-installed as Omanhene of Kumasi. Restoration of the Confederacy Council with the Omanhene of Kumasi as Asantehene did not come until 1935, when a Native Authority Ordinance for Ashanti was enacted.[18] The Council in turn was recognized as the Native Authority for Ashanti.[19] As such, its powers were limited to interposition for the prevention of offenses, compelling the attendance before it of natives, issuing orders dealing with a variety of minor police matters, making rules for the peace, good order and welfare of the natives within the area and maintaining a treasury under the regulatory authority of the Governor. In fact, the functions of the council were almost entirely legislative. It had no executive agents but relied on the divisional chiefs as subordinate Native Authorities to enforce its enactments. Another significant function of the council was to serve as the electoral college for Ashanti members of the Legislative Council when that body was reconstituted in 1946.[20]

The work of the Confederacy Council and the other Native Authorities of Ashanti will not be examined in detail.[21] As Busia has pungently observed, the primary

---

ments had become quite common and had been a source of political unrest. The committee made a number of recommendations for regulations to control such practices. Busia, supra note 1, at 211-12.

[18] The Native Authority (Ashanti) Ordinance, No. 1 of 1935, Cap. 79, 2 Laws of the Gold Coast 1239 (1936).

[19] The Ashanti Confederacy Council Order, Order No. 1 of 1935, as amended, Cap. 79, 3 Laws of the Gold Coast 374 (1936).

[20] The Gold Coast Colony and Ashanti (Legislative Council) Order in Council, sec. 8, 27-30 [1946], 1 STAT. RULES & ORDERS 640 (No. 353), 9 STAT. RULES & ORDERS & STAT. INSTR. Rev. to Dec. 31, 1948, at 673.

[21] See Busia, supra note 1, at 165 et seq.; Hailey, supra note 1, at 232 et seq.

concerns of the Council were cocoa and chiefs,[22] the economic impact of the one contributing to the general insecurity of the other. The recognition of the Council as the Native Authority with legislative powers for the entire region contravened the principle of the older confederation that the divisions were autonomous in matters of their internal law and administration. As in the Colony, the recognition of the chiefs and their councilors as Native Authorities tended to exclude commoners and the better educated members of the community from participation in government, and the progressive breakdown of traditional processes of consultation between the chiefs and their subjects further contributed to suspicion and hostility.[23] Even in their selection, the chiefs became less dependent on the will of the people, since election and installation, according to customary law, did not entitle the person selected to exercise his chiefly functions; that could be done only when he was recognized by the Governor.[24]

The undermining of the traditional respect for the chiefs in Ashanti, however, did not stem solely from identification with the British authorities. Administration of justice in the chiefs' courts was a constant source of complaint. Mismanagement of stool resources was common, though some improvements were effected by an ordinance in 1940 which prohibited, under heavy penalty, the alienation or pledge without the consent of the Chief Commissioner of any stool property and declared such transactions void.[25] Progress in the establishment of a system of regulated Native Authority treasuries improved accounting for revenues and expenditures. Nevertheless, contributions made by the Native Authorities to the provision of local services remained modest, the largest item being contributions

[22] Busia, supra note 1, at 177.   [23] Id., at 193-95.
[24] The Native Authority (Ashanti) Ordinance, No. 1 of 1935, Cap. 79, sec. 2, 2 Laws of the Gold Coast 1239 (1936).
[25] The Stool Property Protection Ordinance, No. 22 of 1940, as amended by No. 25 of 1941, Cap. 101, 3 Laws of the Gold Coast 217 (1951).

to recognized schools.[26] In Kumasi, the principal urban area of Ashanti, limited local service functions were committed to the Kumasi town council which had only a minority of members provided by the traditional authorities.[27]

Finally, in defining the base line from which developments under the government of Ghana will be considered, we turn briefly to the Northern Territories. Detailed data on the organization and functioning of the indigenous societies of the area are fragmentary, and it is therefore difficult to assess adequately the degree of distortion and dislocation of traditional institutions effected after the advent of British administration in 1901. A much earlier fusion of the indigenous people of the Territories with conquering immigrant groups had resulted in a division of governmental functions between religious functionaries (*Tendanas*) of the Earth God and chiefs operating within systems involving varying degrees of centralization. Upon the establishment of the Native Authority system in the Northern Territories in 1932, the *Tendanas* were given no place in the scheme, while the chiefs, both traditional and those actually created by the British, were given an increasing range of powers.[28]

In agrarian-pastoral societies like those of the Northern Territories, the function of allocating and controlling the use of land is of profound significance. The customary view in the Northern Territories was that the land belonged to the Earth God whose priests possessed a ritual jurisdiction to allocate unclaimed land and, among some groups, seemingly to dispossess the lineage then occupying and using it. Among some

[26] Hailey, supra note 1, at 241-43.
[27] The Kumasi Town Council Ordinance, No. 18 of 1943, provided that the council should be composed of an official president, three official members nominated by the Chief Commissioner, one member nominated by the Asantehene and six elected members.
[28] The Native Authority (Northern Territories) Ordinance, No. 2 of 1932, as amended, Cap. 84, 2 Laws of the Gold Coast 1269 (1936).

peoples, for example the Dagomba, these functions of the *Tendanas* were taken over by the chiefs. In the Colony and Ashanti, the indigenous systems of ownership of land were left untouched by the British; for the Northern Territories, however, the Government enacted legislation declaring all lands to be "native lands" and vesting in the Governor all rights in and control over them.[29] Titles acquired before the effective date of the ordinance were protected, however. The Governor was authorized to grant rights of occupancy, excluding mineral rights, for terms not exceeding 99 years on rentals, subject to a continuing power of revision. Stringent restrictions on the alienation of interests in land were imposed. Subsequent legislation vested ownership of all mineral rights, rivers and streams in the Crown, with consequent rights to license and control exploitation.[30] Thus, control of the basic resource of the Protectorate was removed from the traditional religious figures (or in some cases the

[29] The Land and Native Rights Ordinance, No. 8 of 1931, as amended, Cap. 147, 3 Laws of the Gold Coast 581 (1951). The preamble indicated the purposes of the ordinance: "Whereas it is expedient that the existing customary rights of the natives of the Protectorate and the national fruits thereof in sufficient quantity to enable them to provide for the sustenance of themselves and their families should be assured, protected, and preserved:

"And whereas it is expedient that the existing native customary law with regard to the use and occupation of land should as far as possible be preserved:

"And whereas it is expedient that the rights and obligations of the Government in regard to the whole of the land within the Protectorate, and also the rights and obligations of cultivators and other persons claiming to have an interest in such land, should be defined by law."

Insofar as the ordinance was designed to protect the rights of the indigenous people from loss through the exploitation of non-natives, it anticipated any pressing problem. The granting of concessions to non-natives never reached the proportions in the Northern Territories which had appeared in the Colony. This was attributable to the fact that no important mineral discoveries were made in the North and most of the land was unusable for cash crops such as cocoa.

[30] The Minerals Ordinance, No. 20 of 1936, as amended, Cap. 155, 3 Laws of the Gold Coast 631 (1951).

chiefs) and was secularized and centralized in the hands of the Government.

While official action has thus far been emphasized, it was by no means the only factor contributing to the weakening of indigenous institutions of law and government in the Colony, Ashanti and the Northern Territories. Another significant element was the expanding commercial activity centering largely on the cocoa industry. The increase of cash income from cocoa sales or other business activity introduced severe strains into the extended family and its network of rights and obligations. Since the tribal structure, particularly in the Colony and Ashanti, was an organization of family or lineage units, the deterioration of these relations inevitably had profound political consequences. Similarly, since the institution of chieftaincy had important religious aspects, the introduction and growth of Christianity had a corrosive effect.[31] Development of education and the increase in the number of literate Africans tended to increase disaffection with the chiefs, the large majority of whom were illiterate and unwilling to share leadership roles with the better educated and less conservative young commoners. In some measure the greater security of the chieftaincies of the Northern Territories can be attributed to that area's more limited economic and educational development, as well as to the fact that its imported religious veneer is Muslim rather than Christian.

In summary, with the advent of an African national government in 1951, the position of the traditional authorities throughout the areas within modern Ghana had become perilous. This is not to say that historic patterns of allegiance and veneration had been entirely erased. Some persisted, but the extent is impossible to determine. In the remainder of the chapter, our concern will be the legal steps initiated and pursued by the Government under African leadership for the purpose of defining the role of the traditional authori-

[31] Busia, supra note 1, at 135-38.

ties. These developments will be considered under four heads: determination of chiefly status, evolution of local government, status and functions of traditional councils, and economic status of the chiefs. The role briefly assigned to the chiefs in the constitutional structure of central government is considered more fully in Chapters I and III.

THE DETERMINATION OF CHIEFLY STATUS

A fundamental premise of indirect rule was that indigenous institutions should be utilized and guided by the colonial power. This policy in the Gold Coast did not involve, at least in theory, the creation of new tribal structures or the participation of colonial administrators in the selection or installation of functionaries in the indigenous order. To be sure, unfamiliarity with the tribal governmental order did lead to the development of some nontraditional institutions, for example, the court of the Ga Manche, and some chieftaincies in the Northern Territories; also in Ashanti, after the creation of the Protectorate in 1901, British efforts secured the enstoolment of some chiefs having no valid status under customary law. In general, however, the official position was that the Africans determined their own rulers according to traditional law and custom, and the elite group so identified was then enlisted in the scheme of colonial administration.

The first reflection of a shift from this policy came in 1904 when chiefs and head chiefs in the Colony were permitted, at their discretion, to apply to the Governor for confirmation of their election and installation. If the Governor was satisfied that these proceedings had been in accordance with native custom, he was authorized to confirm the applicant, thus determining the lawfulness of his status in all courts of the Colony.[32] Hailey is certainly correct in asserting that "this provision was only intended to render the posi-

[32] The Chiefs' Ordinance, No. 4 of 1904, Cap. 21, 1 Laws of the Gold Coast 151 (1928).

tion of a Chief unassailable in law; it did not enable the Government to maintain that a Chief can exercise no legal powers till formally recognized as a Native Authority."[33] Yet the wedge of governmental participation was thus inserted into the procedures of the indigenous order by which chiefs were elected and installed.

Governmental power to determine chiefly status may be manifested not merely in processes of selection but often more dramatically in deposition. An early ordinance in the Colony authorized the Governor in Council to suspend for a period or depose any chief who appeared to the Governor "to have abused his power, or be unworthy, or incapable of exercising the same justly, or for other sufficient reason."[34] As will be seen, both aspects of governmental power over the determination of chiefly status have been fully developed in subsequent legislation.

There is, however, a significant gap between the claim of a power to render chiefly status unassailable by confirmation or to depose a chief who is found objectionable and the generalized assertion that status as a chief depends on recognition by the Government. Government recognition as the hallmark of chiefly status was first articulated for the Colony by the Legislative Council Order of 1925, but only with respect to head chiefs, later called Paramount Chiefs.[35] This scheme was applied to all chiefs in Ashanti in 1935.[36]

[33] Hailey, supra note 1, at 202.

[34] The Native Jurisdiction Ordinance, No. 5 of 1883, as amended by No. 7 of 1910, Cap. 113, sec. 29, 2 Laws of the Gold Coast 1195 (1928).

[35] The Gold Coast Colony (Legislative Council) Order in Council, 1925, para. xvi [1925], STAT. RULES & ORDERS, 1740.

[36] The Native Authority (Ashanti) Ordinance, No. 1 of 1935, Cap. 79, 2 Laws of the Gold Coast 1239 (1936). Section 2 defines "Chief" as "a person whose election and installation as such in accordance with native law and custom is recognized by the Governor." It may seem strange that a broad power of recognition should depend on such a limited statutory base. Yet such a power, grounded only on the statutory definition of "Chief" was asserted and implemented. See, for a later example, The Para-

84

Thus, when the Nkrumah Government assumed office in 1951 under the Coussey Constitution, only in Ashanti had status as a chief been legally defined in terms of Governmental recognition, though status as a Paramount Chief in the Colony or as a member of a territorial council in any region also depended on recognition or appointment by the Governor.[37]

In the constitutional struggle preceding independence in 1957, the chiefs, particularly in Ashanti, were prominent in opposition to Nkrumah's goal of a unitary government. Among the concessions to this opposition, incorporated in the Independence Constitution,[38] was a House of Chiefs in each region; its functions will be discussed later. The constitution required legislative implementation, however, and this came in 1958 in the House of Chiefs Act.[39] While membership in the new Houses was determined by schedules prepared and promulgated by the Government, these schedules only indicated that the occupants of designated stools should be members of specified Houses.[40] The act did not purport to deal with the problem of determining who the legitimate occupants of these stools might be.

Continued political involvement of the chiefs, and the recurrent efforts through traditional means to depose those who were sympathetic to the Convention People's Party, turned the serious attention of the Government to the problem of recognition and determination of chiefly status. Any constitutional impediments to a legislative attack on the problem were eliminated by the Constitution (Repeal of Restrictions) Act of 1958,[41] which established the supremacy of the national

---

mount Chiefs (Ashanti) Recognition Instrument, 1958, L.N. 179/58 (1958).

[37] The Gold Coast (Constitution) Order in Council, 1950, The Second Schedule [1950], I STAT. INSTR. 831 (No. 2094).

[38] The Ghana (Constitution) Order in Council, 1957, sec. 67 [1957], I STAT. INSTR. 1036 (No. 277).

[39] Act 20 of 1958.

[40] Id., sec. 4 and the First, Second, Third, Fourth and Fifth Schedules.

[41] Act 38 of 1958.

85

legislature. The following year, Parliament enacted the Chiefs (Recognition) Act.[42] This provided that no enstoolment or de-stoolment of a chief after December 18, 1958, should have effect unless recognized by an Order of the Governor General. Thus, for the first time in all of the areas composing modern Ghana, the ultimate determination of who could legally become or remain a chief was vested not in the traditional councils and people, but in the central Government. To buttress this power and provide for every contingency, the Governor General was further authorized, when he deemed it in the public interest, to direct any person purporting to exercise the functions of a chief to desist from doing so and to order any such person to reside outside the state concerned.[43] It was thus made evident that the Government would not tolerate the functioning of "unofficial chiefs."

Extensive though the powers conferred by the Chiefs (Recognition) Act on the Government were, they still limited the Government to the function of approving or refusing to approve actions affecting the status of a person as a chief that had been initiated by traditional processes. Only after these traditional steps had been taken could the Government refuse to recognize a chief and thus prevent his functioning. Similarly, it could refuse to recognize a customary law de-stoolment and thus preserve some functions in a chief who had lost his traditional support. At the level of legal authorization, the Government could not, however, initiate either enstoolment or de-stoolment, but this gap in the array of legal powers was closed in part at least by the Chieftaincy Act of 1961. The act defines a chief as "an individual who—(a) has been nominated, elected and installed as a Chief in accordance with customary law, and (b) is recognized as a Chief by the Minister re-

[42] Act 11 of 1959.
[43] By the Chiefs (Recognition) (Amendment) Act, 1959, No. 48 of 1959, the residence ban authority was changed to permit a direction that the named person "shall not reside within a defined radius of any place named therein."

sponsible for Local Government."[44] The Minister is authorized to withdraw recognition from a chief who has been de-stooled, or when "the Minister considers it to be in the public interest to withdraw recognition."[45] Upon the withdrawal of recognition, the Minister, "if he considers it to be expedient in the public interest," may prohibit a former chief (or a person who has never been recognized) from purporting to function as a chief, require him to live outside a specified area, and prohibit other persons from treating him as a chief.[46] Thus the ring has virtually been closed. Only with respect to the initiation of selection and installation procedures does the present law of Ghana leave full responsibility in the traditional authorities. Their action may be rendered ineffectual, however, by a refusal or withdrawal of recognition. The legal tools of a modern state have operated so effectively on the institution of chieftaincy that one may accurately say that the chief in Ghana today achieves and retains his office only by the sufferance of the national government.

The Ghana Government has now issued regulations establishing procedures to be followed in the de-stoolment of chiefs[47] and in reporting enstoolments, de-stoolments, abdications and other matters affecting chieftaincy.[48] Despite the complex web of Governmental control, status as a chief appears to be extremely unstable. The extent of Government involvement in determining chiefly status, and the insecurity of that status, are reflected in the substantial flow of Executive Orders recognizing enstoolments and de-stoolments and withdrawing such recognition. The Nkrumah Government has sought to assure its participation in the processes for determining chiefly status in large measure by the adoption and extension of devices first employed by the colonial power. The social and economic

---

[44] The Chieftaincy Act, 1961, Act 81, sec. 1(1).
[45] *Id.*, sec. 1(2)(b).   [46] *Id.*, sec. 4.
[47] The Chieftaincy (Destoolment Proceedings) Regulations, 1963, L.I. 309.
[48] The Chieftaincy Regulations, 1963, L.I. 320.

currents which have long tended to undermine the institution of chieftaincy have not subsided. Indeed, those currents have been strengthened by the political relations of the chiefs to the national Government. It is perhaps arguable that the legal controls over status as a chief have made the chiefs less objectionable and less dangerous to the Nkrumah Government—but they have not contributed to the security of chiefly tenure.

THE EVOLUTION OF LOCAL GOVERNMENT

By the late 1940's, it was quite generally recognized that the scheme of indirect rule at the local level required substantial modification. The traditional state councils, operating under legislative fiat as Native Authorities, had justified neither in the range of functions undertaken, in efficiency of operation nor in honesty of dealing with community resources any reasonable hope that they would evolve into acceptable units of local government. The Watson Commission, reporting on its investigations after the 1948 disturbances, could not "envisage the growth of commercialisation in the Gold Coast with the retention of native institutions, save in a form which is a pale historical reflection of the past." The Commission did not find general agreement on the place to be occupied by the chief in the new order but observed: "Among Africans with modern political outlook we found that their conception of the place of the Chief in society was ornamental rather than useful; a man not necessarily of any particular ability, but of good presence, expressing in his person but never in his voice the will of his people; exercising the office of pouring libations to ancestors; remaining always among his people and never speaking save through his linguist; he must either remain on his Stool and take no part in external politics or forgo the office—he should not attempt a dual role."[49] In commenting on the report, the British Government took

[49] Report of the Commission of Enquiry into Disturbances in the Gold Coast, p. 25, Colonial No. 231 (1948).

a more positive view of the status and future of the chief. In the modernization of Native Authorities, the British regarded the ". . . Chiefs as having an essential part to play. In general the Chiefs in the Gold Coast are the traditional leaders of the people. Their functions in regard to local administration are based on popular support; and the transfer or delegation of any of their functions would require popular sanction, since the position of the Chiefs affects the whole system of relationships on which community life is traditionally based."[50]

The 1949 Coussey Committee on Constitutional Reform had strong representation from the traditional elements, and, not surprisingly, it too rejected the Watson Commission view and claimed a place for the chiefs in the new constitutional arrangement. It nevertheless conceded that "the existing system of local government has proved unable to meet the requirements of an efficient and democratic administration," largely because of the narrowly traditional composition of the chiefs' councils, the predominance of illiteracy among the members, the large size of the councils, and the shortage of trained personnel.[51] The Committee therefore recommended a clear separation of the traditional state councils and the new Local Authorities to which local government functions would be committed. In the composition of the local authorities, the Committee recommended an elected majority with reservation of at least one-third of the seats on all Authorities for appointees of the traditional councils.[52] These views of the Coussey Committee were approved by the British Government[53] and by select committees of the Legis-

[50] Statement by His Majesty's Government on the Report of the Commission of Enquiry into Disturbances in the Gold Coast, p. 7, Colonial No. 232 (1948).
[51] Gold Coast: Report to His Excellency the Governor by the Committee on Constitutional Reform, p. 14, Colonial No. 248 (1949).
[52] Id., at 22.
[53] Gold Coast: Statement by His Majesty's Government on the

lative Council appointed to study local government in the Colony[54] and Ashanti.[55]

It will thus be seen that both the British and the traditional leaders of the Gold Coast had endorsed changes in the scheme of local government which would have increased popular representation while retaining a substantial link with the chiefs and their councils. Before these changes could be implemented, however, a profoundly significant political event occurred to alter the expected consequences of the formal structural changes—the electoral victory of the Convention People's Party in 1950. As a consequence, when the new Local Government Bill was introduced in the Legislative Assembly in 1951, it raised the spectre of complete domination of the traditional regimes by the newly organized and aggressive forces of the C.P.P. led by Nkrumah.[56]

The Local Government Ordinance of 1951[57] authorized the establishment of local and urban councils by ministerial instruments, which were also to define the functions of the councils. Each council was to include both popularly elected and traditional members, in a ratio of 2 to 1, unless the Governor in Council deemed some variation expedient, as well as such members representing special interests as the Governor in Council might think desirable. The traditional members were to be appointed by the traditional authorities in the council area. In an effort to expedite the establishment of the new councils, the Government did not attempt

---

Report of the Committee on Constitutional Reform, p. 3, Colonial No. 250 (1949).

[54] Report by the Select Committee on Local Government (Colony), 1950 (1951).

[55] Report of the Select Committee of the Legislative Council Appointed to Make Recommendation Concerning Local Government in Ashanti (1951).

[56] Apter, supra note 15, at 241-56, usefully analyzes in political terms the handling of the Local Government Bill in the Legislative Assembly.

[57] Ord. No. 29 of 1951, Cap. 64, 2 Laws of the Gold Coast 370 (1951).

to rationalize the pattern of council areas but rapidly established local and urban councils on the same area bases as the former Native Authorities. To carry out major services within larger areas, the ordinance also authorized the establishment of district councils, each covering the areas of several local and urban councils and having a membership in which the representatives of the traditional authorities were at most a one-third minority. The existing town councils in Accra, Kumasi, Cape Coast and Sekondi/Takoradi were unaffected by the Local Government Ordinance. In 1953, however, these councils were replaced by new municipal councils on which the appointees of the traditional authorities represented no more than a one-sixth minority in any case.[58] Each council had as president a Paramount Chief, but the post was purely honorary and ceremonial.[59]

It is not necessary here to examine in detail the structure and functioning of the new district, local, and urban councils but only to note the minor role in them assigned to the traditional authorities by the first major legislation introduced by a nationalist African Government. Experience with the new councils was disappointing. To begin with, a large number of them, small in both area and resources, were established.[60]

[58] The Municipal Councils Ordinance, 1953, No. 9 of 1953, secs. 6, 7 and First Schedule.

[59] Id., sec. 15.

[60] In a memorandum given to me by Alan F. Greenwood, he summarizes some of his findings as Commissioner to enquire into local government as follows:

"In this rapid establishment of Local Government [after passage of the 1951 Ordinance] many units were set up which were not only small in area and resources but also in population. In the North eight councils had less than 5,000 inhabitants, and there were 34 between 5,000 and 10,000. In Ashanti the policy of producing small councils was pursued to an extent unsurpassed in any other part of the country. For a population of 740,000 (excluding Kumasi) there were 83 local and urban councils (20 under 5,000 and 31 between 5,000 and 10,000) and 10 district councils. The largest local council had a population of 23,000. In Volta Region (then Trans-Volta Togoland) there were 7 local councils with populations under 10,000, and five district councils. In the other Regions, Eastern and Western, the problem of the

Later, in 1957, a further enquiry into local government produced two principal recommendations for change: the abolition of district councils and the re-grouping and amalgamation of existing local councils into units with sufficient population and resources to become responsible for all local government services in their areas.[61] Commissioner Greenwood reported, however, that most of the chiefs opposed amalgamation:

> A chief whose area of authority coincides with an existing local council feels that if it is joined with its neighbor his status will in some way be affected and make him subservient to the chief of the neighboring area. There is still a deep-rooted feeling—particularly in Trans-Volta/Togoland—that areas of local government and traditional authority must coincide. It is a matter of personal prestige on the part of individual chiefs to have a council which coincides with his area of authority. To countenance an amalgamation would be a blow to that prestige. Moreover, I have gained the impression that in the minds of some chiefs Independence for Ghana means casting aside all forms of local administration established in the past 15 years and reverting to small independent units with themselves in undisputed control.

---

very small units did not arise to the same extent, but the [Greenwood] Commission found that many of the local councils had inadequate financial resources. It was apparent from the Commission's Report that not only were there many small ineffective units but also that the 'two-tier' system, i.e., District Councils and local and urban councils, had not proved successful. The District Councils were not themselves authorised to levy rates and therefore were obliged to call upon the local councils, by a process known as 'precepting,' for money to carry out their functions. In some cases the amount of the precept was more than the local council could raise by its basic rate collection. In these circumstances some of the smaller local councils were only being kept alive by grants which they received from the Central Government."

[61] Report of the Commissioner for Local Government Enquiries, June, 1957 (1960). This is commonly referred to as the "Greenwood Report."

Stool holders feel that if a local council area includes stool land in two separate ownerships they will not receive their fair share of the revenue from their particular pieces of land. Examples of this attitude are to be found in the areas of jurisdiction of existing local authorities, particularly in Ashanti, resulting in a most confused pattern of local government with isolated areas of land cut off by many miles from their parent local council and entirely surrounded by territory within the jurisdiction of another council. Consequently, some of these isolated areas are virtually unadministered.[62]

The decision of the Government to accept the findings and implement the recommendations of the Greenwood Report meant the complete exclusion of the traditional authorities from the processes of local government. This trend was indicated by an Executive Order in 1958 which reduced the number of traditional members on each municipal council to one.[63] When legislation was introduced the following year to eliminate the traditional members of all councils, to abolish district councils and to permit the consolidation of smaller units,[64] the measures caused hardly a ripple in Parliament. In introducing the bills, the Minister for Local Government, Mr. Ofori Atta, himself a member of the royal family of Akim Abuakwa, merely commented that the reasons which had prompted the Coussey Committee to recommend the reservation of council seats for the traditional authorities were no longer valid and that local government bodies should become entirely elective.[65] When an independent member inquired how the proposed legislation could be reconciled with the frequently declared intention of the Government to

[62] *Id.*, at 5.
[63] Municipal Councils (Traditional Members) Order, 1958, L.N. 49/58 (1958).
[64] The Local Government (Amendment) Act, 1959, No. 14 of 1959; Municipal Councils (Abolition of Traditional Members) Act, 1959, No. 15 of 1959.
[65] Parliamentary Debates, vol. 14, 17 March 1959, pp. 332, 344.

93

preserve the traditional authorities, the Minister replied with technical accuracy that there was nothing in the bills to stop a chief from becoming an elected member of a local or municipal council. More realistically, however, another Government spokesman, Mr. Kofi Baako, emphasized "the fact that what we are doing is really consistent with our policy of keeping the chiefs away from politics and making them the fathers of our country through the State Councils and the Regional Houses of Chiefs."[66]

By the time of enactment of the post-Republic Local Government Act of 1961,[67] the re-structuring of local government was virtually complete. The 280 local, urban and district councils had been replaced by 65 urban and local bodies, with membership of all of these, as well as the 4 municipal councils, entirely elective. Local government bodies are now supervised and related to the central Government by administrative personnel responsible in each region to a Regional Commissioner, a political functionary with the rank of Minister, to whom certain local government functions are delegated by the Minister for Local Government. In this re-structuring, the traditional, sacred and local repositories of authority and responsibility have been definitively displaced by secular, representative organs intimately related to the center, under at least formally guiding criteria of rationality and efficiency.

STATUS AND FUNCTIONS OF TRADITIONAL COUNCILS

State councils composed of the chiefs and their councilors played a significant role in legal and governmental affairs of the Akans. These were, of course, traditional institutions, although as has been seen, they were progressively brought within the scheme of secular government under the British policy of designating the councils as the Native Authorities in their areas. As state councils, however, they possessed a range of dis-

[66] *Id.*, at 349.　　　　　　[67] Act 54 of 1961.

crete functions, some conferred by British law, others originating in customary law.

Immediately preceding the advent of the Nkrumah Government, systems of state councils existed in the Colony, British Togoland and Ashanti. The legislation[68] defining and regulating the functions of the councils varied somewhat in detail; only the more significant differences need be noted here.

1. State Councils had jurisdiction to try and determine "matters of a constitutional nature"; these included the election, installation, deposition or abdication of a chief, the right of any person to take part in such procedures,[69] related questions concerning the recovery or delivery of stool property and political or constitutional relations between chiefs under customary law. These matters were not exclusively within the province of the councils, however. A Commissioner representing the Government was authorized in his discretion to withdraw such questions from the state councils and commit them to specially appointed committees of enquiry. Final powers of review and modification of the decisions of either state councils or committees of enquiry on constitutional matters were granted to the Governor. Thus, the Government claimed an important role in the decision of questions ordinarily falling within the competence of the traditional councils themselves.

2. A council on its own initiative or on the require-

[68] The Native Authority (Colony) Ordinance, 1944, No. 21 of 1944, secs. 2, 23-31; The Native Authority (Southern Section of Togoland under British Mandate) Ordinance, 1949, No. 7 of 1949, secs. 22-31. There was no legislation of comparable breadth for Ashanti, but the Ashanti Confederacy Council Order, No. 1 of 1935 as amended, Cap. 79, 3 Laws of the Gold Coast 374 (1936) provides for the composition, procedures and powers of the Confederacy Council. The Council was given the powers with respect to customary law, discussed in the text by the Native Law and Custom (Ashanti Confederacy Council) Ordinance, No. 4 of 1940, Cap. 102, 3 Laws of the Gold Coast 220 (1951), and with respect to constitutional issues by the Native Authority (Ashanti) (Amendment) Ordinance, No. 2 of 1940.

[69] The Colony Ordinance of 1944 (supra note 68) did not include this matter in the definition of constitutional matters; see sec. 2(1).

ment of the Governor was authorized to declare the existing customary law or to recommend its modification.[70] Such action by a council was subject to review by the Governor in Council to determine whether the law as declared or the modification proposed accorded with natural justice, equity and good conscience and did not conflict with any ordinance. If approved on these criteria, the customary law was declared to be in force. Since the great majority of people were subject to customary law, these powers of the state councils might have been used to affect substantially the development of some of the most socially significant legal institutions. In fact, however, the powers were rarely exercised.[71]

3. The provincial councils, and later the Joint Provincial Council in the Colony and the Ashanti Confederacy Council, served as electoral colleges for the election of the traditional members of the Legislative Council.[72] In the general political and legal development of the Gold Coast, this was doubtless the most significant function of the councils of chiefs. This function of the territorial councils was preserved by the Coussey Constitution of 1950 and even extended to Togoland and the Northern Territories.[73]

4. Certain of the councils were expressly granted the privilege of meeting from time to time "for the purpose of deliberating upon matters affecting the welfare or interests of persons" within the area of the council.[74]

[70] Such powers were not granted to state councils in the mandated areas of Southern Togoland. They were granted to the Ashanti Confederacy Council by the Native Law and Custom (Ashanti Confederacy Council) Ordinance, No. 4 of 1940, Cap. 102, 3 Laws of the Gold Coast 220 (1951).

[71] See pp. 101, 249-50.

[72] The Gold Coast Colony (Legislative Council) Order in Council, 1925, sec. XVIII [1925], STAT. RULES & ORDERS 1740; The Gold Coast Colony and Ashanti (Legislative Council) Order in Council, 1946, Parts III, IV [1946], I STAT. RULES & ORDERS 640 (No. 353), 9 STAT. RULES & ORDERS & STAT. INSTR. Rev. to Dec. 31, 1948, at 673.

[73] The Gold Coast (Constitution) Order in Council, 1950, sec. 40 and Second Schedule [1950], I STAT. INSTR. 831 (No. 2094).

[74] For example, The Native Authority (Colony) Ordinance of

Throughout the period of indirect rule, it was commonly difficult to determine whether a state council was acting in that capacity or in its role as a statutory local government body. The effort here has been to isolate the former functions concerning which two summary observations seem warranted: the membership and operation of the state councils as traditional bodies of chiefs had been subjected to appreciable control by the Government; aside from deliberations and decisions on matters directly affecting the status of the chiefs themselves, the councils showed little interest or activity.

Among the early enactments of the Legislative Assembly, upon the assumption of power by the Nkrumah Government, were the 1952 measures for the regulation of state councils in Ashanti, the Northern Territories, the Colony and Southern Togoland.[75] While the ordinances differed in a number of particulars, to accommodate historical and traditional variations, one general pattern was consistently followed. This pattern involved little innovation in the scope of functions of the state councils. The principal functions continued to be the hearing and deciding of constitutional disputes—subject to the ultimate power of the Governor to affirm, vary or reverse—and the declaration or modification of customary law, subject to the Governor's authority to determine compatibility with natural justice, equity and good conscience. The ordinances also reflected substantial Government control over the actual composition of many of the councils, as well as the

---

1944, secs. 28-29, grants such privilege to the Provincial Councils and to the Joint Provincial Council. Technically the grant to the Southern Togoland Council would seem to be made in its role as a representative body of a number of Native Authorities rather than as a traditional council. The Native Authority (Southern Section of Togoland under British Mandate) Ordinance of 1949, No. 7 of 1949, sec. 29.

[75] The State Councils (Ashanti) Ordinance, No. 4 of 1952; The State Councils (Northern Territories) Ordinance, No. 5 of 1952; The State Councils (Colony and Southern Togoland) Ordinance, No. 8 of 1952.

procedures to be followed in their deliberations. While customary sanctions and awards in connection with constitutional disputes were permitted, the actual enforcement procedures required the assistance of a competent court. Provision was made to regulate traditional oath procedures, but, except in constitutional disputes, the use of such oaths initiated no judicial processes in the councils. Rather, the use of oaths merely created an entitlement of the councils to certain traditional fees, stated and limited by the ordinances, while the actual disputes were passed on to the Native Courts. Long-standing concerns were reflected in the provisions prohibiting, under penalty, the charging of excessive fees and such corrupt practices as bribery in connection with council proceedings.

The general pattern of role definition and regulation of the state councils articulated in the 1952 legislation survived until the major readjustments shortly after independence. One important function was taken from the territorial councils, however, when the 1954 Constitution made the entire Legislative Assembly subject to popular election, eliminating the representatives formerly chosen by the territorial councils.[76] The Joint Provincial Council in the Colony was itself dissolved in 1958, and the Asanteman Council was dissolved on October 17, 1958, when the Houses of Chiefs Act came into force.[77] Other significant amendments reflected the increasingly bitter contest being waged in the mid-1950's between the chiefs and the ruling Convention People's Party. It was the belief of Party leaders that chiefs sympathetic to the C.P.P. were being subjected to unwarranted complaints and even de-stoolments. Consequently, legislation was enacted for the Colony, Southern Togoland and Ashanti which not only extended the range of constitutional cases appealable to

[76] The Gold Coast (Constitution) Order in Council, 1954, sec. 28 [1954], 2 STAT. INSTR. 2788 (No. 551).

[77] The Joint Provincial Council (Dissolution) Act, 1958, No. 51 of 1958; The Houses of Chiefs Act, No. 20 of 1958, sec. 47(1) and Tenth Schedule.

the Governor from state councils, from the trial committees which functioned where no state council existed, and from the Asanteman Council, but went so far as to render appealable certain prior decisions that when made had not been subject to appeal. The Governor was also authorized to extend the previously authorized time for appeal.[78] In Ashanti, jurisdiction to hear de-stoolment cases against Paramount Chiefs was removed from the Asanteman Council and vested in committees of enquiry. For the first time in Ashanti, the Governor was authorized to appoint such committees to decide whatever de-stoolment questions and other constitutional matters the Governor deemed inexpedient for decision by a state council or the Asanteman Council.[79]

The Houses of Chiefs Act of 1958, implementing the Independence Constitution, effected sweeping changes in the status and functions of the traditional councils. The constitution itself had provided for the establishment, within twelve months of independence, of a House of Chiefs for each of the five regions of Ghana; these Houses would consider matters referred by a Minister or the National Assembly, offer advice to any Minister and declare the customary law.[80] The implementing legislation did not limit its effect to the establishment of a new tier of Houses or councils, for it simultaneously modified substantially the status and functions of the older state councils. As noted earlier,

[78] The State Councils (Colony and Southern Togoland) (Amendment) Ordinance, 1955, No. 37 of 1955; The State Councils (Ashanti) (Amendment) Ordinance, 1955, No. 38 of 1955. The lodging of appeals even beyond this extended period was permitted on order of the Governor by the State Councils (Ashanti) (Amendment) Ordinance, 1957, No. 3 of 1957, and the State Councils (Colony and Southern Togoland) (Amendment) Ordinance, 1957, No. 8 of 1957.

[79] The State Councils (Ashanti) (Amendment) Ordinance, 1955, No. 38 of 1955, secs. 6, 8. The power to commit constitutional matters to such special committees of enquiry rather than the regular state councils had previously been available in the Northern Territories, the Colony and Southern Togoland.

[80] The Ghana (Constitution) Order in Council, 1957, sec. 67 [1957], 1 STAT. INSTR. 1036 (No. 277).

the Asanteman Council (Ashanti Confederacy Council) itself was abolished as an incident of the creation of a House of Chiefs for Ashanti.

The regional basis on which the new Houses of Chiefs were established followed the earlier divisions of the Gold Coast, except that the Colony was divided into an eastern and a western region.[81] The membership of each House was fixed by a Schedule to the Act which the Governor General (after the Republic, the President) was authorized to amend at any time.[82] Ordinary meetings of a House were limited to two in any financial year, and only the Minister for Local Government could convene an extraordinary meeting.[83] The Houses possessed no revenue sources in their own right; each was required to prepare annual estimates of expenditure which, on receiving ministerial approval, become charges on the Consolidated Fund of Ghana.[84]

The powers and functions of the Houses of Chiefs were not extensive. On reference of any matter by the National Assembly or a Minister, a House might report its views. The Independence Constitution, in fact, required that any bill for the modification of a number of entrenched provisions be referred to all Houses of Chiefs and their views considered by the Regional Assemblies in reaching their decisions on the bills; similarly, any bill affecting the traditional functions or privileges of a chief required reference to the affected House or Houses.[85] It should be emphasized, however, that in neither case was the approval of the Houses of Chiefs required for the enactment of the bill. Their function was purely advisory, and even the requirement of such advice was eliminated by the Constitution (Re-

[81] *Id.*, sec. 63.

[82] The Houses of Chiefs Act, No. 20 of 1958, secs. 4, 46.

[83] *Id.*, sec. 11, as amended by sec. 8 of the Houses of Chiefs (Amendment) Act, No. 8 of 1959.

[84] *Id.*, sec. 32, as amended by sec. 4 of the Houses of Chiefs (Amendment) Act, No. 4 of 1960.

[85] The Ghana (Constitution) Order in Council, 1957, sec. 32 and Third Schedule, sec. 35 [1957], I STAT. INSTR. 1036 (No. 277).

peal of Restrictions) Act[86] later in 1958. Thereafter, seeking the advice of the Houses of Chiefs was entirely within the discretion of the National Assembly and Ministers, though a House might offer advice to a Minister on its own initiative.[87]

The power of declaring the prevailing customary law or recommending its modification was entirely removed from the state councils and vested in the new statutory Houses of Chiefs.[88] Declarations might be made on the initiative of a House or on the request of the Governor General or Assembly, and recommendations for modification could be initiated by a House. The Minister for Local Government, if of the opinion that a declaration of customary law was repugnant to the laws of Ghana, was authorized to require further consideration by the House of Chiefs making the declaration. He could go so far as to direct, by a published order, that the law which the chiefs had declared to be customary not apply to a specified region.[89] On the other hand, if satisfied that the declaration was not "repugnant to the laws of Ghana or contrary to natural justice, equity and good conscience," he could direct that it be in force in a specified area. Strangely, the act did not indicate the procedures for handling recommendations which a House of Chiefs might make for modification of customary law. Only two declarations of customary law have thus far been made, each resulting from a recommendation of a House of Chiefs that the customary law of succession to a stool or skin be modified.[90] In each case the procedure followed was that set out in the act for a declaration of customary law.

The former jurisdiction of state councils in constitutional matters was retained except in instances in-

---

[86] Act No. 38 of 1958.
[87] The Houses of Chiefs Act, No. 20 of 1958, sec. 17.
[88] Id., sec. 47(1) and Tenth Schedule; secs. 16, 17.
[89] Id., sec. 44.
[90] Declaration of Customary Law (Akwapim State) Order, 1960, L.I. 32; Declaration of Customary Law (Dagomba State) Order, 1960, L.I. 59.

volving a Paramount Chief of Ashanti. In fact, the original jurisdiction of state councils in constitutional matters was secured by the repeal of provisions earlier applied in the Colony, Southern Togoland and the Northern Territories which had authorized the Governor to refer such matters to a committee of enquiry if he deemed it expedient. Original jurisdiction in matters involving a Paramount Chief in Ashanti was placed in a committee of the Ashanti Region House of Chiefs.[91] Appeal as of right lay formally to the House of Chiefs of the region from decisions involving a Paramount Chief or dealing with a constitutional matter arising in a state where there was no Paramount Chief, but the actual hearing of the appeal was by an Appeal Commissioner. Subchiefs could appeal from constitutional decisions only with the leave of the Governor General.[92] An Appeal Commissioner was authorized in his discretion to sit with assessors, and, with any clarification requested by the House of Chiefs or its president, the Commissioner's decision was made final.[93] Later legislation eliminated the finality of the Appeal Commissioner's decision, however; he was required to forward his findings to the Minister for Local Government who would then refer the report to the Governor General. The latter was authorized to confirm, vary or refuse to confirm the report. The decision of the Governor General, when published, was final and conclusive.[94] Once again, central political control of the constitutional aspects of chieftaincy was confirmed.

The comprehensive Chieftaincy Act of 1961 consolidated most of the earlier legislation but contained a few innovations. Divisional councils were recognized

[91] Houses of Chiefs Act, No. 20 of 1958, sec. 19.
[92] *Id.*, secs. 18, 19, as amended by sec. 2 of the Houses of Chiefs (Amendment) Act, No. 4 of 1960.
[93] *Id.*, sec. 22(1); sec. 27.
[94] The Houses of Chiefs (Amendment) Act, No. 8 of 1959, sec. 11. This act required the publication not only of the decision of the Governor General but of the ultimate findings. The necessity of publishing the findings was eliminated by the Houses of Chiefs (Amendment No. 2) Act, No. 38 of 1959.

and their customary functions preserved, but the act itself merely authorized the Minister for Local Government to assign to them such functions as he thought fit.[95] The state councils were re-named traditional councils and they retained the major share of their role in hearing and determining matters affecting chieftaincy.[96] All cases in which a Paramount Chief is a party were withdrawn from the jurisdiction of traditional councils, however, and committed to hearing officers, now called Judicial Commissioners.[97] The only other function of the traditional councils, aside from those assigned by customary law, is to make representations to the appropriate House of Chiefs looking to the clarification or modification of customary law.[98]

Under the act, the Houses of Chiefs may still report on such matters as are referred to them by the National Assembly or any Minister,[99] and may declare or recommend modifications of the customary law. In the latter function, however, the role of the central government has been significantly enlarged. Formerly, the Minister merely approved or disapproved the action of the House of Chiefs. Now, he is authorized to make such modifications as he deems necessary and to make effective in the area in question the declaration or modification as presented by a House of Chiefs or as it has been modified.[100] One significant extension of the functions of the Houses of Chiefs involves their participation in the procedures by which certain rules of customary law may be assimilated by the common law of Ghana.[101] This process is discussed in the later chapter on the hierarchy of legal norms in Ghana.

As mentioned above, the role of traditional councils and Houses of Chiefs in the decision of cases affecting chieftaincy has been somewhat reduced. Judicial Commissioners have original jurisdiction to hear and deter-

---

[95] The Chieftaincy Act, 1961, Act 81, sec. 10.
[96] *Id.*, sec. 15.   [97] *Id.*, sec. 40.
[98] *Id.*, sec. 58.   [99] *Id.*, sec. 28.
[100] *Id.*, secs. 59, 60.   [101] *Id.*, secs. 62-64.

mine all causes to which the Asantehene or a Paramount Chief is a party, all causes affecting chieftaincy arising in areas for which no traditional councils exist and even cases affecting chieftaincy falling within the competence of a traditional council if, in the opinion of the Minister, the council has not decided the matter within a reasonable time.[102] An amendment to the Chieftaincy Act grants the Minister absolute discretion to refer any cause affecting chieftaincy, including stool property, to a Judicial Commissioner or to withdraw any case already before a council and refer it to a Commissioner. While the latter action is to be based on the opinion of the Minister that the public interest calls for such withdrawal and reference, the discretion of the Minister is in fact absolute.[103] The Commissioners also hear appeals by leave of the Minister from decisions of the traditional councils.[104] Findings of a Judicial Commissioner are reported through the Minister to the President who may confirm them, order further hearings or amend the findings as he thinks fit. The President's action, when published, is conclusive.[105]

The Houses of Chiefs are avowedly statutory bodies, and the present traditional councils are such in name only. Through a complex evolution of legislative and executive action, the councils of chiefs have, in fact, been stripped of their traditional status and made the limited instruments of the new national state.

THE ECONOMIC STATUS OF THE CHIEFS

In the older customary practices of the Akan people, a chief had no economic life apart from that of his stool. On election as chief, a person was privileged to dispose of property he had acquired, but on his installation any that he had retained became stool property. The new chief received the ceremonial paraphernalia and other personal property of the stool, but more impor-

[102] *Id.*, secs. 40-42.
[103] The Chieftaincy (Amendment) Act, 1963, Act 185.
[104] The Chieftaincy Act, 1961, Act 81, sec. 48.
[105] *Id.*, sec. 39.

tantly, he became the trustee of stool lands, exercising certain types of traditional control and in turn receiving rents and tributes. By Akan custom, income-producing work was deemed inappropriate for a chief, though in Ashanti a venerable practice permitted the Asantehene to provide gold to selected traders who were expected to turn it to good account on behalf of the Golden Stool. For major public expenditures such as war, levies were imposed. In addition to goods and money, an Akan chief could also command a wide range of services from his subjects. In all aspects of his economic life, however, the chief enjoyed his perquisites in his institutional capacity as the occupant of his stool. The stool was in part a pervasive means of economic re-distribution, for it was expected, indeed customary law required, that the chief dispense economic goods liberally among his councilors and subjects.

Changing patterns of social and economic life in the Gold Coast profoundly affected the economic status of the chiefs. Educational development and religious proselytizing weakened traditional feelings of allegiance. The introduction of a major cash crop, cocoa, produced on small holdings by individual farmers, challenged the scheme of rights and duties of the extended matrilineal family on which the institution of chieftaincy ultimately depended. Nor were the chiefs themselves immune from the quickened pace of economic life. The older proscriptions against economic activity and against their owning property in an individual capacity began to break down.[106] The chiefs came to own cocoa farms, rental houses and other business interests, and their retreat from traditional practices served to accentuate the erosion of loyalties which education, economic development and religion had begun in their subjects.

Two other sources of income to which the chiefs resorted had profound significance for the institution of chieftaincy itself. As other sources of income and

[106] For a summary of shifting attitudes on these matters in the Ashanti Confederacy Council, see Busia, supra note 1, at 199-205.

services declined, the revenues realized from the chiefly courts became more attractive. The proliferation of courts, excessive fees, repeated delays and large panels of members anxious to share the profits were all responsible for a diminished confidence in traditional justice and for evoking widespread demands for reform. These developments are fully discussed in the chapter on the judicial system. More pertinent here is the administration of stool lands. The development of the cocoa industry, especially in Ashanti, and increasing interest in the exploitation of mineral and timber resources made the chiefly function of administering unoccupied stool lands an attractive source of revenue and a fertile soil for the growing tension between chiefs and subjects. Particularly in the Colony, but to some extent also in Ashanti, the chiefs developed a lucrative business by granting mining and timber concessions to foreign exploiters. It has been estimated that at one time in the Colony the area of concessions granted by the chiefs exceeded the total area of the Colony itself.[107]

Legal regulation of the economic activity of the chiefs was begun during the colonial period. The Concessions Ordinance of 1900[108] provided for the validation of a concession after a judicial inquiry to determine whether it had been granted by the proper persons without fraudulent or other improper inducements and for an adequate valuable consideration. Certification of validity also required a finding that the customary rights of natives in the concession lands had been protected. It should be emphasized, however, that this ordinance did not attempt to determine the use to which royalties would be put or to impose on the chiefs accountability for the proceeds. Over the years, legislative efforts to regulate the size of Native Courts, to standardize fees

[107] Hailey, supra note 1, at 221.
[108] Ord. No. 14 of 1900, as amended, Cap. 27, 1 Laws of the Gold Coast 260 (1928). A Concessions Ordinance for Ashanti was passed in 1903 (No. 3 of 1903). Both the earlier ordinances were replaced by the Concessions Ordinance, No. 19 of 1939, Cap. 136, 3 Laws of the Gold Coast 486 (1951).

and to enforce accounting for revenues have met only indifferent success.

The principal effort of the colonial regime to deal with the economic aspects of chieftaincy took the somewhat indirect form of pressing for the establishment of regulated treasuries in the various authorities charged with local government responsibilities. In view of the prevailing practice of designating the chiefs and their councilors as Native Authorities, the imposition of a treasury system affected the chiefs and their councils to some extent. In both Ashanti and the Colony, legislative attempts were made to make stool revenues from lands and other sources a part of the Native Authority income and thus subject to accounting through a regulated treasury.[109] Undoubtedly some accountability for stool revenues was achieved by the treasury system, but the Coussey Committee was still able to report in 1949: "It is a well-established fact that in almost all areas, it has been impossible to enforce this provision [for the payment of stool revenue into the treasury] to the full and to ensure that land revenues are brought to account. Moreover, the Ordinances do not stipulate what proportion of the revenue from these sources may be used for local authority services, and in many places the Stool Treasuries receive the monies only to pay them out again as shares to chiefs."[110] It should be remembered that the Coussey Committee was not hostile to the chiefs; in fact, the chiefs and their supporters were well represented on the Committee.

Except in the Northern Territories, most legal regulation of stool resources did not impinge on traditional notions that the chiefs held or owned the land as trustees

[109] The Native Authority (Ashanti) Ordinance, No. 1 of 1935, as amended, Cap. 79, sec. 16, 2 Laws of the Gold Coast 1239 (1936); The Native Authority (Colony) Ordinance, No. 21 of 1944, sec. 32. Similar legislation was enacted in 1949 for Southern Togoland, The Native Authority (Southern Section of Togoland under British Mandate) Ordinance, No. 7 of 1949, sec. 32.

[110] Gold Coast: Report to His Excellency the Governor by the Committee on Constitutional Reform, p. 30, Colonial No. 248 (1949).

for their people. The sole exception outside the Northern Territories involved the Kumasi Town Lands which, after the annexation of Ashanti in 1901, were treated as vested in the Crown by right of conquest. In 1943, however, with the exception of limited areas used for Government residences and railways, these lands were revested in the Asantehene.[111] In the Northern Territories, where land never achieved significant commercial value, the Government early assumed ownership and powers of disposition over native lands.[112] Legal regulation, in general, took the more limited form of imposing accountability for revenues through the treasury system or of defining the legal consequences of transactions into which the chiefs might enter in dealing with stool lands or other property.

Illustrative of measures of the latter type was the Stool Property Protection Ordinance of 1940, applicable only in Ashanti.[113] By the ordinance, it was made unlawful for any Native Authority or other person to alienate, pledge, or mortgage any stool property without the written consent of the Chief Commissioner—and any attempt to do so was declared void. Exempted from this restriction were concessions granted to nonnatives (and regulated by the Concessions Ordinance), as well as pledges or mortgages by a native in his personal capacity of rights in a farm made on stool land. Stool property was also rendered immune from execution or from being sold in satisfaction of a pledge or mortgage unless the security interest was created with the Chief Commissioner's consent. Only in Ashanti had such legal limits on dealing with stool property been imposed prior to the advent of the Nkrumah Government in 1951.

[111] The Kumasi Lands Ordinance, No. 17 of 1943, as amended by No. 14 of 1945, Cap. 145, 3 Laws of the Gold Coast 562 (1951).

[112] The Land and Native Rights (Northern Territories) Ordinance, No. 8 of 1931, as amended, Cap. 147, 3 Laws of the Gold Coast 581 (1951).

[113] Ord. No. 22 of 1940, as amended by No. 25 of 1941, Cap. 101, 3 Laws of the Gold Coast 217 (1951).

At the 1951 base line, the economic position of the chiefs was perilous, although substantial resources remained in their effective control. In all areas, certain dealings in stool property were regulated, but in Ashanti the regulations were especially stringent. In theory, the ordinary revenues of the stools were payable to regulated treasuries, but substantial sums found their way directly into the private purses of the chiefs. Even treasury management of stool revenues did not prevent private use of funds by the chiefs, since the chiefs and their councils were the recognized Native Authorities, and the law did not determine the portion of stool revenues committed to public purposes. In part, at least, the deterioration of traditional taboos against private business activity by the chiefs compensated for the insecurity of their hold on traditional sources of stool income.

The need for change was clearly indicated by the findings and recommendations of the Coussey Committee. While declaring its devotion to the institution of chieftaincy and its belief that the chiefs should have an important role in the emerging constitutional order, the Committee recognized the necessity "to arrange that all revenue from Stool Lands, and all lands held in trust for the people or sections of them, is accounted for and that there is as little opportunity as possible for such monies to go astray. It is also necessary to ensure that not only a fair proportion of this money is appropriated to the services of the community, but also that adequate allowances are provided for the chiefs to maintain themselves in their position of dignity."[114] The Committee itself did not attempt to determine a fair division of stool land revenues between the chiefs and local governmental authorities; this it thought should be fixed by agreements made locally or, in cases of inability to agree, by the Regional Administration. It also

[114] Gold Coast: Report to His Excellency the Governor By the Committee on Constitutional Reform, p. 30, Colonial No. 248 (1949).

recommended that the local government bodies should act as "estate agents" for all stool revenues, but not, however, so as to "deprive the stool of any rights of ownership over their lands."[115]

The support given by the chiefs to the recommendations of the Coussey Committee vanished in the political climate generated by the dramatic emergence of the Convention People's Party. When the Nkrumah Government moved to implement certain of the Coussey recommendations by the Local Government Bill of 1951, it was entirely clear that the newly organized political forces would control the local government agencies on which the chiefs would be a one-third minority. In reaching agreements, therefore, on the division of stool revenues, the chiefs could anticipate hard bargaining, with any impasse subject to resolution by a higher authority also controlled by the C.P.P. The scheme involved not merely a loss of income to the chiefs; it meant also an increase of the resources to be controlled by and used for the programs and prestige of political elements appearing to threaten the very institution of chieftaincy itself.

The Local Government Ordinance of 1951 went beyond the Coussey recommendations in its treatment of stool lands.[116] While any effect of the ordinance on the ownership of stool lands was expressly disavowed, management of these lands was placed in the new urban and local councils which also were to collect the revenues and deposit them in funds in the custody of the Accountant General. Stools could be required to declare their interest in any land; on their failure to do so, or on any disagreement between a stool and a council as to the interest of a stool in land, the issue could be submitted to a Land Court for determination. The distribution of stool land revenues was subject to determination by agreement between the stool and the

---

[115] *Id.*, at 31.
[116] The Local Government Ordinance, No. 29 of 1951, Cap. 64, 2 Laws of the Gold Coast 370 (1951).

local government council, but in the absence of agreement it was to be settled conclusively by the Minister
for Local Government.

Restrictions on the alienation of stool lands, similar
to those previously applicable only in Ashanti, also were
enacted and made general. Any disposition of an interest in land involving the payment of a valuable consideration—or any transfer which could involve such
payment because made to a person not entitled by
customary law to the free use of land—required the
concurrence of the urban or local council for the area,
if the transfer were made by a stool or by any person
who had not paid a valuable consideration for his interest. Persons aggrieved by the refusal of a council to
approve a disposition were accorded a right of appeal
to a special tribunal created by Order of the Governor
in Council.[117]

It must be remembered that the land control provisions of the ordinance were coupled with the transfer
of local government functions to bodies having an
elected majority. The opposition to the ordinance, expressed in the territorial councils of chiefs as well
as in the Legislative Assembly, fully recognized that
the shifts in control over the disposition of land and
the use of its revenues struck at the heart of chieftaincy.
One speaker in the legislative debates declared that
"when a man who is not a subject of a Stool . . . is allowed to control Stool Lands, then the Stool does not
exist." He then asked, "If chieftaincy is not going to
be wiped out, then why are we trying now to take the
powers of the institution itself?"[118] To most, the ultimate
issue was clear, and the protagonists were organizing
for the conflict.

In 1952, legislation affecting state councils imposed

[117] The stool lands provisions of the ordinance were not applicable to the Northern Territories. The modified restrictions on
alienation of stool lands rendered the 1940 Ashanti Ordinance
superfluous and it was later repealed. The State Councils (Ashanti) (Amendment) Ordinance, No. 41 of 1952.
[118] Quoted in Apter, supra note 15, at 248.

further restrictions on the powers of the individual chiefs to deal with stool and skin properties.[119] Any alienation of stool property without the consent of the affected state council was declared void and the maker subjected to criminal penalties.[120] These restrictions were cumulative; they left unaffected the restraints on dealing with stool land imposed by the Local Government Ordinance and the special laws for the Northern Territories.

The responses of the chiefs and their supporters to the threats they saw in the C.P.P. and in the consolidation of powers in the national government are considered more fully in other chapters; they need only be summarized here. Organization of the National Liberation Movement in September, 1954, evidenced the close political cooperation between the chiefs, particularly in Ashanti, and the middle class—intellectual groups opposing the C.P.P. The chiefs thus played a prominent role in the pre-independence controversy over federalism and a second chamber of the legislature.

In succeeding years, government leaders frequently reiterated their support for the institution of chieftaincy while insisting that the chiefs should stay out of politics. The chiefs, on the other hand, publicly denied any partisan identification while giving both open and covert support to the groups opposing the C.P.P. In October, 1957, in response to an invitation from Dr. Nkrumah that they state their positions with respect to party politics, both the Asantehene and the Okyenhene (the Paramount Chief of Akim Abuakwa, Nana Ofori Atta II) in statements to their councils denied partisan involvements. Nevertheless, the Government in October, 1957, suspended Nana Ofori Atta from the exer-

119 The "skin" is the traditional symbol in the Northern Territories, roughly analogous to the "stools" of Ashanti and the southern areas.

120 The State Councils (Ashanti) Ordinance, No. 4 of 1952, sec. 24; The State Councils (Northern Territories) Ordinance, No. 5 of 1952, sec. 15; The State Councils (Colony and Southern Togoland) Ordinance, No. 8 of 1952, sec. 16.

cise of his functions pending the submission of the report of a commission of enquiry into the affairs of Akim Abuakwa State. In February, 1958, a similar enquiry was ordered into the affairs of the Asanteman Council and the Kumasi State Council.

The latter commission reported in September, 1958, that the Kumasi State Council had improperly diverted funds to the National Liberation Movement and that the Asantehene's Lands Department had been guilty of general maladministration. The report of the Akim Abuakwa Commission (I have been unable to procure a copy of this report) alleged, according to a Government White Paper[121] published in 1959, that Nana Ofori Atta II had used his influence to have some £10,000 deducted from the salaries of subchiefs and moneys due to elders, linguists and stool dependents, and that this money had been used to support a body of "Action Groupers"—terrorists who preyed on C.P.P. and Government supporters.

In the light of these developments, it is not surprising that the Government focused on Akim Abuakwa as the pilot project for a new plan to deal with stool revenues and thus with the political activities of the chiefs. On June 20, 1958, the Government introduced the Akim Abuakwa (Stool Revenue) Bill upon a Certificate of Urgency. The Minister of Local Government, Mr. Ofori Atta, himself a member of the royal family of Akim Abuakwa and eligible for election to that distinguished stool, briefly presented the bill. He observed that local authorities had found difficult the task assigned them by the Local Government Ordinance of managing stool lands and collecting revenues "partly because the persons from whom the revenues are collected are apparently under no legal obligation to pay to the local authority and partly, in some cases, to lack of cooperation between the local authorities and the Stools."[122] The more efficient system authorized by the

[121] W.P. No. 10/59, p. 28.
[122] Parliamentary Debates, First Series, vol. 10, col. 137.

bill was to be applied only in Akim Abuakwa, but the Minister significantly added that "if the proposals in it are accepted and prove satisfactory, it may well be desirable to make similar provision for general application later."[123]

In debate, the opponents of the bill made four basic points. The primary argument, which was lost on a ruling of the Speaker, insisted that consideration of the bill violated those provisions of the 1957 Constitution guaranteeing the institution of chieftaincy and requiring that any bill "affecting the traditional functions or privileges of a Chief" must be referred to the House of Chiefs of the region in which the affected chief functioned at least three months before its second reading.[124] When the Akim Abuakwa Bill was introduced, no Houses of Chiefs had been established and the constitution made no provision for an alternative reference. Yet the constitutional prohibition seemed clear. The only issue was whether the bill "affect[ed] the traditional functions or privileges of a Chief." The opposition argued cogently that a central function of the chiefs among the Akans was management of stool lands and control of their revenue. In announcing his ruling, the Speaker declared: "I also hold that there is nothing put before me that the bill seeks to undermine the chief of any state."[125] This, of course, did not address the issue raised by the constitutional language. The Government was permitted to proceed with the bill, but the argument of the opposition made a strong impression; after the repeal of the constitutional limitations on the legislative competence of the Assembly, a bill was passed to remove retroactively any doubts of the validity of the Akim Abuakwa legislation.[126]

The three arguments about the merits of the bill were

[123] *Id.*, col. 138.
[124] The Ghana (Constitution) Order in Council, 1957, secs. 66, 35 [1957], 1 STAT. INSTR. 1036 (No. 277).
[125] Parliamentary Debates, First Series, vol. 10, col. 144.
[126] The Stool Lands (Validation of Legislation) Act, No. 30 of 1959.

repeated in various forms but may now be simply stated. 1. Stool property is private property; thus, by assuming control over stool revenues in Akim Abuakwa, the Government threatened the whole institution of private property in Ghana. 2. The bill was an act of political spite directed at chiefs who had refused to support the C.P.P. Its main objective, therefore, was not to improve the administration of stool revenues for the welfare of the people of Akim Abuakwa but to strengthen the C.P.P. and weaken the opposition. 3. Any inadequacies in the administration of stool revenues in Akim Abuakwa were not attributable to the chiefs but rather to defective legislation hastily pushed through by the Government, or maladministration by local authorities. The unwarranted attack by the Government on the chiefs could thus be explained as only part of a deliberate effort to destroy the institution of chieftaincy itself.

The opposition arguments were made with vigor and occasionally with cogency. The Government had the votes, however, and in less than four hours on June 20, 1958, the Akim Abuakwa (Stool Revenue) Bill passed through all three readings and, without a single amendment, became part of the law of Ghana.

The act[127] authorized the creation of a department within the Ministry of Local Government, headed by the Receiver of Stool Revenue to whom was assigned the full responsibility for the collection of such moneys and the management of stool lands. For purposes of the act, stool revenue was defined to include not merely the various payments due in regard to stool lands, but all levies, dues, fees and rents payable to a Stool in the Akim Abuakwa State in accordance with native customary law or any other law."[128] Under criminal sanctions, all persons and bodies were enjoined to cooperate with the Receiver by providing information and facilities for inspecting and copying records. When

---

[127] The Akim Abuakwa (Stool Revenue) Act, No. 8 of 1958.
[128] *Id.*, sec. 2(b).

collected, funds were to be deposited in a special account against which costs of administration would from time to time be charged. Also from the account such sums as the Minister for Local Government might determine were to be paid to urban and local councils in whose areas income-producing stool lands were located. In making this determination, the Minister was directed to take into consideration the needs of the traditional authorities, but he was given the full responsibility for assessing such needs. The balance remaining after payments to local government bodies was to be used to maintain the traditional authorities, to administer the Akim Abuakwa State and to support scholarships and other projects for the benefit of the people of the State. The actual sums allocated to these several purposes were to be determined by annual estimates made by the Receiver, after consultation with the Akim Abuakwa State Council, and approved by the Governor General. Up to one-third of any excess funds available after covering the estimated expenditures could be used in any manner the Minister for Local Government might approve. Provision was made for the keeping of accounts and for an annual audit to be reported to Parliament. Finally, the Receiver was granted the exclusive right to take part, in the name of the Stool concerned, in any proceedings concerning revenue-producing lands.

Superficially, it might appear that the economic relation of the chiefs to their traditional sources of income was little changed by the Akim Abuakwa Act. Before, the function of managing stool lands and collecting the revenue had been the responsibility, not of the chiefs, but of local government bodies. However, stool revenue from sources other than land was also removed by the new act from the control of the chiefs. In addition to increasing administrative efficiency, the new act effected other significant changes. Under prior legislation, determinations of the division of stool revenues between the traditional authorities and local government agencies were to be made locally by agreement between the parties, with ministerial control operating only in the absence of a local agreement. In theory, therefore, and to some extent in operative fact, the chiefs controlled or influenced the division of resources through locally negotiated agreements. The new act eliminated this element of local control: the share of stool revenues to be paid to local government bodies was fixed by ministerial order. Two aspects of the innovation bear emphasis: participation of the chiefs in the basic division of revenues was eliminated, and the critical decisional process moved from the local level to the office of the Minister in Accra. Contrary to some predictions made in legislative debate, the Minister for Local Government did not permit local government to monopolize the revenues administered under the act. The initial allocation to urban and local councils was 45 per cent but this was later reduced to one-third.[129]

In September, 1958, the Government introduced the Ashanti Stool Lands Bill to control the economic resources available to the chiefs in Ashanti for supporting political opposition. The text of the bill was made available only one day before it was brought up for second reading, the bill being handled on a Certificate of Urgency. Opposition arguments did not differ significantly from those advanced against the Akim Abuakwa Act, and they enjoyed no more success. The Government was fully cognizant that the most direct route to political neutralization of the chiefs lay in the acquisition of firm control over stool lands and their revenues.

The Ashanti Stool Lands Act[130] deals separately with Kumasi Town Lands and other stool lands in Kumasi State. With respect to the former, the property, rights

[129] The Akim Abuakwa (Share of Stool Revenue) Order, 1959, L.N. 187/59, 1959 Laws of Ghana 261; The Akim Abuakwa (Share of Stool Revenue) (No. 2) Order, 1959, L.N. 244/59, 1959 Laws of Ghana 378; Akim Abuakwa (Share of Stool Revenue) Order, 1961, E.I. 162.
[130] Act No. 28 of 1958.

and interests which had been vested in the Asantehene in 1943[131] were transferred to the Governor General to be held and used in trust for the Golden Stool and the Kumasi State. The transfer of ownership in trust to the Governor General also involved the transfer of management functions and the collection of rents from the Asantehene's Land Office to an officer of the central government. Such a shift of administrative responsibility might have been accomplished easily without divesting the "ownership" of the Asantehene. It is significant, however, that the Government used the more dramatic approach; as a consequence, the Asantehene, around whom opposition in Ashanti had revolved, was reduced to a landless chief—the same status his predecessor on the Golden Stool had under British fiat from 1901 to 1943. The revenues from the Kumasi Town Lands were to be spent for the benefit of the Golden Stool and Kumasi State in accordance with estimates prepared by the Governor General's appointee, the Administrator of Stool Lands, after consultation with the Kumasi State Council. The Governor General's approval made the estimates final. Thus, complete control over the ultimate use of the revenues was vested in the central government. The Asantehene and his council thereby were reduced to total economic dependence.

The act did not divest the chiefs of ownership of stool lands in Kumasi State. Rather, powers of land management and collection and administration of revenues were given to the Governor General or the Administrator of Stool Lands, these powers being identical to those developed for the handling of stool revenues in Akim Abuakwa. Although when the act took effect[132] it applied only to the stool lands of Kumasi State, the Minister for Local Government was empowered to

[131] The Kumasi Lands Ordinance, No. 17 of 1943, as amended by No. 14 of 1945, Cap. 145, 3 Laws of the Gold Coast 562 (1951).
[132] The act was brought into operation on September 10, 1958. The Ashanti Stool Lands (Commencement) Order, 1958, L.N. 298/58, 1958 Laws of Ghana 443.

order the extension of the scheme to stool lands in other parts of Ashanti. Through the exercise of this power, by November, 1960, all stool lands in the Ashanti and Brong-Ahafo regions were brought within the scheme.[133] As in Akim Abuakwa, the Minister made one-third of the stool land revenues available to local government agencies.[134]

The usefulness of economic weapons in attacking the traditional citadels of chiefly power and opposition was confirmed by experience. In late 1959, legislation[135] authorized the extension of the scheme of centralized control of stool lands to the remaining regions of Ghana, except the Northern Territories where government ownership and control of land had long been established.[136] The pattern of effective central control of stool lands and their revenues thus was established throughout Ghana.

Further legislation in 1960 authorized the President "where it appears to [him] that it is in the public interest so to do . . . [to] declare any stool land . . . to be vested in him," thus making it lawful for the President "to execute any deed or do any act as a trustee in respect of the stool land."[137] The President has exercised this power to vest stool lands in himself on a

[133] See the following Ashanti Stool Lands (Extension of Application) Orders: L.N. 67/59, L.N. 163/59, L.N. 211/59, 1959 Laws of Ghana 101, 214, 328; L.I. 1/60, L.I. 2/60, L.I. 85/60.

[134] The Ashanti Stool Lands (Share of Revenue) Order, 1959, L.I. 245/59, 1959 Laws of Ghana 379.

[135] The Stool Lands Control Act, No. 79 of 1959. The act was brought into operation in southern Ghana by a series of executive orders: The Stool Lands Control Act (Commencement in Ga State) Order, 1959, L.N. 355, 1959 Laws of Ghana 595; The Stool Lands Control Act, 1959, Commencement Orders, 1960, L.I. 15/60, L.I. 36/60, L.I. 84/60. Under his statutory powers, the Minister has assigned one-third of the stool land revenues to local government units. Stool Lands (Share of Revenue) Order, 1962, E.I. 14.

[136] The State Property and Contracts Act, 1960, C.A. 6, vested the ownership of lands in the Northern Region in the President and defined his powers of administration.

[137] The Stool Lands Act, 1960, Act 27.

number of occasions,[138] with the result that even the formal ownership of stool lands, with whatever symbolic value this might have to the chiefs, has been stripped away in many areas. It does not appear, however, that the vesting of ownership of stool lands in the President significantly added to the arsenal of Government weapons against the chiefs.

Comprehensive legislation was enacted in 1962 on the administration of lands,[139] concessions in stool lands[140] and the ownership and control of mineral resources.[141] In large measure this was consolidating legislation, with amendments of detail, and many of the earlier enactments were repealed. In summary, it may be said that the President retained the power to vest stool lands in himself and the management of stool lands was fully committed to a Minister. The extent to which the traditional authorities will participate in the revenues from stool lands depends on ministerial discretion. Authority is granted to a Minister to terminate an existing concession in stool lands if its terms have been breached, or its area exceeds permitted limits, or it has not been properly developed or exploited, or if the concession holder "unreasonably withholds consent to a variation of such of the terms of the concession as in the opinion of the Minister have become oppressive by reason of a change in economic conditions."[142] Beyond the ministerial powers to induce modifications of concessions, the President is granted summary power to cancel any concession held by non-Ghanaian individuals, corporations or associations "if

[138] See the following Stool Lands Vesting Instruments: E.I. 46/61, E.I. 188/61, E.I. 195/61, E.I. 16/62, E.I. 73/62.

[139] The Administration of Lands Act, 1962, Act 123. See also The Administration of Lands Regulations, 1962, L.I. 232; The Administration of Lands (Appeal Tribunal) Regulations, 1963, L.I. 251; The Administration of Lands Regulations, 1963, L.I. 283; and The Administration of Lands (Amendment) Regulations, 1963, L.I. 295.

[140] The Concessions Act, 1962, Act 124.

[141] The Minerals Act, 1962, Act 126.

[142] The Concessions Act, 1962, Act 124, sec. 3(1)(c).

he considers that it is or may prove prejudicial to public safety or interests."[143] The Minerals Act vests ownership and control of all the minerals in Ghana in the President as trustee for the People of Ghana; it also authorizes him to issue licenses for exploitation of the minerals.

The law of Ghana has altered radically the theoretical structure of stool property and other exploitable resources of the country.[144] Among the most obvious explanations of the legislative development is the Government's realistic awareness that land meant economic power for the chiefs and that economic power nurtured the opposition activities of the traditional authorities. Yet the stool land legislation was by no means limited to economic effects. In the Akan traditions, to say that a chief owned the land was a mere shorthand way of referring to his special relation to the ancestral spirits to whom the land belonged and who provided it for the nurture of the living. To divorce the chief from the land, therefore, struck directly to the heart of the institution of chieftaincy itself, to the conception of the chief not as a secular leader but as the priest whose ritual functions preserved a desirable relation of the living to the dead and of the human to the divine. Today, his status in Ghana is reduced to that of a stipendiary of the central government, dependent in fact for office on official recognition, limited

---

[143] *Id.*, sec. 5.

[144] Our concern here has been entirely with stool property having significant economic value, primarily land. We have not, therefore, discussed the numerous enactments having to do with the custody and control of moveable stool property which has mainly a ritual significance, nor with buildings occupied and used by the stool. It is of interest that the national law has attempted to deal with the latter problem and has vested certain powers of custody and control of stool paraphernalia, some of it regarded as sacred, in nontraditional bodies. These powers are operative particularly in connection with disputes arising from the de-stoolment of chiefs. See The Stool Property (Recovery and Validation) Act, No. 31 of 1959; The Stool Property (Recovery and Validation) (Amendment) Act, No. 51 of 1959; The Chieftaincy Act, 1961, Act 81, secs. 52-57.

to meeting in bodies many of which have no traditional base, under procedures and to perform functions defined by statute. It is thus difficult to see how the chiefs can long remain a significant factor in the social, political or governmental life of the country.

CHAPTER III

THE OPTION FOR UNITY

THE WHITE PAPER presenting to the people of Ghana a draft republican constitution declared "that the present frontiers of Ghana, like so many other frontiers on the African continent, were drawn merely to suit the convenience of the Colonial Powers who divided Africa between them during the last century."[1] This arbitrary quality of national boundaries presents one of the principal challenges to the new states of Africa, and it is one of the hypotheses of this study that it has been a dominant factor in determining how the organized legal force would be used. The effective organizing of public force within the area of Ghana, as it was delivered by colonial hands to an indigenous elite, has necessitated the placing of nationhood high among the values to be implemented by law. This chapter continues the discussion of this problem at the level of general structures: should Ghana be a more or less loosely knit assembly of regional centers of power or a tightly knit unitary state? The discussion will show how Ghana exercised the option for unity.

The territory of modern Ghana possesses no natural unity. Aside from the Gulf of Guinea which forms its southern border, it is not defined by natural boundaries of significance. With its greater extension northward from the coast, it overlays the main geographic divisions of West Africa, the great forest area and the savannah, extending northward toward the Sahara. Although all the people are of Negro stock, there are important linguistic and cultural divisions between the people of the high forest area and the southern grasslands and those of the north. There is also religious diversity; the northern parts have felt the impact of Islam while

[1] Government Proposals For a Republican Constitution, p. 4, W.P. 1/60 (March 7, 1960).

the religion of the south is animist—ancestor worship modified by Christianity.

Throughout most of its history, Ghana has felt little pressure for unity from either Europeans or the indigenous leaders.[2] Though the European presence on the Guinea coast dates from the fifteenth century, its effectiveness was lessened by national economic rivalries and extreme reluctance to assume the responsibilities of civil administration. It was also limited largely to the littoral by these factors as well as by the extreme hardship of life for the white men. A major departure from these patterns began only in the latter half of the nineteenth century when Great Britain finally excluded its European rivals from this part of the Guinea coast.

Indigenous institutions provided no base for the development of a modern national state. The Fante states of the coastal regions were small, territorially organized units which occasionally joined together for military purposes largely under pressure from the Ashantis. In the extreme southeast, political organization among the Ga-Adangbe people was even more elementary, the principal unit being the independent town or village. Further inland, larger and more powerful states did develop, first Akwamu for a brief period, and later the powerful military state of Ashanti. While Ashanti was primarily a confederation for military purposes (with civil government remaining the function of component units), it is significant for present purposes in that it created some perception of a unity larger than the small Akan state in the people of a large central part of modern Ghana. In the Northern Territories, again the pattern was a large number of small relatively autonomous units and fragmentary groups.

In the century between Britain's exclusion of her

[2] An extended historical survey is beyond the purpose of this work. Relevant readings may be found in Bourret, *The Gold Coast* (1952); Fage, *Ghana: A Historical Interpretation* (1959); Ward, *A History of Ghana* (1958); Wight, *The Gold Coast Legislative Council* (1947).

European rivals and her transfer of the powers of government to an independent Ghana, a number of events occurred which augured the drive toward a larger unity. These need be sketched only briefly. During the 1830's, when the British responsibilities on the Gold Coast were in the hands of a group of London merchants, Captain George Maclean, a young Scotsman in their employ, laid the foundations of British government over a larger area; he arranged an acceptable peace between the Fante states and Ashanti and secured the voluntary acceptance by the local rulers and people of himself as judge in a variety of disputes. Maclean's activities lacked a legal foundation, but this was supplied in 1843 by the resumption of British governmental control over the Gold Coast and by the enactment of the Foreign Jurisdiction Act. Shortly thereafter, a number of Fante chiefs, in the so-called "Bond of 1844," acknowledged British jurisdiction in areas adjacent to the coastal forts and accepted the "general principles of British law" as the standard for remolding some of the customs of the country. In the Bond may be seen some concession of the sovereignty of the several native states and their search for a more inclusive organizing structure under the protection and guidance of the British.

British intent, initiative and foresight did not cultivate the seeds implicit in the Bond. Military incursions of Ashanti resumed without effective British response. In 1865, following a parliamentary inquiry, the British Government announced its intention of abandoning the Gold Coast and pursuing a policy which would enable the natives to take over "as speedily as possible." Responding to this apparent invitation, a number of chiefs and educated Africans met at Mankesim and adopted a constitution for the Fante Confederation.[3] Provision was made for executive, judicial and legislative

[3] This remarkable document is reproduced as Appendix C in Casely-Hayford, *Gold Coast Native Institutions* (1903).

functionaries and for the improvement of education, roads and agriculture, as well as for common defense against Ashanti. Again the British vacillated, repressing the unifying drive toward a larger measure of self-government, and the ambitious Mankesim Constitution came to nothing. In fact, on July 24, 1874, the Gold Coast was declared a British colony and such basis as was thereafter laid for the unification of the native states was found within the framework of colonial administration.

New impetus for drawing together diverse elements of the native population came in the 1890's from the reaction to proposals of the Gold Coast Government for legislation that would regulate the granting of mining and timber concessions. Viewing the proposed law as a step toward vesting ownership of "unoccupied land" in the government, the lawyers, businessmen and chiefs of the coastal areas organized the Gold Coast Aborigines' Rights Protection Society to oppose the measure. The proposed land legislation was withdrawn, but the Society remained a unifying political force in the Colony until the mid-twenties. Not all the groups looking toward the formation of wider associations and increased political participation for Africans had a purely Gold Coast focus, however. In the period immediately after World War I, largely under the leadership of J. E. Casely-Hayford, a Cape Coast barrister, the National Congress of British West Africa was formed, with representation from the Gold Coast, Sierra Leone, the Gambia and Nigeria. Early in its existence, the efforts of the Congress were undercut by some of the Gold Coast chiefs; such clashes of interest between the traditional rulers and educated, politically aware Africans were recurrent in the Colony. During certain periods, however, the two groups cooperated—as in the organization in 1930, under the leadership of Dr. J. B. Danquah, of the Gold Coast Youth Conference which met periodically for discussion of the ways to attain social and economic advancement.

All of these movements had their center of gravity in the Colony, though the later ones such as the Youth Conference had representatives from Ashanti. Developments in that important region must be sketched briefly since they not only provide a testimonial to the capacity of African societies to create and operate large and complex governmental structures but also serve to explain one of the principal obstacles encountered by the governing elite of an independent Ghana in creating a viable perception of nationhood. As has been seen, European intervention in West Africa was for centuries limited to a thin area along the coast. Secure in the high forests, the Akan states of the interior were left alone to evolve their own social and political organizations. During the eighteenth century, sparked mainly by the rulers of Kumasi State, the Ashanti Union was formed. Civil government remained the function of the several divisions of the Union under their Paramount Chiefs, but in military operations, first defensive but later aggressive, the Union was an effective, operating unit. The details of its history, largely military, do not concern us here; the important fact is that Ashanti did achieve a higher unity than the characteristic, small territorial state of the Akan. This unity was symbolized by the Golden Stool of Ashanti which was believed to embody the spirit of the entire Ashanti people. The Paramount Chief of Kumasi, as Asantehene, was the custodian of the Golden Stool and thus had the allegiance of the Ashanti people.

The military pressure of Ashanti, impinging as it did on the smaller states to the south, increased the dependence of the latter on the Europeans and explains in part the unifying tendencies epitomized in the Fante Confederation. During the nineteenth century, the British participated in six wars with Ashanti; in the sixth war, although British forces captured and burned Kumasi, they then withdrew almost immediately. In 1896, Kumasi was again occupied, the Asantehene was arrested and deported and a British resident was installed. In 1900, when the Gold Coast Governor, on a visit to Kumasi, demanded the surrender of the Golden Stool, traditional symbol of the unity of the Ashanti people, the seventh and final Ashanti war began. It culminated in 1901 in British annexation of Ashanti, with governmental powers vested in a Chief Commissioner who was responsible to the Governor of the Gold Coast.[4]

Annexation by the British did not immediately affect the institutions of civil government that existed at the divisional level, but the Confederation was in limbo. The significance of Ashanti as a military power was ended; the Golden Stool itself remained hidden until 1920. The British then better appreciated its significance and wisely made no claim to it. With assistance from Rattray's classic studies,[5] the ground was being prepared for the revival of Ashanti unity as an instrument of colonial policy. In 1924, Prempeh I, the Asantehene who had been in exile since 1896, was permitted to return to Ashanti.[6] Two years later, in 1926, he was re-elected Kumasihene, though not Asantehene. Finally in 1935, the Ashanti Confederacy was restored and Prempeh II was recognized as Asantehene. The revitalization of the formal structure of traditional Ashanti unity served to support the region's status under the colonial regime as a separate political and governmental unit. British efforts to unify Ashanti and the Colony did not begin until 1946, when the Burns Constitution granted the Legislative Council

---

[4] The Ashanti Order in Council, 1901, 1 STAT. RULES & ORDERS Rev. to Dec. 31, 1903, at 1.

[5] *Ashanti* (1923); *Religion and Art in Ashanti* (1927); *Ashanti Law and Constitution* (1929).

[6] The campaign for Prempeh's release was led by J. E. Casely-Hayford, a Cape Coast barrister and political leader, and Nana Ofori Atta, Paramount Chief of Akim Abuakwa. This cooperation suggests the interplay of Ashanti and Colony politics. Wight, *The Gold Coast Legislative Council*, 30 (1947).

powers over both areas, with five Ashanti members sitting in the Council in Accra.[7]

The two remaining areas included in modern Ghana are the Northern Territories and Togoland. The former came within British influence in 1897 after the conclusion of agreements with some of the chiefs; its boundaries were subsequently determined, and it was declared a Protectorate in 1901, governed by a Chief Commissioner responsible to the Governor of the Gold Coast. This status was preserved until the Coussey Constitution of 1950 provided Legislative Council representation for the Northern Territories.[8] Thus the north remained in the backwaters of Gold Coast political and governmental development until virtually the eve of independence. The fourth area, Togoland, was a former German colony divided under a League of Nations mandate between France and Great Britain. The southern area of the British mandate was administered as part of the Gold Coast Colony and the northern area as part of the Northern Territories. In 1956, the people of both areas in a plebiscite held under United Nations auspices chose to become part of Ghana upon its achieving independence.[9]

[7] The Gold Coast Colony and Ashanti (Legislative Council) Order in Council, 1946, 9 STAT. RULES & ORDERS & STAT. INSTR. Rev. to Dec. 31, 1948, at 673.

[8] The Gold Coast (Constitution) Order in Council, 1950 [1950], 1 STAT. INSTR. 831 (No. 2094).

[9] The voters in the plebiscite had the choice of union with an independent Gold Coast or separation of the territories from the Gold Coast and continuation under trusteeship with the possibility of ultimate union with the French-administered section of Togoland as an independent state. A total of 194,230 persons was registered to vote in the plebiscite; of these 160,587 voted. The breakdown of the vote was as follows:

	Union	Separation
Manprusi District	17,870	3,429
Dagomba District	28,083	6,549
Gonja District	3,166	2,729
Buem/Krachi District	28,178	18,775
Kpandu District	8,581	17,029
Ho District	7,217	18,981
Total	93,095 (58%)	67,492 (42%)

In summary, one can only conclude that neither indigenous institutions nor colonial developments nurtured a consciousness of higher unity upon which the underpinnings and superstructure of a nation could readily be built. Among the Akan (with the exception of Ashanti), traditional loyalties ran to small, territorially organized states which moved in and out of loose alliances under the exigencies of military pressure. These exigencies resulted mainly from the recurrent threat of Ashanti which thus introduced historic fears and suspicions to complicate the molding of a nation. As later discussion will show, the unification of Ashanti produced allegiances which have erected some of the most difficult obstacles to the recasting of the component elements into a viable national entity. Linguistic, cultural and economic diversities, while perhaps not major factors, have also rendered the task more difficult. Through most of the British experience on the Gold Coast, the practice of administering the several areas as separate entities at least diffused the unifying impact of a single colonial power. It is against this broad background that we turn again to the base line under the Nkrumah Constitution of 1954[10] and other relevant legislation. From that line we will then trace the efforts toward unification under the elite that has manipulated the legal force in independent Ghana.

The 1954 Constitution defined the Gold Coast to mean the Colony, Ashanti and the Northern Territories, and, for purposes of the constitutional allocation of powers, Togoland under British trusteeship as well.[11] The general governmental structure previously described was for the Gold Coast as thus defined.[12] It was made

---

The two districts showing majorities for separation were the Ewe areas. The summary of results appears in 1956 United Nations Yearbook 368. The full report of the UN Plebiscite Commissioner appears in United Nations General Assembly Documents, 11th Session, A/3173.

[10] The Gold Coast (Constitution) Order in Council, 1954 [1954], 2 STAT. INSTR. 2788 (No. 551), hereafter referred to as "1954 Constitution."

[11] *Id.*, sec. 1.　　　　　　　[12] See ch. I.

entirely clear, of course, that the integration of Togoland into the Gold Coast order would not permit any
action by the indigenous legislative or executive organs
that would be incompatible with the responsibilities of
the British Government under its Trusteeship Agreement
with the United Nations. Insofar as those responsibilities
were involved, the metropolitan power reserved ultimate
authority.[13] The National Assembly might legislate for
the entire Gold Coast, but laws repugnant to the Togoland Trusteeship Agreement were, to the extent of the
repugnancy, void. Executive functions, insofar as they
affected Britain's responsibility under the agreement,
were to be exercised on the direction of the Governor.
In defining the Gold Coast proper the 1954 Constitution
merely continued integrations previously achieved.[14]
Nevertheless, it is significant because for the first
time all of the areas of modern Ghana were brought,
to some extent, within a single political and governmental framework. Each area had representation in
the Assembly: 39 from the Colony, 13 from southern
Togoland, 19 from the Ashanti and 26 from the Northern Territories and Northern Togoland; in addition, 7
members represented the municipalities of Accra, Cape
Coast, Kumasi and Sekondi-Takoradi.[15]

Prior to the 1954 Constitution, efforts toward unification had been evident in revisions of the scheme of
local government. For decades, British policy had revolved around efforts to make the chiefs and their
councils effective instruments of local government.[16]
Separate legislation for the three major areas had provided for designating traditional rulers as Native Authorities, defining their powers and providing for the

[13] 1954 Constitution, secs. 16, 17, 36.
[14] As already noted, the 1946 Constitution had provided a
Legislative Council representing both the Colony and Ashanti;
the 1950 Constitution was applicable to the Colony, Ashanti and
the Northern Territories.
[15] Id., sec. 28.
[16] The history of local government is briefly reviewed in Ward,
A History of Ghana, 351-75 (2nd ed. 1958).

establishment and control of treasuries. In this body of enactments, the traditional separateness of the Colony, Ashanti and the Northern Territories is manifest. Ferment for change in local government was stimulated by the report of the Watson Commission[17] following the disturbances in 1948; it also figured prominently in the study and report of the Coussey Committee in 1949.[18] The Coussey recommendations were largely followed in the Local Government Ordinance of 1951, one of the first major pieces of legislation enacted after Nkrumah and the C.P.P. came to power.[19]

The Local Government Ordinance provided for the establishment of a substantially uniform system of local government throughout the entire country. On ministerial order, urban and local councils might be set up, two-thirds of the members of which would be popularly elected while one-third would be appointed by the traditional authorities, unless the Governor in Council determined that it was not practicable or appropriate to maintain this proportion. Substantial legislative and executive functions, including the levying of taxes, were to be exercised by the councils. Council bylaws were not, however, to have effect until approved by the Minister responsible for local government who was also granted the power to amend or revoke bylaws. Provision was also made for district councils composed of representatives of the urban and local councils within the district, the proportion between representative and traditional members to be fixed by the Minister. Adoption of the new system of local government was a signal defeat for the traditional forces, whose orientation was local or regional and politically exclusive, and a major victory for the new elite working within the secular framework of a national polit-

[17] Report of the Commission of Enquiry Into Disturbances in the Gold Coast, Colonial No. 231 (1948).
[18] Report to His Excellency The Governor By The Committee on Constitutional Reform, Colonial No. 248 (1949).
[19] Cap. 64, 2 Laws of the Gold Coast 370 (1951).

ical party and the institutions of modern parliamentary government.[20]

A more dramatic illustration of the conflict between these factions was the dispute over regionalism that reached crisis proportions in the mid-fifties on the eve of independence. Again a brief historical review is essential. In 1948, the Watson Commission had recommended the establishment of regional councils in the three principal areas with largely executive functions, including the supervision of local authorities, but with some power to make bylaws under a definition of function and a delegation of authority from the National Assembly. The Commission thought a taxing power in the Regional Councils might be necessary, though normally the councils were to be financed by grants from the Assembly. A somewhat different membership scheme was proposed for each region, but the common denominator was a limitation on the number of members selected by or identifiable with the traditional authorities. While announcing general agreement on the desirability of developing Regional Councils, the British Government withheld comment on most of the details. Significantly, however, it declared that the Regional Councils should be "developed from" the existing regional councils of traditional authorities—the Joint Provincial Council in the Colony, the Ashanti Confederacy Council and the Territorial Council for the Northern Territories.[21]

The Coussey Committee in 1949 rejected the existing territorial councils as the foundation for new regional organs but continued the pressure for "a large measure of decentralization of functions and of devolution of power by the Central Government." Regional functions in the fields of health, education, public works and social services were envisaged, but without a support-

---

[20] See Apter, *The Gold Coast in Transition*, 241-56 (1955); Ward, supra note 2, at 375 *et seq.*

[21] Statement by His Majesty's Government on the Report of the Commission of Enquiry Into Disturbances in the Gold Coast, Colonial No. 232 (1948).

ing power to tax. Regional administrations were to be financed by central government revenues granted to the regions. The point of emphasis at the moment, however, is the Coussey Committee's underlying theory of the relationship between the central government and each region: while the principle of maximum decentralization should be stated in a new constitution, the regional administrations were to be merely agents of the central government exercising such powers and functions as might be defined by legislation. These recommendations of the Coussey Committee were in general accepted by the Secretary of State for the Colonies.[22]

The Local Government Ordinance of 1951 did not implement the Watson and Coussey recommendations on regional organization. By the time of the Nkrumah Constitution of 1954, which is used here as the base line, the complex of views and political forces affecting this issue had changed radically. In September, 1954, the National Liberation Movement was organized, drawing its main support from the traditional authorities and their supporters, principally in Ashanti, but also profiting from the economic disaffection of the cocoa farmers. The N.L.M.'s importance lay in its transformation of the question of regionalism from the rational allocation of functions between a supreme central government and its regional agents to one involving the very nature and power of the central government itself.

The N.L.M. declared for a federal government under the Independence Constitution then emerging on the horizon. This position was supported by the traditional authorities in Ashanti. On October 21, 1954, the Asanteman Council adopted a resolution endorsing the demand for a federation and requesting the British Government to establish a commission of inquiry to

[22] Statement by His Majesty's Government on the Report of the Committee on Constitutional Reform, Colonial No. 250 (1949).

examine the proposal. The British Government replied that agreement on constitutional structure should result from internal discussions. To that end, Dr. Nkrumah subsequently proposed a round-table discussion, but this proposal was rejected by the Asanteman Council and the N.L.M. on the ground that they would consult with the Governor but not with a mere party leader. Again on December 30, Dr. Nkrumah proposed a conference on fundamental constitutional questions but the proposal was rejected by the N.L.M. and the Asanteman Council on February 5, 1955. On March 9, the Northern People's Party announced that it would support federation. As the movement gained strength during the early months of 1955, there were riots and other forms of violence against C.P.P. supporters in Ashanti, which led to the declaration of a state of emergency there.

On April 5, a Select Committee of the Legislative Assembly was appointed to study the proposals for federation and a second chamber. Its report, submitted on July 27, rejected federation on the grounds of cost and the inadequate number of qualified Africans to fill governmental posts.[23] It recommended, however, that consultative councils be established in the regions to assure collaboration in the planning of development. The Committee also rejected the proposal for a second chamber, suggesting that this might be reconsidered after independence.

The opposition parties decided to boycott the Legislative Assembly debates on the report of the Select Committee because they had taken no part in its appointment or proceedings. This failure had resulted from an earlier decision of the opposition groups to boycott the Assembly proceedings, to refuse to serve on the Select Committee and to reject invitations from the Committee to submit memoranda or give evidence. The demand of

[23] Report from the Select Committee on Federal System of Government and Second Chamber for the Gold Coast (1955).

the opposition was for a constituent assembly to deal with constitutional questions. After debate, the Legislative Assembly adopted the report of the Select Committee.

Following a suggestion made by the Colonial Secretary, Mr. Lennox-Boyd, the opposition parties submitted proposals for a federal structure to the Governor on August 12, 1955. A federation of four regions—the Colony, Ashanti, the Northern Territories and Togoland—was suggested. At the federal level, a parliament would consist of a partly elected and partly appointed upper house and a fully elected lower house. Cabinet government would be based on a working majority in the lower house. Federal power would include making laws for the peace, order and good government of the Union, and the collection of revenue to be divided among the regions. There would also be a federal Supreme Court with appellate powers over regional high courts. Amendment of the constitution would require approval by absolute majorities of both houses of the federal parliament.

At the regional level, the proposals contemplated bicameral legislatures. An upper house would include all chiefs in the region; a lower house would be elected by adult suffrage. All legislative powers other than those specifically assigned to the federal parliament would remain in the regions, each of which would have its own prime minister and cabinet. Regional heads, regional prime ministers, the federal prime minister and the Ministers of Defense, Interior and Justice would form a council of state to advise the Governor General.

In an effort to reconcile the divergent views on the basic allocations of power, Mr. Lennox-Boyd dispatched Sir Frederick Bourne, a former Governor in British India and Pakistan, to the Gold Coast in September, 1955. Bourne was to serve as Constitutional Advisor to the Gold Coast Government and to all parties and organizations interested in the question of devolution of powers to the regions. Before his arrival, however, the opposition parties informed the Governor that they would boycott Sir Frederick unless he was also authorized to inquire into the political crisis in the Gold Coast.

On Bourne's arrival in Accra on September 26, the official announcement of his mandate was broad indeed. He was to advise the Government on the organization and functions of regional councils and to assist in reconciling the competing views so as to resolve the constitutional crisis. Specifically, Sir Frederick was authorized to receive the views of the National Liberation Movement and to place them before the Government with his observations.

Despite this broad mandate, the boycott by opposition groups continued, though on somewhat different grounds. Contending that the Government's pressing passage of legislation dealing with the traditional state councils in Ashanti had impugned the sincerity of the Government in dealing with the constitutional question, the N.L.M. leaders and their supporters in other opposition groups refused to see Bourne officially or to discuss their views with him.[24] The Bourne Report, submitted to the Governor on December 17, 1955, rejected the federalism of the N.L.M., declaring that

[24] The State Councils (Ashanti) (Amendment) Ordinance, 1955, No. 38 of 1955. The critical part of the amendments authorized the Governor to provide for the hearing of matters of a constitutional nature, that is, involving the enstoolment and de-stoolment of chiefs, by a specially appointed committee of enquiry rather than the traditional council, and for the extension of rights of appeal from certain prior decisions of these councils. Nkrumah recognized that many people felt the ordinance was badly timed. In justification of the Government's action he has said: ". . . circumstances in the country at that particular time warranted passing into law an ordinance of that nature, when chiefs were being unjustly destooled for not supporting the federalist idea. They had no right of appeal, and it was high time that the Government took measures to protect them from such unfair treatment. If the bill had been withdrawn, it would have weakened the Assembly, and the chiefs for whose benefit it was being put through would have suffered at the hands of those who dealt in corruption, violence and injustice." *Autobiography*, 243 (1957).

"experience has shown that the fragmentation of existing states is, on general grounds, mistaken: on the contrary the tendency has been toward greater consolidation."[25] The Report did, however, recommend the establishment of regional assemblies, financed by central government grants.[26] These regional bodies would lack the power to tax and would have consultative and deliberative functions as well as certain executive responsibilities.[27] The proposed constitution and any ordinance establishing a regional assembly would make it "clear that the supreme legislative power remained at the centre"; regional legislation would be limited to bylaws and regulations made under delegation of authority to implement national enactments.

The Bourne Report thus rejected the demands for a federal structure in which the powers of the central government were defined and delegated to it while all residual power remained in the regional units. A conference to consider the report was convened at Achimota in February, 1956, but the federalists declined to participate. While varying somewhat in details, the Achimota Conference recommendations and the Gold Coast Government's proposals for an Independence Constitution firmly adhered to the Bourne rejection of federalism. The Government sought[28] the vesting of supreme

[25] Report of the Constitutional Adviser, p. 3 (1955).

[26] The stated purposes of the Regional Assemblies were "(i) to afford an effective link between regions and the Central Government and thereby to remove any danger of excessive centralization; (ii) to provide for the formation and ventilation of local opinion on matters of national importance; (iii) to procure the use of local knowledge and experience to ensure that legislation is devised and implemented and schemes and projects involving expenditure in the region designed, and the required money provided, in a manner suited to the circumstances of the region concerned" p. 5.

[27] The areas mentioned in which these functions might be exercised were local government, agriculture, animal health and forestry, education, regional roads, health, water development, town and country planning, housing and appointment of regional representatives to statutory boards and committees.

[28] Constitutional Proposals for Gold Coast Independence (1956).

legislative power in the national Parliament, a unified national judiciary and legislative devolution of certain functions in specified fields to regional organs. The opposition groups again boycotted the Legislative Assembly when the Government's proposals were debated.

The continuing constitutional dispute in the Gold Coast made the British Government unwilling to move further toward granting independence without a new expression of popular will in the country. Mr. Lennox-Boyd therefore announced in the Commons on May 11, 1956, that independence could be granted only after a new general election. He offered assurance that appropriate steps to grant independence would be taken if requested by a reasonable majority in the newly elected assembly.

Elections were held on July 12 and 17, 1956. The Convention People's Party contested all 104 seats, while the opposition groups were active largely on a regional basis—the N.L.M. in Ashanti and the Northern People's Party in the Northern Territories. Over-all C.P.P. strength in the newly elected Assembly was only slightly reduced, though on the basis of popular votes, the C.P.P. had a minority of votes from both Ashanti and the Northern Territories.[29] On August 3, 1956, Dr.

[29] Summary of popular votes in 1956 election given in per cent of the total population in each region:

	C.P.P.	Opposition	Non-voting
Gold Coast Colony	38	6	56
Ashanti	25	33	42
Trans-Volta Togoland	28	23	49
Northern Territories	20.5	28.5	51

Summary of Assembly totals in 1951 and 1956:

	C.P.P. 1956-1951		N.L.M. 1956-1951		N.P.P. 1956-1951		Others 1956-1951	
Gold Coast Colony	44	41	—	—	—	—	—	3
Ashanti	8	19	12	1	—	—	1	1
Trans-Volta Togoland	8	8	—	—	—	—	5	5
Northern Territories	11	11	—	—	15	14	—	1
Total	71	79	12	1	15	14	6	10

Nkrumah moved a resolution in the National Assembly calling for independence in accordance with Mr. Lennox-Boyd's earlier assurances. The opposition groups again boycotted the Assembly on this occasion, and the resolution was unanimously adopted.

The election results stimulated the agitation of the opposition groups for federation. Professor K. A. Busia issued a statement on August 12, before leading an opposition delegation to London for talks with Mr. Lennox-Boyd, which asserted that the results in Ashanti and the Northern Territories strengthened the case for a federal constitution. The Asanteman Council issued a similar statement on August 16, emphasizing the separate identity of the Ashanti people and their determination to preserve it. Although on September 18 Mr. Lennox-Boyd announced the British Government's intention to grant independence to the Gold Coast on March 6, 1957, he continued his efforts to reconcile the conflicting constitutional views. In the Gold Coast, discussions between the Government and the opposition and Territorial Councils finally took place in October, 1956. Thereafter the Gold Coast Government issued its revised constitutional proposals for independence. After Assembly debate in which the opposition for the first time participated, these proposals were approved by a vote of 70 to 25. On November 20, a joint resolution of the National Liberation Movement and the Northern People's Party demanded "separate independence for Ashanti and the Northern Territories." On November 27, the N.L.M. forwarded to Mr. Lennox-Boyd a plan calling for the establishment of Ashanti or a union of Ashanti and the Northern Territories as an independent state within the British Commonwealth. However, it was not until after the Colonial Secretary had visited the Gold Coast in January, 1957, that seemingly viable compromises were reached. These were reflected in a British White Paper, published on February 8, one day after the Ghana Independence Bill had been passed by the United Kingdom Parliament.[30]

The Independence Constitution represented a compromise between the opposing views, though the major concessions were made by the opposition parties.[31] No provision was made for a second chamber or a council of state. The important innovations were certain limits on the power of the central government, introduced to allay the suspicions of the traditionally oriented groups in Ashanti and the Northern Territories. Those provisions pertaining to changes in the constitution and in the status and functions of the chiefs have been discussed in earlier chapters.[32] Primary attention here is directed to the structure of the regional organizations upon which certain powers and functions might devolve.

The constitution provided for the division of the country into five regions;[33] in each of these there was to be a head of the region chosen by the regional House of Chiefs, except for Ashanti where the Asantehene was to be the head. In recognition of "the need for a body at regional level with effective powers in specified fields," Parliament was required to establish a Regional Assembly in each region. The specified fields were local government, agriculture, animal health and forestry, education, communications, medical and health services, public works, town and country planning, housing, police and such others as Parliament might determine. Within these areas, however, the Regional Assemblies had no

[30] The Proposed Constitution of Ghana, Cmnd. 71 (1957).

[31] The Ghana (Constitution) Order in Council, 1957 [1957], I STAT. INSTR. 1036 (No. 277), hereafter cited as 1957 Constitution.

[32] On constitutional amendment, see ch. I; on the status and functions of chiefs, see ch. II.

[33] The regions were the Eastern Region, made up of the former Eastern and Accra Regions of the Gold Coast; the Western Region, preserved intact; the Ashanti Region, consisting of all of Ashanti; the Northern Region, made up of the Northern Territories and Northern Togoland; and the Trans-Volta/Togoland Region, preserved intact. 1957 Constitution, sec. 63.

actual constitutional power or function. The supremacy of the central government was made entirely clear; the Regional Assemblies would "exercise authority, functions, and powers to such extent as may be prescribed by Act of Parliament."[34]

The only constitutionally assured function of the Regional Assemblies was the review of certain kinds of legislation with the possibility of exercising a qualified veto.[35] Two types of legislation required a special procedure which included approval by the Regional Assemblies: 1) any bill enacting, modifying, repealing or re-enacting the provisions of the constitutional Order in Council defining the basic governmental structure and the public service, guaranteeing regional organizations and chieftaincy and assuring compensation on the compulsory acquisition of property;[36] and 2) any bill abolishing or suspending a Regional Assembly or diminishing its functions or powers. It is noteworthy that this second limitation on parliamentary power did not provide constitutional assurance of any devolution of powers and functions to the Regional Assemblies. Devolution required legislation which could be passed by a simple majority in Parliament. Once delegating legislation was passed, however, it came within the protection of the procedure. Thus, a grant of powers or functions once made to the Regional Assemblies could not be easily revoked.

Bills falling within these two categories were subject to two special requirements. The first was approval by two-thirds of the entire membership of Parliament, the same percentage required in the case of any amendment of the constitution. The second was reference of the bill, after the committee stage in the National Assembly, to each Regional Assembly. Two-thirds of the total number of Regional Assemblies, including any assemblies whose powers or functions were affected by the bill,

[34] *Id.*, sec. 64.   [35] *Id.*, sec. 32.
[36] These "entrenched" provisions are listed in the Third Schedule to the constitutional Order in Council.

had to give their approval before further action on it could be taken by Parliament. In the Regional Assemblies themselves, approval required only a simple majority of those members present and voting. This more modest requirement may have been directed at the tactic often employed by the opposition groups during the disputes occurring since the establishment of responsible indigenous government, i.e., boycott of the proceedings of the National Assembly or special conferences. A similar assurance that dilatory tactics in the Regional Assemblies would not unduly impede the legislative process at the center was provided by the stipulation that unless a Regional Assembly certified to the Speaker of the National Assembly its action on a bill within three months of the reference, the bill would be deemed approved by the Assembly. Further, if a Regional Assembly certified its disapproval of a bill affecting its own powers or functions, the Governor General was authorized to submit the measure to a referendum of the registered electors in the region, and if a majority of the electors voting approved it, the bill would be deemed approved by the Regional Assembly. Thus, in the case of measures affecting the powers and functions of the assemblies themselves, though not in the case of proposed legislation affecting the entrenched provisions, the assemblies were not given an ultimate veto. The central government was able to take the issue to the people themselves.

A further limitation on the central legislative power applied to measures altering the boundaries of regions.[37] The relevant constitutional provisions are extended and rather complex, and for this reason a detailed summary is essential:

 1. No bill effecting any alteration in the boundaries of a region by transferring an area containing less than ten thousand registered electors, other than a bill creating a new region, could be introduced in the

[37] 1957 Constitution, sec. 33.

143

National Assembly unless the alteration had been previously approved by a majority of the members present and voting at a meeting of the Regional Assembly of every region whose boundaries would be affected.

2. If a bill would effect such an alteration in regional boundaries as to transfer ten thousand or more registered electors, it could not be introduced without the prior approval of a majority of the voters participating in a referendum in the region from which the transfer would be made, as well as the prior approval of a majority of the members present and voting in the assembly of the region into which any part of the transferred area would be incorporated.

3. No bill affecting regional boundaries by the creation of a new region could be introduced without prior referendum approval in every affected region and the approval of enough additional assemblies (by majority of those members present and voting) to bring the number of regions in which one form of approval or the other had been given to two-thirds of the total number of regions.

Measures effecting either of these three purposes were required to contain the provisions necessary for the delimitation of new electoral districts or the appropriate modification of existing districts. Thus, significant safeguards were erected around the territorial integrity of the regions specified in the constitution.

When the 1957 Constitution came into force, there were no Regional Assemblies which could merely be preserved. Before such assemblies could be established, basic legislation was required; but until the Regional Assemblies were established, the members of Parliament from each region were constituted an Interim Regional Assembly for that region.[38] These interim bodies were authorized to offer advice to a Minister on

[38] *Id.*, sec. 85.

matters affecting their regions. They could not, however, give the requisite assent to proposed legislation amending the constitution, affecting the existence, functions or powers of the Regional Assemblies or altering regional boundaries (except to create a new region). Where the proposed legislation would create a new region, the Interim Assemblies were expressly authorized to give the requisite assent.[39]

In the establishment of regional organizations and the devolution of powers to them, the study and recommendations of a special commission were contemplated. The constitution provided for the appointment by the Governor General of a regional constitutional commission to be chaired by the Chief Justice or a judge nominated by him and to include Commissioners from Parliament and from the Territorial Councils of traditional authorities as well as others.[40] Upon the report of the commission, implementing legislation was to be introduced. The commission was duly appointed under the chairmanship of Mr. Justice William B. Van Lare of the Supreme Court and received testimony and other evidence from a wide variety of witnesses. Included among them were spokesmen for the traditional authorities and the opposition political parties, the National Liberation Movement and the Northern People's Party.

The commission's report carefully stated the competing views on the relevant issues, evaluated the arguments and formulated its own recommendations.[41] It also incorporated a draft bill to implement these recommendations. In the light of later developments, the commission's conclusions need only be summarized. Regional organizations with substantial powers and functions in the several areas listed in the constitution were envisaged. The commission rejected the proposal for parliamentary structures at the regional level, preferring popularly elected assemblies, with executive functions

[39] *Id.*, sec. 33(3).   [40] *Id.*, sec. 87.
[41] Report to His Excellency The Governor-General by the Regional Constitutional Commission (1958).

being performed by bipartisan committees and a competent professional staff. In the initial period after establishment, the functions of regional organizations would be largely deliberative and supervisory, with executive functions increasing as sound administrative organizations were developed. The steady accretion of powers and functions at the regional level would be at the expense of both the central government and existing local government units. The constitutional status of the new regional assemblies was most clearly articulated in the commission's views on the legislative powers they should enjoy. The commission declared:

> To attempt any sharing of original legislative powers would, we consider, be to strike at the roots of the unitary nature of our constitution and to introduce a quasi-Federal state. We do not recommend that Regional Assemblies should have any original legislative powers.
>
> We consider that Regional Assemblies should have subordinate legislative powers, including the making of bye-laws, such powers being derived from the Act establishing Regional Assemblies or other Acts specifically conferring powers on Regional Assemblies.[42]

The dependent nature of the regional organizations was emphasized by the recommendation that all taxing power be withheld from them at least initially. The Regional Assemblies were to be financed by grants-in-aid from the central government or public corporations, by issuing precepts to local government rating authorities and by borrowing.

The Government's statement on the Commission's Report was quite brief.[43] With respect to the form and organization of the Regional Assemblies, it indicated an intention to prepare amendments to the bill drafted by the commission, dealing only with administrative

[42] *Id.*, at 93.
[43] Statement of the Ghana Government on the Report of the Regional Constitutional Commission, W.P. 4/58 (1958).

detail. With respect to the functions of the Regional Assemblies, however, the Government declared its intention to introduce amendments to the commission's bill which would leave with local government authorities a number of functions the commission would have committed to the regional organizations. The Government's view of the central function of the Regional Assemblies was thus stated:

5. The Government considers that the main value of Regional Assemblies is that there will be, in them, available to the Central Government, directly elected representative bodies which can tender advice either on their own initiative or at the request of the Government. The Government therefore proposes that there should be the fullest development of the advisory powers of Regional Assemblies.

The Government's views of course prevailed in the Regional Assemblies Act of 1958[44] as finally passed. Members of the assemblies were to be elected in regional electoral districts, each parliamentary constituency being divided into two such districts except in Trans-Volta Togoland where each constituency was to be divided into three. Affirmative qualifications for election were the same as those for Parliament, but a person was not eligible if he was a member of Parliament, head of a region, a member of a House of Chiefs, an employee of the central government, of a Regional Assembly, local authority, House of Chiefs or state council, or was engaged in instruction in any educational institution wholly or partly supported by Parliament. The functions of the assemblies were limited to advising and making recommendations to Ministers of the central government in a number of areas. It is not entirely clear from the several relevant provisions of the act whether a Regional Assembly might take the initiative in giving advice and making recommendations or whether even this function was merely to respond to a ministerial

[44] No. 25 of 1958.

147

request. The Government's statement on the Van Lare Commission Report had conceded such an initiative to the assemblies, however.

It is very clear that the act left unimpaired the full substantive control of the central government. This fact is well illustrated by the form of the authorization to a Regional Assembly to make bylaws for the purposes of its functions under the act. The act provided expressly that such "bye-laws shall not have effect until they are approved by the Minister [for local government] who, before approving, may amend them. . . ."[45] While the act contained extended provision for the preparation of estimates of expenditure[46] and the auditing of the accounts of Regional Assemblies, there were no express provisions relating to sources of income. Central government control over regional activity, clearly manifested by the delegated nature of the limited advisory powers of the assemblies, was reinforced by a firm hold on the purse strings.

Elections to the Regional Assemblies were held on October 16 and 21, 1958. The opposition, now substantially unified in the United Party, decided to boycott the elections on the stated ground that the Government had refused to take appropriate steps to check voting malpractices. The U.P. boycott elicited from the Government the curious response of a ban on all rallies of the Party, which lasted from September 26 until October 31, 10 days after the elections were completed. Without significant opposition, the Convention People's Party won 43 out of 44 seats in the Western Region Assembly, 41 out of 44 in the Eastern Region, 41 out of

[45] *Id.*, sec. 50(1).

[46] No expenditure could be made or estimate put into operation "until the estimates have been referred to and approved by the Minister . . . ," sec. 54(1). This is a departure from the Commission's recommendations which had rejected the necessity for central government approval of Regional Assembly estimates, finding adequate control in the central government's determination of what grants-in-aid should be made to each assembly. Report of the Regional Constitutional Commission, p. 101.

42 in Ashanti, 38 out of 39 in Trans-Volta Togoland and all 52 seats in the Northern Region.

Thus, firmly in control of both the organs of central government and the Regional Assemblies, the Nkrumah Government was in a position to abandon the compromises of the Independence Constitution and strike vigorously at the traditionally and regionally oriented groups. In December, 1958, Parliament repealed the restrictions on its legislative power, which had established a special procedure for constitutional amendments and had required reference to the Regional Assemblies and Houses of Chiefs of bills affecting them or the boundaries of Regions.[47] The Speaker duly certified that the bill had been approved by the requisite two-thirds of the entire membership of Parliament, had been referred to all Regional Assemblies and Houses of Chiefs and had been approved by all the Regional Assemblies. Thus, the requirements of the Independence Constitution for such legislation were fully met by the measure which eliminated the requirements for the future. The legislative supremacy of Parliament was now clear. Neither revision of the constitutional Order in Council nor any other measure required more than a simple majority in the Assembly and executive assent. The final blow at regionalism was a gratuity. In early 1959, the existing Regional Assemblies themselves were dissolved and the Regional Assemblies Act repealed.[48]

Subsequent modification of the regional structure is of little interest here. In 1959, Parliament created a new region, called the Brong-Ahafo Region, out of the northern part of Ashanti and a small part of the Northern Region.[49] Later, the name of the Trans-Volta/Togoland Region was changed to the Volta Region.[50] In 1960, the Constituent Assembly divided the Northern

[47] The Constitution (Repeal of Restrictions) Act, 1958, No. 38 of 1958.
[48] The Constitution (Amendment) Act, 1959, No. 7 of 1959.
[49] The Brong-Ahafo Region Act, 1959, No. 18 of 1959.
[50] The Volta Region Act, 1959, No. 47 of 1959.

Region into two new regions, to be known as the Upper and the Northern, and divided the former Western Region into the Central and the Western.[51] These adjustments did not affect the status, functions or powers of the regions, and they remained administrative subdivisions of a unitary government.

The victory of the proponents of unitary government in 1958 and 1959 seemed complete. Nevertheless, with a view toward Ghana's becoming a republic, the fundamental issue of governmental structure and the distribution of power was injected into the plebiscite in 1960. The White Paper presenting to the people a draft constitution declared: "The Government asks the people, by voting for the draft constitution, to show that they believe in the unity of Ghana and reject any form of federalism. The Government will consider a vote in favour of the draft Constitution as a mandate to maintain the unity of Ghana." It is noteworthy that the opposition United Party no longer insisted on a federal structure and, in fact, did not make an issue of regional powers and functions. Dr. J. B. Danquah, in his policy statement for the United Party, did revive the old plea for an upper chamber of Parliament, but on the issue of the distribution of power between the center and the regions he was silent.[52] Indeed, it could be argued that by implication he declared for the complete sovereign power of Parliament. The first on his list of immediate targets when the Government came under United Party control was "to restore to Parliament and affirm for all time its great power and status as the articulate expression of the legislative sovereignty of the country, the representative of the people, responsible not to the President or the Governor-General, but to the Constitution, to the people and to God."[53]

If the results of the plebiscite may be interpreted as the Government proposed, the people firmly rejected

[51] The Regions of Ghana Act, 1960, C.A. 11.
[52] Danquah, *What the People Want* (1960).
[53] *Id.*, at 7.

federalism. Thus, the republican constitution declares that "Ghana is a sovereign unitary Republic" and that the power to change the form of government from that of a unitary republic is reserved to the people.[54]

Thus, the drive toward unity has dominated the structuring and manipulation of public power in Ghana. The full array of legal power has been used to neutralize subnational orientations and power structures. The constitution organizes government on a unitary basis; the traditional authorities have been progressively limited to ceremonial, nongovernmental roles. A unified, national system of courts administers the law which is increasingly national in scope, the customary law with its essential localism now confronting in all cases a rebuttable presumption of nonapplicability. The legal apparatus of political monopoly, to be considered later, can fairly be seen in part as an effort to suppress local and regional divisiveness and to organize political power on the firm basis of the nation-state. Indeed, this entire study might be entitled, "The Legal Aspects of National Unification."

Ghana's role in the broader sweep of Pan-Africanism has been that of the constant agitator, the gadfly whose sting has offended perhaps more often than it has stimulated or attracted. By obvious conviction since his days as a student agitator, Dr. Nkrumah has been an Africanist; as he has gathered the reins of national power into his own hands, he has reached as well for the leadership of a supra-national movement looking ultimately toward the unity of all of Africa. Pan-Africanism in its various aspects, including legal implementation, merits extensive study. It is viewed here from the perspective of Ghana merely as the logical extension of the processes of internal unification that have claimed high priority under the Nkrumah Government. It may therefore be useful to sketch the principal polit-

[54] Republican Constitution, art. 4.

ical moves looking toward supra-national association in which Ghana has been involved.

At the Conference of Independent African States, convened in Accra at the invitation of the Ghana Government in April, 1958, the primary concerns were world peace and the elimination of colonialism and racialism. In his address to the conference, Dr. Nkrumah spoke in general terms of cooperation among the African states in economic and cultural pursuits; he did not, however, stress political association or organization. When the All-African People's Conference convened in Accra in December, 1958, attention was turned more specifically to some form of association. A resolution adopted by the conference called for the formation of a "Commonwealth of Free African States" and expressed the hope that the day would come when "the first loyalty of African States will be to an African Commonwealth." As a first step toward the continental commonwealth, a committee of the conference recommended regional federations in north, west, east, central and south Africa. The conference also decided to establish in Accra a permanent secretariat having as one of its aims the promotion of understanding and unity among the people of Africa.

The subsequent record of Ghanaian efforts to form operative associations with other African states has been a series of political pronouncements with little concrete achievement. On November 23, 1958, Dr. Nkrumah and President Sékou Touré of Guinea announced their agreement, subject to ratification by the respective National Assemblies, to constitute their countries as the nucleus of a Union of West African States. They also invited the other states to join the Union. They agreed, as first steps, to adopt a Union flag and to develop closer contacts so as to harmonize policies, especially in the areas of defense, foreign affairs and economics. The formulation of a constitution for the Union was also envisaged. As part of the initial agreement and also subject to ratification by the National Assemblies, Dr. Nkrumah undertook to provide Guinea a loan of £10,-000,000 as well as technical and administrative aid. After approval of the arrangement by the National Assembly of Guinea on November 28, and of Ghana on December 12, 1958, the two countries also agreed to exchange resident Ministers especially charged with responsibility for coordination and harmonization of policies.

During a visit by Dr. Nkrumah to Guinea in April and May, 1959, the two Presidents reaffirmed their intention to form a Guinea-Ghana Union and also proposed the establishment of a Union of Independent African States. In a statement to the press on May 2, Dr. Nkrumah said that he and President Touré had originally contemplated a "United States of West Africa" but that the rapid pace of events had shifted their thinking to the unity of Africa as a whole.

In July, 1959, Dr. Nkrumah met with President Touré of Guinea and President Tubman of Liberia at Sanoquelli, Liberia. In a communiqué issued at the conclusion of the conference, it was announced that all independent African states and those territories with fixed dates for achieving independence would be invited to attend a conference in 1960 for the purpose of establishing a community of African states. This conference never occurred. However, in November, 1960, Dr. Nkrumah visited Mali for talks with President Modibo Keita; on his return to Accra, he announced that Ghana and Mali had agreed to form a common parliament. A few days earlier, a joint statement based on the Bamako discussions reported that Ghana had granted a long-term loan to Mali, the amount of which was not disclosed.

The scope of Dr. Nkrumah's thought on African unity was clearly revealed in April, 1960. Addressing a conference he had convened in Accra, with representatives from all independent African states and a number of dependent territories, Dr. Nkrumah proposed a common market, a common currency area and better communications facilities as desirable steps toward an African Union. At this stage he was still willing to consider regional groupings as first steps toward continental consolidation. He said: "If countries like the Congo, Nigeria, Ghana, Guinea, Liberia, as well as others, come together in an effective political union in the west for a start, it is not difficult to imagine the impact such an African Union would create on the world. Then consider the weight of our influence if later our brothers of the east throw in their lot with the Union—and greater still the influence if our brothers of the north throw in their lot too. I, for one, am prepared to serve under any African leader who is able to offer the proper guidance in this great issue." Dr. Nkrumah foresaw more rapid economic development, with the assistance of foreign capital, if nonviable national economic units were replaced by united regions and ultimately, by a united continent. Nkrumah's vision and strong pleas, however, did not produce any concrete steps toward unity at the end of the conference.

Another conference of independent African states was convened in Addis Ababa in June, 1960. Ten states, including Ghana, were represented in addition to two countries—Nigeria and Somalia—that were soon to become fully independent. Ako Adjei, then Ghana's Minister for Foreign Affairs, made a strong plea for "the complete political union of African States" and urged the creation of a committee of experts to work out the details of a customs union, a free trade area and an African development fund. For the first time, however, insofar as available reports indicate, the Pan-African activists like Dr. Nkrumah were confronted by clearly conflicting views. The Nigerian representative contended that the idea of a Union of African States was premature and warned of the dangers to Pan-Africanism arising from a Messiah complex in any leaders. The approach favored by Nigeria was more gradual, building on functional ties in economic, social and cultural activities. The conference adopted resolutions recommending the establishment of a Joint African Development Bank, a Joint African Commercial Bank, a Council for African Economic Cooperation and a Council for Educational, Cultural and Scientific Cooperation. Thus, the recommendations supported Nigerian functional gradualism rather than the dramatic moves toward early political unity espoused by Ghana.

Aside from the granting of loans to Guinea and Mali and the exchange of Resident Ministers with Guinea, Dr. Nkrumah's efforts to foster supra-national associations had, by mid-1960, found little concrete expression in the law-government complex of Ghana. Political negotiations supported by the prospect of loans and other aid from Ghana had produced only unimplemented plans for establishing the structures of closer association and a series of presidential announcements that closer ties were desirable. In the development of a republican constitution for Ghana in 1960, Dr. Nkrumah sought stronger internal support for his Pan-African aspirations.

The White Paper that presented the draft constitution to the people asked them "to endorse the conception of African Unity" and "to entrust to Parliament the right to surrender the sovereignty of Ghana so that Ghana can, at any time when this becomes possible, be merged in a Union of African States."[55] The response of the Opposition appears curious indeed against the background of their distrust of national power, the frequent pre-independence references to Ashanti nationhood and their effort to structure governmental power in Ghana as a federation of highly autonomous regions.

Dr. J. B. Danquah, in a policy statement delivered on March 28, 1960, described himself, in contrast to Dr. Nkrumah, as a man "who has never deserted the na-

[55] Government Proposals for a Republican Constitution, p. 5, W.P. No. 1/60 (1960).

155

tional cause for any other cause—has never sought to betray the sovereignty of Ghana, and has never said such a stupid thing as that the freedom of Ghana is meaningless but that only the freedom of entire Africa has a meaning."[56] Among the immediate targets of the United Party, Dr. Danquah included its desire "to stretch out hands of friendship to all other African States, and if there is a true basis for union with any such African State, to so unite with such State or States, but never to sacrifice the sovereignty of Ghana. A federation of certain African States, in particular in West Africa, may be feasible, but the first and foremost need of the present generation of Ghanaians is to establish their country as a stable State, prosperous, happy and productive, and prepared to make a contribution to the progress and survival of Africa and the world."[57] While Dr. Danquah spoke of "immediate targets," his rejection of any surrender of Ghanaian sovereignty appeared to be permanent. He favored "Union" when feasible, but only if this left Ghanaian sovereignty unimpaired. If achievement of Union by the merger of other territories into Ghana is put aside, it would seem that the United Party support for supra-national association was limited to a loose confederation of sovereign states.

The decisive victory in the 1960 plebiscite for Dr. Nkrumah and for the draft constitution placed a firm Pan-Africanist imprint on the republican constitutional order. Article 2 provides: "In the confident expectation of an early surrender of sovereignty to a union of African States and territories, the people now confer on Parliament the power to provide for the surrender of the whole or any part of the sovereignty of Ghana."[58]

[56] Danquah, *What the People Want*, 5-6 (1960).
[57] *Id.*, at 7.
[58] The Constitution (Amendment) Act, 1964, Act 224, sec. 3 adds the following proviso: "Provided that the sovereignty of Ghana shall not be surrendered or diminished on any grounds other than the furtherance of African unity." This amendment clearly emphasizes the causal relation always expected between any surrender of sovereignty and the furtherance of African

The power to repeal or alter this article was reserved to the people and could therefore be granted to Parliament only after majority approval in a referendum ordered by the President. In the text of the solemn declaration before the people, required (in accordance with Article 13) immediately after a President assumes office, the President is required to declare his allegiance to certain fundamental principles, among which are "that the union of Africa should be striven for by every lawful means and, when attained, should be faithfully preserved" and "that the Independence of Ghana should not be surrendered or diminished on any grounds other than the furtherance of African unity."

This constitutional commitment to a larger unity is not unique in Ghana. A similar provision was in the constitution of Guinea in 1958 when Presidents Touré and Nkrumah first agreed on a Guinea-Ghana Union. Less emphatic commitments to African unity may be found in the constitutions of a number of other African states, and aspirations for some form of supra-national unification have found expression in constitutions in other parts of the world.[59]

By early 1961, the African unity movement had entered a more inclusive phase with more divisive potential. In January, 1961, Dr. Nkrumah met in Casablanca with leaders from Morocco, the United Arab Republic, Guinea, Mali and Libya. The Algerian insurgents were also represented, and a representative of the deposed Congolese Premier, Patrice Lumumba, attended as an observer. At the end of the conference, King Mohammed of Morocco and Presidents Nasser, Touré, Keita and Nkrumah signed on behalf of their respective countries an "African Charter," with which all independent African States were invited to associate

---

unity. The proviso thus makes explicit what reasonable interpretation might have found in the original form of Article 2.

[59] Schwelb, "The Republican Constitution of Ghana," 9 American Journal of Comparative Law 634, at 640-43 (1960).

157

themselves. In addition to reaffirming the common interest in nonalignment with any bloc, elimination of colonialism and neocolonialism and opposition to foreign troops and bases in Africa, the charter contemplated the establishment "as soon as conditions permit" of an African Consultative Assembly, a committee for political affairs comprising all Heads of States, a joint African High Command and cultural and economic committees. Dr. Nkrumah regarded the proposed military collaboration as perhaps the most significant development at Casablanca, and he also declared his belief that the conference had "laid the foundations for the political unity of the African continent."

A charter for a "Union of African States," approved by Presidents Nkrumah, Touré and Keita on April 29, 1961, brought the Union formally into being on July 1, 1961. The charter reaffirmed the desire for harmonization of foreign and domestic policies, elimination of all remaining vestiges of colonialism, the preservation of the territorial integrity of the member states through a system of common defense and economic development in the interests of the people. Several consultative media were established, the most important being the Conference of Heads of States which was described as the "Supreme Executive Organ of the Union." The only "executive" function specifically assigned to the conference, however, was the passing of resolutions. Despite provision in the charter for possible membership of other African states, no states have joined. Clearly the the Union did not involve any surrender of sovereignty by its members; it was a "union" only in the sense of a loose association for consultative purposes. Nor has its objective of the development of a common policy through frequent consultations been achieved, as was clearly revealed in the conflicting policies of Ghana and Guinea in dealing with the new government of Togo, which was set up after the assassination of President Olympio in 1963.

The possibilities for the development of competitive

and even hostile blocs within Africa, suggested by some of the discussion at the Addis Ababa conference in 1960 and clearly implicit in the Casablanca meeting, were realized in the Monrovia Conference in May, 1961. In attendance were delegations from nineteen independent African states: the twelve Franco-phonic members of the Afro-Malagasy Organization for Economic Cooperation along with Nigeria, Ethiopia, Liberia, Sierra Leone, Tunisia, the Somali Republic and Togo. None of the states represented at the Casablanca Conference attended, though Guinea and Mali had been among the inviting sponsors and seemingly withdrew later largely on the insistence of Ghana.

The deliberations in Monrovia were secret, the course of discussions only being suggested by an announced agenda and a concluding communiqué that set out certain general principles and specific resolutions. The principles especially are revealing; they declared firmly for absolute equality among African states, condemned territorial expansion by one state at the expense of another, reaffirmed the principle of nonintervention, insisted upon respect for the territorial integrity of all states and condemned the conduct of any state permitting the use of its territory for subversive activity against another country. Instead of the familiar appeal for African unity, the relevant principle was curiously passive: "If an African nation desires to unite with another, no country should do anything to prevent it."

The bases for the division of the African states between the Casablanca and Monrovia groups were complex and the available data leave much to surmise. In part, the division reflected ideological gradations, if not sharp differences, suggesting competition by the major power blocs—the Casablanca group was regarded as the more Marxist and, while opting for nonalignment, cultivated more extensive contacts with the eastern bloc. In large part, however, the division rested on specifically African concerns. The most important of these were the Monrovia group's insistence on respect for the territorial integrity of the national units left by the departing colonial powers and differences of view on the Congo problem. The Casablanca powers, with apparent support from the Sudan, favored to various degrees Morocco's claim to sovereignty over Mauritania. Similarly they tended to support the separatist remnant of the Lumumba regime in the Congo, then operating under M. Gizenga at Stanleyville. The Monrovia Conference, on the other hand, adopted a resolution expressing support for the central Congolese government under President Kasavubu and opposing in general the recognition of separatist regimes.

A further ingredient in the differences between the Casablanca and Monrovia groups was the latter's resentment of the aggressive leadership of Dr. Nkrumah and his insistence on early political unification. In his address opening the Monrovia Conference, President Tubman of Liberia said with obvious reference to Dr. Nkrumah's activism that "the idea of *primus inter pares*, first among equals, is destructive of African unity and peace." The increasing authoritarianism of the Ghana Government, and the effort to project an image of Dr. Nkrumah as the dominant African leader, elicited the suspicion and increasing hostility of leaders in other parts of the continent. While his own ambitions doubtless contributed to Dr. Nkrumah's sense of urgency in developing political unity and the organizations to support it, his long-held conviction concerning the primacy of political considerations was a basic datum. An Nkrumah epigram from the pre-independence period in the Gold Coast enjoined: "Seek ye first the political kingdom and all else shall be added unto it." This view, projected into the politics of continental unification, has caused Dr. Nkrumah to be disdainful of more modest efforts to achieve regional or functional associations oriented toward anything less than the continental sweep of Africa.

The absence of the Casablanca powers from the

Monrovia group continued through another meeting of Heads of State and two Foreign Ministers' conferences held in Lagos in 1962. On December 20, 1962, Foreign Ministers from sixteen of the nineteen Monrovia states signed the charter of the Inter-African and Malagasy Organization. Instead of unity, the charter spoke of co-operation in economic, cultural and political fields. The central feature of the organization was to be an Assembly of Heads of State and Government in which each state would have one vote and which could take decisions only by a four-fifths majority of those present and voting, except on procedural matters which would require only a simple majority. The charter also called for a General Secretariat and specialized agencies for cooperation in economic development, scientific training and research and conciliation and dispute settlement. A budget for the Organization would require ratification by four-fifths of all members and would be underwritten by the contribution of a percentage of each member's national budget. Provision was made for adherence of other states to the charter, as well as renunciation of membership in the Organization.

Before the roots of competitive blocs were firmly established in African soil, steps were taken to eliminate them. Following a decision of the Foreign Ministers of the states of the Afro-Malagasy Organization (taken at Lagos in December, 1962), a conference of Heads of State was convened in Addis Ababa in May, 1963. Although differences in view and emphasis were apparent, these were ultimately subordinated to a widely shared determination that the conference should not end without a continent-wide expression of agreement on certain principles and at least the general structure of an all-inclusive organization. On May 25, 1963, thirty independent African states, including both the Casablanca and Monrovia powers, signed the charter of the Organization of African Unity. Morocco and Togo, although not participating in the conference, later became signatories.

Before the opening of the Addis Ababa Conference, Dr. Nkrumah submitted to the other Heads of State rather detailed proposals for the creation of a Union having a bicameral structure much like the U.S. Congress, with responsibility for development planning, and the creation of an African Common Market, a Central Bank with a common currency and an over-all military command. These proposals did not find sufficient support to reach the agenda of the conference, but in his initial address, Dr. Nkrumah urged early and vigorous steps toward political unification. He stressed the greater ease with which a united Africa could attract development capital without objectionable strings, the benefits of union in resolving the border disputes bequeathed by colonialism and the necessity of union to real African independence.

Aside from a terse endorsement from Prime Minister Obote of Uganda, Dr. Nkrumah's views did not find support at the conference. Rather, the tone of the ultimate consensus was set in the opening address by Emperor Haile Selassie of Ethiopia, in which he said:

> We look to the vision of an Africa not merely free but united. . . . We know that there are differences among us. . . . But we also know that unity can be and has been attained among men of the most disparate origins, that differences of race, religion, culture, and tradition are no insuperable obstacle to the coming together of peoples. . . . There are those who claim that African unity is impossible. . . . Let us confound these and, by our deeds, disperse them in confusion. . . . We are determined to create a Union of Africans. . . . It is our duty and privilege to rouse the slumbering giant of Africa—not to the nationalism of Europe of the 19th century, not to regional consciousness, but to the vision of a single African

brotherhood bending its united efforts towards the achievement of a greater and nobler goal.

Above all, we must avoid the pitfalls of tribalism. If we are divided among ourselves on tribal lines, we open our doors to foreign intervention and its potential harmful consequences. The Congo is clear proof of what we say. . . . But while we agree that the ultimate destiny of this continent lies in political union, we must at the same time recognize that the obstacles to be overcome in its achievement are numerous and formidable. Africa's peoples did not emerge into liberty in uniform conditions. Africans maintain different political systems; our economies are diverse; our social orders are rooted in differing cultures and traditions. Further, no clear consensus exists on the "how" and the "what" of this union. Is it to be federal, confederal, or unitary? Is the sovereignty of individual States to be reduced, and if so, by how much and in what areas? On these and other questions there is no agreement; and if we wait for agreed answers, generations hence matters will be little advanced, while the debate still rages.

We should therefore not be concerned that complete union is not attained from one day to the next. The union we seek can only come gradually as the day-to-day progress which we achieve carries us slowly but inexorably along this course. We have before us the examples of the U.S.A. and the U.S.S.R. We must remember how long they required to achieve their union. . . . Thus a period of transition is inevitable. Old relations and arrangements may for a time linger. Regional organizations may fulfill legitimate functions and needs which cannot yet be otherwise satisfied, but the difference is that we recognize these circumstances for what they are—temporary expedients designed to serve only until we have established the conditions which will bring total African unity within our reach.

There is, nonetheless, much that we can do to speed this transition. . . . There are issues on which we stand united and questions on which there is unanimity of opinion. Let us seize on these areas of agreement and . . . take action now which, while taking account of present realities, nonetheless constitutes clear and unmistakable progress along the course plotted out for us by destiny. . . .

What we still lack . . . is the mechanism which will enable us to speak with one voice when we wish to do so and to implement decisions on African problems when we are so minded. The commentators of 1963 speak . . . of the Monrovia States, the Brazzaville Group, the Casablanca Powers, and many more. Let us put an end to these terms. What we require is a single African organization . . . which will facilitate acceptable solutions to disputes among Africans and promote the study and adoption of measures for common defence and programmes for co-operation in the economic and social fields. . . . Let us not put off for later consideration and study the single act, the one decision, which must emerge from this gathering if it is to have real meaning. This conference cannot close without adopting a single African Charter. . . .[60]

The tone of the Emperor's speech was moderate and conciliatory. Other leaders were more direct in their reaction to Dr. Nkrumah's urgency and the general pattern of Ghanaian activism. President Nasser of the U.A.R. reminded his colleagues that African unity could not be developed overnight. Dr. Nyerere of Tanganyika rejected the idea that African unity could be created by merely saying, "Let there be unity." President Senghor of Senegal warned that unity could not be rushed and urged the development of regional associations as a first step. President Youlou, of the former French Congo, was opposed to a union of African states with a single

[60] 1963 Keesing's Contemporary Archives, 19464.

Parliament and urged consideration of an African Consultative Assembly similar to the European Assembly. President Bourguiba of Tunisia rejected hasty improvisation of African unity which could not in his view be imposed by a dominant force or will.

Sir Abubakar Tafawa Balewa, Prime Minister of Nigeria, in a speech that was temperate in tone but pointed in delimiting the basis of the existing groupings with their attendant suspicions and hostilities said:

> Some of us have suggested that African unity should be achieved by political fusion of the different States in Africa; some of us feel that African unity could be achieved by taking practical steps in economic, educational, scientific, and cultural co-operation and by trying first to get Africans to understand themselves before embarking on the more complicated and more difficult arrangement of political union. My country stands for the practical approach to the unity of the African continent. . . . Nigeria's stand is that if we want this unity in Africa, we must first agree to certain essential things. The first is that African States must respect one another. There must be acceptance of equality by all the States. No matter whether they are big or small, they are all sovereign. . . .
>
> It is unfortunate that the African States have been broken up into different groups by the Colonial Powers. . . . That was not our fault because, for over 60 years, these different units have existed; and any attempt on the part of any African country to disregard this fact might bring trouble to this continent. This is the thing we want to avoid, and for this reason Nigeria recognizes all the existing boundaries in Africa and recognizes the existence of all the countries in Africa. . . .
>
> Many speakers have told us that mere resolutions, mere condemnations, are not enough; it is time for action. I would call upon the Conference to start now

on the real work. It is in our hands to build, to create, and to develop a new Africa, which all of us are anxious to do. . . . I want to be frank; to my mind we cannot achieve this African unity as long as some African countries continue to carry on subversive activities in other African countries. . . .

There has been a suggestion that we should pool our resources together, that we should make arrangements, if necessary, to help the Nationalists in different countries in Africa which are still dependent to fight their way to independence. We in Nigeria are prepared to do anything toward the liberation of all African countries. I have observed that, when we give assistance to another country which is fighting for its independence, some of us are in the habit of imposing obligations on those States. That is wrong. If we give assistance to African people in any dependent territory, we should not ask for any obligation on their part. . . . It is our view that . . . we should appoint a standing committee to go into the details of this matter.

We must take every care to know whom we invite to assist us in the development of our resources, because there is a fear—which is my personal fear—that if we are not careful we may have Colonialism in a different form. . . . Just as we fought political domination, it is important that we fight economic domination by other countries. . . .

I do not believe in African personality but in human personality. The African is a human being, and therefore we have to see to the development of human personality in Africa. I think any talk of African personality is based on an inferiority complex. I do not regard any human being—red, white, brown, yellow, or green—as superior to me. I regard myself as equal to anybody. I am a human being.[61]

Dr. Nkrumah accepted the implicit attacks on his

[61] *Id.*, 19465-66.

policies with apparent good grace and permitted his Foreign Minister to serve on the drafting committee that prepared the charter. The accomplishments of Addis Ababa were in fact depicted by the Ghanaian press as the direct result of the foresight and dynamic leadership of President Nkrumah.

The first significant feature of the Charter of the Organization of African Unity (O.A.U.) is the statement of principles to which each member is committed. These include respect for the sovereign equality and right to independent existence of each state, noninterference in the internal affairs of states, peaceful settlement of disputes, unreserved condemnation of political assassination and subversive activities, dedication to the complete liberation of still-dependent territories and nonalignment. The earlier insistence of the Monrovia powers that the national units left by colonialism must be accepted and respected as basic data of African political affairs thus was clearly articulated in the charter. Ghanaian insistence on early revision of national boundaries, hopefully in the process of Africanization, was rejected. Sponsorship of subversive activities, like those recurrently alleged by Togo and Nigeria against Ghana, was firmly condemned.

The institutional framework created by the charter was simple. Aside from certain specialized commissions to be organized for coordination of effort in such fields as economic development, education, health, defense and scientific research, four bodies were instituted:

1. The Assembly of Heads of State and Government is to be "the supreme organ of the Organization." Its function is to "discuss matters of common concern to Africa with a view to co-ordinating and harmonizing the general policy of the Organization" and to review the structure, functions and acts of all other organs and agencies. In the Assembly, each state has one vote and a substantive resolution requires a two-thirds majority of all members. Procedural questions are subject to resolution by a simple majority.

167

2. The Council of Ministers, composed of the Foreign Ministers or other Ministers designated by member states, is responsible to the Assembly and entrusted with the functions of preparing for Assembly Conferences, implementing Assembly decisions and coordinating inter-African cooperation in accordance with instructions of the Assembly. Again in the Council, each state has one vote, but all matters there are subject to decision by a simple majority.

3. The General Secretariat, under the direction of an Administrative Secretary General, is to perform any functions specified by the charter and regulations approved by the Assembly. In language borrowed from Article 100 of the United Nations Charter, the O.A.U. Charter attempts to make the functionaries of the Secretariat international civil servants, exempt from the instructions or authority of any government or other agency. In an apparent effort to avoid political functions in the Secretary General, his post is formally described as "Administrative." Nevertheless, for more than a year it was impossible to reach agreement on an appointee to this post, and interim direction of the Secretariat was provided by an Ethiopian Officer-in-Charge. At the meeting of the Assembly of Heads of State in Cairo in July, 1964, M. Diallo Telli of Guinea was chosen as the first Secretary General.

4. A Commission of Mediation, Conciliation and Arbitration, instrumental to the undertaking of all member states to settle disputes among themselves by peaceful means, was to be established with such functions and membership as should be laid down in a separate protocol approved by the Assembly.

Any assessment of the Organization of African Unity would be premature. Probably its most significant accomplishment is that it exists. That in the extreme diversities of newly independent Africa, 32 states have recognized sufficient areas of common concern and shared interest to induce the organization of a body of continental scope is an historic and hopeful event.

The signing of the O.A.U. Charter abated the sharpness of the Casablanca-Monrovia split without removing the underlying causes. The continuing divisions were dramatically illustrated by the acid exchange between Dr. Nkrumah and President Nyerere of Tanganyika and Zanzibar at the Heads of State meeting in Cairo in July, 1964.[62] Despite the insistence of some leaders that the charter requires the dissolution of regional groupings, this in general has not been done.[63] The Council of Ministers, meeting in Dakar in August, 1963,

[62] The clash was precipitated by an address by Dr. Nkrumah urging immediate establishment of a United Government of Africa; in this speech he attacked the performance of the Liberation Committee established at Addis Ababa to assist the "Freedom Fighters" in the still-dependent territories. According to Dr. Nkrumah, the Freedom Fighters had been exposed to "espionage, intrigues, frustrations and disappointments," had been denied food, clothing and medicine and proper facilities for training. He complained that the Congo (Leopoldville) rather than Tanganyika was the "logical" training base for Freedom Fighters. In a curious rhetorical question he asked, "What could be the result of entrusting the training of Freedom Fighters against imperialism into the hands of an imperialist agent?" For all these ills, Dr. Nkrumah found the cure in the immediate establishment of a United Government of Africa.

Dr. Nyerere responded with understandable heat. He pointed out that Ghana was the only country that had made no financial contribution to the work of the Liberation Committee; he insisted that Ghana's failure to contribute had not resulted from the inadequate performance of the Committee but that the decision had in fact been made at Addis Ababa when Ghana was not given membership on the Committee and Dar es Salaam had been chosen as the Committee's headquarters. Dr. Nyerere declared that he was becoming increasingly convinced that the African states were divided "between those who genuinely want a Continental Government and will work patiently for its realization; and those who simply use a phrase 'Union Government,' for the purposes of propaganda." Clearly, in his judgment, Ghana fell into the latter category. Dr. Nyerere did "not believe that there is a choice between achieving African unity step by step and achieving it in one act. The one-act choice is not available to us except in some curious imagination."

[63] The Pan-African Freedom Movement for East, Central and Southern Africa (PAF MECSA) was reported to have been dissolved in September, 1963, and replaced by the "Committee of Nine," which had been appointed at Addis Ababa and charged with establishment of a "Liberation Bureau" at Dar es Salaam. Whatever the formal status of the Ghana-Guinea-Mali Union, it clearly has no functional significance.

169

merely recommended that regional groups should "envisage the integration of the existing organizations in the specialized institutions of the O.A.U." The success of the first effort to settle a dispute between member states—the border controversy between Algeria and Morocco that flared briefly into violence—bodes well for the future of this aspect of the Organization's work. The dispatch of Nigerian troops to Tanganyika to replace British forces called in at the time of the mutiny in January, 1964, must also be regarded as an achievement. This inter-African aid was arranged following an emergency meeting of Foreign and Defense Ministers of the O.A.U. states convened at Dr. Nyerere's invitation in February, 1964. Dr. Nyerere recognized the general African interest in the problems raised by the meeting while acknowledging the humiliation that Tanganyika would suffer from having troops of any other nation doing Tanganyika's work for it. He thus evidenced the sensitive nationalism that persists in the grasping for a higher unity.

In attempting to consolidate in Ghana a functioning national unity against the forces of internal division, Dr. Nkrumah has exploited fully his personal charisma, the legal tools of a national state and the surge of nationalistic sentiment generated in the independence movement. As an intelligent and sensitive man, he cannot have failed to appreciate the conflict, actual and prospective, between these means used internally and others that are needed to foster a perception of and movement toward some greater unity—perhaps Africa—in which the aspirations of the African peoples may be more fully realized. On a continental basis, despite the frequently expressed desire for unity, the forces of division are entrenched and powerful. To cope with them, the weapons used within Ghana are not available nor, despite Dr. Nkrumah's passionate pleas for *Union Government Now*, do they appear to be attainable within the near future.

CHAPTER IV

THE LEGAL PROFESSION

THE HYPOTHESIS underlying this chapter is that adequate understanding of a legal system cannot result merely from the study of the legal norms and the structure of courts. The study must also include the professional group which holds itself out to the public as advisers on matters of law and as representatives of litigants in the courts. In this connection, the critical lines of inquiry relate to education and qualification for and admission to the professional group, discipline and control of and exclusion from the group, the availability of the service of the professionals to those desiring their services, the types of function conventionally performed by such professionals either in their individual capacities or through some institutional framework and the view of the professional and his role held widely in the society.

It is not essential here to seek great historical depth. As general background, it may be observed that education abroad early became attractive to Africans from the Gold Coast, and that the study of law has always claimed a significant part of those who decided to study abroad.[1] For many years the African lawyers played an important role in the political ferment among the intelligentsia. The names of John Mensah Sarbah, J. E. Casely-Hayford, J. B. Danquah and K. A. Korsah need only be mentioned in this regard.

The first regulation of the bar to which detailed attention need be given was contained in the Legal Practitioners Ordinance of 1931, which survived the attainment of independence. Its terms will be considered in the later sections on admission and discipline of the profession.

[1] On the early Gold Coast lawyers, see Kimble, *A Political History of Ghana*, 68-70 (1963).

THE GENERAL LEGAL COUNCIL

The Legal Practitioners Act of 1958[2] created the General Legal Council of Ghana. Since its role is critical to all aspects of the profession considered later, the composition and functions of the Council must be first considered.

When first created, the General Legal Council included the Chief Justice as Chairman, a Minister appointed by the Prime Minister, the Justices of Appeal, the Attorney General, the Head of the Faculty of Law at the University College of Ghana, three persons nominated by the Chief Justice, three persons nominated by the Minister responsible for Justice and four members of the bar of not less than five years standing, nominated by the Minister appointed by the Prime Minister on the recommendation of the Chief Justice.[3] In 1960, the membership of the Council was altered slightly, but only one change was significant: the unofficial members from the bar were thereafter to be elected by the Ghana Bar Association rather than appointed by the Minister for Justice.[4] The composition of the Council was again changed in 1964. Membership from the Supreme Court is now limited to the Chief Justice and the three next most senior judges. The nominees of the Chief Justice were eliminated, and the nominees of the Minister for Justice increased from two to three.[5] The effect of these changes was to reduce the relative weight of the judiciary on the Council and to increase that of the executive.

The functions of the General Legal Council are broad: it is to be "concerned with the legal profession and, in

---

[2] No. 22 of 1958.   [3] *Id.*, sec. 2(2) and First Schedule.

[4] The Legal Profession Act, 1960, Act 32, sec. 1(2) and First Schedule. The full membership of the Council under this act included the Chief Justice and all judges of the Supreme Court, the Attorney General, the Head of the Faculty of Law at the University College, two nominees of the Chief Justice, two nominees of the Minister for Justice and four members of the bar elected by the Bar Association.

[5] The Legal Profession (Amendment) Act, 1964, Act 226, sec. 3.

particular,—(a) with the organisation of legal education, and (b) with upholding standards of professional conduct."[6] Originally the Council was made subject, in the performance of all its functions other than the hearing of appeals in discipline cases, to "any general *or specific* directions given to them by the Governor General."[7] At least some members of the Council found this subservience to the executive objectionable. In the 1960 Act, therefore, the relevant provision was altered to provide that "the Council shall in the performance of their functions comply with any general directions given to them by the Minister."[8]

Two aspects of the 1960 provision should be noted: the Council was made legally subject only to general directions, presumably laying down broad policy guides; the earlier exclusion from ministerial direction of the Council's function of hearing appeals in disciplinary cases was eliminated. The latter change was incident however, as will be noted later, to the transfer of this appellate jurisdiction from the Council to the Supreme Court. Thus, the directive powers of the Minister were not increased.

The issue of Council freedom from the specific direction of the executive was sharply raised in November, 1963. The Council had earlier appointed Dr. J. B. Danquah as editor of the Ghana Law Reports. This action evoked from the President a demand that the Council terminate the appointment, under threat that all Governmental subventions for the Council would be terminated if the President's directive were not met. While the Council fully recognized that under the governing law the President lacked power to issue such a directive, it saw no practical alternative to substantive compliance. Instead of dismissing Dr. Danquah, how-

---

[6] The Legal Practitioners Act, 1958, No. 22 of 1958, sec. 2(1); The Legal Profession Act, 1960, Act 32, sec. 1(1).

[7] The Legal Practitioners Act, 1958, No. 22 of 1958, sec. 2(5) (italics mine).

[8] The Legal Profession Act, 1960, Act 32, sec. 1(5).

ever, the Council prevailed upon him to resign. His resignation terminated the issue without the Council's formally acting on the President's directive.

QUALIFICATION AND ADMISSION TO THE BAR

As might be expected in a colonial dependency, the qualifications for admission to the bar under the pre-1958 law were primarily derivative from a metropolitan status. The Chief Justice of the Gold Coast was authorized, in his discretion, to admit and enroll as a barrister and solicitor any person qualified to practice in either of those professions in England, Northern Ireland, the Republic of Ireland or Scotland, who satisfied the Chief Justice that he was a person of good character.[9] Parenthetically, it should be pointed out that the separate professions of barrister and solicitor, characteristic of the United Kingdom, were merged in the Gold Coast.[10] A special annual license was, however, required for practice as a solicitor, and the conditions governing its issuance were prescribed by the Rules Committee established under the Courts Ordinance.[11] The most important of these conditions was a one-year service in the chamber of a local practitioner. The requirement of a qualifying admission was given force by penal and other sanctions against unauthorized practice.[12] Minor deviations from this system of qualification appeared in the Northern Territories where the Attorney General could authorize a police officer to appear for the Crown before the Supreme Court;[13] also, a commissioned officer in the armed forces who was certified to the Chief Justice to be qualified to practice as a barrister, advocate or solicitor in the United Kingdom, Eire or any British possession was authorized to defend any member of the armed forces

---

[9] The Legal Practitioner Ordinance, No. 5 of 1931, as amended, Cap. 8, sec. 3, 1 Laws of the Gold Coast 259 (1951).
[10] *Id.*, sec. 6. [11] *Id.*, sec. 8. [12] *Id.*, secs. 9-10, 35-59.
[13] *Id.*, sec. 67(1).

on a criminal charge brought in any court.[14] In addition, any person holding the office of Attorney General, Solicitor General, Legal Draftsman, Director of Public Prosecutions or Crown Counsel was deemed to be, ex officio, a barrister of the Supreme Court.[15]

After the creation of the General Legal Council, functions involved in the enrollment of persons as legal practitioners were committed to it. Subject to the satisfaction of the Council of good character, the 1958 Act entitled three categories of persons to enrollment:

1. citizens of Ghana holding a qualifying certificate from the General Legal Council;

2. noncitizens qualified as legal practitioners in other countries who fulfilled such conditions as to status or proficiency as might be specified in rules made by the Council with the approval of the Governor General (after the Republic, the President); such persons might be enrolled at the discretion of the Council;

3. until August 8, 1962, citizens of Ghana entitled to practice as barrister, advocate, solicitor or law agent in a country outside Ghana.[16]

The Legal Profession Act of 1960 introduced a number of changes in the qualifying criteria for enrollment. First, the limitation to Ghanaian citizens of qualification by obtaining the certificate of the Council was eliminated. This route was thus opened to noncitizens. Similarly, admission in Ghana at the discretion of the Council by qualification in another country was opened to citizens as well as noncitizens. Whereas the 1958 Act had merely specified qualification "in a country outside Ghana," the 1960 Act required that it be "in any country having a sufficiently analogous system of law."[17]

[14] Military Advocates Ordinance, No. 6 of 1946, Cap. 57, 2 Laws of the Gold Coast 354 (1951).
[15] The Law Officers Ordinance, 1952, No. 1 of 1952, sec. 3.
[16] The Legal Practitioners Act, 1958, No. 22 of 1958, secs. 4-5.
[17] The Legal Profession Act, 1960, Act 32, sec. 3.

Until August 8, 1962, such qualification entitled a citizen to enrollment without Council discretion.[18] The pressure of students studying law in Britain prompted a further liberalization of this provision, enacted after the original cutoff date had passed. An amendment passed in 1963 makes foreign qualification to practice before August 8, 1962, and enrollment as a student in a professional law school prior to January 1, 1961 (approximately the effective date of the Legal Profession Act of 1960) alternative grounds for enrollment without Council discretion.[19]

An interesting provision of the 1960 Act specifies that a citizen of Ghana shall be taken to be qualified to practice in a particular country if he has satisfied the educational tests required for admission, even though he may not in fact have been admitted to practice.[20] The act does not make it entirely clear whether the satisfaction of such tests is determined by the Council in Ghana or by some agency in the other country.

Another innovation of the 1960 Act raises a number of possibly significant questions as to its purposes and effects. Under the 1958 legislation, a person who—after meeting the qualifications stated in the act—was enrolled and thereafter paid the fee prescribed by the Council was entitled to a certificate of enrollment. Except for the annual license required to practice as a solicitor, no other certificate was required. A significant change occurred in 1960, however. No person, with the exception of the Attorney General or a member of his staff, was thereafter entitled to practice, *either as a barrister or solicitor*, except in accordance with a practicing certificate issued by the General Legal Council. It must be remembered that the earlier criteria for qualification related only to enrollment. The practicing certificate after enrollment is a further requirement. In the case of a person not previously licensed as a

---

18 *Id.*, sec. 4.
19 The Legal Profession (Amendment) Act, 1963, Act 166.
20 The Legal Profession Act, 1960, Act 32, sec. 5.

solicitor, the Council is authorized to withhold the certificate or license to practice as a solicitor until the applicant fulfills such conditions as the Council may prescribe. Also, the Council is authorized to withhold certification of any person until he produces "such evidence as the Council may specify showing that he has not been guilty of professional misconduct either in Ghana or in any other country."[21]

Three aspects of this certification should be emphasized: the burden of proof of the broadly inclusive negative—absence of professional misconduct—is on the applicant; certification by the Council appears to be within the range of activities in which the Council is made subject to the general direction of the Minister for Justice;[22] the form of certification specified indicates that the certificate is to be limited to one year.[23] Substantial penal sanctions against unauthorized practice are preserved.

By a series of legislative instruments, the Council has provided further details on the basis for qualification and admission to the bar. These have become more important as an increasing percentage of those seeking admission do not fall within the categories entitled to admission on the basis of a definitive authorization in the act without Council discretion. Since qualification on grounds subject to the Council's discretion is intimately related to programs of legal education in Ghana, brief consideration must be given to this development before concluding consideration of criteria governing admission to the bar.

In connection with its responsibility for certifying applicants for enrollment as legal practitioners, the General Legal Council was authorized to establish a system of legal education, to fix a curriculum and hold examinations.[24] Provision was made for the delegation of immediate administrative and supervisory responsi-

21 *Id.*, sec. 8. 22 *Id.*, secs. 1(5), 56.
23 *Id.*, sec. 8(1) and Second Schedule.
24 The Legal Practitioners Act, 1958, No. 22 of 1958, sec. 12.

bility to a Board of Legal Education consisting of the Chief Justice, the Attorney General, a member of the Council nominated by the Chief Justice, two persons with wide experience in law and other fields nominated by the Minister appointed by the Prime Minister and the Director of Legal Education.[25] In meeting its responsibilities for legal education, the Council was authorized to act either through a school set up by it or through any other educational institution.[26]

Aside from certain law courses taught for economics students in the University College, legal education began in Ghana in late 1958 with the opening of the Ghana Law School. The school, situated near the Supreme Court in Accra, had no university connection. Responsible to the General Legal Council and run by the Director of Legal Education, it offered a program of evening instruction geared to Parts I and II of the English bar examinations. It was also contemplated that in the future the school would provide a one-year Practical Course as transition to practice for both Diploma graduates of the school and those who had taken a law degree in the University College.

The guiding spirit behind the creation of the Law School was Mr. Geoffrey Bing, an English barrister, who until 1961 was Attorney General of Ghana and at one time an influential political adviser of Dr. Nkrumah. Mr. Bing's justification for the Law School, at the same time that a university program in law was being planned, involved two arguments. The first of these was that Ghana needed quickly a number of legally trained persons, not necessarily of university quality, who could play important roles in national development through both Government service and private practice. He pointed to the concentration of lawyers in Accra, Kumasi and Cape Coast and legitimately argued that means must be found for increasing the supply of legal services and dispersing them more satisfactorily throughout the country.

[25] *Id.*, sec. 14.   [26] *Id.*, sec. 12(2).

The second argument advanced by Mr. Bing posited the existence in Ghana of a large number of able people, both interested in and qualified for the study of law, who lacked the financial resources for study in Britain. Many of these persons were civil servants or teachers who could be accommodated by evening instruction in Accra while they continued their regular employment. Fairness to these persons as well as the national interest justified, in Mr. Bing's view, the establishment of a nonuniversity program of part-time legal education in the Ghana Law School.

A third major element which did not appear in the formal argument was political. The existing bar of Ghana was economically and politically conservative. Leading lawyers had long played prominent parts in the intellectual middle-class nationalist movements such as the United Gold Coast Convention and the National Liberation Movement. They provided much of the leadership for the United Party which by the late fifties was the principal opposition group. They had long maintained close, though not always tranquil, relations with the chiefs and traditional rulers who were increasingly regarded by Dr. Nkrumah and his associates in the C.P.P. as the center of dangerous, divisive subnational power. To dilute the existing British-trained bar by a large influx of locally produced lawyers seemed to offer substantial political advantages while increasing the supply and improving the distribution of legal services in the country.

The Ghana Law School was therefore an accomplished fact by the time an International Advisory Committee studied the program of legal education and reported their recommendations in 1959.[27] One of the

[27] The Committee consisted of Professor L. C. B. Gower of Britain, Professor Zelman Cowen of Australia and Professor Arthur A. Sutherland of the United States. Dr. A. A. A. Fyzu of India was also invited. Though unable to participate in deliberations of the Committee, he submitted a memorandum. Most of the information concerning the early development of legal education in Ghana is taken from the unpublished report of the Committee.

Committee's main tasks was to relate the functions of the Law School to those of the Department of Law in the University College, which accepted its first group of students in October, 1959. The Law Department proposed to offer a four-year course leading to the LL.B. degree. The report of the Advisory Committee, accepted by both the University College and the Government, recommended that persons taking the LL.B. should be admitted to practice after completing a one-year, full-time Practical Course in the Ghana Law School. It was also recommended that the part-time instruction in the Law School, leading to the Diploma in Law, should be regarded as a temporary expedient and terminated not later than 1965, and that thereafter the Law School, acting in an undefined capacity as an "Institute of the University," should offer only the final year's Practical Course.

Thus by October, 1959, a two-pronged program in legal education had been set up in Ghana. The only formal link between the two programs was the membership on the General Legal Council, which was responsible for the Law School, of the head of the Law Department in the University. More important, however, was the fact that John H. A. Lang, an English solicitor, was appointed the first Professor of Law and Head of Department in the University; he was also given the position of Director of Legal Education, an office created by the Legal Profession Act of 1960, with operational responsibility for the Law School.

The growing pains experienced by both institutions between 1958 and 1962 need only be summarized. The Law School, with its highly amorphous admission standards, accepted large numbers of students, but the dropout and failure rates were high. The time required for the Diploma in Law was extended from two to three years. When the first group of thirteen students earned their diplomas in 1961, they were required to wait almost a year before a Practical Course was organized for them. In both the Law School and the University College, the shortage of teachers was chronic. Each institution had a small number of full-time teachers, supplemented by part-time lecturers from Government law offices and the private bar. In the University, yearly course programs were largely fixed on an *ad hoc* basis; the first set of course and degree syllabuses was not prepared and approved until the late spring of 1962.

Following the resignation of Professor Lang in January, 1962, the University of Ghana and the General Legal Council invited me to become Professor and Dean of the Faculty of Law of the University and Director of Legal Education. I accepted the invitation for two years, a period that permitted at most the clarification of a guiding philosophy and the organization of basic programs.

The program of legal education projected for Ghana was to be made entirely the concern of the University, with the Ghana Law School to be closed as quickly as fairness to its students would permit.[28] This consolidation was recommended not only with the hope of using the scarce teaching staff in the most economical way, but also by the belief that the education of lawyers should take place in an institution having a commitment to teaching and research in a broad range of humane and social disciplines. No existing foreign system was thought to provide an adequate model for Ghana. Since the British professional division between barristers and solicitors had not been exported and there was no local equivalent of the Inns of Court or the Law Society, Ghanaian university education in law required a broadly professional character unlike its British parent. The concentrated professional education of American law schools was inappropriate, however, for students entering the Faculty of Law directly from secondary schools. Consequently, the planning was

[28] The full text of the statement of views and recommendations of the author is set out in Appendix 1.

eclectic but the projected scheme was a new synthesis, intended to respond to the needs and aspirations of Ghana for a competent and responsible legal profession.

The several recommendations I made were accepted by the General Legal Council and the University. The Council announced that instruction in the Law School would be concluded in July, 1964.[29] It also agreed to delegate to the Faculty of Law of the University responsibility for all legal instruction, both "academic" and "practical." The University undertook to provide five years of instruction in law, divided as follows: a three-year nonprofessional B.A. (Honors) in Law, to include some general, liberal education, study of the basic legal institutions and certain of the less professional specialized courses such as Public International Law. This degree program would cater not only to the prospective professional but also to persons who after three years in the University would make careers in the civil service, diplomatic corps and business concerns both public and private. For those seeking professional qualification, the University would offer a two-year, post-graduate LL.B. degree. The General Legal Council agreed to accept the B.A. and LL.B. from the University as the basis for immediate admission to the bar of Ghana.

The development of local programs of legal education, and the pressure from Ghanaians studying in Britain[30] to continue accepting call to the English bar as a sufficient basis for admission in Ghana, have led to a number of revisions of the legislative instruments in which the General Legal Council has specified the basis for qualification and admission. Only the current

[29] It has been reported that after the author's departure from Ghana in February, 1964, the Government decided to continue instruction in the Ghana Law School. No information concerning the scope or purposes of the continuing program is available.

[30] The grant of independence to African territories has not ended the sense of responsibility in Britain for the legal education of Africans or the flow of African students to the United Kingdom. See "Report of the Committee on Legal Education for Students from Africa," Cmd. 1255 (1961).

instrument need now be considered. The Legal Profession (Enrollment) Instrument of 1964[31] provides that the Council will issue a qualifying certificate if a person has 1) a Diploma in Law from the Ghana Law School, a law degree conferred by the University of Ghana or any degree conferred by an approved university if the holder of that degree has satisfactorily completed instruction in the University of Ghana in certain areas where the law of Ghana is unique;[32] 2) a certificate of professional competence. This certificate is issued to any person who satisfies the Council that he has been satisfactorily examined in a number of specified areas of the law.[33] Provision is also made for comity admissions of persons who have practiced for at least five years in a country having an analogous system of law. In addition to the categories of persons covered by the Instrument, the act itself entitles citizens of Ghana, of good character, to admission if they enrolled in a professional law school prior to January 1, 1961, or if they were qualified to practice in Great Britain or Ireland before August 8, 1962.[34]

In summary, it may be said that admission to the bar in Ghana is governed by the General Legal Council which is authorized with the approval of a Minister to issue regulations on the subject by legislative instrument. Such legislative instruments are made subject to annulment by the National Assembly,[35] but no procedure for laying proposed legislative instruments before the Assembly is provided in the act. As has been noted, the functioning of the Council is made subject to at least general executive direction, and the risk of

[31] L.I. 343.
[32] The four areas specified are the Law of Immovable Property, Equity and Succession, Constitutional Law and Family Law.
[33] The specified fields are: Law of Contract, Law of Tort, Criminal Law and Procedure, Commercial Law, Company Law, Evidence, Civil Procedure, Equity and Succession, Family Law, Conflict of Laws, Law of Taxation, Conveyancing and Drafting and Administrative Law and Practice.
[34] The Legal Profession (Amendment) Act, 1963, Act 166.
[35] The Legal Profession Act, 1960, Act 32, sec. 53(3).

unauthorized specific directions cannot be excluded. This fact, coupled with the procedure for the annual licensing of lawyers, raises the spectre of a serious risk to a strong, truly independent bar, if the government— through the General Legal Council—should seek to curb it. The present legal structure would offer no obstacle to such an effort, but thus far, it has not been attempted by the Government. While certain questions, particularly those relating to comity admissions of lawyers from other countries, are handled on an unduly *ad hoc* basis, internal political tensions have not affected qualification and admission to the bar, except as these factors have motivated the establishment and possible continuation of qualifying programs in the Ghana Law School.

DISCIPLINE AND CONTROL

In determining the status and stature of a bar, it is essential to consider not merely admission to it but also the procedures for supervising professional activity and disciplining those who depart from acceptable standards. Under the pre-independence legislation of the Gold Coast, which is taken here as the base line, disciplinary functions were committed initially to the Legal Practitioners Committee, composed of the Attorney General and Solicitor General ex officio and nine unofficial members who were legal practitioners nominated by the Gold Coast Bar Association.[36] The Committee was authorized to hear witnesses on oath and receive documentary evidence, to compel the testimony of witnesses and the production of essential documentation. Any practitioner whose conduct was called in question before the Committee was entitled to a copy of the charges and other relevant documents, to appear personally at the Committee hearing and to be assisted by counsel. Upon completion of hearings, the Commit-

[36] Legal Practitioners Ordinance, Cap. 8, secs. 40 *et seq.*, 1 Laws of the Gold Coast 259 (1951).

tee was required to report its findings to the judges of the Supreme Court. If the Committee concluded that a prima facie case of misconduct had been established, it was its duty to bring this report and the evidence before the Supreme Court. At a hearing in which the Committee and the practitioner were entitled to appear by counsel, the court might consider the report and evidence presented by the Committee and any further evidence deemed proper. If the court found against the practitioner, it was authorized to impose discipline in the form of suspension from practice for a specified period or by striking the practitioner's name from the Roll of the Court. Similar disciplinary powers for "reasonable cause" were vested in the court even though no inquiry had been made by the Legal Practitioners Committee. The pre-independence system of disciplinary control and ultimate exclusion from the bar thus involved a close cooperation between the bar and the Supreme Court, with the ultimate powers vested in the latter.

The Legal Practitioners Act of 1958 effected a number of significant changes in the disciplinary system.[37] The General Legal Council was authorized to make rules of professional etiquette and standards of professional conduct and to direct that breach of the rules should constitute "grave misconduct." Rules so made by the Council were to be laid before Parliament, which was allowed thirty days within which to annul them. Any legal practitioner guilty of "grave misconduct"—which included but seemingly was not limited to breaches of rules laid down by the Council—or "infamous conduct," which was not defined in the act, was subject to prohibition from practice for a term or to having his name stricken from the Roll of Legal Practitioners. For the purpose of establishing the basis of such disciplinary action, the Council was directed to appoint a Disciplinary Committee of three to seven members,

[37] See Legal Practitioners Act, 1958, No. 22 of 1958, secs. 15-24.

185

consisting of members of the Council, persons holding or who had held high judicial office, or former members of the Council practicing as legal practitioners. The Disciplinary Committee was authorized to hold hearings on charges of unprofessional conduct with investigative powers similar to those of the former Committee. Parties to the hearings were entitled to be heard and represented by counsel. On the completion of the hearing, the Disciplinary Committee might impose discipline of suspension or exclusion from the bar, or postpone indefinitely the making of a decision of whether to impose discipline. In either event, the affected practitioner was given the privilege within 21 days of appealing to the General Legal Council on any question of law and, with the permission of the Committee or the Council, on any question of fact. The types of action open to the Council after hearing the appeal were not specifically defined in the act.

This disciplinary system was preserved by the 1960 legislation[38] with two changes worth noting: the rules of the General Legal Council defining standards of professional etiquette and conduct were no longer required to be laid before Parliament; the function of hearing appeals from the Disciplinary Committee was transferred from the General Legal Council to the Supreme Court. In evaluating the current disciplinary system for lawyers, several contrasts with the pre-independence scheme should be observed:

1. the role of the institutionalized bar has been substantially reduced, being limited to the election of a minority of the General Legal Council which in turn appoints the Disciplinary Committee;

2. the role of the Supreme Court as the ultimate tribunal was eliminated in the period between the 1958 and 1960 Acts but has now been restored;

3. while the procedural aspects of a fair hearing have been preserved, the present system does not

[38] Legal Profession Act, 1960, Act 32, secs. 16-25.

186

require that either the initial proceedings before the Disciplinary Committee or the appeal to the Supreme Court eventuate in a decision. Thus, a practitioner against whom serious charges are pressed bears the risk that even after the full course of disciplinary procedures, these may remain undetermined indefinitely. The possible relation between such undetermined charges and the issuance of the annual practicing certificate by the Council could cause serious concern.

While the formal structure of disciplinary powers over the bar might lend itself to abuse, there is no evidence that this has occurred. In fact, if the system as it operates is subject to any criticism, it would be to complain of the almost total lack of activity of the Disciplinary Committee rather than arbitrary or oppressive oversight of the bar. Complaints against lawyers are normally adjusted or discouraged in an informal, pre-hearing stage. The only formal disciplinary action in recent years resulted in only a mild reprimand, despite findings by the Committee of exceedingly questionable conduct by the lawyer involved. The propriety of more vigorous discipline may be reconsidered later when comment is made on the popular image of the legal profession in Ghana.

THE AVAILABILITY OF LEGAL SERVICES

The existence of a competent and independent bar is meaningless unless its services are readily available to persons against whom or on whose behalf the public force is or should be brought to bear. This observation raises the critical question of the availability of professional legal services to those in need of them.

In this connection, one starts with the fact that in the part of the court system probably closest to the great majority of the people, professional lawyers are entirely excluded. This was true of the older system of Native Courts and remains the rule in the new Local

Courts.[39] A Local Court may, however, permit the litigant to be represented by his spouse or other relative or guardian. In commenting on the exclusionary practice, the Blackall Committee in 1943 made the following observations:

56. Legal practitioners are not allowed to practise before Native Tribunals. A race of "bush-lawyers" has however sprung up who appear for parties under the pretence of being a member of the litigant's family, and it has been suggested that it would be better to regularise the position by allowing licenced pleaders to practise before Tribunals. They should be required to pass an examination in native customary law and Court procedure and their licence would be suspended or revoked if they misbehave. It is contended that the existence of pleaders trained in native law might assist its [the native law] development on lines reconciling traditional usages with modern needs, and it is pointed out that the fact litigants do employ "bush-lawyers" indicates that there is a public demand for their services and that an illiterate litigant may be unable to put his own case properly before the Court.

57. In theory there is a good deal to be said in favour of this proposal, but several practical objections have been raised against it. So far from assisting in the development of native customary law, the average "bush-lawyer's" legal knowledge consists, it is said, of a smattering of English law and the effect of his advocacy is to turn the Native Tribunal into a parody of a British Court. Further, "bush-lawyers" are usually of a poor standard of education and their

[39] Native Courts (Colony) Ordinance, Cap. 98, sec. 22, 3 Laws of the Gold Coast 164 (1951); Native Courts (Ashanti) Ordinance, Cap. 99, sec. 20, 3 Laws of the Gold Coast 196 (1951); Native Courts (Northern Territories) Ordinance, Cap. 104, sec. 20, 3 Laws of the Gold Coast 223 (1951); Native Courts (Southern Section of Togoland) Ordinance, Cap. 106, sec. 22, 3 Laws of the Gold Coast 240 (1951); Local Courts Act, 1958, No. 23 of 1958, sec. 26; Courts Act, 1960, C.A. 9, sec. 104.

sole object being to make money, they tout for business and foment frivolous litigation. It is also pointed out that even if the litigant himself is unable to explain his case properly, it is almost certain that some member of his family will be able to assist (the word "family" is interpreted liberally) and the members of the Tribunal are also ready to help him out. It should also be borne in mind that litigants before Native Tribunals usually confine themselves to facts and that native law is not a technical matter which calls for expert advocacy: it is usually a matter of common knowledge. Lastly, if the employment of licenced pleaders became general it would entail additional expense to litigants for if one side employed a pleader the other would have to follow suit.

58. The general feeling then seems to be that the introduction of licenced pleaders would do more harm than good and the Committee does not propose to recommend any substantial change in the existing law at the present time. We suggest however that the second proviso to section 64 might be clarified by inserting "in its discretion" after "Court" and by providing that where a person appears on behalf of another the opposite party may require him to prove that he is, in fact, within one of the categories of persons entitled to appear.[40]

The Korsah Commission, in 1951, expressed the view that registered practitioners should in general be permitted to practice before the Local Courts. The Commission appreciated, "that courts constituted by honorary lay justices, exercising jurisdiction up to £25 in ordinary civil cases, may find it difficult to follow legal argument and may be embarrassed thereby."[41] For this reason, as well as to reduce expense, the Commission limited its recommendation that practitioners be al-

[40] Report of the Native Tribunals Committee of Enquiry, p. 14 (1943).
[41] Report of the Commission on Native Courts, para. 219 (1951).

lowed to appear to Local Courts other than those constituted by honorary lay justices. In commenting on
the Commission's report, Chief Justice Mark Wilson
recognized the ultimate desirability of admitting practitioners to all courts but felt it then inappropriate for
them to practice in the Local Courts. The interdepartmental committee ultimately accepted the view of the
Korsah Commission.

In its 1955 statement on the report of the Korsah
Commission, the Gold Coast Government indicated
cryptically that under its proposed reforms of the Local
Courts System, legal practitioners would be allowed to
appear before such courts.[42] As already indicated, however, this change was not made by the post-independence legislation, and qualified professionals are still
not permitted to practice in the Local Courts.

The governing law on the availability of legal assistance in matters before the higher courts also presents
certain interesting features. The early Legal Practitioners Ordinance provided that in "civil causes the
employment of a legal practitioner shall be subject to
the approval of the Court, which may disallow such
employment in causes which it considers may more
advantageously be conducted by the litigants in person."[43] In the Northern Territories, however, a separate
provision permitted employment of a practitioner in
all causes, whether civil or criminal, but with the
proviso that in any civil case before any court other
than the Supreme Court, "the presiding officer of the
court may prohibit the appearance of any legal practitioner if he is satisfied that having regard to the
trivial nature of the issues involved, or to the poverty
of the parties, or either of them, it would not be in
the interest of justice that counsel should appear."[44]
A further proviso applicable in the Northern Territories

[42] Statement by the Government on the Report of the Commission on Native Courts (1955).

[43] Legal Practitioners Ordinance, Cap. 8, sec. 12, 1 Laws of the
Gold Coast 259 (1951).

[44] *Id.*, sec. 67(2)(a).

prohibited the appearance of a practitioner before any court in any case on appeal from a Native Court or on appeal from a decision made on appeal from a Native Court.[45] In criminal prosecutions, Court approval of the employment of counsel was nowhere required. At the same time, the courts were under no stated legal obligation to provide counsel for an accused person, no matter how serious the charge.

The foregoing provisions were not affected by the Legal Practitioners Act of 1958, but in 1960 they were repealed by the republican legislation. No new restraints on the employment of counsel were introduced at that time. The provision of legal assistance remained the responsibility of the litigant or accused. The law imposes no obligation to provide counsel in any case, though the Courts Act of 1960 authorizes the Supreme Court to assign counsel to an appellant in any appeal or related procedure where such appears desirable to the court in the interests of justice and the appellant lacks sufficient means to obtain legal assistance.[46]

The question of the right of an accused to counsel was dramatically raised in March, 1963, when seven persons were brought to trial on charges of treason and misprision of treason arising out of the terrorist bombings following the attempted assassination of Dr. Nkrumah at Kulungugu in August, 1962. While in the custody of the police (before their first appearance in court on March 12, 1963), the accused were not permitted to consult counsel. On March 15, the presiding judge on the Special Criminal Division, Sir Arku Korsah, Chief Justice, declared at the beginning of the session that it had come to his attention that some persons had the impression that the accused had been denied counsel. This, he declared, was not true. He explained that it was not the duty of the State to provide counsel to persons accused of plotting against the State. If any attorney wished to come forward and offer his services or if the family of an accused wished

[45] *Id.*, sec. 67(2)(b).   [46] Courts Act, 1960, C.A. 9, sec. 19.

to brief counsel, the court would be entirely willing to hear him.[47]

Under this ruling the defendants remained unrepresented. In private conversations with the author, leaders of the bar expressed both surprise and disapproval of the court's ruling on the appointment of counsel. It was thought contrary to the etiquette of the profession, however, for any lawyer to volunteer his services. Tentative discussions of the desirability for the Bar Association to designate certain lawyers to represent the accused resulted in no action. The seven defendants were ultimately convicted; the judgment of the court did not discuss further the problem of a right to counsel.[48]

In a subsequent treason trial beginning in August, 1963, which involved two former Cabinet Ministers and the former Executive Secretary of the C.P.P., the question of a right to counsel did not arise. On their first appearance in court, all defendants were represented by counsel, who included some of the most prominent members of the bar, and the defense was vigorously conducted.

In civil matters and in connection with other problems requiring the services of professional lawyers, the availability of assistance is seriously affected by both the uneven distribution of lawyers throughout the country and the level of professional fees. It is not surprising to find most lawyers concentrated in the larger cities, particularly Accra and Kumasi, where an economically attractive practice can be developed. Even in these centers, however, legal services depend on the clients' ability to pay. Legal services are expensive in Ghana. The contingent fee contract, which is a commonplace in the United States, is legally foreclosed. No legal-aid clinics have been established. The indigent person con-

[47] *The Ghanaian Times*, March 16, 1963, p. 1, col. 3.
[48] The State v. Teiko Tagoe and others, Unpublished Judgment scd. 1/1963 dated 17 April 1963.

fronting a need for legal services has no recourse except to the charitable inclinations of individual lawyers. No data are available to indicate the amount of work done by lawyers for indigent clients without expectation of fee.

FUNCTIONS OF LAWYERS

The primary function of lawyers in Ghana is the representation of private clients in litigation, both civil and criminal. In this work, the lawyers practice on an individual basis—though there is some sharing of "chambers"—and there is no evidence of specialization. The role of the lawyer as adviser in business and personal affairs not resulting in litigation appears to be relatively undeveloped. This is due in part to the modest level of economic development in the country, as well as to the litigious orientation of both lawyers and clients. The overwhelming majority of Ghanaian lawyers were qualified in Britain as barristers. The first Ghanaian qualified as a solicitor in the early 1950's, and only 10-12 have since achieved this qualification. While lawyers conventionally qualify in Ghana to practice as solicitors as well, the traditional advisory functions of the solicitor, with litigation only a final resort, are relatively neglected.

Lawyers do not now play a prominent role in the public life of Ghana, nor are they apt to do so in the near future. The reasons are not difficult to detect. Lawyers were prominent in the nationalistic movements throughout the 1940's, but very few were attracted to Dr. Nkrumah's Convention People's Party. They represented a more conservative and, as time passed, traditionally oriented segment of the society. Thus, the bar has been regarded by Dr. Nkrumah and the C.P.P. as a seat of political opposition. It is noteworthy that much of the top leadership of the United Party, the last identifiable opposition group, came from leading lawyers like J. B. Danquah, Joe Appiah and Victor Owusu.

The Ghana Bar Association is relatively inactive. Its president makes a ceremonial appearance on the opening of the Judicial Year, and its elected representatives participate in the work of the General Legal Council. As a body, however, the Association appears to have no significance in public life. It has no committees concerned with law reform or similar problems on which the developed views of the profession might have an influence.

SOCIAL IMAGES OF THE LAWYER

Some concluding comment on the general image of the legal profession in Ghana may be justified. This rests on impressions making no claim to scientific validity, formed through a substantial period of involvement in the legal affairs of Ghana. These impressions are supported, however, by the results of an experiment with 28 first year law students in the University of Ghana carried out in December, 1962. Without advance notice, I asked each student to write two essays, one describing his own view of judges and practicing lawyers, the other describing the impression of these persons he believed the general Ghanaian community had. The results were revealing. Almost without exception, what the students claimed for themselves conformed to laudable stereotypes—both judges and lawyers emerged as learned, firm, articulate, patient and bold. The main interest lies in the views attributed to the general community. Three students declared that the community held lawyers in high esteem, respecting them as learned men. The other 25 painted an entirely different picture, in outline as follows. The lawyer usually went to Britain for a rather brief course requiring a modest level of ability for successful completion. He returned to prey upon his less-informed, usually illiterate clients without rendering any meritorious service. The lawyer is a professional liar; many students referred to a common saying that the lawyer is placed in his coffin face-downward as a sign of his mendacity and dim prospect of Heaven. The lawyer's only interest is money. To that end he encourages litigation that he knows his client will lose, extorts exorbitant fees, is willing to defraud and pervert justice. As a consequence, the lawyer is rich, lives ostentatiously and in general is hated and feared. He is a tough, arrogant bully, completely dishonest. Not surprisingly, the number of lawyers was thought to be excessive. Nevertheless, a curious note of respect, admiration and envy of the lawyer crept into many of the essays.

In general, the judge in Ghana projects a more attractive image. He is an august person, highly respected and often feared. Approximately one-third of the students, however, mentioned a common belief or fear that the judge was under the control of the executive, was biased in any case having political overtones and could be influenced by "money or drink." This view was thought generally applicable to courts below the High Court and to apply less to the Supreme Court.

The image of lawyers in many societies has probably, from time to time, resembled that attributed to the people of Ghana. The noteworthy feature of the Ghanaian image of the profession is the extremity and near unanimity with which it appears to be perceived. It is of interest, however, that the image of the profession does not prevent its attracting substantial numbers of new recruits.

CHAPTER V

THE JUDICIAL STRUCTURE

A STUDY of the evolving judicial structure may produce significant insights into the distribution of public power and the order of values achieving implementation in independent Ghana. It should be noted, however, that only recently has this subject figured prominently in the constitutional struggles or internal political controversies. To a considerable extent, lines of development that were clearly projected under the colonial regime have been followed by the independent government of Ghana. Increasing internal pressure on the Nkrumah Government in late 1963 and early 1964 produced the first amendments to the Republican Constitution; one of these profoundly affected the status and role of the superior courts.

With the consolidation of colonial power in British hands during the latter half of the nineteenth century, the groundwork for a nonindigenous system of courts in the Gold Coast was laid. A Supreme Court Ordinance in 1853 built upon the earlier success of Captain George Maclean as a judge in the coastal forts and adjacent indigenous areas.[1] It provided for appeals in more serious criminal cases arising in the protected African states from the judgment of the Judicial Assessor to the Governor and Legislative Council sitting with the Judicial Assessor. The ordinance also created courts to deal with both civil and criminal cases arising within the "settlements" under British jurisdiction. Judicial organs of the indigenous societies were at the same time left intact to administer the applicable customary law. Thus, a pattern was established: a system of British courts administering British law coexisted with a system of traditional courts applying customary law to the native population.

[1] For a brief description of Maclean's work on the Gold Coast see Ward, *A History of Ghana*, 187-88, 190-94.

Basically, this system remained intact until well into the present century.

In 1874, the Gold Coast was formally declared a British Colony, and four years later a Native Jurisdiction Ordinance was issued. This ordinance was not put into effect, however, but was repealed and re-enacted with significant changes in 1883. Under the terms of the Gold Coast Native Jurisdiction Ordinance of 1883, Native Tribunals composed of Head Chiefs and the chiefs of subdivisions or villages were recognized for certain areas specified by proclamation and were authorized to try breaches of bylaws made by the chiefs and their councils and to exercise limited civil and criminal jurisdiction. The civil jurisdiction was limited to land questions under customary law and personal actions in which the subject matter did not exceed in value seven ounces of gold or £25 sterling. Criminal jurisdiction did not permit the imposition of imprisonment but only limited fines; in default of payment of the fine, however, the offender might be detained up to three months. Any person aggrieved by an order of a Native Tribunal might apply for relief to an administrative officer appointed by the Governor. This officer could refer the case to the Divisional Court, and was required to do so in land cases, but could not himself revise the order of the Native Tribunal. Despite numerous efforts of the Government to secure improvements in this system, it remained substantially the same in the Colony until the reforms of 1944. One added control was introduced by the Native Administration (Colony) Ordinance of 1927:[2] certain administrative officials were empowered to transfer cases from Native Tribunals to a court under the control of the Supreme Court.[3]

The defects and inadequacies of the Native Tribunals

[2] Ordinance No. 18 of 1927.
[3] For fuller historical treatment see Hailey, 3 *Native Administration in British African Territories*, 199-203; Report of the Commission on Native Courts (1951).

under this system were indicated by the Blackall Report in 1943[4] and need only be summarized:

1. The Gold Coast chiefs typically believed that they possessed judicial powers and were thus entitled to maintain courts by reason of their election to chiefly office by their own communities. The merits of this view need not now be determined. It was vigorously asserted by the chiefs themselves, and the colonial legislation dealing with Native Tribunals recognized such courts as attaching to the chiefs ex officio. The indigenous law determining the persons properly exercising judicial functions was not clear; the number of tribunals therefore grew rapidly. In 1943, in the Central Province of the Colony, for example, there were 122 Native Tribunals for a population of approximately 546,000, an average of 1 court for each 4,475 people. The Blackall Committee concluded that the location of tribunals depended upon political considerations rather than the needs of judicial business. "This multiplicity of Tribunals who are falling over one another to attract business, encourages frivolous and vexatious litigation and gives rise to numerous law suits about jurisdiction between Chiefs, which waste money that might otherwise be used for the benefit of their people."

2. As has been noted, the chiefs claimed judicial powers as inherent functions of their offices. Since stool eligibility was limited to certain royal lines, judicial office thus came close to being hereditary. Although customary law permitted the inclusion of appointed councilors on a tribunal, the dominant element was the chiefs, relatively few of whom were literate or widely experienced. The educated elements in the societies were thus substantially excluded from the work of the tribunals.

3. Tribunal members were compensated by sharing the fees and fines collected. No adequate system of accounting existed. Since the tribunals were regarded as sources of income for their members, proceedings were

4 Report of the Native Tribunals Committee of Enquiry (1943).

often dilatory so as to augment sitting and adjournment fees, and a marked tendency existed to set every fine at the maximum amount permitted. Since no law prescribed the maximum number of members of a tribunal, it was not surprising that numerous persons sought to share court revenues; courts of fifteen to twenty members were not uncommon.

4. The person most vital to the efficient operation of a Native Tribunal was the Registrar. According to the Blackall Report, the "majority of registrars are, however, semi-educated persons whose only qualification is that they are one-eyed rulers in the country of the blind." Allegations against the Registrars of bribe-taking, alteration or incorrect recording of official proceedings and prior conviction of crimes involving dishonesty were common.

5. In the absence of simple, understandable rules of procedure and evidence for Native Tribunals, many assumed they were bound by the Supreme Court Rules which were beyond their understanding.

The Blackall Report dealt only with the Colony. There is reason to believe, however, that the conditions it described had obtained in the Native Tribunals of the other regions as well.[5] The reform movement which resulted in the Colony Ordinance of 1944[6] had found somewhat earlier expression in Ashanti[7] and the Northern Territories.[8] The Colony Ordinance of 1944 will serve as the basis for discussion here, but significant differences between it and the earlier legislation for Ashanti and the Northern Territories will be noted. A separate ordinance for Southern Togoland,[9] substantially similar to that for the Colony, was enacted in

[5] Hailey, supra note 3, at 243-47, 269-72.
[6] Native Courts (Colony) Ordinance, No. 22 of 1944, Cap. 98, 3 Laws of the Gold Coast 164 (1951).
[7] Native Courts (Ashanti) Ordinance, No. 2 of 1935, Cap. 99, 3 Laws of the Gold Coast 196 (1951).
[8] Native Courts (Northern Territories) Ordinance, No. 31 of 1935, Cap. 104, 3 Laws of the Gold Coast 223 (1951).
[9] Native Courts (Southern Section of Togoland) Ordinance, No. 8 of 1949, Cap. 106, 3 Laws of the Gold Coast 240 (1951).

1949. The following analysis takes account of amendments to the basic ordinances through 1951.

The several Native Courts ordinances firmly rejected the traditional claims of the chiefs to judicial powers as inherent attributes of their offices. Whereas the earlier pattern had involved the *recognition* of courts existing under the indigenous regimes, the reform ordinances provided that Native Courts for prescribed areas were to be *established* by order of the Governor in Council.[10] Appointments of persons as members of a court were to be made similarly. The Colony Ordinance recognized that the Governor in Council might appoint persons who would be members of a court by virtue of their holding certain traditional offices. This does not, however, obscure the fact that authority to serve derived basically from the Government. The only gesture to the traditional authorities formally incorporated in the Colony Ordinance was the requirement that appointments should not be made until the Governor in Council had considered any recommendations offered by the Native Authority exercising authority within the area of jurisdiction of the Native Court. The Native Authority was also authorized to designate the president of the court or a president for each division from among the Governor's appointees.

The relevant provisions concerning personnel for Native Courts in Ashanti and the Northern Territories differed somewhat. Appointments were to be made by the Governor of persons to be, ex officio or otherwise, members of the courts. The Ashanti Ordinance expressly provided that a "Native Court shall consist of the Asantehene, a Head Chief or Head Chiefs, a Chief or Chiefs, or any other person or persons, or a combination of any such authorities and persons" (sec. 4(1)). Similarly for the Northern Territories, the provision was that a "Native Court shall consist of Head Chiefs, Sub-divisional Chiefs or a Sub-divisional Chief, or Chiefs or a Chief,

[10] By the Governor alone in Ashanti, the Northern Territories and Southern Togoland.

or any other person or persons, or a combination of any such authorities and persons" (sec. 4(1)). These different formulations do not seem to alter the substance of the Governor's power. In each area, appointment to a Native Court depended upon the Governor's order and in each case he was authorized to appoint either traditional authorities or others. The express references to such authorities in Ashanti and the Northern Territories, however, indicated the greater strength of traditional institutions there and the continued dominance of chiefly members on Native Courts even under the "reform" legislation.[11]

Neither of the ordinances specified the qualifications necessary for appointment to Native Courts. The discretion of the Governor in Council in the Colony and of the Governor in the other areas was unlimited. In the Colony, the Governor in Council was granted authority to suspend, cancel or vary any appointment without limitation. In Ashanti and the Northern Territories, power to suspend a Native Court judge for a period up to three months was granted to the Chief Commissioner. The Chief Commissioner also had the power, with the approval of the Governor, to suspend for a longer period or to dismiss any member of a Native Court "who shall appear to have abused his power, or to be unworthy or incapable of exercising the same justly or for other sufficient reasons. . . ." Thus, the personnel of the Native Courts were fully subject to the executive sanctions of suspension or dismissal.

The jurisdiction of the Native Courts was defined in terms of both persons and subject matter. The Colony Ordinance subjected to the jurisdiction of the Native Courts three categories of persons:

(a) Persons of African descent, provided that the mode of life of such persons is that of the general community and, that such persons are in their country of origin subject to African customary law how-

11 See Hailey, supra note 3, at 245-46, 271.

soever that customary law may be modified or applied.

(b) Any persons or class of persons whether of African or non-African descent whom or which the Governor in Council may with the approval of the Secretary of State direct to be subject to the jurisdiction of any particular class of Native Court or of any particular Native Court, or to be subject to such jurisdiction in certain causes or classes of causes only. An order made under this subsection shall not come into force without the consent signified by a Resolution of the Legislative Assembly.

(c) Persons whether of African or non-African descent who have at any time instituted proceedings in any Native Court.[12]

Thus, a person might have been within the jurisdiction of a Native Court on the basis of birth and mode of life, voluntary submission or official action, though the latter was never used.[13] The Judicial Adviser, whose functions will be described more fully later, was authorized to issue certificates of exemption from the jurisdiction of Native Courts to entitled applicants, and "any such certificate as the Judicial Adviser may in his discretion issue shall be conclusive proof of the facts stated therein."[14]

It bears emphasis that the jurisdiction of the Native Courts depended in certain instances on factors within the control of the litigants. Obviously this was the case if jurisdiction over the person depended on his voluntary submission through having invoked at some time the aid of the Native Courts. Even in the case of persons of African descent, however, jurisdiction was lost if the person's mode of life was not that "of the general community." Africans otherwise within Native Court

[12] Native Courts (Colony) Ordinance, sec. 10.
[13] While this authorization existed for many years, the Governor General never issued directions bringing additional persons within the jurisdiction of the Native Courts. Report of the Commission on Native Courts, para. 134 (1951).
[14] Native Courts (Colony) Ordinance, sec. 11.

jurisdiction might nevertheless avoid it by an available option as to the applicable law in certain cases. For example, in civil matters, Native Court jurisdiction would not obtain without the consent of the parties where "it shall appear either from express contract or from the nature of the transaction . . . that the parties agreed . . . that the obligations arising out of such transactions should be regulated exclusively by English law."[15] Thus, if a Gold Coast African should purchase a bicycle on installment payments in the shop of a Lebanese merchant who had previously sued in a Native Court, the nature of the transaction itself might imply the option to make English law applicable and thus exclude Native Court jurisdiction.

The formulation determining the persons over whom Native Courts in Ashanti and the Northern Territories should exercise jurisdiction was different, though the substance was much the same. These courts were given jurisdiction in defined subject matter areas when all parties were "natives."[16] A "native" was defined as a person of African descent, except that the term did not include a person not belonging to a class ordinarily subject to the jurisdiction of Native Tribunals. The Governor was given the power, however, to direct that such natives or classes of natives as he might designate should not come within the jurisdiction of the Native Courts.[17] The Ashanti Ordinance also contained a provision[18] for opting out of Native Court jurisdiction where the parties to a transaction either expressly or by implication had chosen to be bound by some law other than native customary law or some other such law was properly applicable. There was no such opting-out provision in the ordinance for the Northern Territories.

In addition to restrictions as to persons, the jurisdic-

[15] *Id.*, sec. 15(b).
[16] Native Courts (Ashanti) Ordinance, supra note 7, secs. 3, 7; Native Courts (Northern Territories) Ordinance, supra note 8, secs. 3, 7.
[17] This is provided by sec. 3(4) of each ordinance.
[18] Sec. 7.

tion of the Native Courts was also carefully delimited as to subject matter. In each area different grades of courts were created (designated A, B, C, etc.). The powers of the grades differed, usually with respect to the value of the subject matter with which each could deal in civil causes or the severity of the punishment they might impose in criminal matters. The technical details of these gradations need not detain us here. The substantive areas of jurisdiction which might be conferred by the order establishing a court need only be summarized with the relevant sections of the ordinances indicated in parentheses:

THE COLONY

1. Civil claims under native customary law such as (secs. 13(2), 15(a) and Second Schedule):
   a. Suits relating to the ownership, possession or occupation of land;
   b. paternity suits except those involving rights arising out of Christian marriage;
   c. suits relating to custody of children other than suits resulting from divorce or matrimonial causes before the Supreme Court;
   d. suits for divorce and other matrimonial causes between persons married under native customary law;
   e. suits relating to the succession to property of a deceased native;
   f. personal suits.
2. The following offenses under customary law (sec. 15(a) and First Schedule):
   a. putting a person into fetish;
   b. sexual connection with a chief's wife or with any woman in an open place;
   c. reckless, unlawful or frivolous swearing of an oath;
   d. knowingly insulting a chief;

    e. withdrawing allegiance owed to a chief by a subordinate chief;

    f. withdrawal by a chief of allegiance owed by his Stool to another Stool;

    g. possessing a poisonous or offensive thing with intent to use it to endanger, destroy, hurt or annoy any person.

3. Causes arising out of the provisions of any ordinance with respect to which the ordinance itself or the Governor in Council by Order granted enforcement powers (secs. 15(c), (d) and 16).

4. Causes arising out of any orders or rules in force by virtue of the Native Authority (Colony) Ordinance of 1944.

5. Offenses under Book II of the Criminal Code[19] except Title 12, including:

    a. offenses against the person;

    b. offenses against rights of property;

    c. misappropriation and frauds;

    d. offenses against public order, health and morality;

    e. miscellaneous offenses such as cruelty to animals.

The substantive jurisdiction of the Native Courts in Ashanti and the Northern Territories was defined along similar lines and need not be detailed.[20]

The Native Courts were related to the rest of the judicial structure and to the colonial administration by a number of control devices that may be summarized, again using the Colony as a model. Three basic types of control were used:

Appeals. Appeal might be made from a lower court to a higher court within the Native Court system and in more limited instances to an appeal tribunal outside the system such as a Magistrate's Court or a Land Court. A further appeal might lie in some cases to a Divisional

---

[19] Cap. 9, 1 Laws of the Gold Coast 276 (1951).

[20] On the Native Courts in Ashanti see Hailey, supra note 3, at 243-47; Busia, *The Position of the Chief in the Modern Political System of Ashanti*, 141-43 (1951). On the courts in the Northern Territories, see Hailey, supra note 3, at 269-72.

Court of the Supreme Court, the West African Court of Appeal or the Privy Council.[21]

Transfers. Either on its own motion or on the application of a party, a Magistrate's Court was authorized to stop proceedings in a Native Court and transfer the matter for trial to another Native Court or to the Magistrate's Court. In land causes and those causes properly within the exclusive jurisdiction of the Divisional Court, the Magistrate, after stopping the proceedings in the Native Court, reported the circumstances to the Land Judge or the Chief Justice who then directed the mode of proceeding. A similar power to transfer cases from lower courts to themselves resided in Grade A Native Courts.

Administrative Control. Both District Commissioners and the Judicial Adviser were authorized on their own initiative to review determinations of Native Courts and to take any amending action which the Native Court could have taken initially or which "the justice of the case requires." District Commissioners were, of course, the administrative officers representing the Government. The post of Judicial Adviser in the Colony was first authorized by the 1944 Ordinance. The Blackall Report which recommended the creation of the post described its functions as follows: "The functions of the Judicial Adviser would be, *inter alia*, to advise native authorities in regard to the improvement of the administration of justice in their Courts by the preparation of model rules of Court dealing with such matters as Court procedure, evidence and the like. He would also suggest to State Councils subjects about which they might usefully make declarations and modifications of customary law . . . and would revise drafts of such declarations. He would be the final authority for reviewing decisions of native tribunals and would be director of the training course for registrars. Lastly he would be a

[21] The system of appeals is well summarized in the Report of the Commission on Native Courts, paras. 70-72 (1951).

link between the Native Courts, the Executive and the Judiciary."[22]

The 1944 Ordinance did not in fact make the Judicial Adviser the final reviewing authority, though he was given certain review powers. In case a Native Court objected to review by the District Commissioner, any decision to review required confirmation by the Judicial Adviser.

The same three types of control devices were provided by the ordinances applicable to Ashanti and the Northern Territories, though details differed in a number of respects.

Significant improvements in the law relating to the finances of Native Courts in the Colony were made by the 1944 Ordinance. No Native Court was to be constituted unless the Governor in Council was satisfied that a Native Authority had made adequate provision for the payment of honoraria to the members of the court, the remuneration of the Registrar and other officers and the proper accommodation and equipping of the court. All revenue of the court was to be paid to the responsible Native Authority.[23] Under his power to make regulations, the Governor issued a schedule of authorized fees applicable in all Native Courts.[24] In Ashanti and the Northern Territories, members of the courts were paid salaries or prescribed sitting fees. In Ashanti and Togoland—but not in the Northern Territories—executive orders prescribed the fees to be charged and the records to be kept by the courts.[25]

In this system of courts, justice was administered to the great mass of the population. It bears re-emphasis that the jurisdiction of these courts over persons was defined basically along ethnic lines. In terms of subject

[22] Report of the Native Tribunals Committee of Enquiry, pp. 6-7 (1943).

[23] Native Courts (Colony) Ordinance, supra note 6, sec. 9.

[24] The Native Courts (Colony) Procedure Regulations, 1945, Regulations No. 10 of 1945, Part 12 and Second Schedule.

[25] Hailey, supra note 3, at 246, 271. Report of the Commission on Native Courts, paras. 114-116 (1951).

matter, powers were limited to dealing with petty crimes and small civil claims. Moreover, the system was avowedly tutelary. The personnel of the Native Courts were called "members" and not "judges," and they lacked completely the security of tenure and other guarantees of independence normally associated with the judiciary in the Western tradition. Proceedings in the Native Courts were subject to review and modification by administrative officers[26] as well as by judges of the higher order of courts yet to be described. Recurrent efforts to improve the system had been made since the establishment of the Gold Coast as a Colony in 1874, and undoubtedly some of these efforts were partially successful. It remains to evaluate the impact of the reform legislation up to the advent of responsible indigenous government in 1951.

Concern over the judicial order did not figure prominently in the constitutional ferment of the late forties and early fifties. In its chapter on law reform, the Watson Commission gave little attention to the courts and limited itself largely to a recommendation that the

[26] The powers of administrative review were relatively little used. The Report of the Commission on Native Courts, para. 82 (1951) provides the following summary:

"(a) Colony and Southern Togoland

	1946-47	1947-48	1948-49	1949-50	1950-51
Total Cases	50,342	59,299	63,400	63,767	56,788
Reviews by District Commissioner	117	unknown	90	120	115
Reviews by Judicial Adviser	6	8	3	11	4
Percentage of Cases Reviewed	0.24		0.15	0.20	0.21

(b) Ashanti

	1949-50	1950-51
Total Cases	29,230	21,369
Reviews	179	112
Percentage of Cases Reviewed	0.88	0.54

No accurate statistics are available for reviews in the Northern Territories. They number about forty or fifty a year, or between one-half and one per cent of the cases heard."

question be considered of "whether the time has not arrived when the jurisdiction of Native Courts might not be entrusted to African lawyers versed in customary laws and appointed by the Government to act as Stipendiary Travelling Magistrates."[27] The primary objective of this suggested reform was the clarification and development of customary law so that it might be assimilated into a general body of national law. In 1949, the Coussey Committee offered a number of suggestions on the improvement of the system of Native Courts, including the appointment as members of more persons who were not members of state councils or Native Administrations, the establishment of local advisers on appointments, reduction in the number of grades of courts, supervision of the Native Courts by the Chief Justice and judicial officers working under him and direct appeals from these courts to the Supreme Court.[28] The Committee did not urge its views very strongly and simply suggested that a special committee be set up to examine the whole question of local courts.

The latter suggestion of the Coussey Committee was accepted and a commission under the chairmanship of Mr. Justice (later Chief Justice) K. A. Korsah was appointed in 1950. Pending its report, the constitutional proposals of the Coussey Committee were acted on and a new constitution brought into effect.[29] The new constitution affected only the executive and legislative branches of the government and left the entire judicial order intact.

The Korsah Commission, all of whose members were African, made it entirely clear that the reform movement of the thirties and early forties had not solved the problems of the Native Courts.[30] Restriction of mem-

[27] Report of the Commission of Enquiry into Disturbances in the Gold Coast, p. 72, Colonial No. 231 (1948).

[28] Gold Coast: Report to His Excellency The Governor by the Committee on Constitutional Reform, pp. 32-33, Colonial No. 248 (1949).

[29] The Gold Coast (Constitution) Order in Council, 1950 [1950], I STAT. INSTR. 831 (No. 2094).

[30] Report of the Commission on Native Courts (1951).

bership on courts to persons of chiefly status was still widespread. While the percentage of nonchiefs on courts in the Colony had reached 45 per cent and in Southern Togoland just over 50 per cent, virtually no progress in this direction had been made in Ashanti or the Northern Territories.[31] The predominance of chiefly members on the Native Courts was of course intimately related to the incidence of illiteracy. Only 2 per cent of members of Native Courts in the Northern Territories were literate. Elsewhere the situation was somewhat better: 12 per cent in Ashanti, 20 per cent in Southern Togoland and 27 per cent in the Colony. While the appointive power was formally lodged in the Governor in Council, the initiative in proposing names was left mainly to the Native Authorities. In many areas, the Native Courts were inadequately housed and in general the quality of the court staffs was inadequate. Financial provision for the Native Courts was the responsibility of the Native Authorities who in turn received the fees and fines of the courts. It is not surprising that many courts were poorly provided for in order that a profit on their operations could be realized.

Aside from the Northern Territories, the Commission concluded that there was general popular dissatisfaction with the administration of justice in the Native Courts. Evidence of specific delinquencies was difficult to obtain, but the Commission entertained no doubt that many courts were tainted by "the vice of corruption, and the other defects . . . —dilatoriness, somnolent inattention, illiterate incomprehension, using the court as a political weapon." These, in the Commission's view, stemmed "largely from the too close connection between

[31] Report of the Commission on Native Courts, paras. 61-62, indicates that aside from one man on the Yeji Court, all members in the Northern Territories were "officials of some sort; that is, chiefs and sub-chiefs of the ruling caste or autochthonous people of the area, or headmen of 'stranger' communities, or religious officials, Mohammedan or pagan." In Ashanti the only nonchiefly members of Native Courts were in Bekwai and Obuasi. The Asanteman Council firmly resisted the appointment of nonchiefs.

courts and the Native Authorities, which in all territories, are composed very largely or entirely of chiefs and elders. As long as men become court members *ex officio*, without regard to their probity, personality, education or experience, so long will these defects appear."[32] Many witnesses before the Commission urged that chiefly status should be made an absolute disqualification for membership on a Native Court.

The Korsah Commission recommended sweeping changes in the Native Court system. Its major proposals were as follows:

1. A new system of local courts under the control and responsibility of the Chief Justice should be established to replace Native Courts.
2. Local courts should have unrestricted jurisdiction as to persons.
3. Until such time as all local courts could be served by stipendiary professional justices, both laymen on stipends and honorary justices should be appointed.
4. Neither sex nor chiefly status should be a disqualification for appointment but no chief should be appointed ex officio. In Ashanti, the Colony and Southern Togoland, however, no chief who was a hereditary territorial ruler should be appointed. While members of local or state councils should not be absolutely barred, their appointment should in general be avoided.
5. Registered legal practitioners should be permitted to appear before all local courts except those constituted by nonstipendiary, lay justices.

The Government chose not to consider the report of the Korsah Commission directly; rather, it was submitted to an interdepartmental committee composed of a representative of the Governor's Office, representatives of the Ministries of Justice, Defense and External Affairs and Local Government, and representatives of

[32] Report of the Commission on Native Courts, para. 141.

the Chief Regional Officers.[33] After preliminary discussions, the Committee referred the report to Chief Justice Mark Wilson for comment. The ultimate conclusions of the Committee, submitted to the Cabinet in mid-1953, differed in a number of details from the recommendations of the Korsah Commission, largely on the ground of practical feasibility. The only departures from the major recommendations were on the following points: 1) Local courts should continue to be staffed by honorary lay justices. Professionals were thought unavailable for these posts and the Committee did not favor stipendiary lay justices. 2) While no chief or ruler should be appointed as a lay justice ex officio, there should be no disqualification on the ground of being a chief or hereditary ruler.

The Korsah Commission report, with the interdepartmental committee's gloss, summarizes both the accomplishments and defects of the Native Court system to the time in 1951 when responsible African government under Dr. Nkrumah began. Before considering the fate of the Korsah Commission's recommendations under that leadership, the structure of the superior courts should be outlined. It will suffice for our purposes to consider the major court system as defined by the Courts Ordinance of 1935 and the amendments reflected in the revised edition of the laws of 1951.[34] The relevant data will be presented under the following subheads: the hierarchy of courts; qualifications, appointment and tenure of judges, and powers and functions of the courts.

THE HIERARCHY OF COURTS

The Courts Ordinance made provision for four basic types of courts. At the top of the hierarchy was the Supreme Court of the Gold Coast which for convenience

[33] It is perhaps worthy of note that all members of the Committee were expatriate officers of the Colonial Government. The report of the Committee is in unpublished cyclostyled form.
[34] Cap. 4, 1 Laws of the Gold Coast 25 (1951).

in transacting its business was organized in Divisional Courts on a territorial basis. One division of the Supreme Court, called the Lands Division, was to be assigned a specialized responsibility for hearing land causes. At the local level, and subordinate to the Supreme Court, was a system of courts of summary jurisdiction called Magistrate's Courts. The Governor was authorized to constitute by order Special Juvenile Courts. Finally, in Ashanti and the Northern Territories, there were Chief Commissioner's Courts with a specialized jurisdiction. Beyond the scope of immediate interest were two tribunals to which, in limited instances, appeals from the courts of the Gold Coast might be taken: the West African Court of Appeal,[35] and the Judicial Committee of the Privy Council.[36]

QUALIFICATION, APPOINTMENT AND TENURE OF JUDGES

The Courts Ordinance specified two overlapping qualifications for appointment as a judge of the Supreme Court of the Gold Coast: qualification to practice as an advocate in a court of unlimited jurisdiction in civil or criminal matters in England, Scotland, Northern Ireland, some other part of Her Majesty's dominions or the Republic of Ireland, and qualification to practice as an advocate or solicitor in such a court for at least five years.[37] No qualifications were stated in the ordinance for the appointment of Magistrates or members of the Chief Commissioner's Courts in Ashanti and the Northern Territories. In practice, however, appointment to these courts did not require either legal education or experience.

Judges of the Supreme Court were appointed by the Governor by royal letters patent. In addition to those

[35] West African Court of Appeal Ordinance, No. 11 of 1935, Cap. 5, 1 Laws of the Gold Coast 227 (1951).

[36] West African (Appeal to Privy Council) Order in Council, 1930, 11 STAT. RULES & ORDERS & STAT. INSTR. Rev. to Dec. 31, 1948, at 457.

[37] Courts Ordinance, Cap. 4, sec. 5, 1 Laws of the Gold Coast 25 (1951).

judges specifically appointed for the Gold Coast, the Court also included as members ex officio the Chief Justices and judges of the Supreme Courts of Nigeria and Sierra Leone and the judge of the Supreme Court of the Gambia.[38] All other judicial officers of the Gold Coast Courts were appointed by the Governor. The ordinance was completely silent on the terms of Supreme Court judges and other judicial officers. Only one provision relating to tenure in office was expressed; this applied to Juvenile Court Magistrates and provided that the Governor could at any time remove them from office.[39]

POWERS AND FUNCTIONS OF THE COURTS

The Supreme Court of the Gold Coast was granted all the jurisdiction and powers capable of being exercised in England by the High Court of Justice and, within the Gold Coast, all the powers of the Lord High Chancellor of England.[40] In addition to its original jurisdiction in all the more important civil and criminal matters, it possessed exclusive jurisdiction to hear and determine all suits between chiefs of the Colony and Ashanti and between chiefs of Ashanti and the Northern Territories, relating to the ownership, possession or occupation of land.[41] Finally, the Supreme Court had broad appellate jurisdiction and supervisional powers over Magistrate's Courts, including Juvenile Courts, but not the two Chief Commissioner's Courts.

Magistrate's Courts had civil jurisdiction in smaller civil matters, usually where the value involved did not exceed £150, and criminal jurisdiction over less serious criminal offenses where the sanction was limited to a fine not exceeding £100 or imprisonment for twelve months or both, plus whipping in those cases where the law permitted this penalty. In addition, those Magistrate's Courts constituted by District Commissioners had jurisdiction to hear appeals from Native Courts.[42]

[38] Id., sec. 4. [39] Id., sec. 63(2). [40] Id., secs. 15, 16.
[41] Id., sec. 20. [42] Id., sec. 51.

Juvenile Courts where constituted were given the exclusive power among courts of summary jurisdiction to hear matters affecting persons under the age of sixteen years.[43]

The Court of the Chief Commissioner in Ashanti served only as a court of appeal from decisions of the Ashanti Confederacy Council dealing with offenses against the lawful power and authority of any Native Authority in Ashanti.[44] The Chief Commissioner's Court in the Northern Territories, on the other hand, had original jurisdiction in land cases between chiefs of different divisions or between a chief and his subject, as well as certain appellate jurisdiction from Magistrate's Courts and Native Courts. Decisions and orders of the Chief Commissioner's Court in the Northern Territories could be appealed to the West African Court of Appeal.[45]

This completes our survey of the judicial order of the base line, that is, 1951 and the advent of responsible indigenous government. In brief summary, that order involved a system of Native Courts applying customary law and a selected body of minor legislation. Created by order under the authorization of ordinances, they remained by virtue of their organization, staffing and supervision predominantly a facet of administration. The judicial order was dual, however, for a system of superior, largely British, courts also existed. Even these courts in the lower ranges were closely identified with the administration by reason of the judicial powers of District Commissioners.

While the far-reaching recommendations of the Korsah Commission on Native Courts, as modified by the interdepartmental committee, were under consideration, the inexorable constitutional movement toward independence continued. The 1951 (Coussey) Consti-

---

[43] *Id.*, secs. 61-73.
[44] *Id.*, sec. 76. The Supreme Court took the place of the Ashanti Chief Commission's Court as a court of appeal for other purposes in November, 1949.
[45] *Id.*, sec. 80.

tution had left the judicial order untouched. The Nkrumah Constitution of 1954, however, included a number of significant provisions affecting the courts:

1. The Chief Justice was to be appointed by the Governor after consultation with the Prime Minister. Other judges of the Supreme Court were to be appointed by the Governor after consultation with the Judicial Service Commission until July 31, 1955, and thereafter the Governor was required to act on the recommendation of the Commission.[46]

2. The tenure of the judges of the Supreme Court was protected by a provision that a judge should not be removable "except by the Governor on an address of the Assembly carried by not less than two-thirds of the Members thereof, praying for his removal on the ground of misbehaviour or of infirmity of body or mind."[47]

3. The salaries of judges of the Supreme Court were to be fixed by the Legislative Assembly, charged on the general revenues and assets of the Gold Coast and not subject to diminishment during their terms of office.[48]

4. A Judicial Service Commission was established consisting of the Chief Justice, the Attorney General, the senior Puisne Judge, the Chairman of the Public Service Commission and another present or former judge of the Supreme Court appointed by the Governor.[49]

5. The power to appoint, promote, transfer, dismiss and discipline judicial officers was vested in the Governor acting after consultation with the Judicial Service Commission. After July 31, 1955, however, the Governor acting in these matters was bound by the recommendation of the Commission.[50] For this purpose, a "judicial officer" was defined to mean the holder of any judicial office in the public service except judges of the

[46] The Gold Coast (Constitution) Order in Council, 1954, secs. 60(1), 63 and Part II of the Third Schedule [1954], 2 STAT. INSTR. 2788 (No. 551).

[47] *Id.*, sec. 60(2).   [48] *Id.*, sec. 60(6).   [49] *Id.*, sec. 61.

[50] *Id.*, sec. 63 and Part II of the Third Schedule.

Supreme Court or officers exercising judicial functions by virtue of appointment to some other office in the public service.[51] Thus, District Commissioners acting as District Magistrates under the Courts Ordinance remained, as before, subject to administrative control.

Aside from these five modifications, the judicial order was unaffected by the Nkrumah Constitution. Yet one should not discount the significance of the innovations of 1954. For the first time the judiciary was dealt with in a constitutional document. Provision was made for the appointment of most judges on the basis of recommendations of a specialized body on which the Supreme Court itself was heavily represented. Substantial safeguards of tenure and economic independence for judges of the Supreme Court were instituted. Nevertheless, the old dual system with all its shortcomings persisted, and the African Government gave little indication that major reform of the system ranked high among its priorities.

In 1955, the Government of the Gold Coast issued a brief statement on the report of the (Korsah) Commission on Native Courts.[52] Suggesting that the four-year delay in responding to the Commission's report was due to the far-reaching recommendations and their many implications, the statement indicated that reform of the Native Courts had in fact been proceeding by the reconstitution of Native Court panels and the changing of jurisdictional areas, as well as by improving the qualifications and efficiency of Registrars and providing better physical facilities for the courts. Largely because of the impossibility of immediately staffing a radically different system, the Government announced its intention to lay down a program of reform for gradual implementation. This program need not be summarized from the Government's statement, since it will be spelled out from the legislation subsequently enacted.

[51] *Id.*, sec. 1(1).
[52] Statement by the Government on the Report of the Commission on Native Courts (1955).

In the rush toward independence, court reform was not pressed. There was no relevant legislation in 1955 and only one act effecting minor technical amendments in 1956.[53] In the Government's constitutional proposals for Gold Coast independence,[54] published in 1956, those relating to the courts provided:

1. that after independence, legislation should be enacted to establish a unified judiciary consisting of Magistrates, Puisne Judges and Justices of Appeal, headed by the Chief Justice;

2. that the Chief Justice should be appointed by the Governor General on the advice of the Prime Minister;

3. that the functions of the Judicial Service Commission should be continued but its membership reduced to the Chief Justice, the Chairman of the Public Service Commission and a present or former judge of the Supreme Court appointed by the Governor General, thus eliminating the Attorney General and one judge from the previous membership.

4. that any judge should be liable to removal on an address of Parliament carried by a two-thirds majority of the members present and voting, on the ground of misbehavior or infirmity of mind or body; this proposal would have altered significantly the 1954 Constitution which required a vote of two-thirds of the entire membership of the Assembly;

5. that the West African Court of Appeal should cease to exercise jurisdiction in the Gold Coast;

6. that appeals to the Judicial Committee of the Privy Council should be retained.

These proposals were not fully accepted by the British Government. The re-ordering of the judicial structure that was effected by the Independence Constitution, two ordinances which took effect on independence

[53] The Courts (Amendment) Ordinance, 1956, No. 34 of 1956.
[54] Constitutional Proposals for Gold Coast Independence (1956).

and one of the early acts of Parliament, must be discussed in some detail.

Provision was made by ordinance that the Supreme Court after independence should consist of the High Court of Justice and the Court of Appeal.[55] The High Court of Justice, comprising the Chief Justice and a number of Puisne Judges,[56] was granted the original jurisdiction of the former Supreme Court as well as its appellate jurisdiction from Magistrate's Courts.[57] The Court of Appeal, consisting of the Chief Justice, not more than two Justices of Appeal and the Puisne Judges of the Supreme Court,[58] was granted appellate powers in the major cases from all lower courts, including Native Courts.[59] It thus assumed the jurisdiction over Gold Coast cases formerly enjoyed by the West African Court of Appeal, and the ordinance relating to that Court was repealed.[60] Appeal from the Supreme Court of Ghana to the Judicial Committee of the Privy Council was authorized.[61] It should be noted that the old system of Native Courts was left intact.

Judicial appointments and safeguards for tenure were dealt with by the Independence Constitution. Appointments of the Chief Justice and the Justices of Appeal were to be made by the Governor General acting on the advice of the Prime Minister, though with respect to the Justices of Appeal, the Prime Minister was required to consult the Chief Justice.[62] All other judicial

[55] The Courts (Amendment) Ordinance, 1957, No. 17 of 1957, sec. 2.
[56] The Courts (Amendment) Act, 1957, No. 8 of 1957, sec. 3.
[57] The Courts (Amendment) Ordinance, 1957, No. 17 of 1957, sec. 9.
[58] The Courts (Amendment) Ordinance, 1957, No. 8 of 1957, sec. 4.
[59] The Court of Appeal Ordinance, 1957, No. 35 of 1957, secs. 3-12.
[60] *Id.*, sec. 23.
[61] The Ghana (Appeal to Privy Council) Order in Council, 1957 [1957], I STAT. INSTR. 1197 (No. 1361).
[62] The Ghana (Constitution) Order in Council, 1957, sec. 54(1)(2) [1957], I STAT. INSTR. 1036 (No. 277), hereafter cited as 1957 Constitution.

appointments, that is, of Puisne Judges of the Supreme Court and other judicial officers, were to be made by the Governor General acting on the advice of the Judicial Service Commission.[63] The earlier definition of "judicial officer" which excluded those exercising judicial functions by virtue of administrative office was continued, however.[64] The substantive power of promotion, transfer, dismissal and disciplinary control of judicial officers was vested in the Judicial Service Commission, but without articulated limitations on such powers.[65]

The tenure of all judges of the Supreme Court was protected by a provision for removal only on an address of the Assembly, carried by not less than two-thirds of the entire membership, asking removal on the ground of stated misbehavior or infirmity of body or mind.[66] It will be recalled that the Gold Coast Government had proposed a requirement of only two-thirds of the Members present and voting, but this relaxation was rejected by the British Government.[67] Judges were further protected by a guarantee against reduction of salary during their terms of office.[68] It bears re-emphasis that no such safeguards were provided for judicial officers below the Supreme Court level.

The Judicial Service Commission was preserved with the same functions. The proposals of the Gold Coast Government for the elimination of the Attorney General and one Supreme Court judge from the Commission were not implemented. The membership of the Commission remained at five, the only change being the substitution of the senior Justice of Appeal for the senior Puisne Judge.[69]

All the provisions of the 1957 Constitution relating to the judiciary were entrenched. No bill for their mod-

[63] *Id.*, secs. 54(1) and 56(1).   [64] *Id.*, sec. 1(1).
[65] *Id.*, sec. 56(1).   [66] *Id.*, sec. 54(3).
[67] The Proposed Constitution of Ghana, para. 19, Cmd. 71 (1957).
[68] 1957 Constitution, sec. 54(7).
[69] *Id.*, sec. 55(1).

ification or repeal could become law unless passed by two-thirds of the entire membership of the National Assembly and approved by at least two-thirds of the Regional Assemblies.[70]

On balance, it does not appear that the modifications of the court system incident to the attainment of independence were significant. The former dual system was retained. Appointive powers remained substantially as they were, and the safeguards of tenure and independence of the judiciary were not extended; they continued to be limited to the Supreme Court.

Probably the most important innovation of the 1957 Constitution relevant to the status and powers of the courts was the grant to the Supreme Court of a limited power to review the validity of legislation. It will be recalled that the constitution imposed certain limits on the legislative power of Parliament:[71]

  a. no law was permitted to make the persons of any racial community liable to disabilities to which other such communities were not liable;
  b. no law could deprive any person of freedom of conscience or the right freely to profess, practice or propagate any religion, except insofar as restriction might be necessary to preserve public order, morality or health;
  c. no law could authorize the taking of property without compensation, the amount of which was to be judicially determined.

Jurisdiction to review legislation to determine its validity under these restraints was granted to the Supreme Court. It may be argued that this jurisdiction was not an innovation since the 1954 Constitution had included the prohibition against racial discrimination and had declared any law in contravention of the restraint to be "void."[72] No grant of power was made to the courts to declare that "voidness," however, and the mere limita-

[70] Id., sec. 32.   [71] Id., secs. 31, 34.
[72] 1954 Constitution, sec. 36(2)(3).

tion of legislative power in a written constitution does not necessitate judicial review. Thus, it is suggested that the 1957 provisions authorized a significant extension of the powers and functions of the Supreme Court or at least formally validated a pre-existing implied power.

Although the major attempt to reform the system of Native Courts did not come until 1958, a start was made in 1957 with the abolition of the Chief Regional Officer's (formerly Commissioner's) Court in Ashanti and the Northern Territories and the assignment of the jurisdiction of the latter to the High Court of Justice.[73] The major effort to implement the recommendations of the Korsah Commission and the Government's statement thereon came in the Local Courts Act of 1958.[74] The changes authorized by this legislation were substantial, but much of the basic structuring of the old system of Native Courts was left intact. It will suffice here to discuss only the more significant changes in the system.

Preliminarily, it should be observed that the new system of Local Courts was not brought fully into being with the commencement of the enabling legislation. Existing Native Courts were to cease to function only on the establishment of Local Courts for their areas, and the ordinances providing for the Native Courts system were to be repealed only on the later proclamation of the Governor General.[75] Thus, the new system was to be only gradually implemented, the rate depending primarily on the availability of qualified personnel.

The new Local Courts, to be established for each area by an instrument issued by the Minister for the Interior,[76]

[73] The Statute Law (Amendment) Act, 1957, No. 22 of 1957, sec. 3. See also secs. 9 and 10 for other minor modifications of the Native Courts system in Ashanti and the Northern Territories.
[74] The Local Courts Act, No. 23 of 1958.
[75] The repeal was proclaimed by The Native Courts (Repeal) Proclamation, 1960, L.I. 37, to become effective on July 1, 1960. Thus, the repeal coincided with the advent of the Republic and the new Courts Act, discussed later.
[76] All of the powers conferred by this act on the Minister for

were to be nationally uniform, each court possessing the same jurisdiction. The hierarchy of a number of grades which characterized the Native Courts system was abandoned. The extent of this jurisdiction need not be detailed; it was substantially that jurisdiction over minor civil causes and petty crimes, plus the enforcement of a few ordinances, formerly granted to Grade A Native Courts.[77]

Local Courts were to be presided over by Magistrates appointed by the Minister for the Interior. The Minister was authorized to set up local advisory committees to recommend the names, qualifications and experience of persons to be appointed as Local Court Magistrates, but the Minister was under no obligation to accept these recommendations.[78] The power to promote, transfer, dismiss and discipline Magistrates was also vested in the Minister, and the act imposed no limits on his discretion in the exercise of this power. Magistrates' salaries were to be fixed by the Minister but paid by the local government authorities which in turn received all revenues of the courts. Any excess of proper Local Court expenditure over revenue was underwritten by the central government.

One significant innovation, recommended by the Korsah Commission, was the effort to eliminate the racial criterion for jurisdiction over persons, which had applied in the Native Courts. The act provided that, except for matters in which the Government of Ghana or any public officer in his official capacity was a party, or any cause in which government revenues or the

---

the Interior were transferred in 1959 to the "Minister responsible for Local Courts." The Local Courts (Amendment) Act, 1959, No. 13 of 1959. Local Courts were established in the Eastern Region and the Accra District in 1959. On the creation of the Republic in 1960, 109 Local Courts were established throughout Ghana. The Local Courts Instrument, 1960, L.I. 83.

[77] The civil jurisdiction is now fixed by the Courts (Amendment) Act, 1962, Act 130, sec. 27.

[78] The view appears to be widely accepted in Ghana that Local Court appointments have become political sinecures for partisans of the Convention People's Party.

actions of a public officer were in issue, "Local Courts shall have unrestricted jurisdiction as to persons."[79] This change was largely formal, since most of the substantive jurisdiction of the courts still depended on the application of customary law.[80] Insofar as the Local Courts were authorized to enforce ordinances or acts, however, they could exercise jurisdiction over non-Africans.

An effort to maintain a higher quality of operation in the Local Courts is clearly apparent in the act. The Registrars and other officers of the courts could be appointed only with the approval of the Minister who was authorized to lay down standards of proficiency. The provision of courses of instruction for Magistrates and court officers, the supervision of the arrangements made by local governmental authorities for the courts and the inspection of court records were some of the functions of the Senior Local Courts Adviser. As has been pointed out, the remuneration of Magistrates and officers was the obligation of local authorities, and their income did not depend on sharing the revenues of the courts. No fees or fines in excess of those legislatively sanctioned could be charged.[81]

Powers of review and other supervisory control over the Local Courts were vested in District Courts established under the Courts Ordinance. In more important cases, appeals could be further pursued to the High Court of Justice and the Court of Appeal. The power to transfer causes from one Local Court to another was also granted to District Courts. All Local Courts were required to file monthly returns on matters decided by or brought before them with their District Magistrates who were granted wide powers of review and modification. The act expressly provided, however, that a "Government Agent shall not exercise any jurisdiction

---

[79] The Local Courts Act, 1958, sec. 8.

[80] *Id.*, secs. 10, 15.

[81] For some reason, not immediately apparent, this restriction was repealed in 1959. The Local Courts (Amendment) Act, 1959, No. 13 of 1959, sec. 5.

whether by way of appeal, transfer, review or otherwise in any cause or matter in a Local Court."[82] The term "Government Agent," though not defined by the act, referred to the officer formerly called the District Commissioner who was authorized by the Courts Ordinance to exercise the powers of a District Magistrate. The termination of his power over Local Courts therefore necessitated the repeal of Section 51 of the Courts Ordinance.[83]

A tentative assessment of the significance of the Local Courts Act is in order. It contributed to the general process of nation-building by making provision for a nationally uniform system of Local Courts. It further manifested the overriding power of the central government by vesting broad powers over personnel of the Local Courts in a Minister of the central government and review and supervisory powers in the national superior courts. An effort was made to put the Local Courts on a nonracial basis and to reduce the justification for persistent charges of corruption and inefficiency. The Magistrates remained laymen in the law, however, except insofar as in-service training might provide expertise, and no statutory safeguards of their tenure or independence were provided.

It will be recalled that legislation in 1958 eliminated the special procedures required by the 1957 Constitution for its amendment. By ordinary legislation in 1959,[84] a number of constitutional amendments affecting the judiciary were enacted. The most important of these dissolved the Judicial Service Commission and provided that for references in the constitution or legislation to the Commission there should, in general, be substituted references to the Chief Justice.[85] In connection with the demise of the Commission, the mode of appointment of Puisne Judges of the Supreme Court was changed to provide for the appointment by the

[82] The Local Courts Act, 1958, sec. 70.
[83] Id., sec. 76 and Third Schedule.
[84] The Constitution (Amendment) Act, 1959, No. 7 of 1959.
[85] Id., sec. 7.

Governor General acting on the advice of the Prime Minister after he had consulted the Chief Justice. The procedure for appointing Justices of Appeal was also altered by eliminating the requirement that the Prime Minister first consult with the Chief Justice.[86] Powers of appointment, dismissal and disciplinary control over magistrates and other judicial officers were granted to the Governor General, acting on the advice of the Chief Justice, but with a proviso that before tendering any advice on appointment, the Chief Justice should consult with the Prime Minister.[87] The definition of "judicial officer" in the 1957 Constitution was further clarified to exclude a Magistrate appointed under the Local Courts Act of 1958.[88] The effect of these constitutional amendments was to increase substantively the power of the national executive in the selection and appointment of judges of the higher courts.

The courts and judicial order had a far from prominent place in the deliberations and political actions leading up to the creation of the Republic in 1960. The articles relating to the courts in the draft constitution submitted to the people[89] were almost completely redrafted in the Constitution Bill submitted to the Constituent Assembly. These changes were largely formal, however. The analysis here will deal with the articles as finally incorporated in the Republican Constitution. The Courts Act[90] and the Judicial Service Act[91] also enacted by the Constituent Assembly in 1960 will be treated later.

The Republican Constitution conferred the judicial power of Ghana on a Supreme Court and a High Court, designated the superior courts, and such inferior courts as might be created by law.[92] The Supreme Court was made the final court of appeal, thus eliminating the

[86] *Id.*, sec. 5.   [87] *Id.*, sec. 6(1).   [88] *Id.*, sec. 6(3).
[89] Government Proposals for a Republican Constitution, W. P. No. 1/60 (1960).
[90] Courts Act, 1960, C.A. 9.
[91] Judicial Service Act, 1960, C.A. 10.
[92] Republican Constitution, art. 41.

former appellate jurisdiction of the Judicial Committee of the Privy Council.[93] In addition to other powers which might be conferred by law, the Supreme Court was given original jurisdiction in all matters involving a question of the validity of legislation under the constitutional limitations on the power of Parliament and of the first President. Should such a question arise in any other court, the hearing must be adjourned and the question referred to the Supreme Court.[94] The jurisdiction of the High Court, both original and appellate, was left for statutory determination.

The power to appoint all judges of the superior courts was vested in the President.[95] No qualifications for appointment were specified, nor was any such appointment subject to the review or confirmation of any other body. From among the judges of the Supreme Court, the President was authorized to designate a Chief Justice,[96] who was entitled to such additional compensation or allowance as the National Assembly might determine.[97] No judge of the Supreme Court or the High Court could be removed from office, except by the President on the basis of a resolution passed by at least two-thirds of the Members of Parliament on stated grounds of misbehavior or infirmity of mind or body.[98]

[93] The Constitution (Consequential Provisions) Act, 1960, C.A. 8, sec. 22 and First Schedule. By agreement between the Government of the United Kingdom and the Government of Ghana, appeals registered in the Privy Council office before the date on which Ghana became a republic would be heard. Exchange of Letters, Cmd. 1190 (1960). See also the Constitution (Consequential Provisions) Act, 1960, C.A. 8, sec. 16.

[94] Republican Constitution, art. 42. To be validly constituted to determine the validity of an Act of Parliament, the Supreme Court must comprise at least three judges of the Supreme Court. For its other judicial work, including determining the validity of any legislative enactment of the first President under Article 55, the Supreme Court is properly constituted if it comprises at least one judge of the Supreme Court and two other judges. Art. 43.

[95] Republican Constitution, art. 45(1).

[96] Id., art. 44(1).

[97] Id., art. 46(2). This provision for supplementary allowance or compensation was repealed by The Constitution (Amendment) Act, 1964, Act 224, sec. 9.

[98] Republican Constitution, art. 45(3).

While thus protected in his tenure as a judge of the Supreme Court, the Chief Justice was nevertheless subject to dismissal from that office, and thus to deprivation of its special perquisites, at the discretion of the President.[99] A memorandum annexed to the Constitution Bill as submitted to the Constituent Assembly explained the removability of a judge from the Chief Justiceship on the ground that his "capacity as Chief Justice makes him the administrative head of the Judicial Service, and in relation to such non-judicial functions it is considered that the President ought to be in a position to ensure that the Chief Justice will give his loyal co-operation."

The salaries of judges of the superior courts were to be determined by the National Assembly and were not subject to diminution during their terms.[100] While a retirement age of sixty-five for Supreme Court judges and sixty-two for judges of the High Court was specified, tenure could be extended by the President.[101]

The articles of the constitution establishing the Supreme Court and the High Court and specifying the mode of appointment and removal of judges were entrenched, that is, they could be modified only by the special procedure involving a popular referendum.[102]

It will be seen that there was little innovation in the Republican Constitution with regard to the court system and judicial order. Substantially the same can be said of the Courts Act passed by the Constituent Assembly. This was a comprehensive consolidation of existing legislation with slight modification of detail. Some court names were changed (the former Court of Appeals became the Supreme Court, the High Court of Justice, merely the High Court); and a new system of Circuit Courts was introduced between the High Court and the District Courts, to exercise the jurisdiction

[99] Id., art. 44(3).   [100] Id., art. 46(1).
[101] Id., art. 45(4). See also the Constitution (Consequential Provisions) Act, 1960, C.A. 8.
[102] Id., arts. 41, 44 and 20.

previously granted to Senior District Magistrates.[103] The basic system in those aspects relevant here remained unchanged, however.

Somewhat more significant was the Judicial Service Act, also enacted by the Constituent Assembly. This provided that the President should be the appointing authority for all posts in the Judicial Service. Before filling a vacancy, however, the President was required to consult the Chief Justice, to whom he was also authorized to delegate the appointing power with respect to Circuit Judges and District Magistrates.[104] Standing as a legal practitioner was specified as a qualification for appointment of all judges from the Supreme Court down through the District Courts.[105] This qualification was especially significant in relation to District Magistrates, most of whom had in the past been administrators without formal legal qualifications. The act also made the President the disciplinary authority for Circuit Judges and District Magistrates, but authorized a delegation of these powers to the Chief Justice.[106] Certain safeguards of a fair hearing such as a written charge, the privilege of calling witnesses and compelling their testimony, and a final appeal to the President were provided in disciplinary proceedings.[107] It should be emphasized, however, that the Local Courts and their Magistrates were not covered by the Judicial Service Act and thus enjoyed none of these safeguards.

The general structure of judicial power established by the Republican Constitution and the basic statutes passed by the Constituent Assembly remained intact until

[103] By Legislative Instrument 45 of 1960, the Chief Justice divided the country into seven circuits, each circuit composed of one of the regions as defined in the Regions of Ghana Act, 1960 (C.A. 11), except that the Northern and Upper Regions were combined into one circuit.

[104] Judicial Service Act, 1960, C.A. 10, sec. 7.

[105] Id., sec. 8(3). The periods of standing as a practitioner required for appointment were as follows: Judge of the Supreme Court, 10 years; Judge of the High Court, 5 years; Circuit Judge, 5 years; District Magistrate, 18 months.

[106] Id., sec. 18(1).   [107] Id., sec. 20.

early 1964, though a number of detailed adjustments were made.[108] Within that structure, significant developments have taken place. All European judges have been replaced. The number of judges in the Supreme Court was increased in September, 1962, from five to nine. There have been continuing efforts to improve the personnel of the lower courts by in-service training programs and to strengthen lines of supervision over them. Unfortunately, these efforts have been in large measure defeated by the appointment on political grounds of unqualified and noneducable magistrates for the Local Courts.

Internal political tensions (discussed more fully in Chapter VII) first affected the judicial structure in 1961 when Parliament made provision for the creation of Special Criminal Courts. The act authorized the creation of a Special Criminal Division of the High Court, comprising a presiding judge and two other members, constituted by the Chief Justice on the request of the President.[109] The substantive jurisdiction of the Special Criminal Division included offenses against the safety of the state or against the peace as these offenses were defined in the Criminal Code and any "offense specified by the President by legislative instrument." On its face, the latter provision is highly ambiguous. Does it merely authorize the President to bring within the jurisdiction of the Special Division other offenses already defined by the Criminal Code? Or does it authorize the President to define new crimes, making criminal acts not otherwise covered by the criminal law of Ghana? In presenting the bill to the National Assembly, the Minister for the Interior declared that it "gives the President no power to amend the Criminal Code so as to create any new offence or to impose any special punishment for any existing offence. The power given to the President is no more than to make such modifications in the established procedure as are needed to bring it into

---

[108] See the Courts (Amendment) Act, 1962, Act 130.
[109] The Criminal Procedure (Amendment) Act, 1961, Act 91.

conformity with the terms of the bill."[110] The Minister's assurances do not resolve the ambiguity on the face of the statute, however.[111]

Proceedings in the Special Division are to be instituted by the Attorney General. The President is authorized, after consulting the Chief Justice, to adapt the Criminal Procedure Code in any way he thinks proper to give effect to the act establishing the Special Court. Subject to such instrument, the court itself is authorized to give directions on procedure. Unless modified by the President or a direction by the court, the appropriate procedure is that applicable to summary trials in the High Court, except that the provisions of the Criminal Procedure Code concerning trial by jury or with assessors are made inapplicable to the Special Court.[112]

The decision of the Special Criminal Division is determined by the majority. The decision is announced by the presiding judge and the act prohibits the disclosure of any minority opinion. The decision when reached is final. No appeal is permitted to any court, but the President's power of mercy may of course be invoked.[113]

In 1963, the President issued regulations[114] governing proceedings in the Special Criminal Division. The procedures require the issuance of a summons to the accused person and, if the accused person cannot be found, service may be made by leaving a copy with a person at the accused's usual or last known place of abode, by posting a copy on the house in which the accused ordinarily resides or by publication in the *Ghana Gazette* or another journal or newspaper ap-

[110] Parliamentary Debates, 16 October 1961, col. 38. Similar assurances were given by the Minister for Justice, cols. 72, 75.

[111] Thus far, the President's power to bring additional offenses within the jurisdiction of the Special Court has been exercised twice. In these instances the added offenses were already defined by the Criminal Code. See The Special Criminal Division (Specified Offences) Instruments, 1963, L.I. 245 and L.I. 246.

[112] Criminal Procedure Code, 1960, Act 30, secs. 242-45.

[113] Republican Constitution, art. 48.

[114] The Special Criminal Division Regulations, 1963, L.I. 244.

proved by the court. Such service permits the court to proceed to trial, even in the absence of the accused, on an assumed plea of not guilty. The court may, however, permit an advocate to appear on behalf of such an absent accused, "on sufficient explanation for the absence of the accused being given, if the Court is satisfied that such advocate has been instructed to represent the accused." The general Criminal Procedure Code also permits trial in the absence of the accused in certain circumstances.[115] When this is done, however, a regular court has the power to set aside any conviction on being satisfied that the absence of the accused was from "causes over which he had no control, and that he had a probable defence on the merits."[116] Regulations governing the Special Criminal Division deprive the court of this power to vacate convictions of persons tried *in absentia*. The power of the Special Court to proceed to trial in the absence of the accused has not yet been exercised.

Creation of the Special Criminal Division was part of the aftermath of the political strikes originating in Sekondi-Takoradi and the readjustment of leadership within the C.P.P., incident to the expulsion of Mr. Gbedemah and Mr. Botsio. In presenting the bill to the National Assembly, Mr. Boateng, then Minister for the Interior and Local Government, sought to justify it as a necessity for protecting the security of the state. At the same time, the Minister and other supporters of the bill contended that no power was granted by it to define new crimes. In the light of this assurance, the justification for the bill from the Government's viewpoint arose from certain procedural advantages:

1. elimination of the necessity for a preliminary hearing before a District Magistrate and foreclosing of appeals from the Special Court, thus expediting the trial and sentence of offenders;

[115] Criminal Procedure Code, 1960, Act 30, sec. 170.
[116] *Id.*, sec. 170(3).

2. elimination of a jury or assessors from the trial procedure;

3. granting of control over procedure, including modes of proof, to the President, thus restricting the applicability of the Criminal Procedure Code.

Perhaps the most revealing comment in support of the bill was made by Mr. Tawia Adamafio, then Minister of Information and Broadcasting: "In the courts we do not get justice, we get law. It is justice that we want and that is what is going to be created."[117] It was evidently the Government's belief that those engaged in anti-State activity had been able in the past to escape proper punishment because of the technicalities of ordinary criminal procedure.

On only two occasions has the jurisdiction of the Special Criminal Division been invoked. On the first, in March, 1963, the court comprised Sir Arku Korsah, Chief Justice, and Justices Van Lare and Sarkodee-Addo of the Supreme Court. Charges against the seven defendants included treason, conspiracy to commit treason, misprision of treason and unlawful possession of arms. Counsel did not appear on behalf of any of the defendants. On the third day of the trial, the Chief Justice announced that it had come to his notice that the impression had been created that the accused had been denied counsel. Denying that this was the case, he ruled that it was not the duty of the State to assign counsel to defend persons accused of plotting against the State. He added, however, that if any lawyer wished to offer his services to the accused or was briefed by relatives, he would be entirely free to represent the defendants. The defendants remained without counsel throughout the trial.

The trial was public and the atmosphere of the courtroom was decorous but relaxed. The defendants gave no impression of intimidation, and appeared to be alert, interested in the proceedings and capable of fol-

[117] Parliamentary Debates, 16 October 1961, col. 66.

lowing them. The proceedings were conducted in English, which all of the defendants except one spoke with apparent ease and comprehension. For the non-English-speaking defendant, a Ga interpreter was provided. The defendants interrogated prosecution witnesses and each other as they testified.

All of the accused made damaging, uncautioned pre-trial admissions to the police, but contended at the trial that these statements had been coerced by threats or actual violence. The court nevertheless permitted the statements to be read into the record. Three possible explanations of the admission of this evidence might be advanced: (1) the court chose not to believe the defendants' accounts of police misconduct; (2) the defect arising from the fact that the accused gave their original statements without proper cautions was removed by the reaffirmation of the statements after proper caution had been given; (3) although informed by the Chief Justice in open court that they might remain silent, make an unsworn statement to the court or take an oath and testify as a witness subject to cross examination, all of the defendants chose the third course. From the witness box they repeated admissions substantially in line with those given earlier to the police. It is impossible to determine from the available record which explanation or combination of explanations is proper.

The two defendants charged with unlawful possession of arms pleaded guilty to this charge. At the conclusion of the trial, all defendants were convicted by the court of all charges against them. The five convicted of treason were sentenced to death, the remaining two to prison terms of eight and five years respectively.

The second trial before the Special Criminal Division, beginning in August, 1963, involved charges of treason and conspiracy to commit treason against Tawia Adamafio and Ako Adjei, both former Ministers, H. H. Cofie Crabbe, formerly Executive Secretary of the C.P.P., Robert B. Otchere, a former Member of Parliament, and Joseph Yaw Manu, a former civil servant and trader. Both Otchere and Manu had been identified with political opposition groups. The court included Chief Justice Sir Arku Korsah and Justices Van Lare and Akufo-Addo. Throughout the trial, which continued for more than three months, all defendants were represented by counsel. The defendants Otchere and Manu were convicted on both counts. Adamafio, Adjei and Crabbe were acquitted on both counts, however, and discharged by the court. Although the order was given to release them, under the authorization of the Preventive Detention Act, they were returned to prison where they had been for almost a year before the beginning of the trial. The question of the guilt or innocence of the several defendants is not of concern here. Rather, it is the effect of the judgment of the Special Criminal Division on the general judicial structure of Ghana.

The reactions of the Government and Party to the acquittal of the principal defendants were immediate and extreme. The Attorney General described the judgment as a "mockery of justice." In typical vein, the C.P.P. *Evening News* referred to the judges' "open subversion and treachery against [the workers'] class and cause" and added:

> The courts, ideally an instrument of Socialist education and discipline not of class insolence and subversion, ye have made a den of thieves, robbers, assassins and corruption.
>
> And the voices of the people say—Away with them! No more shall we entrust such vital machinery in the hands of the class enemy![118]

The reaction of the President involved direct action against the court. The judgment of the Special Criminal Division was announced on December 9, 1963; on December 11, the President, exercising his powers under the Republican Constitution, dismissed Sir Arku Korsah from the Chief Justiceship. While the revocation of his appointment as Chief Justice left Sir Arku a judge of

[118] *Evening News*, Dec. 12, 1963, p. 1, col. 1.

the Supreme Court, he immediately resigned from the Judicial Service. Mr. Justice Van Lare, the second senior judge of the Supreme Court, who had also sat on the Special Criminal Division in both trials, resigned from the Judicial Service a few days later. The third member, Mr. Justice Akufo-Addo, was not immediately affected.

Reaction to the judgment of the Special Criminal Division was not limited to steps against the individual judges involved. On December 24, the act which had established the Special Criminal Division was amended retroactively to provide that "where it appears to the President that it is in the interest of the security of the State so to do, he may by an executive instrument declare the decision of the Court to be of no effect, and the instrument shall be deemed to be a *nolle prosequi* entered by the Attorney General before the decision in the case was given. . . ."[119] Exercising this power, the President on December 24 declared all of the proceedings of the second treason trial void, thus invalidating the acquittal of Adamafio, Adjei and Crabbe as well as the conviction of Otchere and Manu.[120]

The most significant adjustment of the judicial structure in the aftermath of the Special Court's judgment required an amendment to the constitution. In accordance with the constitutional requirement, the President ordered a referendum seeking the approval of the people for an amendment granting to the President summary powers to dismiss judges of the Supreme Court or High Court.[121] This approval being given, the following clause was inserted in Article 45(3) of the Republican Constitution:

Provided that the President may at any time for reasons which to him appear sufficient remove from

---

[119] The Criminal Procedure (Amendment) (No. 2) Act, 1963, Act 223.

[120] Special Criminal Division Instrument, Ex. Inst. 161/63. All five defendants were later retried under a revised procedure and on February 8, 1945, were convicted of treason and sentenced to death. The sentence was later commuted to imprisonment.

[121] Referendum Order, 1963, L.I. 329.

office a Judge of the Supreme Court or a Judge of the High Court.[122]

The amendment received presidential assent on February 21, 1964; on March 2, the President without explanation dismissed three judges of the Supreme Court: Mr. Justice Akufo-Addo, the sole survivor of the panel that had sat in the second trial as the Special Criminal Division, and Justices Adumua-Bossman and Blay.[123] Earlier, Justice Sarkodee-Addo had been appointed to succeed Sir Arku Korsah as Chief Justice of Ghana. To replace the three dismissed justices, three judges were promoted from the High Court. On March 16, 1964, Dr. Nkrumah revoked the appointment of Justice Henry K. Prempeh of the High Court; no reasons were given.

Concluding comment on the actual operations of the courts of Ghana must be brief and impressionistic. Evaluation of the judicial labors of the superior courts is made difficult by the unavailability of recent reports. The 1959 volume of the Ghana Law Reports is the last that has appeared, and unfortunately, there is no immediate prospect for significant improvement of the reporting system.

The superior courts are generally regarded with respect. Below the High Court level, however, the prestige of the courts rapidly dissipates. The most unsatisfactory situation exists in the Local Courts, for here, chiefs and other traditional officials, whose primary qualification was familiarity with the customary law, have now generally been replaced by political appointees.

---

[122] The Constitution (Amendment) Act, 1964, Act 224, sec. 6(c).

[123] By the Judicial Service (Amendment) Act, 1964, Act 245, a judge of a superior court who has been removed, resigned or retired is permitted to practice as a lawyer in Ghana but may not appear before a court, a judge in chambers or any tribunal performing judicial functions. This limitation is far more stringent in Ghana than it would be in other countries where the counseling aspects of the profession are more fully developed.

The educational level of these magistrates is so low that in-service training programs are of questionable value.[124] Suspicions of bribery and corruption in the Local Courts seem no less prevalent than they once were with respect to the old Native Courts. With differences only in degree, however, the same suspicions affect public regard for the Magistrate's Courts and even the Circuit Courts. To a considerable extent, these views reflect a widespread belief that any person in authority, whether public or private, will use that authority for his own profit. On occasion one is tempted to conclude that such beliefs are not merely descriptive but are approaching the normative. It would be most useful to determine, if possible, how much fact supports these attitudes of the people toward the lower courts. Whether fully supported by fact, the belief is prevalent that the courts who administer "justice" to the great mass of the population are in fact for sale to the highest bidder. The recent constitutional changes and the related actions of the President and dominant Party strike directly at the confidence in the integrity and independence of the superior courts.

[124] While serving as Dean of the Faculty of Law of the University of Ghana, I proposed the establishment of brief courses for Local Court Magistrates, to be offered during the University's long vacations and staffed by members of the Law Faculty. The Minister of Justice rejected the offer on the ground that the incumbent Magistrates were noneducable.

CHAPTER VI

THE HIERARCHY OF LEGAL NORMS*

EVERY LEGAL system presents the problem of relating its constituent norms to each other so as to form
a coherent and harmonious whole. Even if one imagined
a highly unified system in which all norms were laid
down by a single lawgiver or legislative body, some
standard would nevertheless be required for resolving
the conflict or inconsistency among those norms that
human frailty would sow and partisan ingenuity would
discover. In any modern system of law, the problem
of interrelating norms is far more complex. No single
agency creates all norms, and the variety of sources is
matched by a variety of forms or classifications of
norms. The layman as well as the lawyer readily dis-
tinguishes constitutional rules and doctrines from statutes. In the process of adjudication, courts are regularly called upon to interpret constitutional or statutory
language and to fill gaps in the existing body of law.
Few, if any, modern theorists would deny that in this
process, law creation occurs. Even in a nonfederal system, lawmaking functions are shared by delegation with
executive agencies of the central government and local
government bodies.

Norms from these several sources have been considered in earlier chapters without emphasis on the
problem of relating them in an orderly system. Familiar
and widely accepted notions on the status and function
of constitutions, on the supremacy of the legislature over
the courts in lawmaking and on the principle of delegation prevent difficulty. The problems of relating legal
norms, to be considered in this chapter, arise from the
fact that the legal order in Ghana is in a special sense

* An earlier version of this chapter was published as the major
part of an article entitled "The Evolution of Ghana Law since
Independence" in 27 Law and Contemporary Problems 581
(1962).

239

pluralistic, encompassing not merely law derived from the former colonial power, now greatly supplemented by post-independence legislation, and a system of courts to apply that law, but also a body, or more properly, bodies of indigenous or customary law applied mainly in the Native, now Local, Courts. To avoid chaos, some scheme was necessary to delimit the sphere of operation of each body of law and each system of courts and, insofar as these spheres coincided or conflicted, to determine which should prevail.

Two basic methods for interrelating the component elements in a pluralistic legal system may be distinguished. The first involves the definition of discrete substantive areas of operation for each element in the system, with each element entirely uncontrolled by the other so long as it remains within its assigned sphere. Thus, for example, it is conceivable that the definition of major crimes such as murder, rape and robbery might be made the function of English law or a nationally legislated norm and the application of that law assigned to a system of superior courts, while all other crimes and the interpersonal relations of which the law takes account are left entirely to a body or bodies of customary law, applied in courts established by the indigenous regimes. Such a division of function between the two systems may be referred to as involving horizontal ordering.

The other type of order is hierarchical or vertical. In this type the bodies of law and the applying courts are related as superiors and inferiors. While hierarchical ordering may permit some horizontal division of function, at least in the early stages of law application, it allows ultimate resort to the higher courts applying the superior or ultimately governing body of law in an appeal or some other type of supervisory proceeding. Such a distinction of types of ordering relations is useful for some analyses, but it would appear that in every pluralistic system there is an irreducible minimum of hierarchical or vertical ordering, since some overriding set of norms must at least define authoritatively the spheres of operation and application of the several bodies of law.[1]

The general standards defining the relations between English-derived law and native customary law in the pre-independence Gold Coast were found in the Courts Ordinance.[2] It bears emphasis that these general standards were posited by the imperial power. Thus, any ordering of the relations of English and indigenous law of the horizontal variety fitted into an over-all hierarchical pattern dominated by imperial law. Within that general structure both horizontal and hierarchical ordering were used, however.

The Courts Ordinance, Sec. 83, provided that "subject to the terms of this or any other Ordinance, the common law, the doctrines of equity, and the statutes of general application which were in force in England on the 24th day of July, 1874, shall be in force within the jurisdiction of the Courts." The specified date derived its significance from the fact that the Gold Coast then became a British Colony with a Legislative Council. English law made applicable in the Gold Coast by this Section consisted of four elements: local ordinances, common law, doctrines of equity and statutes of general application in force in England on the cutoff date. It is entirely clear, of course, that English statutes of general application that came into force after July 24, 1874, were not per se applicable to the Gold Coast.

The question may be raised whether the same cutoff date applied to the common law and doctrines of equity, so that norms from these sources were applicable in the Gold Coast only as developed and articulated

---

[1] For a useful application of this distinction to international order, see Falk, "International Jurisdiction: Horizontal and Vertical Conceptions of Legal Order," 32 Temple Law Quarterly 295 (1959).

[2] Courts Ordinance, No. 7 of 1935, as amended, Cap. 4, secs. 83-89, 1 Laws of the Gold Coast 25 (1951).

up to the cutoff date. The language of Section 83 and the punctuation suggest that the cutoff date applies only to statutes of general application, thus making common law and equity doctrines as developed later by English courts also part of the Gold Coast law. Unless, however, one assumes an eternal completeness and immutability of common law and equity, these being merely discovered but not created by the courts, the same rationale underlying a cutoff date for statutes of general application would appear applicable to common law and equity as well.

Current acceptance of the view that courts do create law in the decision of cases on a common law or equity basis suggests that English developments in these spheres after July 24, 1874, were not applicable in the Gold Coast. This conclusion finds some support in Section 17 of the Courts Ordinance which provided that the Supreme Court of the Gold Coast should exercise its jurisdiction in probate divorce, and matrimonial matters "in conformity with the law and practice for the time being in force in England." Evidently the draftsmen of the ordinance were entirely competent to find language appropriate to an intention that the law in the Gold Coast should be continuously related to the current state of the law in England. It is thus arguable that the cutoff date in Section 83 applied not only to statutes of general application but to common law and equity as well. This question was never authoritatively settled, however, while the Courts Ordinance remained in force.[3]

A further contribution of English law to the legal order of the Gold Coast consisted of "Imperial laws declared to extend or apply to the jurisdiction of the Courts" (Sec. 85). Such laws were to apply only within the limits of local jurisdiction and to the extent local

---

[3] This problem and the related question of the extent to which English decisions were binding on Gold Coast Courts are analyzed in Allott, "The Authority of English Decisions in Colonial Courts," 1 Journal of African Law 23 (1957).

circumstances permitted. These relatively vague criteria necessitated more precise definition by judicial determination of the applicability of imperial laws. Similarly, courts in the Gold Coast were authorized to construe imperial laws with such alterations not affecting the substance of the enactment as would facilitate their application.

To handle cases of conflict among the norms derived from English law, a distinct hierarchy was required. Clearly, the paramount norms were those provided by imperial laws made expressly applicable to the Gold Coast or extended to it by Orders in Council. Next, in descending order, were those norms provided by local Gold Coast legislation. English statutes of general application in force in 1874 were received in the Gold Coast as legislation. Prevailing ideas of legislative supremacy would therefore cause these statutes to prevail in cases of conflict with common law or equity doctrines. In the final case of conflict between law and equity, which were concurrently administered in the superior courts of the Gold Coast, the rules of equity were to prevail (Sec. 86).

This hierarchical order of English norms coexisted with a number of bodies of customary law in force in various parts of the Gold Coast.[4] The standards that determined the relation of customary law to English law

---

[4] The Courts Ordinance did not use the term "customary law." Rather, it spoke of "native law or custom" and "local law or custom." Neither of these terms, which do not seem to differ in substantive meaning, was defined in the ordinance. However, the Native Courts (Colony) Ordinance, No. 22 of 1944, as amended, Cap. 98, sec. 2, 3 Laws of the Gold Coast 164 (1951), defines "native customary law" as "a rule or body of rules regulating rights and imposing correlative duties, being a rule or body of rules which obtains and is fortified by established native usage and which is appropriate and applicable to any particular cause, action, suit, matter, dispute, issue or question, and includes also any native customary law recorded or modified in accordance with the provisions of sections 30 and 31 respectively of the Native Authority (Colony) Ordinance, 1944." The procedure for the declaration or modification of customary laws by the traditional authorities will be discussed later.

in a horizontal order were provided by Section 87 of the Courts Ordinance and were primarily ethnic. In causes or matters in which the parties were "natives," the primary law presumptively applicable was customary law. A party could, however, lose the benefit of customary law if it appeared either from an express contract or from the nature of the transaction out of which the question arose that the party had agreed to have his obligations regulated exclusively by English law. If, on the other hand, the parties to the cause or transaction included both natives and nonnatives, English law was presumably controlling. Even in such a case, however, the courts were authorized to apply customary law if they determined that "substantial injustice would be done to either party by a strict adherence to the rules of English law."

Overriding this horizontal relation of English and customary law, based on ethnic criteria, was a hierarchical relation of customary law to certain limiting principles. Not all native law and custom existing in the Gold Coast was retained, but only such as was not "repugnant to natural justice, equity, and good conscience" and not "incompatible either directly or by necessary implication with any ordinance for the time being in force."[5] Determinations of repugnancy or incompatibility were to be made by the courts. In the main, the courts that actually invoked these limiting criteria were the superior courts, staffed principally by English personnel, though it was possible for a Native Court to exclude customary law on such grounds.[6] Clearly, in the cast of incompatibility with any ordinance, the standard invalidating the customary law

[5] Courts Ordinance, supra note 2, sec. 87(1).

[6] Matson, "Internal Conflicts of Laws in the Gold Coast," 16 Modern L. Rev. 469 (1953), indicates that the repugnancy standard has been used occasionally to deal with procedural irregularities in native courts, but that the two principal categories of repugnancy cases are those involving slavery or practices analogized to slavery and cases involving disturbance of long-continued, bona fide possession of land.

was supplied by the colonial power. The "brooding omnipresence" of English law was further strengthened by the overriding standards of "natural justice, equity and good conscience" which impliedly were incorporated in English law or were at least revealed to the eyes of English judges. Natural justice, equity and good conscience also served as the basis for decision in any case within the jurisdiction of the Native Courts to which no express rule of the customary law was applicable.[7]

This pluralistic system created an appalling number of problems, most of which were neither clearly nor satisfactorily solved prior to the repeal of the Courts Ordinance. These difficulties need only be touched upon here. A serious issue was posed by the common law doctrine of precedent or *stare decisis*, whereby the decisions of higher courts are binding on lower courts in the hierarchy. In applying this doctrine, much uncertainty existed as to the binding effect on Gold Coast courts of decisions of the English High Court, the Court of Criminal Appeals and the House of Lords which were not in the hierarchy through which decisions of courts in the Gold Coast could be appealed.[8] We have already noted the question whether the cutoff date in Section 83 of the Courts Ordinance applied to common law and equity as well as to English statutes of general application. There were also difficulties related to the reception of such statutes themselves. What statutes fell within this category? Might parts of a statute be "of general application" and thus be applicable though other parts clearly were not? As a purely practical matter,

[7] See Matson, supra note 6, at 475-76, for the suggestion that in certain types of cases between natives—for example, those involving the use of abusive or derogatory remarks—the courts have applied the English law of torts with "no pretence that the law is the embodiment of 'justice, equity and good conscience,' applied in the absence of any 'express rule' of customary law; they [the courts] do not consider the possibility that such a rule may exist."

[8] On this problem see Allott, supra note 3; Elias, "Colonial Courts and the Doctrine of Judicial Precedent," 18 Modern L. Rev. 356 (1955).

how easily could a lawyer in the Gold Coast discover the English statutes in force in 1874?[9]

The problems created by the application of customary law were probably even more difficult. Standards for solving the perplexing problem of excluding customary law in causes between "natives" on the basis of express or implied agreement that English law should govern were never adequately developed by the courts. When was such an agreement to be implied?[10] When not all of the parties were "natives," in what circumstances would the court's perception of injustice to one of the parties foreclose the application of English law and warrant resort to native law and custom?[11]

Perhaps most difficult of all was the matter of ascertaining the customary law in situations where the general hierarchy of norms indicated its applicability. The Courts Ordinance, Sec. 87(2), provided that a court might "give effect to any book or manuscript recognized in the Gold Coast as a legal authority" and might "call to its assistance Chiefs or other persons whom the Court considers to have special knowledge of native law and custom." The courts were also authorized (Sec. 89) to refer questions of native law and custom to a competent Native Court for determination. Decisions of Native Courts on such referred questions were not appealable, but the referring court was in no way bound by them; it could accept or reject them, in whole or in part.

The methods for ascertaining customary law were entirely different in the superior or English courts and in the Native Courts. In the latter, customary law was assumed to be known to the members of the court who could apply it on the basis of their own, ordinarily local,

[9] See Atiyah, "Commercial Law in Ghana," The Journal of Business Law 430 (1960).

[10] For examples of judicial treatment of this problem see Kwesi-Johnston v. Effie, 14 W.A.C.A. 254 (1953) and Ferguson v. Duncan, 14 W.A.C.A. 316 (1953).

[11] For cases in point see Koney v. Union Trading Co. Ltd., 2 W.A.C.A. 188 (1934); Nelson & anor. v. Nelson & othr., 13 W.A.C.A. 248 (1951).

knowledge, although a party relying on a particular custom was free to call witnesses to prove it.[12] In the British courts, however, magistrates and judges could not be presumed to be familiar with the indigenous customary law; indeed, they were foreclosed from relying on such personal knowledge as their prior experience might provide. The party relying on customary law was therefore required to lay by allegation and proof an adequate basis for the court's application of customary law. The West African Court of Appeal held that "where a party intends to set up and rely upon a Native Law and Custom it must be specifically alleged and pleaded."[13] This requirement was confirmed by court rules necessitating the pleading not merely of the substantive effect of the native law or custom but also the geographic area and the tribe or tribes to which it related.[14]

Once adequate pleading opened the door, proof of the customary law itself remained difficult. By dictum in the case of *Angu* v. *Attah*, the Privy Council declared that customary law "has to be proved in the first instance by calling witnesses acquainted with the native customs until the particular customs have, by frequent proof in the Courts, become so notorious that the Courts take judicial notice of them."[15] The evidence contemplated by the first branch of this rule might come from chiefs, linguists or others who could be qualified as experts on customary law. As mentioned earlier, the Courts Ordinance also permitted proof of customary law by the use of "any book or manuscript recognized in the Gold Coast as a legal authority" (Sec. 87(2)), and by reports from Native Courts on questions referred to them (Sec. 89).

Incidentally, it may be noted that the use of text-

[12] Ababio II v. Nsemfoo, 12 W.A.C.A. 127 (1947).

[13] Bonsi v. Adjena II, 6 W.A.C.A. 241 (1940).

[14] Supreme Court (Civil Procedure) Rules, Order 19, Rule 31, 2 Laws of the Gold Coast 251 (1954).

[15] (1915) Gold Coast Privy Council Judgments, 1874-1928, 43 at 44. This dictum was later approved by the Judicial Committee in Amissah v. Krabah, 2 W.A.C.A. 30 (1931).

books or documents for the proof of customary law highlighted a further complication. Such law was not uniform throughout the Gold Coast; on the contrary, major differences existed between the principal cultural or tribal groups, and, even within the same group, local variations were always a possibility. Thus, even after a decision was reached that a cause was governed by customary law, a frequently difficult choice of law problem remained. Yet these complex problems were often overlooked by the courts. This was particularly true when customary law was proved by the use of textbooks. The most prominent of such works in the Gold Coast were the books of Sarbah on Fanti law.[16] The Fantis, a branch of the larger Akan group, are concentrated in the south-central and southwestern areas of the country. Sarbah had declared that "Fanti laws and customs apply to all Akans and Fantis, and to all persons whose mothers are of Akan or Fanti race."[17] This seems a most doubtful generalization when one considers that the Ashanti are also Akans. Even the author made no pretension, however, that he described the laws of the Ga-Adangbe, Ewe or other non-Akan peoples of the Gold Coast. Yet not infrequently the British courts accepted Sarbah's work as indicative of the applicable customary law between non-Fanti and even non-Akan parties.[18]

Determination of customary law as fact by the introduction of evidence is inconvenient and time-consuming as well as productive of uncertainty. The second branch of the dictum of *Angu* v. *Attah* suggested the possibility of dispensing with evidence when "the particular customs have, by frequent proof in the Courts, become so notorious that the Courts take judicial notice of them." Yet sixteen years after the decision in *Angu* v. *Attah*, the Privy Council observed that "their Lord-

[16] Sarbah, Fanti Customary Laws (1897); Sarbah, Fanti Law Report (1904).

[17] Sarbah, Fanti Customary Laws 16.

[18] See Matson, supra note 6, at 478-81, for a review of relevant cases.

ships have not been informed of any customary law so established; and they may observe that it would be very convenient if the Courts in West Africa in suitable cases would rule as to the native customs of which they think it proper to take judicial notice specifying, of course, the tribes (or districts) concerned and taking steps to see that these rulings are reported in a readily accessible form."[19] While this method of establishing the content of the customary law has the advantages of convenience and certainty, it could also involve the disadvantage of freezing the development of customary law, separating it from the on-going life of the community and in fact entirely changing the basis of its obligatory quality. In general, customary law is deemed binding because it reflects the consensus of the community as manifested in actual usage. When the custom becomes subject to judicial notice, however, it arguably derives its force not from usage but from the acceptance and implementation by the courts. If, as has been suggested,[20] it was open to a party to show even after judicial recognition that a custom was no longer supported by established usage, much of the advantage of convenience and certainty attributable to judicial notice of oft-proved customary law would be lost. The admission of such proof would mean that judicial recognition of a custom had done little more than shift the burden of proof in a lawsuit.

Another device for establishing customary law without proof of usage was provided by legislation authorizing certain traditional authorities to make declarations of customary law or recommend its modification. An example of such legislation was the Native Law and Custom (Ashanti Confederacy Council) Ordinance of 1940,[21] which authorized the Confederacy Council to

[19] Amissah v. Krabah, 2 W.A.C.A. 30 at 31 (1931).

[20] Allott, "The Judicial Ascertainment of Customary Law in British Africa," 20 Modern L. Rev. 244 (1957).

[21] Native Law and Custom (Ashanti Confederacy Council) Ordinance, No. 4 of 1940, Cap. 102, 3 Laws of the Gold Coast 220 (1951).

declare what in its opinion was the native law and custom within the confederacy relating to any subject. If the Governor in Council was satisfied that the declaration truly recorded the custom and was not repugnant to justice, equity or good conscience or incompatible with any ordinance, he was authorized to declare it to be in force, with the result that every court would be required to accept it as determinative of the customary law on the specified subject. The same ordinance authorized the Confederacy Council to recommend modifications of native law and custom, which, subject to the same criteria, the Governor in Council might accept and implement.[22] These powers were little used by the traditional authorities. It appears clear, however, that insofar as they were used, the law so declared ceased in fact to be customary law in the strict sense and became a form of legislation, deriving its force like any positive law from being authoritatively laid down by official agencies.[23]

This brief sketch by no means exhausts the problems presented in administering the pluralistic legal order of the Gold Coast. The purpose here is only to outline the various sources and kinds of legal norms and to indicate their relations in a general hierarchical and horizontal structure. It remains to consider the extent to which that structure has been modified in the post-independence legal order of Ghana and to look briefly at the contribution the changes may have made toward

[22] Similar legislation for other divisions of the Gold Coast is the State Councils (Northern Territories) Ordinance, No. 5 of 1952, secs. 12, 13; the State Councils (Colony and Southern Togoland) Ordinance, No. 8 of 1952, secs. 13, 14. The post-independence Houses of Chiefs Act, Act No. 20 of 1958, sec. 16(1), authorized a House of Chiefs to submit to the Governor General or to the Speaker of the Assembly "a written declaration of what in its opinion is the customary law relating to any subject in force in any part of the area of its authority." The act was silent, however, as to the status such a declaration would have in the courts or the functions it would perform for the legislative or executive branch.

[23] For a discussion of these problems, see Allott, supra note 20.

solution of the practical problems of administering justice.

The hierarchy of legal norms was not greatly affected by the grant of independence on March 6, 1957. After that date, of course, the supreme position in the hierarchy was occupied by the constitutional Order in Council. Next came local legislation in the form of Acts of Parliament. No British statute enacted after independence extended to Ghana unless the Parliament of Ghana requested and consented to the enactment. Otherwise, the pre-independence body of law was left intact.[24] This structure of legal norms remained until the advent of the Republic on July 1, 1960, when the Republican Constitution and certain acts of the Constituent Assembly made significant changes.

The basic statement on the new order of legal norms in Ghana is found in the constitution, Article 40, which provides:

> Except as may be otherwise provided by an enactment made after the coming into operation of the Constitution the laws of Ghana comprise the following—
> (a) the Constitution,
> (b) enactments made by or under the authority of the Parliament established by the Constitution,
> (c) enactments other than the Constitution made by or under the authority of the Constituent Assembly,
> (d) enactments in force immediately before the coming into operation of the Constitution,
> (e) the common law, and
> (f) customary law.

The constitutional list is suggestive of a hierarchical ordering, but this is not made clear in the constitution itself. For clarification of the new structure of norms,

[24] Ghana Independence Act, 1957, 5 & 6 Eliz. 2, c. 6, sec. 1.

it is necessary to consider also two enactments of the Constituent Assembly—the Interpretation Act (1960, C. A. 4) and the Courts Act (1960, C. A. 9).

The Interpretation Act of 1960 (Sec. 17 (1)), provides that the common law received as part of the law of Ghana includes, in addition to the rules generally known as the common law, the doctrines of equity and "rules of customary law included in the common law under any enactment providing for the assimilation of such rules of customary law as are suitable for general application." The effect of this provision for assimilation is not yet clear. A Ghanaian scholar has suggested that the assimilation device may "have been the sugar-coating which served to enable the drafters or their instructors to administer the common-law pill to Ghana's lawmakers." The same author continues: "Short of legislative enactment by the national legislature, it is not easy to see how it can be left to the courts to decide which customary law rules to assimilate and generalize, and how communities subject to a different system of customary law of which they are equally proud are going to be induced to drop their own rule merely because the court has seen fit, in some particular case before it, to declare that a particular rule of customary law in one system is suitable for universal application and should be assimilated into the common law. This would seem to indicate that it would be preferable for the national legislature rather than the courts to tackle the general problem of customary law."[25] It must be observed that the Interpretation Act did in fact contemplate legislation on the subject of assimilation of customary law. Basic implementing provisions were incorporated in the Chieftaincy Act of 1961.

The statute commits the task of assimilating customary law into the common law not to the courts but

[25] Bentsi-Enchill, "Ghana Faces Constitutional Problems," 31 Harvard Law Record, No. 8, pp. 9, 13.

to the chiefs, the traditional rulers, subject to the ultimate discretion of the executive. On the initiative of
either a Regional House of Chiefs or the Minister for
Local Government, a joint committee drawn from the
Houses of Chiefs of all the regions may be convened
to consider whether a customary law rule should be
assimilated by the common law. If the joint committee
favors assimilation, they may draft a declaration "with
such modifications as they may consider desirable" for
submission to the Minister.[26] After consulting the Chief
Justice, if the Minister is satisfied that effect should be
given to the draft "either as submitted or with such
modifications as he considers necessary," he may effect
the assimilation by a legislative instrument.[27] The resulting common law rule of customary origin then has
priority of application within its scope over other rules
derived from the common law or any system of customary law.[28] The Minister has discretion to devise
transitional provisions relating to cases pending when
the assimilation instrument is made.[29]

It is noteworthy that this assimilation scheme consciously sanctions legislative adjustments in the customary and common law. The chiefs may recommend assimilation of an existing customary law rule or some modification. The Minister may decree the assimilation of the
rule recommended by the chiefs or modify it as he thinks
necessary. Thus, significant powers to effect legal
change are lodged in persons outside the conventional
legislative and judicial structure. It does not appear,
however, that these powers have been exercised up to
this time.

The courts of Ghana inevitably have some leeway for
creative activity in deciding cases not covered by statute
or well-established common law rules. Insofar as they
draw inspiration for their decisions in such novel cases
from some local custom they may be said to have as-

[26] Chieftaincy Act, 1961, Act 81, sec. 62(2).
[27] *Id.*, sec. 62(3).   [28] *Id.*, sec. 63(2).   [29] *Id.*, sec. 64.

similated customary law into a body of national common law. This in fact is the historic method of the Anglo-American common law, and its use in the new order in Ghana may reasonably be expected. On the other hand, if the generalization of customary law is left to legislation or to the procedures outlined in the Chieftaincy Act, there seems to be little reason for categorizing the resulting rule as either common law or customary law; such a rule would derive its force from the enacting statute or legislative instrument. Determination of the significance of the assimilation procedure for legal change in Ghana must await developments.

Although the Courts Act of 1960 repealed the old Courts Ordinance, the common law, doctrines of equity and statutes of general application in force in England on July 24, 1874, were retained. Section 17(1) of the new Interpretation Act defines the common law as including doctrines of equity, and both were therefore retained in the new legal order of Ghana by Article 40 of the Republican Constitution. Statutes of general application were also retained, though somewhat circuitously. The Courts Act, Sec. 154(4), kept in effect such statutes of general application in force in England on the cutoff date as applied in Ghana immediately before the act became effective. Thus, these statutes were preserved by the provision of Article 40 of the constitution covering "enactments in force immediately before the coming into operation of the Constitution." The new Interpretation Act, Sec. 17(3), further provides that these retained statutes of general application shall be treated as part of the common law and shall stand in the hierarchy of norms above any rule of the common law other than a rule assimilated from customary law. The net result of this circumlocution is to preserve the statutes of general application in very nearly the same position relative to the common law that they occupied in the former hierarchy of norms, except that now they are regarded as a preferred part of the common law.

A rule of equity, in case of inconsistency, is to prevail over any rule other than an assimilated rule. Thus, it might appear that in the new hierarchy of norms equity doctrines have been raised above rules derived from English statutes of general application, if the latter are treated as part of the common law. On the other hand, the statute expressly states that rules derived from statutes of general application prevail over all other parts of the common law except rules assimilated from customary law. Since equity is defined as part of the common law, this suggests that statutes of general application have retained their precedence over equity doctrine. In this regard the provisions of Sec. 17(2) and (3) of the new Interpretation Act may appear to present inconsistent views on the hierarchy of norms. A possible reconciliation might be effected by regarding the statutes of general application as technically not part of the common law, Sec. 17(1), and therefore deriving priority of application only from the specific rule of Sec. 17(3) which ranks them above all common law rules except assimilated rules.

The enactments adopted on the creation of the Republic contain a novel set of provisions dealing with the administration by the courts of a common law system. As noted earlier, part of the English legacy to the Gold Coast was the doctrine of precedent or *stare decisis*. In the old order, the courts in the Gold Coast were bound by the decisions of the West African Court of Appeal and of the Judicial Committee of the Privy Council. On the other hand, decisions of the English Court of Appeal and the House of Lords were in theory not binding, since they were outside the hierarchy that included the Gold Coast courts, but in practice were treated as if they were. There was much uncertainty over the effect of their dates on the status of English decisions even from courts within the immediate hierarchy—that is, did it matter whether they were handed down before or after the date of the reception of English law in the Gold Coast. Some clarification on these points comes from the new constitution. The appeal previously allowed from the courts of Ghana to the Judicial Committee of the Privy Council was eliminated; thus, the Supreme Court of Ghana became the tribunal of last resort.[30] Consequently, after the establishment of the Republic, no English court by its decisions could bind the courts of Ghana. The stability of legal institutions and the normal conservatism of judicial attitudes make it inevitable, however, that English decisions will long enjoy a high degree of persuasiveness in Ghana.

Within the hierarchy of Ghanaian courts, the constitution provides that

> The Supreme Court shall in principle be bound to follow its own previous decisions on questions of law, and the High Court shall be bound to follow previous decisions of the Supreme Court on such questions, but neither Court shall be otherwise bound to follow the previous decisions of any court on questions of law.[31]

The Interpretation Act of 1960 further provides (Sec. 17(4)) that "in deciding upon the existence or content of a rule of the common law, as so defined, the Court may have regard to any exposition of that rule by a court exercising jurisdiction in any country."

When one turns from the status of foreign decisions under the Republican Constitution, much of the certainty of the foregoing provision of the constitution disappears. If only the decisions of the Supreme Court are in the future to be binding, what is the "Supreme Court" for this purpose? Is the Court as constituted under the Republican Constitution to be deemed to be a new court, so that only decisions of the Republican Supreme Court are binding? Or is a theory of antecedent

---

[30] Republican Constitution, art. 42(1).   [31] *Id.*, art. 42(4).

and continuing existence to be applied. If the Supreme Court is deemed to have had a pre-Republic existence, should this be traced back to independence in 1957 or some earlier date? Thus far the Supreme Court has not answered these questions.

At first impression it appears that the Supreme Court of Ghana is committed by the constitution to a doctrine of precedent similar to that prevailing in England. There the House of Lords is bound by its own prior decisions and therefore lacks the power, normally assumed by American courts, to correct its prior mistakes by over-ruling previous decisions either of common law or statutory interpretation. The same doctrine of judicial restraint or impotence is often said to apply to the English High Court with respect to its own prior decisions. To the extent, if any, that this doctrine has been accepted in Ghana, it clearly seems to be limited to the Supreme Court. A question may be raised as to the significance of the constitutional provision that the Supreme Court shall be bound "in principle" to its prior decisions. In prevailing common law theory, the only aspect of a decision binding in later cases is its "principle" or *ratio decidendi*. Only by determining this principle can a court fix the authority, the binding aspect, of a case. In the process of articulating the principle, a court therefore has a range of flexibility and may succeed in distinguishing the present case so that it lies outside the authoritative principle. At least this much freedom is surely left to the Supreme Court of Ghana. Another possible interpretation of the constitutional provision, however, would equate the phrase "in principle" to "in general" or "ordinarily." Such an interpretation would bring the doctrine of *stare decisis* in Ghana much more closely in line with that prevailing in the United States. Here, the values of doctrinal stability and predictability of decision are recognized and ordinarily are protected. At the same time, however, these values may be sacrificed by judicial adaptation of the law to changed circumstances or by the correction of serious prior error. The pre-Republican constitutional discussions throw no light on this problem of interpretation, nor do decisions of the Republican Supreme Court thus far.

In the pre-Republican legal order of the Gold Coast and Ghana, it was recognized that beyond the range of local and English decisions, binding under the accepted doctrine of precedent, lay a further range of English and Commonwealth decisions which might be recognized as highly persuasive. For example, in appropriate circumstances, decisions of the English High Court or House of Lords, of the East African Court of Appeal or of the Supreme Court of India might be accepted as correct declarations and applications of the law in force in Ghana as well. Despite their common legal roots, however, it is by no means common for courts in the English tradition to refer to American decisions. The possibility of greater resort to these resources is at least suggested by the Interpretation Act of 1960 which authorizes the courts of Ghana, in deciding the existence or content of common law rules, to "have regard to any exposition of that rule by a court exercising jurisdiction in any country." Whether this possibility will be realized can be determined only by observing the conduct of the courts of Ghana for the next several years.

Another interesting though probably academic question in the administration of Ghana's common law system concerns the power of the Supreme Court under the new dispensation to modify or abandon rules provided by the old English statutes of general application. As discussed earlier, these are now categorized as part of the common law. Furthermore, such rules were not created by prior decisions of the Supreme Court and are not therefore protected by the stringent doctrines of precedent that one interpretation of the constitution may have imposed on the Supreme Court. Arguably, therefore, the Supreme Court could modify such rules, as it might change rules forming part of the common law because laid down by prior decisions of the former High Court or of English courts. This seems unlikely to occur to any considerable extent, however; such law reform will result, if at all, from legislation in Parliament.

The problem remains of determining the status of customary law in the new hierarchy of norms. As has been seen, the former Courts Ordinance made customary law applicable in causes between natives, unless an agreement could be found to have English law apply, and in causes between natives and nonnatives if the court should decide that injustice would result to either party from the strict application of English law. Understandably, an effort has been made in the new legislation to abandon an avowedly ethnic criterion for determining the applicable legal rules and also to deal with the complex problems of conflict between bodies of customary law and of determination of the content of customary law rules.

Standards for determining the choice between common law and customary law and between different systems of customary law are provided by a series of rules in Section 66 of the new Courts Act. The six rules must be quoted in full text:

> Rule. 1. Where two persons have the same personal law one of them cannot, by dealing in a manner regulated by some other law with property in which the other has a present or expectant interest, alter or affect that interest to an extent which would not in the circumstances be open to him under his personal law.
>
> Rule 2. Subject to Rule 1, where an issue arises out of a transaction the parties to which have agreed, or may from the form or nature of the transaction be taken to have agreed, that such an issue should be determined according to the common law or any system of customary law effect should be given to

the agreement. In this rule "transaction" includes a marriage and an agreement or arrangement to marry.

Rule 3. Subject to Rule 1, where an issue arises out of any unilateral disposition and it appears from the form or nature of the disposition or otherwise that the person effecting the disposition intended that such an issue should be determined according to the common law or any system of customary law effect should be given to the intention.

Rule 4. Subject to the foregoing rules, where an issue relates to entitlement to land on the death of the owner or otherwise relates to title to land—

(a) If all the parties to the proceedings who claim to be entitled to the land or a right relating thereto trace their claims from one person who is subject to customary law, or from one family or other group of persons all subject to the same customary law, the issue should be determined according to that law;

(b) if the said parties trace their claims from different persons, or families or other groups of persons, who are all subject to the same customary law, the issue should be determined according to the law;

(c) in any other case, the issue should be determined according to the law of the place in which the land is situated.

Rule 5. Subject to Rules 1 to 3, where an issue relates to the devolution of the property (other than land) of a person on his death it should be determined according to his personal law.

Rule 6. Subject to the foregoing rules, an issue should be determined according to the common law unless the plaintiff is subject to any system of customary law and claims to have the issue determined according to that system, when it should be so determined.

It should be noted that Rules 1 and 5 expressly employ the concept of "personal law" which is defined in Sec. 66(1) as "the system of customary law to which [a person] is subject or, if he is not shown to be subject to customary law, . . . the common law." In general, it would appear that one's personal law is determined en bloc by reference to his status and mode of life in the community of which he is a part. This is to be contrasted with the narrower bloc determination of the applicable law on a transactional basis by agreement between the parties or in some instances on a unilateral basis, as provided in Rules 2 and 3. Rule 4 does not expressly use the concept of "personal law" but admits it in substance by making the choice of law depend on whether a critical person is "subject to customary law" or all members of a relevant group are "subject to the same customary law."

Any appearance of clarity and certainty presented by this catalog of rules on the choice of law problem is misleading. The use of the concept of personal law in a legal order based primarily on the concept of territoriality of laws introduces great complexity. Many of the legal norms of Ghana are applicable within the geographic boundaries of the nation. The common law and the several systems of customary law are "personal," however, and their application depends on the particular persons involved. Surprisingly, the Courts Act is entirely silent as to the criteria by which one's "personal law" is to be determined. Presumably this determination must still be made on the basis of such ethnic factors as determined the jurisdiction of the former Native Courts—that is, is the person of African descent? Is his way of life that of a native community? If so, of what native community is he a member? While the legislative draftsmen were able to avoid the use of the word "native," the concept of personal law seemingly commits the courts to criteria reminiscent of the colonial period in answering the choice of law questions.

It should be observed that the new legislation actually improves the status of common law, or rather, law derived primarily from England, in its competition with indigenous legal norms. Formerly there was a presumption favoring the applicability of customary law in all cases where the parties were "natives" or "of African descent." Customary law might also control in certain other cases even though some of the parties were nonnatives. Under the new legislation, the initial presumption favors the application of common law in many instances where previously a contrary presumption would have prevailed. While both common law and customary law are categorized as "personal law," the basic definition of this concept indicates that it is the former that is to be applied, unless the person affected shows that he is subject to some body of customary law that provides an applicable rule.[32] This point is reemphasized by Rule 6 in Section 66, which declares that "subject to the foregoing rules, an issue should be determined according to the common law, unless the plaintiff is subject to any system of customary law and claims to have the issue determined according to that system, when it should be so determined." None of the six rules delimiting the choice between customary and common law compels the court on its own initiative to seek out a basis for applying customary law. The court is entitled to apply common law, unless the affected party establishes the propriety of applying a personal law from the indigenous systems.

A difference in the phraseology of Rule 6 from that employed in the first five rules suggests a further limitation on the application of native custom as personal law. Rules 1 through 5 deal with the law applicable in certain property transactions and in cases where the parties have agreed, either expressly or by implication, that a certain law should apply. Within the scope of these rules, either party apparently may claim the benefit of the appropriate personal law or transactional law and establish the basis for its application. In the

[32] Sec. 66(1).

residue of cases, covered by Rule 6, the literal language seemingly would entitle only the plaintiff to negative the presumption of applicability of common law. Why the important issue of choice of law should be thus determined by the vagaries of the line-up of parties in an action is by no means clear. In any event, it appears that the six rules of Section 66 have shifted earlier boundaries between the English derived common law and customary law to the prejudice of the latter.[33]

[33] Mr. Gordon R. Woodman, Gonville and Caius College, Cambridge, who has examined an earlier version of this chapter with much-appreciated care, agrees with my analysis of the 1960 Courts Act but not of the pre-1960 law. He thus believes that I have made too much of the verbal changes made in 1960. His comments, which I quote with his permission, deserve careful consideration. "Under the Courts Ordinance (Cap. 4) sec. 83, the basic law of the Supreme Court was 'English law.' Sec. 87 was strictly an exception to this basic rule, so that any party wishing to claim the benefit of customary law had to establish that the necessary conditions were fulfilled. This was normally done by showing that both parties were natives. In practice it was extremely easy to do this, as an allegation to this effect was almost never challenged. However, the burden was on the person claiming the benefit of customary law, just as it is today on the person claiming that someone's personal law is customary law. Since the criteria are the same as they used to be in this respect, one would suppose that it should be neither more nor less difficult to discharge the burden, and that an allegation to this effect will rarely be challenged." I would make the following observations on Mr. Woodman's views. While Section 83 of the old Courts Act did make English law the basic law of the Supreme Court, the section explicitly provided in an introductory phrase that this was "subject to the terms of this or any other Ordinance." The provisions of Section 87 on the application of customary law would seem, therefore, to have equal stature and to be "basic law" "in causes and matters where the parties thereto are natives." I think it significant that Section 87 provides that customary law "shall be deemed applicable" in the specified causes and does not make the choice of this law dependent upon a claim by the parties for its application. Thus, it would seem that the court could properly be expected to apply customary law *sua sponte* when it determined that the criteria for application were met. In contrast, the 1960 Act expressly makes the application of customary law conditional upon a claim by a party for its application. Therefore, I conclude that it is appropriate to insist that the starting presumption on the applicable law was reversed in 1960.

Mr. Woodman and I are in complete agreement that it is no more difficult today than formerly to establish the grounds for resorting to customary law, at least as far as the formal standards

A further inroad on the area of application of customary law was introduced by the Courts Act of 1960. As already noted, the new Interpretation Act, Sec. 17(1), suggested the possibility of a later enactment to provide for the assimilation by the common law of certain rules of customary law found suitable for general application. The Courts Act, Sec. 66(2),[34] provided that where, under any of the six rules previously discussed, customary law was applicable but a relevant rule of customary law had been assimilated by the common law, the rule thus assimilated should be applied. The effect of this provision in further curtailing the customary law may be illustrated by the following imaginary case. In Fanti law, intestate succession to property is matrilineal, while the basic rule among the Ga people provides for patrilineal succession. Assume that the appropriate authority determined that the Ga rule was more in keeping with the modern economic and social conditions of Ghana and should be assimilated by the common law. In a subsequent case between Fantis involving Fanti lands, the rules of Section 66 of the new Courts Act would indicate that the case should be determined by Fanti customary law. However, since a "relevant" rule, that is, a rule dealing with the kind of problem presented, had been assimilated, the rule assimilated by the common law from the Ga custom would be applicable. To insist that this is still the application of "customary law" is to permit a label to blind one to substance. Insofar as the Fanti parties are concerned, their custom would have been rejected in

---

and what we know of actual practice are concerned. Therefore, there is no reason to anticipate that the 1960 shift of presumption will necessarily affect the results in a wide variety of cases. The primary significance of the 1960 changes arises from their reflection of general attitudes of the lawmakers toward the relations between component parts of the legal system.

[34] Although Sec. 66(2) of the Courts Act was repealed by Sec. 69(1) of the Chieftaincy Act (Act 81 of 1961), the substance of the earlier provision discussed here appears to have been reenacted by Sec. 63(2) of the Chieftaincy Act.

favor of a national rule. Arguably, it would in the circumstances mean no more to them that the national rule was a generalization from an African (Ga) custom than if it were derived from English law. In view of the jealousies and historic differences among the indigenous people of Ghana, the nationalization of one tribal rule might be even less acceptable than similar treatment of an English doctrine.[35]

One final limitation of the new Courts Act on the application of customary law should be noted. Section 66 in conclusion provides that notwithstanding the earlier provisions of the section, which in general seek to delimit an area of application for customary law,

[35] Gordon R. Woodman, for whose knowledge of Ghanaian customary land law I have great respect, has sent me the following comments on these observations, which I quote with his permission: "I think the difficulty can be answered. There are in fact many principles common to all the systems of customary law in Ghana. This may not appear at first sight: for example, what could be more different from a matrilineal family system than a patrilineal system? In the former a man's family consists of an entirely different group of persons from those in the latter. But even here there are even more fundamental principles which are common. Thus in each case a man's immovable property is inherited on his death intestate as family property; in each case a man has a right to share the enjoyment of family property with the other members of the family, and that right is secured in the same way in each case; and there are many other rules common to both systems. The family consists of a different set of relatives in each case, but otherwise there is little difference. Moreover, it is likely that membership of this set of relatives is determined by the same principles in each case, apart from the fact that in one case only matrilineal relationships are taken into account, and in the other case only patrilineal relationships. I think it was probably rules such as these, common to all systems, that were contemplated by the assimilation provisions."
Unfortunately, no reliable legislative history is available that would either support or refute Mr. Woodman's speculation on the intention of the proponents of the assimilation technique. It seems sufficient now to observe that the statute does not limit assimilation to supposed common principles. Since the technique has not yet been used, its limits are not suggested by experience. I continue to believe that the illustration offered in the text would be entirely consistent with the basic legislation; it is also compatible with the thesis advanced here that assimilation is to be viewed as part of the many-faceted attack on local particularity and subnational loyalties.

two sets of legal rules derived from English law shall apply: (1) the rules of private international law shall apply in any proceedings in which an issue concerning the application of law prevailing in any country outside Ghana is raised; (2) "the rules of estoppel and such other of the rules generally known as the common law and the rules generally known as the doctrines of equity as have heretofore been treated as applicable in all proceedings in Ghana shall continue to be so treated."[36] The first of these categories is not of primary interest here. The use of conflicts (private international law) rules derived from English or other non-African law in those cases involving an issue of non-Ghanaian law would affect only a thin stratum of Ghanaian society, primarily those persons engaged in some way in international business transactions. The second category of rules is of greater general interest. The underlying premise is that in pre-Republican Ghana and the Gold Coast, certain rules derived from English common law and equity were applicable in all legal proceedings, even those otherwise governed by the indigenous customary law. All such rules are to be retained in the new legal order. What are these rules and doctrines? The statute provides only one illustration: the rules of estoppel. In general, it may be said that these rules represent particularizations by the courts of the general ideas of "natural justice, equity, and good conscience" which in the old legal order set bounds to the application of customary law and also provided the basis for decision where the customary law was thought not to offer a relevant rule.

In summary, it appears clear that the new legal order has not in any way enlarged the scope of application of customary law. On the contrary, in the competition between customary law and English law (common law, equity and statutes of general application), English law seems somewhat advantaged by the new ordering. This

---

[36] Courts Act, 1960, C.A. 9, sec. 66(3)(b).

treatment of customary law must be viewed in the larger perspective of the relations between the traditional tribal institutions and the power centers of a new national state. In the new order, the center of activity in creation and adaptation of norms will not be the courts administering an amorphous, pluralistic system of customary and common law, but rather Parliament, developing a body of national legal norms.

One more feature of the 1960 legislation must be examined. This deals with the problem of determining the content of customary law in those cases governed by it. The earlier view regarded customary law as a matter of fact, at least in the superior courts, to be established by proof. The dictum of *Angu* v. *Attah* had suggested that some rules might become sufficiently "notorious" through frequent proof that judicial notice would be taken of them, but this suggestion does not seem to have been followed. The Courts Act (1960), declares, however (Sec. 67(1)), that the question of the existence or content of a rule of customary law is a question of law for the court and not a question of fact. The important aspect of this provision is not the clear assignment of the finding function to the court rather than to assessors or jury. Even when customary law was deemed a matter of fact, the function of finding it was assigned to the court.[37] The important change is that customary law is to be found *as law* rather than as fact. If the normal consequences of this categorization are to prevail in Ghana, a court may determine the applicable customary law rule from its own knowledge or assumed knowledge or from investigation conducted by the court but in no way reflected in the record, short of the court's announcement of the rule to be applied.

While seeming to free the courts from the necessity of building a record to support their findings of customary law, Parliament realistically recognized that in many cases in which claims for the application of

[37] See Allott, supra note 20, at 248.

customary law are made, the courts will need to inquire concerning the existence and content of the applicable norm. Under the Courts Act (Sec. 67(2)(3)), the extent and methods of inquiry are left largely to the court's discretion. Techniques suggested by the statute include considering such "submissions" as may be made by the parties, consulting reported cases, textbooks and such "other sources as may be appropriate," calling and hearing such witnesses as the court may deem proper, and requesting a written opinion from a House of Chiefs, State Council "or other body possessing knowledge of the customary law in question." It seems obvious that a court has discretion to determine which one or more of these techniques will be used; it seems equally obvious that the court is not bound to accept any particular opinion. The statute is silent, however, as to whether a court that has decided to hear witnesses or request written opinions on the customary law must preserve the testimony and documents in the record for use by a reviewing court. No such necessity would seem to exist if customary law is indeed to be found as law and if the testimony and opinions of witnesses and the submissions of the parties are analogized to the legal memoranda or oral arguments on the law adduced in a trial court in England or the United States. Regardless of whether the trial court's inquiry into customary law is preserved in the record, it would seem that any reviewing court may utilize the same techniques as were available to the trial court for supplementing its assumed knowledge of customary law. A further consequence of the categorization of customary law as law would therefore appear to be that a trial court's determination of the applicable rule would enjoy no presumption of accuracy or reliability on appeal or other review.

Experience alone will determine the actual effect of the new provisions on the finding of customary law. The initial analysis suggests the possibility that in operation they will gradually erode variable local customs in favor of a national "customary law." The similarity between the possible, clearly authorized handling of customary law in the courts of Ghana and the development of the common law in England is striking. To Blackstone, the common law of England rested in general custom, but it was known and its validity determined by the judges, "the depositories of the laws; the living oracles who must decide in all cases of doubt. . . ."[38] Local custom, variable throughout the realm, could indeed be given effect subject to rather stringent criteria, but, when relied on, allegation and proof were, in general, required and the issue thus raised was ordinarily for the jury.[39] Thus, the treatment of customary law under the new Courts Act of Ghana more closely resembles that of general common law in England than local custom. The commitment of the decisional function to the courts as on questions of law augurs the demise of local particularity and the emergence of a body of national Ghanaian common law.

To a considerable extent, the actual impact of the formal changes in the structure of the operative legal norms of Ghana remains speculative. Continuing study of legislative developments and the judicial process is essential. It may be suggested, however, that the grant of independence and the adoption of a Republican form of government have not served to revitalize that part of the legal order derived from the indigenous societies. On the contrary, this component of the legal order seems to have suffered continued attrition in favor of legal institutions and legal norms received from non-indigenous, primarily British sources and incorporated in a rapidly growing body of national legislation. Insofar as "Africanization" of the legal order is to occur, it is

[38] Blackstone, Commentaries (Andrews-Cooley, 4th ed., vol. 1) 69 (1899).
[39] *Id.*, at 75-76.

to be expected mainly from the activity of Parliament. The extent to which legislative reforms draw inspiration from indigenous institutions or remain more broadly eclectic can be determined only by detailed analysis of the numerous enactments since independence.

There has been a high level of legislative activity in Ghana, particularly since the creation of the Republic. While much of this has involved technical adjustments of governmental structure and much reflects the possibly transient problems of neutralizing subnational centers of power, a substantial residue has concerned basic law reform. Many of the old enactments received from England have been repealed. Those which in substance have stood the test of time and still seem appropriate in Ghana's circumstances have been put in modern language and re-enacted by Parliament. Some statutes have been passed to make applicable in Ghana, with such modifications as seemed appropriate, legislation enacted in Great Britain after the reception date and never extended to the Gold Coast. Some partial codifications have been attempted, as in the Contracts Act of 1960.[40] In some instances, legislative efforts have been preceded by major studies which examined the relevant problems in depth and proposed solutions.[41] The scope of the legislative activity is suggested by a partial catalog of basic post-Republic enactments: Apprentices Act (Act 45), Arbitration Act (Act 38), Bills of Exchange Act (Act 55), Bills of Lading Act (Act 42), Copyright Act (Act 85), Capital Investments Act (Act 172), Civil Liability Act (Act 176), Companies Code (Act 179), Incorporated Private Partnerships Act (Act 152), Insolvency Act (Act 153), Sale of Goods Act (Act 137) and Workmen's Compensation Act (Act 174). In addition, a new Criminal Code (Act 29) and Crim-

[40] Act 25.
[41] See for example, Final Report of the Commission of Enquiry into the Working and Administration of the Present Company Law of Ghana (1961); Report of The Commission Appointed to Enquire into The Insolvency Law of Ghana (1961).

inal Procedure Code (Act 30) have been enacted. In relatively little of the reform legislation has there been great innovation; familiar models, particularly from Britain or Ireland, have been preferred, though to a limited extent American experience has also been considered.

CHAPTER VII

THE LEGAL TOOLS
OF POLITICAL MONOPOLY

A MAJOR PART of the British legacy to Ghana was the institutional structure of parliamentary democracy. Though the changes incident to the creation of the Republic in 1960 necessitate qualification of the term "parliamentary," it remains true that the basic governmental structure is that of a representative democracy. This applies at the local and the national level; both legislative and executive agencies are in theory selected, directly or indirectly, by the people to whom the officials must return periodically for judgment of performance and the renewal or withdrawal of their mandate. This theory of government finds its highest expression in the Republican Constitution which declares that the "powers of the State derive from the people, as the source of power and the guardians of the State, by whom certain of those powers are now conferred on the institutions established by this Constitution and who shall have the right to exercise the remainder of those powers, and to choose their representatives in the Parliament now established . . ." (Art. 1).

Underlying the institutions of representative government are certain assumptions as to the scope and kind of political participation available to the members of the community. The purpose of this chapter is to identify those assumptions and determine the extent to which they find support in the legal order of Ghana.

THE RIGHT OF FRANCHISE

The minimum political participation assumed by representative institutions is the right of franchise. Wide variations can, of course, exist in the size of the group within which this right exists. The representative quality of governmental institutions must therefore be assessed by reference to the criteria determining who may vote.

The base line for the present study is the Coussey Constitution of 1950 which created the first Legislative Assembly with a majority of elected members.[1] The Assembly consisted of 3 ex officio members, 6 special members chosen by chambers of commerce and the chamber of mines and 75 elected members.[2] Of the elected members, 37 were to be chosen by the Paramount Chiefs and other representatives of the Native Authorities.[3] The remaining 38 members were popularly elected in single-member districts. Qualifications for the franchise varied slightly between municipal and rural districts. In both, the voter was required to be a British subject or British protected person. In municipal districts the second criterion was owning, renting or occupying assessed premises within the district for at least six months prior to registration.[4] In rural districts the further criteria were residence within the district for at least six months immediately before application to register and, when applicable, the payment of the local Native Authority tax for the current or preceding year.[5] Though *prime facie* entitled to be registered and to vote on the basis of these criteria, a person was disqualified by sentence to major criminal punishment, adjudicated lunacy or conviction of election offenses.[6] No discrimination on the basis of sex was authorized. In summary, while only a minority of the members of the Legislative Assembly under the Coussey Constitution were popularly elected, the fran-

---

[1] The Gold Coast (Constitution) Order in Council, 1950 [1950], I STAT. INSTR. 831 (No. 2094), hereafter cited as 1950 Constitution.

[2] *Id.*, secs. 33, 38-40.

[3] *Id.*, sec. 40 and Second Schedule.

[4] Elections (Legislative Assembly) Ordinance, 1950, No. 29 of 1950, Cap. 270, sec. 9, 5 Laws of the Gold Coast 395 (1951).

[5] *Id.*, sec. 10.   [6] *Id.*, sec. 11.

chise for these seats was widely distributed and could be lost only on the basis of significant, objective factors.

The Nkrumah Constitution of 1954 enlarged the Legislative Assembly to 104 members and substantially altered the basis of representation.[7] The ex officio members, the representatives of economic groups and the members chosen by the traditional authorities were entirely eliminated. All members of the Assembly were elected in single-member constituencies by popular suffrage. Although in preparation for the election of a new Assembly, an Electoral Provisions Ordinance had been enacted in 1953,[8] in substance, the basis of the franchise was changed very little. Provision was made for a common role of electors for both National Assembly and local government elections.[9] A single set of criteria was established for registration and voting in municipal and rural electoral districts. These included 1) status as a British subject, a British protected person, or a member of the armed forces or police force of the Gold Coast; 2) attainment of twenty-one years of age; 3) ownership of immovable property or residence for at least six of the twelve months preceding application for registration in the ward where application was made; and 4) payment of the local government rate.[10] The same substantive grounds of disqualification for registering and voting were retained from the earlier ordinance.[11] A person already registered was disqualified from voting if his basic local government tax was not paid.[12]

[7] The Gold Coast (Constitution) Order in Council, 1954 [1954], 2 STAT. INSTR. 2788 (No. 551). Hereafter this will be cited as 1954 Constitution.

[8] The Electoral Provisions Ordinance, 1953, No. 33 of 1953.

[9] An interesting insight into the problems encountered in utilizing the methods of modern democratic government in the Gold Coast is provided by an amendment to the Local Government Ordinance in 1955 (No. 39 of 1955), which makes punishable the use of oaths, fetishes, invocations and spells in relation to voting or refraining from voting.

[10] The Electoral Provisions Ordinance, supra note 8, sec. 14.

[11] Id., sec. 15(1).

[12] Id., sec. 15(2). This provision was repealed by the Electoral

Legal provisions for broad, popular suffrage were further strengthened by the Independence Constitution of 1957. Every citizen of Ghana, "without distinction of religion, race or sex" was entitled to be registered as an elector for members of Parliament and to express his preference by secret ballot if he was at least twenty-one years of age, subject to no statutory incapacity on the grounds of nonresidence, unsoundness of mind, crime or corrupt or illegal practices, or nonpayment of rates or taxes, and either owned immovable property or resided for a stipulated period within the district of application.[13] Two significant changes were made in the implementing legislation. The criteria of qualification for registration as an elector and voting were modified to omit any dependence of the franchise on the payment of taxes.[14] The liberalized basis of the franchise applied in all elections, those for local government posts as well as elections for the National Assembly.[15] The limitation of the franchise to citizens of Ghana, inevitable at independence, was not unduly restrictive since the new citizenship was broadly available to the same categories of persons who had enjoyed the franchise under Gold Coast law before independence.[16]

The trend toward universal adult suffrage found its highest expression in the Republican Constitution of 1960. After declaring that the powers of the State derive from the people, Article 1 lays down the principle on which the people shall exercise their nondelegated powers and choose their representatives:

Provisions (Amendment) (No. 3) Ordinance, 1954, No. 10 of 1954.

[13] The Ghana (Constitution) Order in Council, 1957, sec. 69 [1957], 1 STAT. INSTR. 1036 (No. 277), hereafter cited as 1957 Constitution.

[14] The Electoral Provisions (Amendment) Ordinance, 1957, No. 4 of 1957.

[15] The Electoral Provisions (Amendment) (No. 2) Ordinance, 1957, No. 14 of 1957.

[16] The Ghana Nationality and Citizenship Act, 1957, No. 1 of 1957.

That, without distinction of sex, race, religion or political belief, every person who, being by law a citizen of Ghana, has attained the age of twenty-one years and is not disqualified by law on grounds of absence, infirmity of mind or criminality, shall be entitled to one vote, to be cast in freedom and secrecy.

The power to repeal or alter this provision is reserved to the people (Art. 3).

ACCESS TO POLITICAL OFFICE

The significance of the franchise depends directly, of course, on the opportunity to cast votes for candidates substantively and not merely formally representative. The privilege of casting a vote for a single approved list of candidates or for a choice that is unduly limited leaves little meaning in the franchise. It is therefore necessary to examine the criteria determining eligibility to stand for and hold the major political offices whose occupants play the critical roles in shaping the law and determining how the public force shall be applied. This inquiry will be limited to national institutions. Until the Republic, the critical criteria affected membership in the Legislative or National Assembly; thereafter the office of President acquired paramount importance.

Under the Coussey Constitution of 1950, three affirmative qualifications were imposed for membership in the Legislative Assembly. Any person who was a British subject or British protected person, at least twenty-five years of age, and sufficiently proficient in the English language to take an active part in the proceedings of the Assembly, was eligible for election.[17] A number of grounds of disqualification were specified, however:[18]

[17] 1950 Constitution, sec. 42.
[18] *Id.*, sec. 43.

1. acknowledging allegiance, obedience or adherence to a foreign power;
2. holding any public office or the office of Speaker;
3. except in the case of special Members chosen by certain economic interests, being related in any of several ways to contracts with the government, unless adequate disclosure of the relation was made;
4. being an undischarged bankrupt;
5. disqualification by competent authority from practicing a profession for which qualification had existed;
6. adjudicated unsoundness of mind;
7. sentence to a major criminal penalty unless a pardon had been given or the imprisonment had been completed more than five years;
8. in the case of most elected Members, not being qualified for registration as an elector;
9. holding an office concerned with elections or electoral registers;
10. conviction of election offenses.

Questions as to the right of a person under these criteria to be a member of the Assembly were to be determined by the Supreme Court of the Gold Coast.

The same provisions determining qualification for membership in the Legislative Assembly were preserved in the 1954 Constitution.[19] The Independence Constitution of 1957 retained the substance of both the affirmative criteria of qualification and the grounds for disqualification, while substituting Ghanaian citizenship for status as a British subject or British protected person and changing the geographic focus of the disqualifying grounds from the earlier "in any part of Her Majesty's dominions" to "in Ghana."[20]

A major revision of the law relating to membership in the National Assembly was enacted in 1959. The National Assembly Act retained the three affirmative

[19] 1954 Constitution, secs. 29, 30, 32.
[20] 1957 Constitution, secs. 24, 25.

qualifications for membership[21] but changed in a number of respects the grounds for disqualification for election to the Assembly and the bases for termination of membership. Five of the earlier grounds were dropped:[22] acknowledging allegiance to a foreign power; involvement in government contracts; being an undischarged bankrupt; not being qualified for registration as an elector; and holding an office concerned with elections or electoral registers. Two new grounds of disqualification were introduced: conviction of an offense involving dishonesty,[23] unless a pardon had been given or at least five years had elapsed since termination of imprisonment or since conviction, if no sentence of imprisonment was imposed; being or having been within the previous five years under a Preventive Detention Act order.[24]

In addition to the grounds of disqualification for election to the National Assembly, the act further specified a number of reasons for termination of a member's tenure. These included all the grounds for disqualification for election, as well as the following additional bases:[25] expulsion from the Assembly under Section 40 of the act, which permitted such action on a resolution supported by at least two-thirds of the Members of the Assembly finding "conduct which, whether or not it amounts to contempt of Parliament, is so grossly

[21] The National Assembly Act, 1959, No. 78 of 1959, sec. 4(1).
[22] *Id.*, sec. 4(2).
[23] Whether an offense involved dishonesty was to be determined by the Chief Justice and his certificate on the question was made conclusive for all purposes. The National Assembly Act, supra note 21, sec. 4(3). The act made no provision for a hearing prior to this determination.
[24] The Preventive Detention Act, 1958, No. 17 of 1958, will be discussed fully later in this chapter. An order issued under this act was first made a ground of disqualification for membership in the National Assembly by the National Assembly (Disqualification) Act, 1959, No. 16 of 1959, which was repealed by the later National Assembly Act.
[25] The National Assembly Act, supra note 21, sec. 5(2). The second and third of these bases for terminating membership were first provided by the National Assembly (Disqualification) Act, 1959, No. 16 of 1959.

improper as to indicate that [a person] is unfit to remain a member . . ."; absence from twenty consecutive
sittings of the Assembly in the same session without
leave of absence from the Speaker, unless the Assembly
orders this provision not to apply;[26] a public declaration
in the course of Assembly proceedings of the member's
"intention of systematically refraining from attending
the proceedings of the Assembly," if the Speaker or presiding officer confirmed that the declaration was made
in his hearing. The Speaker, to whom the act assigned
significant functions in determining the application of
the sanction of exclusion from membership in the Assembly, was elected by majority vote of the Assembly for
a term which could be ended by a two-thirds vote of no
confidence and which terminated before the first sitting
after a dissolution.[27] In addition to the major sanction
of exclusion from membership, lesser penalties such as
exclusion from a day's sitting or reprimand and suspension for a period up to nine months could be imposed
in appropriate circumstances.[28]

The Republican Constitution of 1960 did not alter
the existing law relating to membership in the National
Assembly. In 1961, however, the 1959 legislation was
repealed by the National Assembly Act which, in the
main, preserved the former criteria for election to and
membership in the Assembly.[29] It did, however, re-
institute conviction of election offenses as a ground
for disqualification.[30]

The office of President was established under the Republican Constitution, and, for the first time since independence, executive power was lodged in an official

---

[26] In 1959, when Dr. Kofi A. Busia, leader of the United Party,
was on a three-month lecture tour of Europe, he was denied permission to absent himself from Parliament. No reason was given
for the Speaker's denial of leave of absence. *New York Times*,
July 6, 1959, p. 27, col. 2. On missing the specified number of
sittings, he was ousted from Parliament. *New York Times*, July
28, 1959, p. 5, col. 5.

[27] The National Assembly Act, supra note 21, sec. 8.

[28] *Id.*, secs. 37-39.   [29] Act 86.   [30] *Id.*, sec. 1(2).

who was not a member of the Assembly. The specified qualifications for election as President were minimal however: Ghanaian citizenship and attainment of thirty-five years of age.[31]

In summary, it may be said that the law of Ghana leaves access to responsible political office broadly open to those who can garner the support of the electorate. No ethnic, economic or religious barriers have been erected to limit the choice by the people of the chief executive or of their representatives in the legislative branch. The present legal provisions dealing with disqualification for election to the National Assembly and with exclusion from membership in that body are in the main rational and objective. They open significant opportunities, however, for a parliamentary majority or the executive to foreclose the election of persons unsympathetic to the dominant party and the government or to exclude them, even after election, from membership in the National Assembly. Primary examples are found in the disqualification of persons against whom Preventive Detention orders have been issued and of those found guilty of conduct falling short of contempt but so "grossly improper" as to indicate unfitness of membership in the Assembly. Thus far the Preventive Detention Act has been the principal vehicle for exclusion and disqualification for election.

THE FREEDOM AND RATIONALITY OF POLITICAL CHOICE

In the narrowest sense, representative institutions do not necessitate an assumption that the choice of representatives has resulted from rational processes of examination of evidence, discussion and persuasion. Probably the minimum assumption is that the choice on whatever basis made has been voluntary. Thus, in the assessment of supposedly representative institutions, it is essential to examine the safeguards, legal and other-

[31] Republican Constitution, art. 11(2)(a). Presidential Elections Act, 1960, Act 1, secs. 4, 5.

wise, of freedom of choice of political representatives. A part of this examination has already been made since the availability of the franchise and the criteria of eligibility for political office speak directly to the range of choice an electorate enjoys. Although the further assumption that choice of legislative representatives and executive officers involves rational communication and deliberation may be to some extent an idealization, it seems clear, at least, that to the extent these processes are curtailed for those inclined to use them, the underpinning of representative institutions has been seriously distorted. The objective of this section is to examine the extent of such distortion in the evolving legal order of Ghana. The discussion will be organized around the claims to reasonable freedom of movement, of assembly and association and of communication. Since denial of these claims by government frequently involves the processes of criminal law, it seems appropriate to examine certain of the procedures leading to penal sanctions in order to determine what safeguards have been erected against arbitrary action.

The most widely publicized enactment in post-independence Ghana is the Preventive Detention Act of 1958. Before proceeding to an analysis of the act itself, the deprivation of individual freedom of movement by order of executive agencies should be placed in a broader historical perspective. Historical antecedents of such executive power need not be traced beyond the disturbances in the Gold Coast in 1948. Under regulations[32] promulgated by the British Governor authorizing such action if he was "satisfied" that it was "expedient for securing the public safety and the maintenance of public order," six leaders of the United Gold Coast Convention, including Mr. Nkrumah, were arrested and

[32] Regulations 28 and 29 of the Emergency (General) (Amendment) (No. 2) Regulations. No. 2 of 1948. These regulations were issued pursuant to the Emergency Powers Order in Council, 1939, printed as Appendix in [1952], 1 STAT. INSTR. 621. Regulation 29 is reproduced as Appendix 9 to the Watson Commission Report, Colonial No. 231 (1948).

detained. The regulation under which the Removal Orders were issued provided that "no action, prosecution or other legal proceeding calling in question the legality of anything done under or by virtue of, or in pursuance, of this regulation or any Order or direction made or issued thereunder shall be brought, instituted or maintained, or shall be entertained by any Court at any time." The arrest and the detention of the six nationalist leaders were therefore carried out entirely as executive action, with no formal charges being made against the detainees and with no opportunity for review, judicial or otherwise, of the propriety of this action. The Watson Commission, after investigating the disturbances, recognized the reality of the emergency and concluded that the Government had acted in good faith. It declared, however, "that in so far as Regulation 29 purports to deprive His Majesty's Judges in the Gold Coast, of jurisdiction to entertain an application by a subject, detained otherwise than pursuant to a warrant issuing out of a Court of competent jurisdiction, the assumption of such a power was excessive to the occasion and we unhesitatingly condemn it."[33]

On the grant of independence to the Gold Coast in 1957, the Constitutional Order in Council continued in force for one year the Emergency Powers Order in Council of 1939 under which the detentions on executive order had been carried out in 1948.[34] Such special powers were, of course, no longer to be exercised by the metropolitan power; rather, they were formally exercisable by the Governor General, but in substance by the Prime Minister and Cabinet. Any regulations issued on the proclamation of an emergency by the executive were required to be laid before Parliament and, unless approved by resolution of Parliament within 28 days, were to cease to have legal effect.

The subsequent history of emergency powers legisla-

[33] Watson Commission Report, supra note 32, at 16.
[34] 1957 Constitution, sec. 82.

tion in Ghana will be considered later. As the 1948 experience demonstrated, such legislation could provide an adequate legal basis for the arrest and detention without charge of persons whose continued freedom of movement was disturbing to the Government. Instead of relying on this basis, however, the Nkrumah Government moved directly in mid-1958 for the enactment of special preventive detention legislation. Even in this step the Ghana Government did not innovate, for there was a long history of similar legislation in British India, and the Indian constitution of 1950 expressly granted to both the Union and the States authority to utilize preventive detention.[35] Of its genre, the Preventive Detention Act of Ghana[36] is quite stringent, and its provisions must be analyzed in detail.

The act authorized the Governor General (after the Republic, the President) to order the detention of any citizen of Ghana if he was "satisfied that the order is necessary to prevent that person acting in a manner prejudicial to (a) the defense of Ghana, (b) the relations of Ghana with other countries, or (c) the security of the State." The only rights afforded a person so detained were the right to be informed of the grounds of his detention within five days of its beginning and the right to make representations in writing to the Governor General (now the President) with respect to the detention order. In general, the maximum period of detention permitted by the original act was five years, and a person who had been detained under the act was not subject to any further order except on the ground of activities carried on since the first order was made. However, in certain circumstances, detention up to ten years was authorized. The Minister for Defense could, by published notice, direct any person against whom an order had been made and who the Minister had reason to believe was attempting to evade arrest to report

[35] See Tripathi, "Preventive Detention: The Indian Experience," 9 American Journal of Comparative Law 219 (1960).
[36] The Preventive Detention Act, 1958, No. 17 of 1958.

to the police; if the person failed to comply, he could be detained when arrested "during the Governor-General's pleasure for a period not exceeding double the period specified in the order." The Governor General was authorized to suspend the operation of any detention order subject to such conditions as he might specify for requiring the detainee to keep the authorities informed of his movements and for giving security for compliance with the conditions. The initial term of the Preventive Detention Act was five years, but resolutions of the National Assembly could renew it for further three-year terms.

The legislative authorization for preventive detention was thus straightforward and uncomplicated. The satisfaction of the Governor General (after the creation of the Republic of the President), of the necessity of detention to prevent action prejudicial to the three stated interests was not expressly made subject to review of any kind. Nor was any antecedent declaration of an emergency necessary. The "grounds" of detention of which the detainee had a right to be advised could conceivably range in their particularity from a general statement that possible conduct of the detainee imperiled one of the general interests, such as the defense of Ghana, to some particularization of the anticipated conduct. In a country where possibly 80 per cent of the population are illiterate, the opportunity to make written representations to the executive is of questionable value, particularly since the act makes no provision for the assistance of counsel in preparing the representations.

The first use of the Preventive Detention Act was made in November, 1958, in connection with an alleged conspiracy to assassinate Dr. Nkrumah and overthrow the Government. Political threats of this kind have been cited most frequently by the Government to justify detentions, but in September and October of 1960, a number of persons were detained on the ground of "gangsterism," which seemingly included molesting, beating and robbing people without any asserted political motivation.

It is impossible to present an accurate count of the persons detained under the Preventive Detention Act. Estimates range from a few hundred to thousands. In the first years of the act, detentions were publicly announced, but this practice has been discontinued. While some of the earliest detainees are still imprisoned, a number of persons have been released. For example, Dr. J.B. Danquah was detained after the Takoradi strike in October, 1961, released in June, 1962, and detained again in January, 1964. In May, 1962, Dr. Nkrumah announced the release of 160 detainees, most of whom had been engaged in the strikes in September, 1961. Another 152 persons were released in June, 1962. With further arrests to offset the releases, it seems likely that from 400 to 600 persons are still imprisoned under the Preventive Detention Act. An indeterminate additional number are held on short-term detentions under Criminal Procedure Code authorizations.

Attempts have been made to challenge the legal validity of the Preventive Detention Act and arrests made under it. Applications for writs of *habeas corpus* have relied on the contention that the English Habeas Corpus Act of 1816 subjected the grounds of detention to judicial review. In an opinion dated January 9, 1961, Mr. Justice Adumua-Bossman in the High Court, Accra, held that the English Act of 1816 was not in force in Ghana and that the applicants had no common law right to have the grounds of their detention reviewed.[37]

The principal challenge to the validity of the Preventive Detention Act relied on the Republican Constitution of 1960. The appeal from the refusal of the High Court to issue writs of *habeas corpus* was argued in the Supreme Court of Ghana in June, 1961. Baffour Osei

[37] In the Matter of the Arrest and Detention of Emmanuel Obed Kofi Dumoga and 12 others, High Court, Eastern Judicial Division, 9 January 1961 (Misc. 19/60).

Akoto, Senior Linguist to the Asantehene, and seven other Kumasi residents had been detained in November, 1959, under an order declaring the satisfaction of the Governor General that the order was necessary to prevent the detained persons from acting in a manner prejudicial to the security of the State. Application for a writ of *habeas corpus* on behalf of the detainees was made to the High Court and denied; appeal was then taken to the Supreme Court. There the argument for the appellants was made by Dr. J.B. Danquah, and for the Government by the then Attorney General, Mr. Geoffrey Bing. In support of his contention that the Preventive Detention Act was invalid under the new constitution, Dr. Danquah sought to make the President's declaration in Article 13(1) of the Republican Constitution into a bill of rights creating justiciable rights in individuals.[38] Specifically, he cited the declarations that

[38] "13(1) Immediately after his assumption of office the President shall make the following solemn declaration before the people—

"On accepting the call of the people to the high office of President of Ghana I .... solemnly declare my adherence to the following fundamental principles—

That the powers of Government spring from the will of the people and should be exercised in accordance therewith.

That freedom and justice should be honoured and maintained.

That the union of Africa should be striven for by every lawful means and, when attained, should be faithfully preserved.

That the Independence of Ghana should not be surrendered or diminished on any grounds other than the furtherance of African unity.

That no person should suffer discrimination on grounds of sex, race, tribe, religion or political belief.

That Chieftaincy in Ghana should be guaranteed and preserved.

That every citizen of Ghana should receive his fair share of the produce yielded by the development of the country.

That subject to such restrictions as may be necessary for preserving public order, morality or health, no person should be deprived of freedom of religion or speech, of the right to move and assemble without hindrance or of the right of access to courts of law.

That no person should be deprived of his property save where the public interest so requires and the law so provides."

"freedom and justice should be honoured and maintained"; "that no person should suffer discrimination on grounds of sex, race, tribe, religion or political belief"; and "that subject to such restrictions as may be necessary for preserving public order, morality or health, no person should be deprived of freedom of religion or speech, of the right to move and assemble without hindrance or of the right of access to courts of law." On the premise that these declarations established constitutionally protected individual rights limiting the legislative power of Parliament, Dr. Danquah urged that the Supreme Court exercise the power granted to it by Article 42(2) to adjudicate the question "whether an enactment was made in excess of the powers conferred on Parliament by or under the Constitution" and declare the Preventive Detention Act void. He recognized that certain of the "rights" articulated in Article 13 were subject to such restrictions "as may be necessary for preserving public order, etc.," but contended that the President should be required to show such necessity. He argued that the Preventive Detention Act, in permitting the President to issue detention orders "if satisfied" that critical interests were in danger, went beyond the constitutional competences of Parliament. It is of interest that Dr. Danquah made extensive use of American constitutional cases and materials in urging upon the Supreme Court an extensive power of judicial review of legislation.

Mr. Bing for the Government rejected the contention that the President's declaration on assumption of office was in legal effect a bill of individual rights limiting the power of Parliament. To him, the declaration was "a solemn statement of principles intended to prevent any person who cannot subscribe to them becoming President," a "goal to which every President must pledge himself." The declaration did not, in his view, affect legal relations cognizable by the courts, except perhaps in providing a generalized policy guide in the interpretation of ambiguous legislation. Rather, it merely imposed on the President a moral obligation, to be sanctioned, if at all, at the polls. The only restriction recognized by the Attorney General on the legislative competence of Parliament was imposed by Article 20, which foreclosed amendment of the entrenched clauses of the constitution without prior referendum approval and amendment of the nonentrenched clauses other than by an act exclusively devoted to that purpose. Consequently, the argument of the Attorney General limited the Supreme Court's power of review under Article 42(2) to determining whether these limits of Article 20 had been exceeded.

The judgment of the Supreme Court in the *Baffour Osei Akoto* case was a total victory for the Government.[39] The Court, speaking through the Chief Justice, Sir Arku Korsah, accepted the view that the English Habeas Corpus Act of 1816 is a statute of general application and thus in force in Ghana.[40] Nevertheless, it held that the act did not authorize a court to enquire into the truth of the grounds stated for executive action or into the reasonableness of the belief that such action was necessary, where the enabling legislation vested plenary discretion in the official taking the action.[41] While the Court conceded that the "good faith" of the action might become a justiciable issue, it carefully shifted the burden of proof to the party attacking the action on the ground of bad faith. "The courts must presume that high officers of State have acted in good faith in the discharge of their duties. It will be wrong

[39] Civil Appeal No. 42/61, dated 28 August 1961.

[40] The Habeas Corpus Act, 1964, Act 244, terminates the application of English *habeas corpus* legislation in Ghana and authorizes inquiries into the lawfulness of detention to be made by the High Court or, if the application calls into question the constitutionality of an Act of Parliament, by the Supreme Court. This act does not extend the scope of review in Preventive Detention Act cases beyond that allowed by *Baffour Osei Akoto*.

[41] The principal authority relied on by the court in support of this conclusion was the wartime English case of Liversidge v. Anderson [1941], 3 All Eng. Rep. 338.

288

in principle to enquire into the bona fide [sic] of Ministers of State on a mere allegation of bad faith by a petitioner. The court can only look into allegations of bad faith if there is positive evidence, which is singularly absent in this case."

The major contention of the detainees, that the Preventive Detention Act itself was unconstitutional, was firmly rejected by the Court. The argument rested on the view that the Presidential declaration in Article 13(1) of the Republican Constitution was a justiciable bill of rights limiting the legislative power of Parliament. In the view of the Court, such a contention was based "on a misconception of the intent, purpose and effect of Article 13(1) the provisions of which are . . . similar to the Coronation Oath taken by the Queen of England during the Coronation Service. In the one case the President is required to make a solemn declaration, in the other the Queen is required to take a solemn oath. Neither the oath nor the declaration can be said to have a statutory effect of an enactment of Parliament. The suggestion that the declarations made by the President on assumption of office constitute a 'Bill of Rights' in the sense in which the expression is understood under the Constitution of the United States of America is therefore untenable. . . .

"It will be observed that Article 13(1) is in the form of a personal declaration by the President and is in no way part of the general law of Ghana. In the other parts of the Constitution where a duty is imposed the word 'shall' is used, but throughout the declaration the word used is 'should.' In our view the declaration merely represents the goal to which every President must pledge himself to attempt to achieve. It does not represent a legal requirement which can be enforced by the courts.

"On examination of the said declarations with a view to finding out how any could be enforced we are satisfied that the provisions of Article 13(1) do not create legal obligations enforceable by a court of law. The declarations, however, impose on every President a moral obligation, and provide a political yardstick by which conduct of the Head of State can be measured by the electorate. The people's remedy for any departure from the principles of the declaration, is through the use of the ballot box, and not through the courts."

Thus far, the *Baffour Osei Akoto* decision is the only pronouncement by the Supreme Court on the Republican Constitution. The importance of the view adopted on Article 13(1) extends well beyond the problem of preventive detention. The decision is explicit that the only limitations on the legislative power of Parliament are those expressed in Article 20 of the constitution: that the entrenched clauses cannot be altered except on the authorization of the people expressed in a referendum and nonentrenched clauses except by an act stated to be one to amend the constitution and containing only provisions effecting the amendment.

The impact of the Preventive Detention Act is not exhausted in the actual arrest and detention of citizens. Even after detention has been terminated, it can have an important influence on the political role of the former detainee, and indirectly on larger groups in the society, in limiting the range of their political choice. As has been noted, the National Assembly (Disqualification) Act (1959)[42] provided that no person should be qualified for election as a Member of Parliament against whom a Preventive Detention Act order was in force or had been in force at any time within five years preceding the election. The same act provided that the seat of any Member of Parliament should become vacant if an order under the Preventive Detention Act should be made against him. Both provisions were retroactive, that is, applicable in relation to any detention order

[42] No. 16 of 1959. This act was repealed by the National Assembly Act, 1959, No. 78 of 1959, but its substantive provisions were incorporated into the repealing act. These provisions are now incorporated in the National Assembly Act, 1961, Act 86, secs. 1, 2.

even though made prior to the passage of the National Assembly (Disqualification) Act. Thus, the executive is able to control quite fully the continued membership of opposition members in the National Assembly. A similar basis of disqualification for membership in various local government councils was provided by the Municipal and other Councils (Disqualification for Membership) Act (1959), but this disqualification resulted only from Preventive Detention Act orders currently in force.[43]

The Preventive Detention Act was significantly amended in 1962. The original provision had limited the ground for issuance of a second detention order against a person to "activities in which that person may have been concerned and which have been carried on at times subsequent to the date on which the first . . . order was made."[44] This limitation was repealed in 1962 and the following language substituted: "The President may, by executive instrument in the form of an order, if he is satisfied that any person who has been released after being detained under this act has subsequently concerned himself with activities prejudicial to [the defense of Ghana, the relations of Ghana with other countries or the security of the State], in respect of each time he so concerns himself, detain such person for a period not exceeding five years."[45] Persons against whom such orders were made were disqualified from voting in an election for, and for election to, the National Assembly or any local government council.

The original act had expressly limited its life to five years, subject to the possibility of extensions for periods of three years by resolution of the National Assembly. This entire provision was repealed by the 1962 Act.[46]

[43] No. 26 of 1959. This provision is now included in the Local Government Act, 1961, Act 54, sec. 7.
[44] The Preventive Detention Act, 1958, No. 17 of 1958, sec. 4(1).
[45] The Preventive Detention (Amendment) Act, 1962, Act 132, sec. 3.
[46] *Id.*, sec. 4.

Thus, the legislation authorizing preventive detention was established on the books as a continuing act, the repeal of which would require a regular Act of Parliament. This change did not necessarily assure longer life to the system of preventive detention in Ghana. It may, however, have symbolic significance, indicating an acceptance of the system as a continuing and not *prima facie* transient aspect of Ghanaian life.

The necessity for the 1962 amendments is not readily apparent from the text. As has been noted earlier, legal authorization for using Preventive Detention Act orders to effect political disqualification already existed. Similarly, the continued life of the act could be assured under its original terms. The remaining problem, which may have prompted the 1962 amendments, was the retention of detainees beyond the five-year period originally authorized. The central amendment in 1962 does not directly meet this problem, since literally it was limited to persons who had been released after detention. The duration of the period of release was not specified, however, and it is therefore arguable that the Government could release a detainee only to pick him up under a second order at the prison gate. Such an approach finds some support in the much less definite language dealing with grounds of a second order used in the 1962 amendment. It will be recalled that the original act required that any second order should be based on "activities in which [the detained person] may have been concerned and which have been carried on at times subsequent to the date on which the first mentioned order was made." The amendment merely required that the person released have "subsequently concerned himself with activities prejudicial, etc." Arguably, "concern" does not necessitate any activity, any objective involvement; interest or sympathy might arguably suffice. If the Government's intention was to deal with the problem of detention beyond five years through the 1962 amendments, there appears to have been a later determination that that intention was not effectively carried out. In November, 1963, the solution was accomplished directly by an amendment which expressly authorized the extension of an earlier detention for a further five years.[47]

A comprehensive new Preventive Detention Act was passed in May, 1964, and the earlier legislation was repealed.[48] The new act consolidated with certain amendments the former enactments, but the scheme of preventive detention was not greatly changed. When satisfied that it is necessary to prevent action prejudicial to the defense of Ghana, relations with other countries or the security of the State, the President is authorized to issue detention orders or restriction orders. The latter have the effect of restricting the movements of the affected person for a period not exceeding five years within such place or area as the order may specify. A restriction order may also impose conditions on employment or business and on the restricted person's association or communication with others. The President is authorized to extend the period of detention or restriction, at any time before the expiration of the initial order, for a further period of five years. Power is continued in the President to order any person who he believes is attempting to avoid arrest after the issuance of an order against him to report to the police. Failure to report in such circumstances can result in detention or restriction for ten years. The act is not limited in duration and appears to be a stable feature of Ghanaian law.

In addition to detentions under the Preventive Detention Act itself, other possibilities were opened up by an amendment to the Criminal Procedure Code in 1962.[49] This granted to the police the power to detain persons arrested without warrants for 28 days or such longer

[47] The Preventive Detention (Amendment) Act, 1963, Act 199.
[48] The Preventive Detention Act, 1964, Act 240. See pp. 446-48 below.
[49] The Criminal Procedure (Amendment) (No. 3) Act, 1962, Act 139.

period as the Attorney General may determine. The written consent of the Attorney General to such detentions is formally required. While official figures are unavailable, it appears that extensive use of this detention power was made during the disturbances in late 1962 and thereafter. It seems doubtful that the police regularly secured the consent of the Attorney General to such detentions, though reliable evidence on this point is unavailable. Informal and illegal police detentions for periods exceeding 28 days seem to have been tolerated out of fear that any challenge would provoke a formal Preventive Detention Act order.

The Preventive Detention Act can be used only against citizens of Ghana. The traditional method of dealing with undesirable aliens is deportation, for which legislative authorization existed under the colonial regime in the Gold Coast. The deportation of aliens was authorized either on the recommendation of a judge or magistrate after conviction of an offense for which the court had power to impose imprisonment without the option of a fine, or when the Governor in Council deemed it "conducive to the public good to make a deportation order against any alien."[50] If the latter provision was invoked, the ordinance provided for no judicial intervention in the entire proceedings; nor was provision made for notification to the person affected of the grounds on which his deportation was ordered. A separate ordinance authorized deportation of British subjects, other than natives of the Gold Coast, if they had been connected with certain serious crimes, were destitute or had been conducting themselves "so as to be dangerous to peace, good order, good government or public morals."[51] The burden of proof that a person was a native of the Gold Coast, and thus exempt from deportation, was on the person claiming the exemption.

[50] Aliens Ordinance, No. 20 of 1935, as amended, Cap. 49, 2 Laws of the Gold Coast 223 (1951).

[51] Immigrant British Subjects (Deportation) Ordinance, No. 26 of 1945, as amended, Cap. 50, 2 Laws of the Gold Coast 227 (1951).

In the case of British subjects, however, that ordinance required notice to the person affected of the grounds of the deportation order and a judicial hearing in which the person or his attorney had the right to cross-examine the witnesses against him and to call witnesses in his own behalf. The findings of the court in such a hearing and the court's recommendation, if any, were not binding upon the Governor in Council, who might nevertheless order the deportation if satisfied that such an order could be lawfully made.

Although the pre-independence ordinances were retained in force by the 1957 Constitution, shortly thereafter they were repealed by a new Deportation Act.[52] Under this legislation, no citizen of Ghana was liable to deportation, but the burden of proving citizenship was placed on the person claiming the exemption.[53] The grounds upon which deportation could be ordered were 1) conviction of certain major crimes and recommendation of deportation by the convicting court; 2) judicial ascertainment that a person was destitute, without visible means of support, of unsound mind or a mental defective, or a prostitute, and 3) declaration by the Governor General that the affected person is one "whose presence in Ghana is not conducive to the public good."[54] It should be noted that the first two grounds required judicial action in a hearing in which the affected person presumably enjoyed a full opportunity to be represented by counsel, to cross-examine the witnesses against him and call witnesses of his own, and to have some access to higher courts for review. The third ground, however, required only executive action, and the person whose continued presence in Ghana was declared contrary to the public good was not entitled to notification of the specific charges against him nor to a review of the declaration and order, judicial or otherwise. It is also worthy of note that any deportation order might include the dependents of the person to

[52] The Deportation Act, 1957, No. 14 of 1957.
[53] *Id.*, sec. 3.   [54] *Id.*, sec. 4.

295

be deported if the Governor General so ordered.[55] This seemingly was true without respect to which of the three principal grounds of deportation was used. The powers granted to the Governor General by the Deportation Act became exercisable after the creation of the republic by the President.

In 1959, the Deportation Act was amended to permit the Governor General, in instances where a deportation order was not executed within six months or he was satisfied that deportation was for any reason impracticable, to suspend the deportation order and substitute a supervision order. The latter, if issued, could contain conditions relating to the area within which the person would be required to reside, his involvement in political activities and his periodic reporting to the police.[56] Criminal penalties were provided for violation of such a supervision order. The Governor General was also authorized to cancel the supervision order, thereby reviving the deportation order. Supervision orders were permitted to continue in effect for five years.

The pre-Republic deportation statutes have been continued in effect. The powers that before the Republic were formally vested in the Governor General are now vested in the President acting on the advice of the Cabinet.[57]

Since independence in 1957, the Ghana Government has made substantial use of deportation. While occasionally directed at foreign businessmen, or at the Anglican Bishop of Accra, and in February, 1964, against six members of the academic staff of the University of Ghana, deportation has in most instances been used against Africans, many of them long-term residents of Ghana, who were believed to be associated with political opposition to the Government. Two instances of such deportations and the supplementary legal techniques invoked by the Government may be mentioned.

[55] *Id.*, sec. 5(3).
[56] Deportation (Amendment) Act, 1959, No. 65 of 1959.
[57] Constitution (Consequential Provisions) Act, 1960, C.A. 8, sec. 23 and Second Schedule.

In July, 1957, deportation orders were issued against Alhaji Amadu Baba and Alhaji Othmen Larden Lalemie, who were prominent in the Moslem Association Party in Ashanti. The Government contended that both men were Nigerians. Claiming Ghanaian citizenship and therefore immunity from deportation, Baba and Lalemie sought an injunction against the execution of the deportation orders. When the matter came up for hearing in the High Court in Kumasi, a large crowd of opposition supporters demonstrated around the court. Mr. Geoffrey Bing for the Government assured the court that the deportations would not be carried out pending investigation of the claims of Ghanaian citizenship, and on this basis, the hearing was recessed. The two men, under arrest, were transferred to Accra.

On August 23, 1957, Parliament received and enacted a special bill authorizing the deportation of Baba and Lalemie "notwithstanding the provisions of the Deportation Act, 1957."[58] Proceedings in any court to impugn the validity of the earlier deportation orders were declared "automatically determined." Further, ministerial orders issued to implement the special act were immune from review in any court. On this authorization, Baba and Lalemie were deported to Nigeria. The Government justified this summary action by saying that the deportations were necessary in the public interest and that the abuse of counsel and the court incident to the hearing on the challenge to the deportations had created a deplorable situation. On resumption of the hearing in Kumasi, the High Court held that it had no authority to inquire into the validity of the special act under which the deportations had been carried out, and the proceedings were thus terminated.

Four other persons against whom deportation orders were issued in October, 1958, claimed Ghanaian citizenship. On their behalf a *habeas corpus* proceeding was begun to establish their citizenship and thus protect

[58] The Deportation (Othman Larden and Amadu Baba) Act, 1957, No. 19 of 1957.

them from deportation. While the action was pending, the four were deported. Thereupon the court issued contempt citations against the Minister for the Interior (Krobo Edusei) and the Police Commissioner (E.R.T. Madjitey). When the court found these officials to be in contempt, Parliament promptly responded with an act providing that they should "be indemnified from all penalties for contempt of court and exonerated from all other liabilities in respect of any action taken by them in carrying out the deportation orders. . . ."[59] While deploring what it described as "the Executive's interfering with its functions," the Divisional Court regarded the Indemnity Act as fully sufficient to foreclose any action consequent to its finding of contempt.

In determining the incidence of the Preventive Detention Act and the Deportation Act, the question of citizenship is critical. In addition to citizenship by birth and descent, the Ghana Nationality and Citizenship Act[60] provided for the acquisition of Ghanaian citizenship by citizens of Commonwealth countries and British protected persons through a registration procedure and acquisition of citizenship by aliens through naturalization. Citizenship so acquired could be taken away by ministerial order on a number of more or less objective grounds such as fraudulent application, trading with the enemy or sentence to imprisonment for at least twelve months. In the present context, however, the relevant ground of deprivation of citizenship is the "satisfaction" of the Minister that the citizen "has shown himself by act or speech to be disloyal *or disaffected* towards Her Majesty or the Government of Ghana."[61] (Italics mine.) The act gave no indication of the meaning of the term "disaffected." Republican legislation substituted "Ghana" for "Her Majesty,"[62] and

[59] The Deportation (Indemnity) Act, 1958, No. 47 of 1958.
[60] The Ghana Nationality and Citizenship Act, 1957, No. 1 of 1957, now replaced by The Ghana Nationality Act, 1961, Act 62.
[61] *Id.*, sec. 17(3)(a).
[62] Constitution (Consequential Provisions) Act, 1960, C.A. 8, sec. 23 and Second Schedule.

the later Ghana Nationality Act of 1961[63] substitutes "disloyal or disaffected toward the Republic or its Government." The dichotomy thus preserved between "the Republic" and "the Government of Ghana" and between "disloyalty" and "disaffection" raises the question whether political opposition to the incumbent Government may be a sufficient ground for depriving naturalized persons of their citizenship. Unfortunately, no data on such deprivations are available.

Significantly, the present Nationality Act makes no provision for an antecedent hearing in connection with the Minister's order depriving a person of his citizenship. Indeed, the act expressly provides that "the Minister shall not be required to assign any reason for any decision taken under any provisions of this Act, and no such decision shall be subject to appeal to or to review in any court."[64] While the Minister is authorized to issue implementing regulations, which might appropriately establish orderly and fair procedures for reaching critical decisions, it appears that no regulations have ever been issued under the 1961 Act.

We turn now to a consideration of another basic freedom relating to the rationality of political choice and the reality of representative institutions. This is the freedom of persons to assemble and form associations for the protection and advancement of common interests. The first relevant observation is a general negative —none of the constitutional instruments of the Gold Coast or Ghana has expressly recognized and protected a right of assembly and association. The President's solemn declaration before the people, required by Article 13 of the Republican Constitution, affirms the right to move and assemble without hindrance, but, as has been noted, this lacks juridical effect. The status of such a right has therefore always depended upon the legislative will. In fact, however, neither during the colonial period nor since independence have the

63 Act 62, sec. 11(d).   64 *Id.*, sec. 14.

legislative organs attempted to define generally the scope of the privilege of assembly and association. The usual assumptions of a democratic society would in these circumstances, therefore, lead to the conclusion that freedom to assemble and form associations exists except insofar as curtailment may be authorized in specific circumstances. We thus turn to the various enactments which may authorize some limitation of the assumed freedom.

The Ghana Criminal Code defines an unlawful assembly as a gathering of three or more persons with "intent to commit an offence, or [persons who] being assembled with intent to carry out some common purpose, conduct themselves in such a manner as to cause persons in the neighbourhood reasonably to fear that the persons so assembled will commit a breach of the peace, or will by such assembly needlessly and without reasonable occasion provoke other persons to commit a breach of the peace."[65] Participation in such an assembly is a misdemeanor. On the other hand, obstructing or dispersing with violence or disturbing any lawful assembly is also a misdemeanor.[66] Aside from the troublesome possibility of characterizing an assembly as unlawful solely because it may "needlessly and without reasonable occasion" provoke others to breach the peace, the basic criminal law restriction on assembly should create no difficulty for persons wishing to assemble for conventional political activities.

Perhaps the most effective control of assembly for political purposes has been achieved under police regulation of the use of loud-speakers and the collection of money at meetings. The use of loud-speaker vans by political parties to attract a crowd has an obvious relevance to the police responsibility for the control of traffic, and legislation authorizing such control has long existed.[67] During the mid-fifties, police licensing of pub-

[65] Criminal Code, 1960, Act 29, sec. 201(1).
[66] Id., sec. 204.
[67] Police Force Ordinance, Cap. 37, sec. 54(3), 2 Laws of the Gold Coast 98 (1951).

lic meetings and processions and the use of sound equipment was fully covered by regulations.[68] Without loud-speaker vans, the assembly of more than a few people was extremely difficult or impossible. A police permit was also required for any collection of money at a public meeting, and at the end of each year the organization making the collection was required to report to the police its total receipts. Through such collections much political activity was financed. Denial of permits for collections therefore imposed an effective restriction on meetings for political purposes. The necessity of applying to the police for a permit to hold a meeting or procession in a public place is now imposed by the Public Order Act of 1961,[69] which also authorizes the Minister for the Interior to impose a curfew when he is "satisfied that it is necessary in the interests of public order or the maintenance of the public peace."[70] Under the reasoning of the Supreme Court in the *Baffour Osei Akoto* case, the grounds of the Minister's satisfaction are not reviewable.

Mention has been made already of the Emergency Powers Order in Council (1939), which the 1957 Constitution of Ghana continued in force for twelve months. It is quite clear that under regulations issued by the Governor (after independence by the Governor General) under this order, assemblies could be forbidden or otherwise regulated, as was done during the disturbances of 1948.[71] There would seem to be no doubt that such regulations legally could have forbidden or curtailed the freedom to form associations as well. Shortly

[68] The Public Meetings and Processions Regulations, L.N. 415 of 1954.
[69] Act 58, secs. 6, 7, as amended by The Public Order (Amendment) Act, 1963, Act 165.
[70] *Id.*, sec. 11(1).
[71] Emergency (General) Regulations, No. 13 of 1948, Laws of the Gold Coast, 1948, with amendments, Nos. 15, 19, 20, 21, 23 and 25 of 1948; terminated by Emergency (General) (Revocation) Regulations, No. 46 of 1948.

after independence, the operation of the Order in Council in Ghana was terminated by a new Emergency Powers Act.[72] On the declaration by the Governor General (after the Republic, by the President acting on the advice of the Cabinet) of a state of emergency of either type, he acquired power to issue such regulations, superseding ordinary law, as might appear to him "necessary or expedient for securing the public safety, the defence of Ghana, the maintenance of public order and the suppression of mutiny, rebellion and riot, and for maintaining supplies and services essential to the life of the community."[73] Any regulations issued by the Governor General were required to be put before Parliament and if not confirmed by Parliament within 28 days, they would cease to have effect. The specific but non-exhaustive list of subjects with which regulations might deal did not mention assembly and association, but there is no reason to doubt that they could be regulated.

The 1957 legislation was repealed by the Emergency Powers Act of 1961.[74] This was largely a simplified redrafting of the earlier act, differing little in substance. One change of interest, however, is the elimination of the former requirement that emergency regulations be confirmed by Parliament within 28 days. The current act merely requires that any regulations issued by the President be laid before Parliament.

Only limited use has thus far been made of emergency powers in Ghana. A local emergency declared in parts of Accra in 1958 illustrates, however, the impact of these special powers on freedom of assembly

[72] The Emergency Powers Act, 1957, No. 28 of 1957. Detailed analysis of this act is unnecessary here. It suffices to say that the act distinguished a general state of emergency from one limited in nature or local in scope.

[73] *Id.*, sec. 5(1). These are the purposes of regulations in a general state of emergency. If the emergency declared is limited or local, a somewhat narrower pattern of interests is at stake and the regulatory power is somewhat more limited.

[74] Act 56.

and association.[75] The regulations[76] prohibited the holding in specified areas of any public meeting or procession, as well as the use of any loud-speaker van or public-address system. Later, the regulations were amended to permit the use of such amplifying equipment on the issuance of a permit by the Commissioner of Police.[77]

At the time of the politically motivated strike in Sekondi-Takoradi in September, 1961, an emergency was declared and a sweeping pattern of emergency controls was imposed on the area. These prohibited public processions and meetings imposed a 6 P.M. to 6 A.M. curfew, authorized stringent traffic controls and the requisitioning of certain kinds of property such as foodstuffs and fuels.[78] These restrictions were revoked, however, after only four days of operation.[79]

The most extensive use of emergency powers occurred after the assassination attempt on President Nkrumah at Kulungugu in August, 1962. An emergency was declared in the Accra and Tema areas[80] and stringent regulations were issued.[81] The Minister responsible for internal security was given authority to ban processions and meetings either public or private. In addition to other powers existing under the Preventive Detention Act, the President was given power to detain persons who he was satisfied were concerned in acts inimical to public safety and order. Power to issue removal orders requiring residence in an approved place was also granted to the President. More limited powers to detain suspected persons for periods up to ten days were

[75] Proclamation, L.N. 147/1958. This emergency was declared ended and the regulations canceled after about six weeks. Proclamation, L.N. 189/1958.

[76] The Local State of Emergency (Accra) Regulations, 1958, L.N. 148/1958.

[77] The Local State of Emergency (Accra) Regulations (No. 2), 1958, L.N. 175/1958.

[78] L.I. 143/1961, L.I. 144/1961 and Ex. Instr. 150-155/1961.

[79] L.I. 148/1961, L.I. 149/1961 and Ex. Instr. 163-168/1961.

[80] Proclamation, L.I. 214, effective September 22, 1962.

[81] The Emergency Regulations, 1962, L.I. 215.

given to the police. While the curfew imposed on Accra and Tema was lifted after approximately one month, the emergency continues and the special powers are still available.

In the exercise of powers under the Emergency Powers Act, executive action affects other freedoms relevant to this inquiry as well as assembly and association. For example, particularized restraints on freedom of movement have been imposed. During local emergencies in Dormaa State[82] in 1958 and in Kumasi[83] in 1957, named persons were prohibited from entering designated areas under threat of penal sanctions. The limitation on communication during the local emergency in Accra has been mentioned earlier.

A major legislative impingement on freedom of association was the Avoidance of Discrimination Act of 1957.[84] Such legislation was first publicly proposed in September, 1957, by the then Minister for the Interior, Krobo Edusei, after several weeks of intense political tension arising from the arrest and deportation of the two Muslim leaders in Kumasi.[85] Prior to the passage of the act, three political parties and three regional groups that might have fallen within its restrictions joined together to form the United Party, which they believed would not be vulnerable to the strictures of the proposed act.[86] The act has not in fact been used by the Government, but nonetheless it remains a part of the law of Ghana. Its relevance to this study necessitates an analysis of its provisions.

The preamble to the act declares its purpose to be "to prohibit organizations using or engaging in tribal,

[82] Proclamation, L.N. 326/1958; The Local State of Emergency (Dormaa State) Regulations, 1958, L.N. 327/1958; Local State of Emergency (Dormaa State) (Amendment) Regulation, 1961, L.I. 115.
[83] Proclamation, L.N. 261/1957; The Local State of Emergency (Kumasi Municipal Area) Regulations, L.N. 236/1959.
[84] The Avoidance of Discrimination Act, 1957, No. 38 of 1957.
[85] *New York Times*, Sept. 29, 1957, p. 35, col. 1.
[86] *New York Times*, Dec. 12, 1957, p. 20, col. 6.

regional, racial or religious propaganda to the detriment of any other community, or securing the election of persons on account of their tribal, regional, or religious affiliations and for other purposes connected therewith." In considering the substantive provisions of the act, two important definitions should be kept in mind. "Community" is defined as including "any body or group of persons, having a common tribal or racial origin or because of their birth or upbringing in any region, locality or place whether in Ghana or any other country, associating together in Ghana." "Organization" includes any "club, institution, political party, or other association of persons by whatever name called." The basic provision of the act makes it an offense for "any organization whose membership is substantially limited to one community or religious faith to have as one of its objects the exposure of any other organization however constituted or of any part of the community, to hatred, contempt or ridicule on account of their community or religion." Persons participating in the management or control of offending organizations are subject on conviction to criminal sanctions. Further, the fact that an organization or part of a community has been exposed by another to hatred, contempt or ridicule is made *prima facie* evidence of the latter's object. Organizations whose leaders are convicted of an offense under the act are subject to prohibition by the Minister for Local Government. Before considering other important prohibitions of the act, the foregoing provisions should be analyzed more carefully. Superficially, the offense created appears to involve racial or religious bias whose elimination would contribute directly to social harmony and the rationality of political choice. If the terms of the act are examined carefully, however, in the light of the structure of Ghanaian society and political forces, the possibilities for using the act for political suppression emerge.

It should be remembered that much of the opposition to the Convention People's Party has been regionally organized and has found its basic loyalties in the tribal order, an order that has profound religious overtones as well. Thus, for example, an organization in Ashanti would be apt to restrict its membership substantially to one "community" as defined above, and, since that community has religious significance, to one religious faith. Would criticism by such an organization of a political party like the Convention People's Party expose it to prohibition under the act? It will be noted that the criticized or ridiculed organization need not be constituted in any particular way; it is necessary only that it be exposed to hatred, contempt or ridicule because of its "community or religion." One element of Ashanti suspicion of the C.P.P. has been the fear of domination by the coastal area, the pre-independence Colony, where C.P.P. strength has always been heavily concentrated. Any political activity against the C.P.P. invoking this fear might arguably be criticism on account of the "community" of the C.P.P. Such interpretative possibilities are obviously speculative, since the act has not been authoritatively interpreted by the courts. The illustration merely suggests the hazard in such vague grants of power to control organizations.

Even more directly aimed at the regional opposition to the C.P.P. is the provision permitting the President, on the advice of the Cabinet, to declare illegal any organization "established substantially for the direct or indirect benefit or advancement of the interests of any particular community or religious faith." Such organizations are prohibited from organizing or operating for the purposes of engaging in any election. Symbols or names identifiable with any particular community or religious faith are also prohibited. Jurisdiction is granted to the High Court for supervising the dissolution of any prohibited organization. A highly significant provision authorizes the Minister for Local Government to require any organization which in his opinion engages in politics to disclose to him its rules and whether it permits the use of a particular symbol or name. If the rules of the organization are found in any way discriminatory as to membership by reason only of community or religion, the Minister may require amendment under threat of penal sanctions. Perhaps more important than the ultimate threat of these sanctions is the possibility of using these provisions to require significant disclosures by opposition political groups. Finally, it should be noted that only with the consent in writing of the Attorney General can prosecutions under the act be initiated.

Thus far, the merger of several opposition groups into a single United Party has forestalled use of the powers granted the Government under the Avoidance of Discrimination Act. The loss of leaders in the United Party, largely through the Government's use of the Preventive Detention Act, may again create a situation in which political opposition, if any, will be carried out through smaller regional or local groups. At such time the act may take on fresh significance in the political life of the country. It should be noted that, unlike the Preventive Detention Act in its original form, this anti-discrimination legislation was not enacted for a term.

The possibility that political activity will in the future be organized in regional, religious or social groups, not political parties, was further strengthened by the amendments to the Republican Constitution effected in 1964. Since the plebiscite of 1960, the United Party has existed in name only; no national election has been held and the United Party has not contested Parliamentary by-elections or local government contests. In fact, if not in law, Ghana has been for several years a one-party state.

A private member's motion calling for the establishment in Ghana of a one-party system was adopted by the National Assembly in September, 1962. While Dr.

Nkrumah expressed support for such a move, no legal steps to implement the motion were taken immediately. In ordering the referendum on constitutional amendments in January, 1964, however, the proposal for a one-party system was put before the people.[87]

Following approval of the amendments in the referendum, the constitution was altered to insert the following Article (1A):

> (1) In conformity with the interests, welfare and aspirations of the People, and in order to develop the organisational initiative and the political activity of the People, there shall be one national party which shall be the vanguard of the People in their struggle to build a socialist society and which shall be the leading core of all organisations of the people.
>
> (2) The national party shall be the "Convention People's Party."[88]

Subsection (1) which provided for a national party was entrenched, while the designation of the C.P.P. as the national party was not. Thus, the C.P.P. is constitutionally the national party, but in this respect the constitution is subject to amendment by ordinary legislation in the form required by Article 20(2).

While the intention of the amendment clearly seems to have been to constitute Ghana a one-party state, the language adopted is curiously ambiguous. Provision is made for "one national party" to which certain functions are attributed, but it would not be inconsistent with the literal terms to recognize the legitimacy of other "national parties" distinguished only by the lack of those functions. Furthermore, it could be argued that regional parties, as distinguished from national parties, remain permissible under the constitutional amendment. At this time, no occasion for resolving these ambiguities is in prospect. If in fact any political

[87] Referendum (Amendment) Order, 1964, L.I. 332.
[88] The Constitution (Amendment) Act, 1964, Act 224, sec. 2.

party other than the C.P.P. is now illegal in Ghana, new significance may be attached to the Avoidance of Discrimination Act as a device for controlling substitute forms of organization.

The possibility of proliferation of organizations without avowed political purposes but potentially serving as the focal points of opposition seems to have motivated a significant addition to the Criminal Code after the constitutional amendment on a one-party system was adopted. The new section provides as follows:

(1) Whenever the President is satisfied with respect to any organisation either—
   (a) that its objects or activities are contrary to the public good; or
   (b) that there is danger of the organisation being used for purposes prejudicial to the public good, he may, if he thinks fit, by executive instrument declare that organisation to be a prohibited organisation.

(2) Where an organisation is declared under the foregoing subsection to be a prohibited organisation no person shall—
   (a) summon a meeting of members or managers of such an organisation;
   (b) attend or cause any person to attend any meeting in the capacity of a member or manager of such an organisation;
   (c) publish any notice or advertisement relating to any such meeting;
   (d) invite persons to support such an organisation;
   (e) make any contribution or loan to funds held or to be held by or for the benefit of such an organisation or accept any such contribution or loan; or
   (f) give any guarantee in respect of such funds as aforesaid.

(3) Any person who contravenes any of the pro-

visions of the foregoing subsection shall be guilty of an offence and shall, on conviction, be liable to a fine not exceeding one hundred pounds, or to imprisonment for a term not exceeding one year or to both such fine and imprisonment.

(4) Upon application being made by the Attorney-General the High Court may with respect to any organisation declared under this section to be a prohibited organisation, make such orders as appear to the Court just and equitable for the winding up and dissolving or the disposition of any property or assets held by such organisation.

(5) For the purposes of this section "manager" means, in relation to any organisation, any officer of the organisation, and any person taking part in the management or control of the organisation or holding or purporting to hold a position of management or control therein.[89]

The reservoir of practically unlimited and nonreviewable discretion created in the President by this enactment justifies the conclusion that no right of association or organization exists under the law of Ghana today.

The various civil liberties affecting the rationality of political choice are inextricably interwoven. Virtually all must be recognized for any one to be meaningful. Freedom of movement has limited value for political activity if the speech of the person moving is effectively bridled; nor does free speech mean much within the walls of a prison. Only for analytical purposes, are the several liberties dealt with separately. With this caution we turn now to the status of free speech and other expression in Ghana.

Again it is appropriate to start with a negative. During neither the colonial nor the post-independence period has freedom of speech been constitutionally protected. Arguably the provision of the 1957 Constitution that "subject to such restrictions as may be imposed for the

[89] The Criminal Code (Amendment) Act, 1964, Act 228, sec. 5.

purposes of preserving public order, morality or health, no law shall deprive any person of his freedom of conscience or the right freely to profess, practise or propagate any religion"[90] guaranteed freedom of expression within at least a narrow area. The primary objective of this provision seems to have been religious freedom, however, rather than freedom of expression or communication within the wider context of political activity. The Republican Constitution of 1960 requires the President to include in his declaration before the people a statement that "subject to such restrictions as may be necessary for preserving public order, morality or health, no person shall be deprived of freedom of religion or speech, of the right to move and assemble without hindrance or of the right of access to courts of law."[91] As interpreted by the Supreme Court in *Baffour Osei Akoto* this is merely an executive declaration of political ideals which lacks juridical effect in guaranteeing individual rights. Within Parliament itself, the Republican Constitution does guarantee freedom of speech, the entrenched Article 21(3) declaring: "There shall be freedom of speech, debate and proceedings in the National Assembly and that freedom shall not be impeached or questioned in any court or place out of the Assembly." Even prior to the Republican Constitution, however, statutes had offered assurance of free expression in the National Assembly.[92] No similar guarantee for free expression in the wider context of political, intellectual or literary activity is provided.

In a number of ways the law of Ghana has imposed particularized restraints on freedom of expression or communication. The year 1959 was especially productive of such legislation. On his arrival in Britain on June 29, 1959, Dr. K. A. Busia, leader of the op-

[90] 1957 Constitution, sec. 31(3).
[91] Republican Constitution, Art. 13(1).
[92] The Legislative Assembly (Powers and Privileges) Ordinance, 1956, No. 20 of 1956; The National Assembly Act, 1959, No. 78 of 1959.

position United Party, was reported to have said that his life was in danger in Ghana, that police called regularly at his home and that he was uncertain whether he would return to Ghana; he tried, however, to avoid any impression that he had run away.[93] There would seem to be a direct connection between the Busia interview and Parliament's enactment of the Offences Against the State (False Reports) Act, 1959.[94] This act amended the Criminal Code to provide that "whoever communicates to any other person, whether by word of mouth or in writing or by any other means, any false statement or report which is likely to injure the credit or reputation of Ghana or the Government of Ghana, and which he knows or has reason to believe is false, shall be liable to imprisonment for a term of not more than fifteen years." The act was expressly made inapplicable to anything said in proceedings of the National Assembly, to anything done in preparation for or in civil or criminal proceedings in the courts, and to fair reports of such proceedings. It was to be no defense to a charge under the act that the person did not know or have reason to believe that his statement was false, unless he proved that before making the statement he "took reasonable measures to verify the accuracy of the statement or report." It is of interest that the offense could be committed by a citizen of Ghana by statements made outside the country as well as within.[95]

Shortly after the passage of the False Reports Act, Parliament enacted a number of highly significant changes in the Criminal Code relating to the offense of sedition. The crime of sedition had, of course, been defined by the law of the Gold Coast during the colonial

[93] *New York Times*, June 30, 1959, p. 2, col. 5.

[94] Offences Against the State (False Reports) Act, 1959, No. 37 of 1959. This act was repealed by Criminal Code, 1960, Act 29, sec. 318, but its substance was retained by sec. 185.

[95] The substance of the 1959 Act was incorporated in the Criminal Code, 1960, Act 29, sec. 185 and the earlier act was repealed.

period.[96] A wide variety of related offenses were recognized, such as conspiring to carry out a seditious enterprise, printing, publishing or uttering seditious words, selling, distributing, reproducing or importing seditious documents or merely possessing them. In delineating the substantive aspects of these offenses, the critical provision is that defining "seditious intention." In order to indicate the scope and significance of the changes in 1959, the earlier definition should be quoted in full:

"A seditious intention" is an intention—
(1) to bring into hatred or contempt or to excite disaffection against the person of Her Majesty, Her Heirs or successors, or the Government of the Gold Coast as by law established; or
(2) to bring about a change in the sovereignty of the Gold Coast; or
(3) to excite Her Majesty's subjects or inhabitants of the Gold Coast to attempt to procure the alteration, otherwise than by lawful means, of any other matter in the Gold Coast as by law established; or
(4) to bring into hatred or contempt or to excite disaffection against the administration of justice in the Gold Coast; or
(5) to raise discontent or disaffection amongst Her Majesty's subjects or inhabitants of the Gold Coast; or
(6) to promote feelings of ill-will and hostility between different classes of the population of the Gold Coast.

It is not a seditious intention—
(a) to show that Her Majesty has been misled or mistaken in any of Her measures; or
(b) to point out errors or defects in the government or Constitution of the Gold Coast as by law established or in legislation or in the

[96] Criminal Code, Cap. 9, sec. 344(2), 1 Laws of the Gold Coast 276 (1951).

administration of justice with a view to the reformation of such errors or defects; or

(c) to persuade Her Majesty's subjects or inhabitants of the Gold Coast to attempt to procure by lawful means the alteration of any matter in the Gold Coast as by law established other than that referred to in paragraph (2) of this subsection; or

(d) to point out with a view to their removal, any matters, which are producing or have a tendency to produce feelings of ill-will and enmity between different classes of the population of the Gold Coast:

Provided that none of the acts or things mentioned in paragraphs (a), (b), (c), and (d) shall be deemed to be lawful if they are done in such a manner as to effect or be likely to effect any of the purposes (1) to (6) which are declared in this section to be a seditious intention.

In determining whether the intention with which any act was done, any words were spoken, or any document was published, was or was not seditious, every person shall be deemed to intend the consequences, which would naturally follow from his conduct at the time and under the circumstances in which he so conducted himself.[97]

In the structure of the definition, it will be noted that "seditious intention" is first defined in terms of intention to accomplish certain stated purposes. Immediately, however, it appears that a wide range of political discussion along reasonably moderate lines is not to be ascribed to seditious intentions, except for one specified subject: urging a change in the sovereignty of the Gold Coast was entirely excluded from political debate. The appearance of saving a broad spectrum of political debate from the charge of seditious intention is somewhat misleading, however. The proviso after paragraph (d)

[97] *Id.*, sec. 344(8).

immunizes the several activities described in paragraphs (a) through (d) from a charge of seditious intention only if they are not done in such a manner as to effect or be likely to effect the purposes described in paragraphs (1) through (6). Thus it would seem, for example, that pointing out errors in the "administration of justice with a view to the reformation of such errors" could still ground a charge of seditious intention if the conduct were likely "to bring into hatred or contempt or *to excite disaffection* against the administration of justice in the Gold Coast." (Italics mine.)

We turn now to the 1959 Act amending the law relating to the crime of sedition.[98] By referring to the definition of seditious intention quoted above, we can easily and precisely point out the changes effected. Although there were a number of formal changes such as the substitution of "Ghana" for "the Gold Coast" and the elimination of references to "Her Majesty," our concern is with the substantive changes. Of the original list of purposes ascribed by the old ordinance to a seditious intention, paragraph (2) was omitted in the new act. Two new purposes were, however, added to the list:

(a) to advocate the desirability of overthrowing by unlawful means the Government of Ghana as by law established; or

. . . .

(g) falsely to accuse any public officer of misconduct in the exercise of his official duties, knowing the accusation to be false or reckless whether it be true or false.

The impact of the new paragraphs is clear enough. The grammatical construction of subsection (g) indicates that the basic requirement for its application is that the accusation against the public officer be false. In

98 Sedition Act, 1959, No. 64 of 1959. The substance of this enactment is now included in the Criminal Code, 1960, Act 29, sec. 183(11).

such a case, it is further required that the accuser know the falsity of the accusation or act without proper regard to the question whether it is true or false. It is reasonably clear that an accusation made recklessly is not seditious if in fact it is true.

Under the new act the provisions purporting to protect legitimate political discussion remained the same with one exception. Since paragraph (2) of the old ordinance was eliminated, the reference to it in paragraph (c) was also eliminated. The opening of the subject of change in sovereignty to political advocacy in this manner is perhaps attributable to the recurrent pan-African ideal which found its fullest articulation in the Republican Constitution where Parliament was expressly authorized to cede Ghanaian sovereignty to a union of African states.[99]

The only other change of significance made by the 1959 Act was a substantial increase in the severity of the penalty for seditious activity. Whereas the previous ordinance made imprisonment for three years the most severe penalty in any circumstance, and that only for repeating offenders, the new act increased the penalty even for first offenders to imprisonment for fifteen years. Further, a minimum sentence of five years imprisonment became mandatory for most seditious offenses.

In summary, it may be said that the most significant change effected by the 1959 Sedition Act was the increase in penalties. In terms of proscribed conduct, the new act effected one liberalization in opening to political discussion the subject of change of sovereignty. It also identified two new purposes that could be ascribed to seditious intention, thus somewhat narrowing the scope of political debate. The use of such vague concepts as "disaffection," "ill-will and hostility" in both the colonial ordinance and the new act commit expression in the context of political debate and agitation to essentially indeterminate hazards.

[99] Republican Constitution, art. 2.

Perhaps the most pointed threat to free political discussion was introduced in 1961 by the following amendment to the Criminal Code:

> Any person who with intent to bring the President into hatred, ridicule or contempt publishes any defamatory or insulting matter whether by writing, print, word of mouth or in any other manner whatsoever concerning the President commits an offence and shall be liable on summary conviction to a fine not exceeding five hundred pounds or to imprisonment for a term not exceeding three years or to both such fine and imprisonment.[100]

The amendment was made retroactive to the effective date of the Criminal Code of 1960. It should be noted that neither the truth of the publication nor any idea of fair comment provides a defense if the requisite intent is present and the publication can be deemed to be "defamatory or insulting." The central role of President Nkrumah in all aspects of Ghanaian political life makes this statute a practically general restraint on political discussion and debate in the country.

The crime of treason was also re-defined by legislation in 1959. Under the laws inherited from the colonial regime, the English law of treason was made applicable in the Gold Coast with death the prescribed penalty, while certain other related offenses such as instigating invasion, attacking or preparing to attack with armed force persons within or without the Gold Coast, and using armed force against the Government or its officers were separately defined and made punishable by life imprisonment.[101] Under the 1959 Act, these several offenses were brought within a new definition of treason and all made punishable by death.[102] The law of England, including all "the enactments, pro-

---

[100] The Criminal Code (Amendment) Act, 1961, Act 82.

[101] Criminal Code, Cap. 9, secs. 337-343, 1 Laws of the Gold Coast 276 (1951).

[102] Treason Act, 1959, No. 73 of 1959. This act in substance is now the Criminal Code, 1960, Act 29, sec. 180.

visors, requirements, and limitations" relating to the offenses were made inapplicable in Ghana. One immediately apparent change effected by the new act was to re-classify certain types of conduct as treason and to increase the severity of the penalty from life imprisonment to death. Nothing in the present statutory definition forecloses a finding of treason where the defendant's conduct has been limited to speech. In the two treason trials under the act, however, other overt acts of a treasonable nature were charged.

Sedition legislation has an obvious impact upon freedom of expression. Yet such an offense requires charge and trial under the usual processes of the criminal law with the safeguards there provided. Our interest now turns to limitations of freedom of communication imposed prior to the act of communication and usually by executive and not judicial action. Under the pre-independence Criminal Code, the Governor in Council was authorized to prohibit the importation into the Gold Coast of any newspaper, book or document when the Governor in Council was "of the opinion that the importation . . . would be contrary to the public interest."[103] The importation, sale and even possession of such prohibited documents were subject to criminal penalties.[104] Domestic publications were not subject, however, to prior restraint by executive action. By legislation in 1960, after the creation of the Republic, the authorization of executive restraint on freedom of communication was greatly extended. The act provides:

Whenever the President is of opinion—
   (a) that there is in any newspaper, book or document which is published periodically a systematic publication of matter calculated to prejudice public order or safety, or the maintenance of the public services or economy of Ghana, or

---

[103] Criminal Code, Cap. 9, sec. 344(1), 1 Laws of the Gold Coast 276 (1951).
[104] Id., sec. 344(2).

(b) that any person is likely to publish individual documents containing such matter.

he may make an executive instrument requiring that no future issue of the newspaper, book or document shall be published, or, as the case may be, that no document shall be published by, or by arrangement with, the said person, unless the matter contained therein has been passed for publication in accordance with the instrument.[105]

Violation of the orders in such instruments are subject to criminal sanctions. It will be noted that the restraint may be imposed on established publications appearing periodically or on the occasional publication of an individual. In fact, in 1962 the individual dispatches of press correspondents were subjected to a prior censorship.[106] The only condition of the President's power is his "opinion" on the specified matters. No review of that opinion, judicial or otherwise, is required, and seemingly, under the general rationale of *Baffour Osei Akoto*, review would be beyond the competence of a court.

Since the formation of the Republic, executive powers over publications have been used formally against only three publications. The importation of the magazine *Drum* was prohibited for a brief period.[107] The importation of one newspaper has also been prohibited.[108] Perhaps most significantly, *The Ashanti Pioneer*, a so-called independent newspaper usually critical of the Government, was placed under censorship on three occasions

[105] The Criminal Code (Amendment) Act, 1960, Act 5. This was later incorporated in the new Criminal Code, 1960, art. 29, as sec. 183(2).

[106] The Press Correspondents' Instrument, 1962 (Ex. Instr. 274).

[107] Prohibition of Importation ("Drum") Order, 1960 (Ex. Instr. 83); Revocation of Prohibition on Importation of Periodical ("Drum") Order, 1960 (Ex. Instr. 145).

[108] Prohibition of Importation of Newspaper (Mia Denyigba) Order, 1960 (Ex. Instr. 225).

in 1960 and 1961.[109] Each control order provided that "no issue of the newspaper . . . shall be published . . . unless the matter contained therein has been passed for publication by such person as may be nominated in that behalf by the Minister responsible for information." My own inquiries in Ghana shortly before the issuance of the control order of 1960 suggest that the principal factor behind it was the news and editorial treatment by *The Pioneer* of worker unrest and demands for higher pay made during that period. *The Pioneer* ultimately ceased publication altogether after an abortive move by the Government to purchase its printing plant.

Complete control over newspaper publication was assumed by the Government in 1963. The Newspaper Licensing Act imposes the requirement of a license for the publication or circulation of any newspaper.[110] On the failure to comply with any condition included in the license, the Minister of Information is authorized to revoke or suspend the license for such period as he thinks fit. Failure to comply is also made a criminal offense. Regulations issued to implement the act provide for the issuance of licenses on an annual basis.[111] Standard conditions are not specified in the regulations, but the license form contains blank spaces for such conditions as the Minister in his discretion may fix.

Four newspapers are now published in Ghana. The *Daily Graphic*, now owned by the Government, is the most temperate; the *Ghanaian Times*, the *Evening News* and the weekly *Spark* are organs of the Convention People's Party. None of the papers carries critical comment on Government policy or action. The Party press not infrequently criticizes individual officials who are believed to oppose Party dogma or to be delinquent

[109] The "Ashanti Pioneer" (Control) Instrument, 1960 (Ex. Instr. 195); The "Ashanti Pioneer" (Control) (Revocation) Instrument, 1961 (Ex. Instr. 83); Control Instrument, 1961 (Ex. Instr. 156); Revocation Instrument, 1961 (Ex. Instr. 169); Control Instrument, 1961 (Ex. Instr. 171).

[110] Newspaper Licensing Act, 1963, Act 189.

[111] Newspaper Licensing Regulations, 1963, L.I. 296.

in furthering Party objectives. The journalistic level of the press is generally low. The *Daily Graphic* and *Spark* are technically the best productions, the *Evening News* clearly the worst. Since Radio Ghana is also owned and fully controlled by the Government, no news medium within the country provides a vehicle for objective presentation of facts and the critical discussion of issues of public concern.

No body of law is clearly revealed by an analysis of its formal provisions. It is essential that the procedures applicable in its administration be examined to determine what safeguards of fair play have been erected. Since the criminal law is extensively used to effect the controls already discussed, the law of criminal procedure has major importance. In such a study as this a thorough examination of the relevant rules of criminal procedure of Ghana is too large a task. It must suffice here to say that the new Code of Criminal Procedure[112] carefully delimits the rules relating to such vital subjects as arrest and search with or without a warrant, the use of indictment, the mode of trial, including trial by jury, and appeals. In general, these rules evidence a respect for the person of the putative offender and for the elements of a fair hearing, to which reasonable exception could not be taken. To be sure, certain provisions are stringent, such as those authorizing the Attorney General to compel disclosures for the purposes of detecting the commission of offenses against the State without any guarantee against self-incrimination.[113] In general, however, the most significant impingements of the Government of Ghana upon the basic freedoms underlying rational political choice do not utilize the ordinary procedures of criminal law as applied in the courts. Rather, they arise from the increasing reliance on executive action immunized from judicial review.

[112] Criminal Procedure Code, 1960, Act 30.
[113] *Id.*, secs. 50-53. These provisions were first enacted in the Investigation of Crime Act, 1959, No. 33 of 1959.

The developments in Ghana since independence sketched in this chapter should not have been unanticipated. In 1956, Dr. Nkrumah wrote: "But even a system based on social justice and a democratic constitution may need backing up, during the period following independence, by emergency measures of a totalitarian kind."[114] David Apter has reported an even earlier personal interview with a leader of the Convention People's Party in which the suggestion was made that if Nkrumah's power later waned, parliamentary structures themselves might be dismissed "as British and imperialist," and a more totalitarian system modeled after Marxist practice might be instituted.[115] The continued existence of Parliament is not the root of the problem. Experience has already shown that the formal structures of parliamentary government and independent courts can be maintained while authorized and unreviewable executive action, supplemented perhaps by unofficial terror tactics, seriously undermines the basic assumptions of representative institutions and rational political choice.[116]

The title of this chapter suggests the thesis that certain legal tools have been used in Ghana to create a

[114] Nkrumah, *Autobiography* x (1957).

[115] Apter, *The Gold Coast in Transition* 215 (1955).

[116] In 1959, Joe Appiah, deputy leader of the Parliamentary opposition, charged that C.P.P. supporters drove United Party candidates away from a district headquarters in Ashanti and made it practically impossible for them to file nomination papers in a by-election. *New York Times*, Sept. 22, 1959, p. 3, col. 3. While in Ghana in mid-1960, I heard many reports of intimidation and actual violence carried on by supporters of the C.P.P. against United Party rallies and individual voters at the polls during the pre-Republic plebiscite. It was frequently charged that units of the Builder's Brigade, a paramilitary organization with purposes somewhat similar to those of the American Civilian Conservation Corps during the depression of the thirties, were used for such purposes. The full facts were impossible to establish. I concluded tentatively that terror and intimidation of political opponents had in fact been used by the C.P.P., but that the United Party had not been entirely innocent of such conduct. Which party took the initiative and which acted defensively could not be ascertained.

political monopoly for the Convention People's Party. Thus far we have examined those tools; we turn now to the evidence of the results achieved. In the general election of 1954, 59 per cent of the registered electors voted.[117] Of these, 391,720 voted for C.P.P. candidates; all other candidates received 324,822 votes. The resulting party distribution in the National Assembly was as follows:

Convention People's Party	71 seats
Independents (including C.P.P. expellees)	16 seats
Northern People's Party	12 seats
Togoland Congress	2 seats
Ghana Congress Party	1 seat
Moslem Association Party	1 seat
Anlo Youth Organization	1 seat

In the general elections of 1956, the last held for the National Legislature, about 697,000 votes were cast, of which the C.P.P. took 57 per cent. This gave the C.P.P. 71 seats with the remaining 33 distributed among the opposition groups. It is worth noting, however, that in both Ashanti and the Northern Territories the C.P.P. remained a minority party.[118]

Without a general election, the C.P.P. majority in Parliament has increased since 1956. This increase can be attributed to defections from the opposition, expulsion of opposition members because of unexcused absences or disqualification under Preventive Detention Act orders, followed by the uncontested choice of C.P.P. candidates in by-elections, as well as the election by the Parliament itself of ten special women members.[119] The current political position is suggested by the following summary of the results of local govern-

[117] The data on the 1954 elections are taken from Apter, supra note 115, at 231.
[118] *New York Times*, July 20, 1956, p. 3, col. 8; *New York Times*, July 23, 1956, p. 8, col. 1.
[119] See pp. 36-37.

ment council elections in the year following the creation of the Republic in mid-1960.[120]

No. of Council Seats Available	566
No. of Seats Contested	16
No. of Seats Uncontested	550
C.P.P. Votes in Contests	5,506
Other Votes in Contests	2,619
C.P.P. Seats	566
Other Seats	—

The figures speak for themselves. The dominance of the C.P.P. has been total. Two subordinate facts are also worth noting. Most of the contested elections occurred in the first half of the period covered; indeed, since January 1, 1961, only one local council seat has been contested. It is also of interest that in the sixteen contested elections only three candidates standing against the C.P.P. took a party designation; these associated themselves with the United Party. The remaining thirteen candidates running against the C.P.P. chose to describe themselves as "Independents."

Perhaps the most telling evidence of political monopoly in Ghana comes from the announced results of the referendum on constitutional changes held in January, 1964. The proposed amendments were designed to make the C.P.P. the "national party," to adopt the C.P.P. flag as the national flag and to grant to the President summary power to dismiss superior court judges. Despite the multiplicity, complexity and possibly controversial nature of the proposals, voter response was limited to the simple choice between a "yes" and a "no" vote. Official figures on the referendum (*Ghana Gazette*, February 14, 1964, p. 109) disclosed the following results:

[120] Data on local government elections are compiled from The Local Government Bulletin, an official publication. My files do not include Bulletin No. 5 of February 3, 1961; if election results were published in that issue, my figures are to that extent inaccurate.

Registered electorate	2,988,598
"Yes" votes	2,773,920
"No" votes	2,452
Percentage of electorate voting	92
Percentage of "yes" votes	99.9

While there was no organized opposition to the proposals, the nearly unanimous approval does not seem likely, or even possible in a free election. In Ashanti, for example, where opposition to the C.P.P. had traditionally been strongest, not a single "No" vote was reported. Opportunities for voter intimidation were ample; each ballot was marked with the voter's serial number as recorded in the electoral register. The Party press warned voters that they could not hide behind the so-called secrecy of the polling booth. Observers reported that in many polling places no box for "No" votes was available or the slot in this box was sealed. The high percentage of the electorate voting may be in part attributable to warnings in the Party press against staying at home and promises that "the people's wrath is apt to descend without mercy upon those who are not with us."[121]

The evidence of political monopoly by the Convention People's Party in Ghana is compelling. It must be pointed out, however, that only inference supports a conclusion that there is a causal connection between this monopoly and the legal devices limiting political activity described in this chapter. It is theoretically possible that the increasing dominance of the Government Party is attributable to widening popular support.[122] My own impression, however, formed in visits

[121] *Ghanaian Times*, Jan. 24, 1964, p. 1, col. 2.

[122] The term "Government Party" has a special significance and appropriateness in Ghana since leading members of the Party have on more than one occasion declared that it is meaningless to suggest a distinction between Party and Government. Nkrumah is quoted as saying that "the [ruling] party is Ghana." *New York Times*, July 4, 1959, p. 4, col. 1. Mr. Ako Adjei, when Minister of Labor, in defending the legislation bringing Ghana's labor movement under Government control insisted that it was

to Ghana and an extended period of residence there, is that popular support for the C.P.P. has steadily declined. In any event, the C.P.P. monopoly is not sustained solely by the legal tools of political suppression. The perquisites, economic and otherwise, that the Government is able to confer on individuals and communities manifesting sympathy and support create heavy handicaps for any political opposition.

In the years since the Republic, one can find considerable evidence of disaffection with Government policy. Workers have demonstrated for more pay; a major political strike has been organized; bombings have occurred in Accra and elsewhere; two attempts to assassinate Dr. Nkrumah have failed. It is difficult to believe that this disaffection would not have been more actively manifested in direct, conventional political activity if the hazards arising from the legal machinery available to the Government had been less acute.

Adequate evaluation of the legislative development described in this chapter must not be divorced from the factual situation in which the development occurred. What was the threat to which the new enactments responded? Was the security of the State in fact imperiled? If so, was the danger such as to require measures of the stringency of those described? We turn now to a record of some events that may provide partial answers to these questions.

On December 19, 1958, officers of the Ghana Army and police arrested Captain Benjamin Awhaitey, commandant of the army camp in Accra, and R. R. Amponsah, an opposition Member of Parliament, in connection with a suspected conspiracy to stage a *coup d'état*. Shortly thereafter, another opposition Member, M. K. Apaloo, was also arrested. Subsequently, Awhaitey was tried by court-martial on a charge of failure to report

---

"nonsense" to distinguish between the Government and the Convention People's Party, adding "Party rules Government." *New York Times*, April 7, 1959, p. 8, col. 3.

what he knew of the matter. Following conviction for neglect of duty under Section 69 of the British Army Act, which had been made applicable by legislation to the Ghana Army, he was dismissed from the service. Amponsah, Apaloo and Awhaitey were detained under the Preventive Detention Act.

Following these events, the Government appointed a commission of enquiry to look into the matters involved in the court-martial as well as the surrounding circumstances. The make-up of the commission and its mode of procedure must be described since they are important in evaluating its report and the Government's response. The chairman of the commission was Mr. Justice Granville Sharp of the Supreme Court of Ghana, an Englishman who had had judicial experience in the United Kingdom as Recorder of Kings Lynn. Mr. Maurice Charles from British Guiana, when appointed to the commission, was a Senior Magistrate in Ghana. The only African member of the commission, Sir Tsibu Darku, had served for many years as a member of the Gold Coast Legislative Council and Executive Council; only he lacked judicial experience.

The commission held public hearings to decide questions of procedure. The task of collecting evidence was undertaken by the Attorney General's department, and the then Attorney General, Mr. Geoffrey Bing, with two members of his staff, acted as counsel to assist the commission. Persons appearing to the commission to have an interest in the subject of inquiry were permitted to be represented by counsel. The commission also directed that persons having reason to believe they were affected should be entitled to attend the hearings. Such persons were also entitled to testify and to call witnesses. The commission ordered that the persons concerned who were detained under the Preventive Detention Act should be given reasonable and timely opportunity to consult with their legal advisers. Full opportunities for the cross-examination of witnesses were accorded. After the initial hearing on procedure, the commission sat for 28 days hearing evidence and argument.

The structure of the final report of the commission is of interest.[123] In a unanimous part of the report, the commission first summarized the evidence and made certain factual findings. Agreement was not total, however, and on certain crucial matters the majority of the commission—Sir Tsibu Darku and Mr. Charles—re-examined the evidence and made findings. Justice Granville Sharp filed a minority report on these matters. It would be inappropriate here to review in detail the large body of conflicting evidence; the substantive conclusions in each of the three parts will be summarized, however.

The commission unanimously found, largely on the basis of the purchase of certain military insignia by Amponsah in London in June and July, 1958, that since June, 1958, Amponsah and Apaloo had been "engaged in a conspiracy to carry out at some future date in Ghana an act for an unlawful purpose, revolutionary in character." On the question whether the leadership of the opposition United Party was part of this conspiracy, the full commission concluded that "there is no evidence whatsoever that Dr. Busia, Mr. Appiah, Mr. Owusu and Mr. Dombo were involved in these transactions." On the role of Government leaders and other official agencies, the commission unanimously found that "there is no justification whatever for any suggestion that the Cabinet of Dr. Nkrumah, or any Member of it, was interfering with the course of justice." Further, they held that the senior officers of the army and police had only done their duty, "and were not connected with any design to implicate innocent persons."

[123] Report of the Commission Appointed to Enquire into the Matters Disclosed at the Trial of Captain Benjamin Awhaitey Before a Court Martial, and the Surrounding Circumstances (1959). The report is commonly referred to as "The Granville Sharp Report."

Other unanimous findings were subordinate and need not be recounted here.

The specific charge against Captain Awhaitey had involved his failure to report his knowledge of a conspiracy involving Amponsah and Apaloo to assassinate the Prime Minister, Dr. Nkrumah, on December 20, 1958, when he arrived at the Accra airport to emplane for India. It will be recalled that the commission had found unanimously that earlier in 1958, Amponsah and Apaloo had been involved in a revolutionary conspiracy, but the commission was not in full agreement on the relation of that earlier conspiracy to the alleged plans for December 20, nor did they agree on Awhaitey's role. The majority of the commission concluded, however, that Awhaitey, Mr. Amponsah, Mr. Apaloo and Mr. John Mensah Anthony (Apaloo's half-brother, a Ghanaian by birth who had long resided in Lome, French Togoland) were engaged in a conspiracy to assassinate the Prime Minister and carry out a *coup d'état*. On this crucial issue, and on the related question of how Amponsah and Apaloo could explain their presence at certain places if they were innocent of the specific conspiracy charged, Mr. Justice Granville Sharp filed his minority report.

Sharp concluded that "there was no conspiratorial association between Mr. Amponsah and Mr. Apaloo in association with Awhaitey," and specifically that "there did not exist between Mr. Amponsah, Mr. Apaloo and Awhaitey a plot to interfere in any way with the life or liberty of the Prime Minister of Ghana on the airport before his departure for India on the 20th December." Thus, he concluded that the earlier conspiracy in which Amponsah and Apaloo were involved had been abandoned. He fully rejected the contention that these men were "at any time between the second week of November and the 20th December associated together or with any other person or persons in a conspiracy to carry out any *coup d'état*." How then did

Amponsah and Apaloo come to be at the road junction outside Accra at which the former was arrested and where, the Government contended, they had arranged to meet Awhaitey to complete their sinister plans. Mr. Justice Sharp's conclusion, though clothed in the language of judicial restraint, was unmistakable: they were "framed" by unknown persons who lured them there by false messages. In Sharp's analysis, the evidence tended to suggest some complicity of Awhaitey and a Lt. Amenyah, the officer who had first reported the alleged conspiracy to the higher army command, but the evidence was not such as to permit a finding on the actual role of these men. It should be remembered that Mr. Justice Sharp participated in the unanimous finding of the commission that Dr. Nkrumah, his Cabinet and the higher officers of the army and police were not involved in the "frame-up."

If Amponsah and Apaloo were in fact the victims of a sinister plot to make them appear as conspirators against the life of the Prime Minister and the security of the State, who were the plotters? While Sharp concluded merely that they were "persons unknown," the implication is clear that they were persons sympathetic to the C.P.P. and the Nkrumah Government. He argued: "If, as we have found, two persons of the stature and importance of Mr. Amponsah and Mr. Apaloo could, without the knowledge of their leaders or of any other important associate of theirs, indulge in the kind of exploit such as that connected with the purchase of [military] accoutrement, surprise need not necessarily be expressed at the suggestion that in other circles also were to be found persons capable of taking matters into their own hands, without the knowledge of others, in the belief that they were rendering some service to their cause by causing the downfall of two persons, each of whom they knew to be *persona non grata*."

The Government's statement on the commission report not unnaturally accepted the conclusions of the majority and rejected the minority findings of Mr. Justice Sharp. The importance of the statement lies, however, in the effort of the Government to place the Awhaitey affair in a broader context and thereby to explain and defend the pattern of enactments discussed earlier in this chapter. By way of general introduction, the statement declared:

> The Government believes in, and is determined to maintain, the system of free elections and the maintenance of a regime based upon the will of the people expressed through the use of the ballot-box.
>
> . . . .
>
> The western conception of a two-party system with an opposition capable of forming an alternative government if they obtain the support of the majority of the electorate becomes meaningless if the opposition party devotes itself as a party to conspiracy, boycotts Parliament and abandons all but a token interest in the ballot-box.
>
> The problem which a government has to face when the opposition, or a powerful section of it, goes over to conspiracy and violence as its policy, is therefore an extremely serious one.[124]

The Government's thesis was thus clearly revealed—the Awhaitey-Amponsah-Apaloo affair was not to be viewed as an isolated episode but as only one part of a broad scheme adopted by the opposition parties and groups to abandon the constitutional, political routes to power in favor of a general scheme involving unfounded charges of corruption against government officials, exploitation of racial and tribal differences and violence.

To support these broad charges against the opponents of the C.P.P., the Government reviewed the record of events since 1954. The various allegations with some

---

[124] Statement by the Government on the Report of the Commission Appointed to Enquire into the Matters Disclosed at the Trial of Captain Benjamin Awhaitey Before a Court Martial, and Surrounding Circumstances, p. 1, W.P. No. 10/59 (1959).

indication of the supporting evidence should be briefly summarized.

In the election of 1954, the Opposition Members of the National Assembly "were elected not on the basis that they could form an alternative Government, but that they should represent various tribal, religious and regional interests." The C.P.P. victory in that election was so overwhelming that the opposition despaired of ballot-box success and therefore "reorganized themselves . . . upon a basis of violence rather than upon any rational appeal to the electorate." The National Liberation Movement, founded in 1954, "relied upon the support of chiefs who could use both their spiritual and their temporal authority to coerce their subjects into giving it political support at election time, and upon organized violence based upon hired gangsters who were often of Nigerian or French West African origin. The policy of the National Liberation Movement was to revive tribalism under the guise of regional autonomy or federalism and they therefore allied themselves with the Togoland Congress, a party which wishes to split off from Ghana entirely that part of Togoland which was under United Nations Trusteeship but which had been politically united to the Gold Coast since 1915. On the same principle they also allied themselves with the Northern People's Party which stood for the maintenance of unchanged chiefly rule in the North, and the exclusion from the Northern Region of Ghana of Ghanaians of different tribal or racial origin from the peoples of the North." This combination of forces engaged in a campaign of violence, refused to participate in discussions of a proposed constitution, declined to confer with the Constitutional Adviser, Sir Frederick Bourne, boycotted the All-Party Achimota Conference that had been called to consider constitutional proposals, even after independence, refused to contest the Regional Assembly elections and from time to time boycotted the National Assembly.

Even in the face of the C.P.P. victory in the 1956 election, the opposition, in an effort to influence the British Government to delay independence and to achieve a federal structure of government, threatened civil war. As a compromise "the Government accepted the 1957 Constitution with the greatest reluctance on the ground that it was . . . quite unworkable. . . ." In order not to delay independence, the Government accepted the constitution intending to modify it later by the constitutional methods provided.

Prior to independence, separatist elements in British Togoland developed plans for military training and attacks on Government facilities in the hope that the ensuing chaos would bring about a United Nations inquiry and an independent government for British Togoland. Subsequently, the Government had reason to believe, the Togoland Congress Party considered implementing this plot in connection with disturbances being planned by the National Liberation Movement. Following the disturbances in early 1957, which in fact involved attacks on police by armed and disciplined men, two Members of Parliament representing the Togoland Congress Party, S. G. Antor and Kojo Ayeke, and a number of other leading Party figures were charged and tried for conspiring to attack persons with armed force. Ten persons, including the two Members of Parliament, were convicted, but the convictions were quashed on appeal on the ground of errors by the trial judge. "Quite irrespective, however, of the question of the guilt or innocence of any particular individual, the evidence given at this prolonged trial contains, in the Government's view, ample judicial proof of the organization of revolutionary activity in Trans-Volta Togoland."

In April, 1957, there was organized in Accra the Ga Shifimo Kpee, "a political organization frankly based on tribal affiliations. Its objects were in essence to drive out of Accra all those who were not of Ga origin."

333

Following a riot in Accra on August 21, 1957, provoked by this organization, in which 40 persons were injured, the Government procured the passage of the Avoidance of Discrimination Act.

A commission of enquiry was appointed in November, 1957, to determine whether there had been abuses of power by the traditional rulers of the State of Akim Abuakwa. The commission found that Nana Ofori Atta II, Omanhene of Akim Abuakwa, had used his influence to have deducted from the salaries of lesser state officials the sum of £G 10,000 and that this money was used to pay for certain "action groupers" who committed various acts of violence, to pay the fines of those convicted of such offenses, to support the dependents of those imprisoned, and to pay compensation when the convicted persons were released. The commission of enquiry had declared, "There is evidence that this body of action groupers were recruited largely by the energies of Nana Ofori Atta II and his Ayasehene." While this fact was not expressly mentioned in the Government's statement, it may be observed that Nana Ofori Atta II was of the same family as and closely associated with Dr. J. B. Danquah, a prominent leader of the opposition United Party.

In February, 1958, a commission was appointed to make similar inquiries in Kumasi. The commission found that the Kumasi State Council had abused its powers by paying £G 19,000 of public money to the National Liberation Movement. Evidence before the commission indicated that the money was used to pay "Action Troopers" and to pay fines of those convicted of acts of violence in the service of the Movement.

In response to the disturbances in Togoland and the campaigns of violence supported by leading chiefs and the National Liberation Movement, the Government procured passage in August, 1958, of the Preventive Detention Act. In a public speech, Mr. M. K. Apaloo declared: "Let us all prove to the C.P.P. Government that

334

the implementation of this act will be an open invitation to violence. People will take revenge by attacking Ministers in their offices, homes and elsewhere." Dzenkle Dzewu, a member of the United Party executive group, was quoted as saying at a U.P. rally on July 27, 1958: "We, in Accra, are prepared to revolt against the Government; we are prepared. Once the Government tried to arrest any opposition member there would be trouble in all regions. We, in Accra, will march straight to the castle despite police, army and dogs on guard, and catch Kwame Nkrumah. We will have to arm ourselves with guns, machetes and cutlasses." Certain members of the Accra Regional Executive of the United Party, including Dzenkle Dzewu, began organizing terrorist groups of young criminals called "Tokyo Joes." It seemed probable, the Government contended, that their activities were to some extent approved by the leadership of the United Party. In November, 1958, about 40 persons, including the organizers and certain members of these terrorist and revolutionary groups, were detained under the Preventive Detention Act. This was the first use of the act.

As one ground for their refusal to contest the Regional Assembly elections in 1958, the opposition contended that the elections would be unfairly conducted. Specifically, allegations were made that the Government, supported by the police, was conniving in the printing of extra ballot forms to be used in stuffing ballot boxes. Although informed of the results of a police enquiry that had determined the falsity of these charges, R. R. Amponsah had repeated the accusation. Consequently, prior to his arrest in the Awhaitey affair, Amponsah was arrested, tried for sedition but acquitted. The trial judge had held that, though the accusation was false and Amponsah had no reason to believe it to be true, his words were not seditious under the existing law of Ghana.

The Government had reason to believe that dissident

335

elements in Ghana were able to muster support, including large financial backing, from elements outside Ghana that were anxious to show that the newly independent country could not be governed responsibly through the use of free, democratic institutions. "Those who are prepared to assist from outside, subversive movements in Ghana are, however, not troubled by any such problems. To them it is immaterial whether the conspiracy which they seek to promote succeeds or fails. If it succeeds, naturally a most serious blow will have been dealt to the conception that a freely elected African Government has the ability and the strength to govern. If, on the other hand, the conspiracy fails, it will be due to the fact that the Government has had to take exceptional measures to deal with the conspiracy, and these measures can then be used by the very persons who assisted in provoking the occasion for them as a justification for their own repressive rule." Possibly in support of its view that large outside financial support was available to aid subversion in Ghana, the Government recounted "the strange affair of Dr. Oppavar." The details of this case need not be considered here. In essence, it appeared to the Government that Dr. Oppavar was in some way involved in the purchase of a large quantity of grenades for shipment to Ghana and possible use there. The Government concluded that "while the Dr. Oppavar incident cannot be said to provide any definite proof of anything, it does illustrate the need for the utmost security precautions being taken by the Government and the utmost vigilance being exercised in regard to anyone who may be suspected of attempting to overthrow the Government by force."

In May, 1958, certain documents were mailed to persons in Ghana and elsewhere that purported to be "secret cabinet papers." The import of the papers was that leading members of the Government were planning actions highly prejudicial to certain tribal groups in Ashanti, the Northern Region and elsewhere. These papers were completely spurious. Their authors were not ascertainable, but three persons employed in the Government Statistician's Office were tried and convicted of having printed the documents during office hours and on Government premises. The Government suggested a "close association" between two of these persons and Dzenkle Dzewu, already identified as a member of the Executive Group of the United Party in Accra. Both Dzewu and R. R. Amponsah testified in a parliamentary enquiry that they believed the documents to be genuine.

The Government recounted in some detail the alleged facts of an involved plan carried out in part by a certain Emil Savunda to defraud the people of Ghana by the sale of worthless corporate securities. The plan was foiled by Government action, but out of it arose "wild and fantastic allegations of wholesale bribery" of Government officers. The Government did concede that one official was involved in the fraudulent scheme, Mr. S. I. Iddrisu, a Member of Parliament who was also Parliamentary Secretary to the Ministry of Information and Broadcasting. The opposition, led by Dr. Busia, demanded a commission of enquiry and the prosecution of a number of persons, including Cabinet Ministers, on charges of corruption. Dr. Busia, in an interview in London, repeated charges that "the present state of affairs offers no good prospects either for investments in Ghana from abroad or for a parliamentary government which requires respectable standards of honesty of its public officers." The Government vigorously denied the charges of widespread corruption but rejected the demand for a commission of enquiry. It saw the charges as an excuse for a *coup d'état* with the assistance of foreign interests.

To what extent were these various activities carried on by or with the approval of the top leadership of the Opposition, thus reflecting established policy? To what extent were they attributable to an extremist fringe?

337

In the description of the critical events and their causes, the Government's statement is not consistent on these issues. As has been noted, in some instances such opposition leaders as Dr. Busia were directly charged. In other cases, primary responsibility was attributed to secondary figures in the opposition, but in at least one instance the argument was made that the top leadership approved the extreme action. Unknown persons were charged with responsibility for some of the attacks against the C.P.P. and the Government. On the specific question of the involvement of major opposition figures in the Awhaitey affair, the Government took the view that leaders such as Dombo, Appiah and Busia participated in or knew of the revolutionary plot and either failed to discourage it or attempted to conceal the real facts from the investigating authorities. In this respect, it is significant that the Government went beyond and in essence rejected the unanimous findings of the Granville Sharp Commission.

An effort has been made here to summarize fairly the Government's view of the situation. By the time the White Paper was issued, the Preventive Detention Act and the Avoidance of Discrimination Act had been passed. The Government announced its intention to procure re-definitions of the crimes of treason and sedition and to revise the scale of punishment for sedition, to amend the criminal law relating to the making of false statements, to strengthen the hand of the Attorney General in investigating crimes against the State and to increase the powers of the National Assembly to discipline its own members. These steps were taken in the enactments analyzed earlier in this chapter.

What independent verification can be found for the Government's general conclusion that its opposition had in effect abandoned constitutional political processes in favor of terrorist activity, defamation of governmental officials and revolutionary plotting of a *coup*

d'état? In a number of respects, the particulars of the
Government's case are confirmed by the public record.
The opposition groups did refuse to participate in constitutional discussions; they did boycott the National
Assembly and refuse to contest certain elections. Clearly,
too, many in the Opposition were oriented toward the
traditional tribal order and seemingly felt primary loyalty to their chiefs and tribes rather than to the new
nation. The Opposition did charge the Government with
corruption and suppression of democratic freedoms.
There were, in fact, riots and other acts of violence
from time to time, particularly in Ashanti. Yet by and
large, the critical evidentiary facts to support the Government's case are not available. Such phrases as "the
Government has reason to believe," "the evidence given
at the trial contains, in the Government's view, ample
judicial proof of the organization of revolutionary activity," "documentary evidence in the possession of the Government shows" are recurrent in the White Paper. It is
significant, however, that in the case considered by the
Government to be most clearly revolutionary, the
Awhaitey affair, an investigating commission, after
hearing all the available evidence, could not agree
unanimously that the plot ever existed. Indeed, the
chairman of the commission not only denied the existence of the plot but found affirmatively a conspiracy
to implicate two innocent members of the opposition
United Party. More generally, it might be said that the
Government has courted frustration when it invoked
the ordinary processes of criminal law, as evidenced
by the failures in the prosecutions of Antor, Ayeke and
Amponsah. To some extent these failures may be attributed to inadequacies, from the Government's viewpoint, of the substantive definitions of criminal offenses.
Other difficulties were encountered, however, in the
procedural safeguards of ordinary criminal prosecutions
and in marshalling evidence sufficient to satisfy the
requirements of English-derived criminal law.

Reference has been made to the strike in Sekondi-

Takoradi in September, 1961. My own inquiries in Ghana leave no doubt that the objective of the strike was the replacement of the Nkrumah Government. Following these difficulties, several of the principal leaders of the Opposition, including J. B. Danquah, Joe Appiah and Victor Owusu, were detained. Late in 1961, in connection with charges that he was plotting a *coup d'état*, Komla Gbedemah, Minister of Finance, was removed from office, but before further action could be taken against him, Gbedemah fled the country. No persuasive evidence to support the charges against him was adduced by the Government. A White Paper issued in December, 1961, summarized events from the Government's viewpoint and attempted to justify the measures taken in connection with the Sekondi-Takoradi strike.[125] The White Paper contributed little beyond the factual interpretations and arguments presented in the Government's Statement on the Granville Sharp Commission Report and resolved none of the questions that had been left open.

In August, 1962, on his return from a state visit to Upper Volta, President Nkrumah was the victim of an assassination attempt in the village of Kulungugu in the Northern Region. Though slightly wounded, he returned immediately to Accra and shortly thereafter ordered the detention of Tawia Adamafio, Minister of Information and Broadcasting, Ako Adjei, Minister of Foreign Affairs and H. H. Cofie-Crabbe, General Secretary of the C.P.P. The usual charges of a plot to stage a *coup d'état* were made by officials and the newspapers. Between September, 1962, and January, 1963, hand grenades were exploded on three occasions in gatherings of C.P.P. supporters in Accra. The apprehension of some of the terrorists who admitted their involvement in the Accra bombings led to the conviction of five persons for treason and two for misprision of treason. The alleged link of the terrorists to the recognized opposition

[125] Statement by the Government on the Recent Conspiracy, W.P. No. 7/61 (1961).

was one Obetsebi-Lamptey, a former official of the United Party in Accra, who unfortunately died one month before the trial began.

The first treason defendants also named Adamafio, Adjei, Cofie-Crabbe, Gbedemah and several Ministers still in the Government as participants in the alleged conspiracy. When the first three were brought to trial for treason, however, they were fully acquitted by the Special Criminal Division.[126] While this judgment had the support of the majority of lawyers who had followed the evidence adduced in the trial, it aroused the vehement condemnation of Government spokesmen and the C.P.P. press who demanded strong retaliation. As has been noted, Sir Arku Korsah was immediately dismissed from the Chief Justiceship by President Nkrumah and parliamentary steps were begun to remove from the bench the three members of the Special Court. On January 2, 1964, another unsuccessful attempt to assassinate Dr. Nkrumah was made by a member of the police force in the guard detail at the President's residence.

While the extent and sponsorship of violence and subversive activity in Ghana are subject to question, there is no doubt that the Nkrumah Government has been confronted with the problem of dealing with dissident groups that have not limited themselves to political activity of a constitutional and democratic kind. The nature of the forces opposing Nkrumah and the C.P.P. explains in some measure the resort to such methods. These forces have been largely composed of persons oriented toward the traditional order where authority was status-determined and to whom mass political organization and methods are alien. That they should be frustrated in their attempts to develop such organizations and employ such methods, and that this frustration should lead to violence would not be surprising. It should be observed, however, that the very nature of Nkrumah's leadership and the significant poli-

[126] See pp. 234-36 above.

cies implemented by his Government have served to stimulate the kind of action to which the Government has responded in an increasingly authoritarian manner. The charismatic quality of Nkrumah's rule,[127] while initially highly effective in organizing discrete elements in the Gold Coast into a disciplined, functioning organ to accomplish the transfer of power from British hands, is, on a long-range basis, incompatible with the democratic political processes of criticism, performance-evaluation and peaceful role-transfer by which a loyal opposition may hope to achieve power. Furthermore, the vigor of the C.P.P.'s attack on the traditional order, and the substantial exclusion of the chiefs and traditional authorities from governmental roles, even largely honorific ones which could be easily reconciled with their traditional functions, have served to embitter them and their followers and to increase their distrust of the political institutions and processes through which the power of Nkrumah and the C.P.P. are exercised.

[127] See Apter, supra note 115, especially 291 *et seq.*

CHAPTER VIII

VALUE COMPETITION IN
GHANAIAN LEGAL DEVELOPMENT

THE EARLIER chapters have described and analyzed the body of law that allocates, channels and controls public power in Ghana. An effort has been made to trace the development from the indigenous order through the contributions of the colonial period, in order to establish a base line from which innovations under an African government in the Gold Coast and Ghana can be understood and assessed. To the extent permitted by the available data, legal developments have also been related to a wider range of political, economic and social experience. It is hoped that the earlier chapters will be of use to lawyers and social scientists interested in Africa, whose concerns do not include the value structures implicit in the legal development or who would view those structures quite differently from the analysis to be offered here.

For those whose interests may include the value orientation of the public law of Ghana, a somewhat fuller statement of the theoretical underpinning of the following analysis may be useful. For the purposes of this study, law has been taken to mean a technique of social ordering deriving its essential characteristic from its ultimate reliance on the reserved monopoly of systematically threatened or applied force in politically organized society. Some implications of this definition must be noted. First, the definition emphasizes the purely instrumental character of law—law is a tool, a technique. Thus viewed, it does not involve any particular value assumptions or any particular set of functions within the broad scope of arranging, channeling and directing forces within the social group. The technique can be used within the context, and to implement the value assumptions of western democracy, Soviet

343

communism, Nazism, or any other ideology, and still appropriately and fully qualify as law. If anything that might be called a value is necessarily implicit in the concept, it is the element of order, in the sense merely of some kind of purposeful channeling of social energies.

The essential characteristic of law or the legal technique is its ultimate reliance on the force of politically organized society. Two aspects of this proposition require explication. The first is the centrality of force, an aspect of law that is seen most clearly in the prohibitions of the criminal law. If a man commits murder, the public force will be applied to take the offender's life or imprison him. Yet the ultimate reliance on force characterizes civil law as well. If one breaches his contract, the public force may at the suit of the aggrieved party be applied to take the defaulter's property for compensation or to compel specific performance by forcible detention until he performs his duty. I do not mean, of course, that law necessarily involves the actual use of force; on the contrary, most legal orders are viable only because resort to this ultimate sanction is needed relatively rarely. Nor is there implicit in this analysis any factual assertion as to why law is obeyed. Coincidence of the substance of the legal norm with that provided by religion, ethics or popular morality may explain conformity far more satisfactorily than fear of the ultimate sanctioning force. The reference to force is intended merely to identify the legal technique. A device for social ordering is law, as here defined, if the persons who deviate from the ordered pattern are confronted with a threat, express or implicit, of being compelled through the application of official force to suffer in some significant interest because of their deviation.

It should be emphasized that this concept of law is value-neutral. Law is merely technique. The values, claims, desires or demands in aid of which the technique may be employed are as variable as human experience. They are data extrinsic to law in the strict conceptual sense, and, therefore, neither an irreducible minimum of values nor an order of priorities of values is used as an essential identifier of law.

The effort to view law as essentially value-neutral and as deriving its value content from extrinsic sources perhaps cannot be entirely successful. Two words of caution are essential. First, while the technique of law may in its strictest sense be stripped of all value overtones, certain values are so commonly associated with its use that they may come to appear as inevitable concomitants. For example, it is commonly accepted that a legal standard should be promulgated in advance of its application. Indeed, for most effective operation to the end of social ordering, such promulgation would seem to be required. The requirement of prior promulgation immediately suggests, however, a concern not merely with efficiency of technique, but also with fairness to those who may be affected by the sanction attached to the standard. Thus, a value coloration comes to be associated immediately with the technique. To be sure, this value is not always implemented. One recalls the biting comment of Bentham that the common-law approach is similar to the training and discipline of a dog—wait until he has acted, then beat him so that he will not repeat the offense. Perhaps this criticism is overstated, but it does serve to emphasize the common expectation of an association between the legal technique and the value implications of fair notice.

The second word of caution is required by another observable aspect of the use of law. Most if not all legal systems show a marked tendency toward stability in the substantive content of their norms as well as in their methods. It is indeed a commonplace that every legal system faces a constant challenge of introducing enough flexibility to accommodate within tolerable limits the pressure of social change and to counterbalance the built-in stability, even rigidity, of the system. In strong support of the stability of law is the emotional pattern found in most societies that nurtures respect, often veneration, for "the law of the land." Yet, as will be observed later, one of the most persistent value competitions in any society and any legal order is that between stability and change, between the familiar and the novel. The legal technique in its usual operation appears to weight the balance heavily in favor of the former. One may recognize this fact, however, while insisting that the value of stability does not always prevail and that new values may find implementation through the legal technique.

To look outside the law for the sources of its value acceptances does not commit one to an unduly passive characterization of the legal technique. At least in a democratic society one does expect the value content of legal norms to reflect the acceptances present, though perhaps amorphously, in the society. It is possible, however, for law to draw its value content from the acceptances of an elite group that has succeeded in monopolizing the function of manipulating the technique and is using it to achieve social change. In such circumstances the regime would doubtless appear quite authoritarian, since the social acceptance of the value content of legal norms and the frequency and severity of resort to the ultimate force lying behind the legal order will, in secular terms at least, probably vary inversely. Even in a democratic society, however, there is some range of creativity, some function of social modification, through the manipulation of legal norms, left to those entrusted with the power to commit the public force. One of the regrettable failures of legal and social science scholarship thus far is that so little is known, as Pound once put it, of the limits of effective legal action for social engineering in the context of either a democratic or authoritarian regime.

This concept of law opens wide vistas of fruitful social inquiry. Since law involves no necessary set of value acceptances, the opportunity is available to the manipulators of the technique to determine what value judgments will be implemented. The assumption will be made in this study that those values which the manipulators undertake to nurture or preserve and implement by law rank high in their hierarchy of goods. They are not left to unorganized social pressures, nor are they dependent solely on the flexible and varied compulsion of religion or ethics. I do not suggest, of course, that the process of value choice for legal implementation is unadulterated rationality, that the order of desires or claims of men in society is first determined and then fed, fully articulated, into the legal machine. On the contrary, the materials of the law—constitutions, statutes, legislative enactments, judicial decisions and administrative orders—reflect the struggles of competing values for expression and realization. It is for this reason that the study of law can provide significant insights into the structure and processes of the society as a whole, into the wellsprings of social change which lie outside the technically defined domains of law.

Viewed in this way, law is a product of social factors which fix its content and to a considerable extent its procedures as well. Thus it is an effect of social change. To be sure, social movement does not stand in relation to legal institution as temperature to a thermometer. As noted already, inherent in the technique of law is a peculiar quality of stability, at times almost of intransigence. As a consequence, it is quite possible for tensions to develop between the claims or demands of the social group, or significant parts of it, and legal institutions. Careful study of legal data, the flow of litigation, legislative debate and enactment, the applications of executive power, will reveal those tensions and assist the investigator in assessing the direction of social movement, its force and speed.

Many students of society have used their claim to status as scientists to explain and justify a disregard of the problems of values. Since this study is concerned in part with the value orientation of a particular legal order, the compatibility of scientific legal scholarship with value analysis must be considered. Two points are vital: clarification of the concept of value as used in this study, and the distinction between value analysis of law and evaluation of law.

When one turns to the concept of value, the dangers of reification are great. The Platonic notion of absolute, eternal and immutable Ideas, independent of human experience, has persisted. Thus, it is difficult to focus on what a particular individual or group at some point in time perceives to be good and therefore desirable without raising the spectre of *The Good* and thereby becoming embroiled in epistemological speculation on the cognitive nature of values. In this study I would hope to avoid this difficulty.

Whether there is a world of absolute values is here irrelevant, in the sense that this study does not raise the question and therefore takes no position on it. Equally irrelevant is the question whether such values, if they exist, are within human cognition. These problems are avoided by taking a value to mean merely an interest, claim, desire or demand felt or made by men in society. Whether these are good or of value in relation to an absolute standard, if such exists, is thus beyond the range of discussion. The concept of value, thus restricted, subsumes data that are subject to cognition and are within the range of scientific investigation.

It is necessary here to maintain the distinction between evaluation of law and the value analysis of law. Evaluation is an important aspect of legal scholarship, though it is not among the purposes of this study. Rather, the purpose is to analyze the development of certain legal institutions in Ghana over a period of time in order to determine what values, as delimited earlier, have guided that development. In a sense, therefore, the ultimate focus will not be on law but on the society, the elite manipulators of the technique, the claims and demands they advance, and the processes by which their value acceptances have been reflected in the legal technique.

A study of this kind would ideally be divorced from the value acceptances of the researcher. That divorce can never be total, however, since the researcher's own value position at least dictates what is "of value" for study. That I investigate legal institutions in Ghana rather than drum music reflects not merely my assumed competencies but also my perceptions of value. More particularly, that I concentrate on constitutional structure and the norms affecting political activity rather than the law of contract or commercial transactions reflects similar perceptions. At some points where my own value acceptances perhaps assume greater importance, as in the chapter on "The Legal Tools of Political Monopoly," I have tried to articulate the guiding value assumptions.

At the level of value analysis, a further caveat must be attached to any claim of scientific objectivity. My purpose is clear—to identify the value acceptances that have guided and shaped the legal institutions under study and, insofar as possible, to determine the locus and scope of the acceptances. At this point, however, an important element of subjectivity enters, and this must be acknowledged. A research scholar encountering in a society other than his own an institution that appears familiar may see in it implicit value judgments like those that produced similar developments in his own society. Thus, he runs the risk of too ready attribution of familiar value motivations to familiar institutions. Such attribution may be appropriate, but independent evidence to support it should be sought.

A parallel risk arising out of the researcher's own social background and value set is that he will fail to see or to weigh accurately important value judgments in the society he studies merely because in his own they are unfamiliar or unknown; thus arises the danger of the partial view with its enormous potential for distortion. If the investigator is aware of these risks, he improves the prospects for contributing significant knowledge and new insights. He cannot provide absolute guarantees, however, against the effects of his personal and societal subjectivity.

Most men would feel great diffidence if suddenly confronted by a demand that they articulate definitively the essential elements of the good life. Within any social group, it will surely be the rare individual or association that has consciously and comprehensively worked out a scheme of wants or desires so that the scheme can be urged in its full coherence on an embryonic law-government order. In their particularized form these wants are numerous and probably subject to frequent change. By no means will all of them be presented to the law-government order for support and, hopefully, satisfaction. Of those presented, not all can be implemented through law. The present study does not, of course, attempt to examine the resulting competition through the full range of Ghanaian law. The value competition relevant here is that which has influenced the shaping of basic governmental structures, the allocation of powers and functions and the relation of the citizen to law-government processes.

It must not be assumed that the resolution within a particular law-government order of the competition among the claims presented to it results in a single, totally consistent scheme of values. Rather, as one seeks to discover behind the multitude of particular enactments a greater design or ordering of values, he soon discovers a number of basic antinomies. In the various streams of legal theory and in actual legal systems, these same antinomies tend to recur. A system is viable to the extent that the antinomic tensions are controlled by processes of compromise and adjustment among the members of the social group and the elite who exercise the greatest influence or power in shaping the law. The analyst traces the value profile of a particular legal order as he discovers the shifting fulcrum points at which various value acceptances are counterbalanced or outweighed by their antinomic competitors. With great humility, I will attempt in this chapter to suggest the more important antinomies and the shifts that have occurred in the developing legal order of Ghana.[1]

The dominant antinomy thus far opposes the value of the small, intimate law-government units characteristic of the traditional order to the value of nationhood, I use the term "nationhood" rather than "nationalism" to avoid some of the conventional implications of the latter. Of primary interest here is the effort to create within modern Ghana a popular perception of a new value, the nation, and to organize its expression internally, rather than to implement externally a set of developed national values and aims. Vigorous external expression of Ghanaian aims and efforts to realize them have thus far occurred mainly in the context of the movement toward African unity. In the fullest sense, therefore, the antinomic competition to be considered first opposes traditional localism to nationhood and both to the embryonic value of African unity.

Traditional law-government in the area defined by the boundaries of modern Ghana was totally oriented to the values of small, ethnically homogeneous groups. While innumerable differences among these groups could be detected, they appear to have had two critically important common characteristics. The first of these was the dependence of law-government on a *Weltanschauung* shared by the group. Civil government and the enforceable norms of social intercourse were merely one facet of a system that included Divinity in its several manifestations, the physical world inhabited by the group, the ancestors, the chiefs and their councilors, the lineages and ultimately each member of the group. In such a system, the law-government functions of an elite could not be isolated, for their religious and

[1] This theme was developed very briefly in my Inaugural Lecture in the University of Ghana. See Harvey, "A Value Analysis of Ghanaian Legal Development Since Independence," 1 Univ. of Ghana L. Jour. 3 (1964).

ritual functions were intertwined and equally important. The second characteristic of the traditional order was a consequence of the first: law was personal; it governed a person because he was a member of the group and thus enmeshed in its total religious-legal-social life.

The advent of sustained British colonial power on the Gold Coast did not, in theory at least, undertake to change this general ordering system. The initially limited range of British interest and activity and, as that range was extended, the use of the system of indirect rule, left the law-government complex of the traditional order substantially intact in a formal sense. British efforts to validate and support the indigenous law-government system were in large measure self-defeating. This result was in part due to the efforts of the colonial government to sustain and use indigenous functionaries who had never had or had lost their traditional status and support. More importantly, however, it was due to the increasing association of these functionaries with a system of power that lay quite outside the self-contained world of the traditional order. That association tended to demand of the indigenous rulers new functions and attributed to them novel powers. The corrosive effect of this association on the status of the chiefs, and thereby on the total order of which they were an indispensable part, was reinforced by educational, economic and religious factors intimately related to the colonial regime. The development of local schools and broadened opportunities for study abroad, the introduction of cocoa cultivation as a widespread source of cash income and religious proselytism (particularly by the Christian sects) challenged the *Weltanschauung* that supported the traditional regimes and thus undermined the value of the various indigenous groups as effective instruments of social order.

Until virtually the advent of independence for the Gold Coast, British colonial policy did not seem to be concerned to nurture some central value perception that could substitute for the traditional localism. Unlike France or even Portugal, whose policies tended to be integrationist, Great Britain never offered the British "nation" as an organizing value around which the developing aims and aspirations of the African people could be pursued. Nor was a new, essentially African synthesis provided. Historical factors reflecting the economic struggles of the European powers alone explain the aggregating of areas and peoples under British dominion. Within these areas, schemes of administration reflected such considerations as the mode of acquisition, certain niceties of British law supporting the government of overseas territories, as well as administrative efficiency and convenience. Thus, through most of the period of British responsibility on the Gold Coast, the overlay of British law-government was separately defined for the Colony, Ashanti, the Northern Territories and Trans-Volta Togoland. Only in 1946 were Ashanti representatives brought into the Legislative Council in Accra; only in the Coussey Constitution of 1950 was provision made for the inclusion of Northern Territories members. It is, therefore, impossible to find in colonial policy any effort to nurture an organizing value perception of wider inclusion than the small states, towns, divisions or tribes of the traditional order. It might fairly be added that British policy was hostile to the attempts at wider association made by the indigenous people. For example, the Mankesim Confederation, though inspired in part by British expressions of disenchantment with the responsibilities of government on the Gold Coast, was promptly suppressed. In Ashanti, where the Confederacy represented the largest and most developed law-government institution of the indigenous order, the period from 1896 to 1935 found it in total disarray, with the Asantehene in British-imposed exile through most of the period.

Since 1951, when a government under Dr. Nkrumah was granted substantial internal power and began pressing rapidly toward independence, the value of nationhood has been the fundamental assumption behind virtually all of the enactments considered in this study. Indigenous institutions had not totally lost their vitality, however, and the values implicit in them constantly challenged the efforts to organize law-government effectively on a national basis. Consequently, tension and conflict, sometimes violent, have characterized Ghana's brief national existence.

As I suggested in an earlier chapter, this entire study illustrates the competition between traditional localism and nationhood. That competition may be seen most sharply, however, in a limited range of examples. Chief among these is the 1957 Independence Constitution which resolved the issue against federalism, with its heavy reliance on local loyalties, in favor of a unitary national government. Another example is found in the progressive transfer since 1951 of local government functions to secular, elective bodies under the supervision of a Minister, from which representatives of the traditional authorities have been completely excluded. Yet another is provided by the several enactments by which the new national government has extended its control over matters affecting chiefly status and the functions and economic resources of the chiefs. Finally, the growing body of national law administered in a nationally uniform system of secular courts should be mentioned. The seeds planted by the colonial power in importing English statutes, common law and equity, have been nurtured by the independent Government of Ghana. Republican legislation now creates an initial presumption of the applicability of the common law, rather than a personal customary law, and thus advantages the regime of national law grounded, not on personal status under the traditional order, but on the territoriality of the nation.

While law-government developments since 1951 have tended to emphasize the value of nationhood, the older loyalties and values underlying the traditional order have also been reflected. In some instances the reflection was transient, dictated by passing considerations of expediency, as in the restrictions on national legislative power imposed in the interests of regional and traditional forces by the Independence Constitution. Yet the Republican Constitution still requires an incoming President to pledge that "Chieftaincy in Ghana should be guaranteed and preserved" (Art. 13(1)). The chiefs still meet in their Regional Houses, though regulated and controlled by national law. Most important of all, customary law, though restricted, still represents a vital element of the legal order—indeed, it is the element most intimately related to the great mass of the people.

The analysis thus far merely suggests that the value of nationhood has guided law-government developments. The available data do not establish the extent to which this value is actually accepted by the people. If the views of an ordinary citizen in Enchi, Bawku, Lawra or Keta could be accurately analyzed, it seems doubtful that the value associations of "Ghana" would dominate his perceptions of the good. It seems more likely that the dominance of nationhood depends upon the perceptions of the relatively small elite, led by Dr. Nkrumah, that has determined the mainstream of law-government developments since 1951. It must also be emphasized that no conclusion can now be reached on the potential effectiveness of the legal enactments and institutions oriented to the value of nationhood in instilling and nurturing within the people a perception of that value. Insofar as the enactments discussed in the chapter "The Legal Tools of Political Monopoly" are a factor, it seems clear that, in the short run at least, they are dysfunctional to the development of national unity and to an appreciation of the value of nationhood.

A developing antinomy in Ghana, and indeed throughout Africa, opposes the value of nationhood to the broader good of African unity. Aside from the authorization to Parliament to cede Ghanaian sovereignty to a union of African states, the value of African unity has thus far been reflected very little in the law-government institutions of Ghana. To be sure, certain loans have been made in connection with political pronouncements of prospective close association with Guinea and Mali; Guinea and Ghana have exchanged Resident Ministers; and the Parliament of Ghana has ratified the Charter of African Unity. Nevertheless, the nation-states as spun off by departing colonial regimes are now the critical law-government structures of Africa and show every prospect of remaining such for the foreseeable future.

African political leaders like Dr. Nkrumah are torn by a cruel dilemma. They understand, and Dr. Nkrumah more clearly than many, that the realization of widely felt aspirations for rapid economic development, education, health care, and greater independence of external, nonpolitical controls will be furthered by closer association among the African states. The form of that association might fall at many different points on a continuum marked at one extreme by treaties between two or more sovereign states and at the other by true political unity on a continental scale. The appropriate point has not yet been settled to the satisfaction of all, but it is clear that the present Charter of African Unity is much closer to the first extreme than to the second. The fact, however, that the Organization of African Unity even exists so early in the experience of independent Africa is a cogent testimonial to the acceptance by African political leaders of an organizing value overarching nationhood.

In reality the value of the nation stands to African unity as the localism of the traditional societies stands to nationhood. Tension and conflict are inevitable. Law-government measures reflecting and fostering the value of nationhood, as well as political actions designed to support the charisma of national leaders like Dr. Nkrumah, are dysfunctional to the competitive value of a more inclusive unity. Yet clearly, such measures are now demanded by the elite's knowledge that African aspirations cannot be realized in a continent fragmented into groups typical of the traditional order and that the small, nation-states left by colonialism are the best immediately available vehicles for organizing public power. Yet the long-range inadequacies of the states are readily apparent. Followers of Hegel might sense here the stately movement of the dialectic. Implicit in the thesis that nationhood sets against the traditional order is its own antithesis which is not yet fully revealed. For the present, however, the thesis of nationhood governs law-government in Africa.

One of the most persistent antinomies of legal theory, and one that can engender the most profound tensions in the practical orientation of a legal order, opposes individualist to collectivist values. Of course, such tensions are not inevitable, since the individual and the collective need not be made absolute or ultimate values. If they are not, it is possible to establish certain rational relations between them and thus facilitate accommodation. Absolute individualism could produce a Hobbesian state of nature; most people would therefore recognize that the greatest well-being of the individual requires some concern for the interests of the group of which the individual is inevitably a part. Conversely the exponent of group values must recognize that the collectivity benefits from the well-being of its members and thus must seek to protect certain interests that can be deemed individual. Further, Roscoe Pound's jurisprudence of interests long ago emphasized that most individual claims and interests can be meaningfully stated in terms of social interests and vice versa. Nevertheless, there are significant, practical differences in the structure and operation of law-government orders dependent upon whether the individual or the community is more commonly the dominant value, when an actual choice must be made.

The indigenous law-government order of Ghana resolved this issue in favor of the community. It would hardly be an overstatement to say that in this order there was no operative concept of the individual. The family or lineage was the basic unit of social organization. Status within that group and the higher organizations built upon it fully determined each person's obligations and rights.

Insofar as British colonial policy attempted to support and utilize indigenous institutions, it weighted the scales on the side of collectivist values. As has been seen, however, within certain limits, the colonial regime also contributed new governmental structures and procedures and an alien body of law which were dominated by individualist values. Introduction of cash crops also emphasized individual initiative and strengthened the claims of the nuclear family that usually assisted in the production of cash income, rather than the claims and obligations of the traditional extended family. The influence of Christianity was also individualizing; sin and salvation are individual, not group, experiences. As the Gold Coast approached independence under British tutelage, the influence of English governmental models increased. The traditional order was by this time in sufficient disarray that its priority for group values offered little deterrent to an accelerating development of law-government predominantly grounded on individualistic values.

These values are reflected in governmental structures involving at both national and local levels the exercise of legislative powers by popularly elected bodies. Wide dissemination of the franchise, access to legislative and executive office limited by only a few objective criteria rationally related to qualification, the recruitment of a public service also on objective criteria of qualification and the refinement of a body of private law to facilitate a broad range of individual economic activity are some of the developments in which a strong emphasis on individualistic values is reflected. If the law-government structure of the traditional order is accepted as the reference point, it seems entirely clear that the movement of the individual toward the center of the stage, begun under the influence of the colonial regime, has been continued in independent Ghana.

The decline of the collectivist values supporting the traditional order has been more than balanced however by a new collectivist orientation toward the nation-state. Therefore, it is in relation to this new collectivity that the status of the individual in modern Ghana must now be assessed. One of the customary approaches to such an assessment is in terms of fundamental private rights and the machinery for their enforcement or protection against the state or its functionaries.

Only one fundamental right is clearly articulated in the current law of Ghana. This is the right to the franchise for the selection of officials and for the modification of the basic scheme of allocating and controlling public power, where this function has been reserved to the people. While this right is constitutionally "guaranteed," however, the only realistic conclusion today is that it is purely formal; it is systematically denied, and no effective procedure for its enforcement exists. This fact is best illustrated by the constitutional referendum in January, 1964.

The 1957 Constitution articulated two other basic rights, to freedom of conscience, religious profession and practice and to compensation for property taken for public purposes. These guarantees were reduced to statutory level by the removal in 1958 of the restrictions on parliamentary power to amend the constitution. The present Republican Constitution contains no statement of individual rights, other than the franchise; the closest approach is the presidential statement of political ideals, required by Art. 13(1), which lacks juristic effect. Aside from areas where popular power is entrenched, the status of the individual, his interests and claims, is fully subject to the collective will as expressed in Acts of Parliament. Furthermore, as recent experience has shown, the entrenchment device itself is not an effective deterrent to fundamental changes in the law-government structure.

Three categories of relatively recent enactments illustrate well the triumph of collectivist values over individualism: 1) measures restricting freedom of movement, association, speech, etc., the imposition of such restrictions often depending upon non-reviewable executive discretion; the Preventive Detention Act is the most dramatic example of this category; 2) measures effecting a merger of executive and legislative power; cogent illustrations of these are found in the special legislative powers of Dr. Nkrumah under Article 55 of the Republican Constitution and the increasing reliance on the delegation of legislative powers to executive officers; 3) measures terminating or gravely threatening the independence and integrity of the judiciary; the cardinal example here is the 1964 constitutional amendment granting to the President complete discretionary power to dismiss superior court judges. An independent judiciary cannot protect individual interests if the law itself demands the dominance of collective values. It can however maintain certain safeguards by demanding that officials justify their actions under the law. In the absence of an independent judiciary, even this minimal protection of individual interests is lost.

The individualism-collectivism antinomy is closely related to the competition between democracy and autocracy. Both the incompleteness of data and the fact that the available evidence strongly suggests significant variations among the groups now included within the country make generalization on the latter antinomy in the traditional orders of Ghana difficult. For example, the institution of chieftaincy seems to have been more strongly autocratic in the Northern Territories than in Ashanti and the Colony. If the Akan, representing the largest population group, are considered, however, one finds a delicate balance between democratic and autocratic features.

In both the processes of selection of an Akan chief and the direction of state affairs after his enstoolment, widespread consultation and efforts to achieve a consensus were characteristic. These processes were carried out through a hierarchy of at least partially representative persons or groups, starting with the lineage head and eventuating in the council of the Paramount Chief. The important role played by the companies of commoners and their elected representatives should also be noted. Democratic control of chiefly conduct was ultimately asserted in the power to de-stool a chief who, after fair warning, continued actions not approved by his people.

These democratic features were woven into a fabric with significant autocratic elements. The sacred nature of Akan chieftaincy was a fundamental limitation on indigenous democracy. Chiefly authority was validated not solely by the consent of the governed but by the special relation of the chief to God in all His manifestations and to the spirits of the departed ancestors. This relation served to limit the choice of a law-government elite to candidates provided by certain stool-eligible families. Even significantly democratic processes in the system were often carried out behind an autocratic façade. Thus, the election of a chief resulting from extensive consultation was announced by the Queen Mother as if the choice were hers alone. Similarly, important decisions of state policy representing a patiently sought consensus were declared by the chief's linguist as if they sprang full-blown from the brow of Jove.

Both democratic and autocratic values were vital to the system. The balance between them was delicate, and it is not surprising that it was disturbed profoundly by British efforts to use traditional institutions in the scheme of colonial administration. Perhaps deceived by some of the external appearances of autocracy, colonial administrators often attributed to the chiefs powers and functions to which the indigenous order did not entitle them. Similarly, governmental efforts to support loyal and cooperative chiefs deeply disturbed the processes of consultation and consensus-formation on which chiefly status and the viability of the order depended. Thus, the system of indirect rule operated so as to subvert the democratic values implicit in the traditional order and to support its autocratic aspects.

It was not simply by distorting the traditional system that colonialism weighted the scales in favor of autocratic values. By its essential nature, colonialism is autocratic. An alien elite, able to relate its power to govern to the consent of the governed only by the most palpable rationalization, is inevitably autocratic. That elite may be relatively benevolent; it may justify its role on laudably altruistic grounds; it may nurture a respect for individual values; it may in fact attempt to educate the subject people to appreciate, adopt and operate limited and democratic government. In varying degrees all these traits were shown by British colonialism on the Gold Coast. The conclusion is inevitable, however, that as long as the colonial power was exercised, the dominant value was autocratic, in the sense that British power over the African people was self-generated and, in the last analysis, absolute.

The autocratic face of colonialism was shown in many ways: in the official majority maintained in the Legislative Assembly until 1946, in the vesting solely in the British Governor of legislative powers over Ashanti until 1946 and over the Northern Territories until 1951, in the substantial reservations of metropolitan powers in all constitutions until independence. It was manifested also in such actions as the discretionary and unreviewable detention of nationalist leaders, including Nkrumah, in 1948. Virtually every legal technique of autocratic, authoritarian government, employed in more recent years by the Government of Ghana under Dr. Nkrumah, finds its historic precedent in the colonial Gold Coast.

As has been noted, however, the colonial regime also reflected and attempted to nurture democratic values. This statement became truer as the date for granting independence approached. Democratic ideas of law and government surely prevailed in the national governmental structure, closely patterned on Westminster, with which Ghana entered its independent existence. The progression, culminating in the 1957 Constitution which completely terminated the power of an alien elite, had a number of earlier phases worth noting: the termination of the official majority in the Legislative Council in 1946, the spelling out in 1953 of a broad popular franchise with articulated guarantees against discrimination on the ground of race, sex, religion or political belief and the transfer under the Local Government Act of 1951 of responsibility for local government and services to popularly elected, secular councils.

The democratic, basic framework of government with which Ghana entered independence has been, in general, preserved. The present Republican Constitution articulates a theory of popular sovereignty and makes the people the repository of all power not expressly delegated to the several organs of government. Both national and local legislative bodies are elective, and the franchise implements at least formally the principle of one man-one vote. Qualifications for the franchise and eligibility for election to office, as well as stated grounds of disqualification, are for the most part objective and rationally related to the privilege they condition. One may fairly conclude that in the formal allocation and channeling of law-government powers and in the philosophical position expressed to justify the scheme, democratic values have been dominant.

The democratic underpinning of the formal law-government structure has been progressively drained of meaning, however, by the realities of political life in Ghana and by the rapid accretion of practically absolute powers, particularly in the executive. The constitution itself accords independent legislative powers to the first President, Dr. Nkrumah. He also enjoys absolute power over the tenure of all judges of the High Court and Supreme Court. Legislative authorizations of preventive detention, deportation and controls over assembly, association, speech and other expression gravely restrict or deny the necessary operative assumptions of a democratic society. These powers have been exercised in aid of one political party over which a single charismatic leader presides. Autocratic powers created and allocated by law have been increasingly supplemented by extralegal or illegal techniques for the suppression of political diversity and the consolidation of unquestioned, indeed unquestionable, powers in the revolutionary elite of the Convention People's Party. The differential allocation of perquisites by the Government, intimidation of political opponents and the vigorous use of all available information media for Party propaganda exemplify these techniques.

Thus, the antinomy between democratic and autocratic values is pervasive in the law-government structure of Ghana. If democratic values have clearly dominated the basic structuring of public power, it is equally clear that autocratic values have determined the realities of political life and have directed a rapidly growing body of particular enactments.

Roscoe Pound's oft-quoted statement that "law must be stable and yet it cannot stand still"[2] reflects one of the basic antinomies of any legal order. Though one rejects, as I do, the proposition that stability is an essential characteristic of some objective idea of law, it must be recognized that stability and the attendant values of certainty and predictability usually find prominent expression in any legal system. No society is completely static, however, though the pace of change may vary greatly in different societies. The on-going stream of social life introduces a demand for change that must be accommodated if the legal system is to remain viable. Beyond the demands for change presented to a legal order by individuals and groups within the society, a further, more sharply focused demand may be presented by an elite group seeking to use the law-

[2] Pound, *Interpretations of Legal History* I (1923).

government technique to reshape the society itself. Thus, law-government institutions may be both cause and effect of broader societal changes. It is important to locate the sources of the pressure for change and the effective ordering of that value in relation to the ever-present demands for stability.

The indigenous law-government orders of Ghana reflected the dominant value of stability. Indeed, this seems a necessary consequence of the fact that law-government institutions were only one part of a universal, divinely ordained system. Their systemic relation to God, the spirits of the departed ancestors and the physical world did not encourage attempts to modify law-government structures and norms in the interest of the present inhabitants of this vale of tears. Direct legislation, the legal technique most apt for innovation, was used by the chiefs and their councils, but immemorial custom was the mainstream of the law. Change inevitably occurred under the modest pressure of gradual social movement, but there is no evidence that anywhere in the indigenous order a demand for change from either the governing elite or the larger social group fundamentally disturbed the strong tendency of the system toward stability.

The British option for indirect rule was intended to support the stability of the traditional order. As has been seen, however, the colonial experience had a corrosive effect on chieftaincy and thus the legal order of which it was a prominent part. Economic, social and even religious factors introduced under the colonial system further sapped the strength of traditional institutions and sharpened popular awareness of the desirability of change. The range of functions allocated by the colonial government to the traditional authorities also involved implicit demands for a re-shaping of the system. Perhaps unfortunately, the indigenous order and its elite members never demonstrated a capacity for creative response to the newly awakened needs and desires of the people or to the expectations of the colonial power. The result was increasing tension between the traditional law-government order and the society.

By introducing new structures of secular government at both national and local levels, the colonial power provided the means for accommodating the growing social pressure for change. It also provided the tools to be employed by a new African elite in their effort to achieve rapid, planned social reconstruction. At the time of independence, following the controversy over federalism, certain deterrents to rapid change were built into the constitutional structure. The national legislative powers over basic governmental structures were limited by the necessity for concurrence of regional bodies with a more strongly traditional orientation. In 1958 these restrictions were eliminated and a fully sovereign Parliament was created. The entrenchment device of the present Republican Constitution forecloses a claim to full Parliamentary sovereignty, and the necessity for a referendum as a prerequisite to fundamental changes in the law-government structure evidences a continuing appreciation of the value of stability. The success of the Nkrumah elite in 1964 in overcoming the entrenchment deterrent and accomplishing profoundly important reallocations of public power indicates that such legal safeguards of stability are relatively insignificant in the power complex of Ghanaian politics.

This entire study is evidence of the dominance of the value of change. For almost two decades, constitutional changes have been frequent. Unlike the United States or Britain, "the Constitution" has not become in Ghana an emotive symbol generating passions for stability. Both basic law-government structures and particular enactments have been modified readily as perceptions of need have changed. No significant reliance has been placed on the courts as agencies for adapting the law to new social needs. Both the English tradition of judicial passivity, which has obtained in Ghana, and the existence of an aggressive political elite in firm control of executive and legislative organs have acted to assign this function almost entirely to the legislature under effective executive control. The large body of enactments in both public and private law, particularly since the Republic, attests to the present strength of the value of change.

It is significant, however, that even in this revolutionary period, changes have been accomplished in an unbroken chain of legality. While it is surely appropriate to speak of the Ghanaian revolution, there has been at no point a definitive break with the past. Even in transferring the ultimate locus of legal power on the grant of independence in 1957, care was taken to justify the new order under the legal postulates of the old system. The same was especially true in the selection of procedures to be followed on the creation of the Republic in 1960. While the office of President is novel, it is an amalgam whose antecedents can be found in Great Britain, the United States and France. For most of the new legislation, even that which has elicited the greatest criticism elsewhere, models can be found either in colonial enactments for the Gold Coast, in the law of the United Kingdom or, less frequently, in the law of Eire or the United States. Finally but most significantly, despite the attractions of a uniform body of national law, most of the people continue to be affected mainly by the various regimes of customary law.

In summary, it appears that legal developments in Ghana have shown the increasing aggrandizement of the values of nationhood, collectivism, autocracy and change over their antinomic competitors. The victory of these value accceptances is not total. The value of a higher unity, perhaps of Africa, is perceived fairly clearly by the elite and therefore may help to prevent the necessary process of nation-building from developing into an aggressive nationalism. The indigenous order, and much of the British legacy, tended to instill an appreciation of democratic values that continues to be reflected in the formal structuring of law-government powers. The indigenous soil was probably least propitious for the values of individualism, and the present drive toward rapid development—while public order is still precarious—does not encourage the individualistic seeds sown during the colonial period by British education, patterns of economic activity and theories of government. The present dominance of change reflects the urgency and pace of general social movement, not a rejection of the value of stabilizing and protecting a legal order that has finally demonstrated its capacity to respond to the developing needs of the people it serves.

LEGAL EDUCATION IN GHANA

THE VIEWS expressed in this memorandum are grounded on a set of premises which should be stated preliminarily. The views themselves project a rational plan for development only insofar as the premises can be defended. At this time we will state the premises with little elaboration or argument. If they appear to be of doubtful validity, we would, of course, be glad to defend them further.

1. Law is a learned profession. This is not merely a traditional cliché. The statement should be understood to mean that the professional lawyer who is faithful to the highest standards of his profession is not merely a skilled craftsman manipulating a technique for social ordering. Rather, as adviser to individuals in many of the most intimate and important concerns of their lives and as counselor in various aspects of social and political organization, he achieves his full professional stature only if he is a man of broad and liberal education. He must be sensitive to the values of the cultural tradition of which he is a part and alert to the pressures and needs felt at the growing edge of his society. Thus, the never-ending education of the lawyer comprehends far more than acquiring familiarity with a body of positive legal norms, substantive and procedural. It includes as well a substantial exposure to the learning of the humanities and the social sciences, and a constant effort to relate his more strictly professional work to the full range of individual and social interests, demands and claims.

2. If the education of the lawyer is seen from this

* The following paper was prepared by the author and in November, 1962, presented on behalf of the Faculty of Law to the Academic Board of the University of Ghana. It states the guiding philosophy to be applied in the development of legal education in Ghana and covers the specific recommendations made to the University and to the General Legal Council.

perspective, it is clear that the study of law will have a wider range of utility than catering to the prospective professional. We are profoundly convinced that the legal order of any society is a rich storehouse of data of general social and humanistic significance. For example, a study of the Law of Contract should be most revealing of the development of a market economy. The Law of Torts reveals graphically the individual and social pressures of urbanization and growing technology. The Law of Crimes tells much of the philosophical underpinning of a society, of the values which seem to it most important. Thus, study of such legal subjects has utility for many who seek merely a liberal education with no thought of professional qualification.

3. If the foregoing premises are valid, it seems beyond question that instruction in law is legitimately part of a university's concern. Indeed, it appears clear that adequate education in law can be provided only within the framework of an institution having a commitment to research and teaching over a spectrum as wide as a university can provide.

4. The circumstances of certain of the new countries may justify "crash programs" for the training of minimally qualified legal technicians. We see no persuasive evidence that these circumstances obtain in Ghana today. Therefore, in projecting its program, Ghana is entitled to concentrate on the production of lawyers who are soundly and liberally educated, entitled to full acceptance and respect in the international legal community.

5. No existing system of legal education provides a model fully responsive to Ghana's conditions and needs. British university education in law, which achieves magnificently in the development of analytical skills and historical perspective, can perhaps afford to be extremely nonprofessional in view of the ancient instructional programs of the Inns as well as the pre-

professional apprenticeships and courses of study required of solicitors. In America the university law schools long tended toward excessive, narrowing professionalism. A high degree of professionalism can be defended there, however, in view of the fact that law is post-graduate education, the student having pursued his general studies beyond the secondary school level and very commonly having earned a B.A. or equivalent degree before entering law school. The German system involves an interesting combination of legal and non-legal instruction. The universities are able, however, to shape their programs in reliance on the student's having three years of referendar study and practical observation after leaving the university and before entering his profession. Thus, the underlying assumptions of the various foreign models are not valid in Ghana. This country must devise its own model, borrowing from abroad whatever is useful but feeling no initial commitment to any pattern merely on the basis of familiarity.

6. A basic consideration in planning is the conservation and most effective use of limited resources. Monetary costs are important but probably more so is the cost in scarce manpower. That part of Ghana's qualified manpower which can be committed to legal education is relatively small. For a time there must be reliance on some expatriate staff while strenuous efforts are made to interest able young Ghanaians studying law in preparing themselves for an academic career. During this early period of relative scarcity of resources, it is necessary to concentrate on sound basic programs, leaving until later extensions of activity which may now be legitimate elsewhere. In the latter category fall programs of part-time study largely directed toward civil service advancement or general adult education. The only alternative to such concentration is a dissipation of resources and a commitment to mediocrity or less.

BACKGROUND INFORMATION

We assume there is general familiarity with the Report of the International Advisory Committee on Legal Education in Ghana which led to the establishment of the present bifurcated program. Two routes to the bar have been provided: (i) a four-year degree program in the University followed by a year of "practical" study in the Ghana Law School, and (ii) a diploma program, now structured for three years in the Law School, followed by the so-called "practical" year. The University will grant the first LL.B. degrees in July, 1963, and these graduates will then be ready for their final phase. The diploma program in the Law School has thus far produced only 13 diplomas. Of these, 10 are now embarked on a "practical" course which presumably will be completed in March or April, 1963. There are 32 students in the Law School reading for Part I of the Bar Examination and 24 reading for Part II. No new students have been admitted to the diploma program of the Law School since January, 1962, pending decisions on merger with the University.

Brief mention should be made of the academic qualifications for admission to the University Law Department and the Law School. The basic qualification for admission to the former is the Higher School Certificate or two advanced level passes on the Certificate of Education examinations. Students who entered the Department in October, 1963, were also required to perform acceptably on a special Departmental entrance examination largely directed toward reading comprehension and compositional skill. There is evidence that the incoming group of students (about 30) is the best the Department has ever had. The educational criterion for admission to the Law School is quite open-ended. As formally stated, it requires that the student pass an entrance examination set by the Law School and obtain either a West African School Certificate, a Certificate which the Board of Legal Education accepts as the equivalent thereof, or the Board's exemption from the educational requirement. The actual preadmission educational levels of the students in the School cannot be effectively summarized. It suffices to say that the educational spectrum covered is very wide—ranging from completion of a commercial course in accounting to a Bachelor's degree. We think one is entitled to raise seriously the question whether the existing admission criterion is compatible with the study of law at a satisfactory level.

The present curricula of the Law Department of the University and of the Law School are set out in the following table:

A. UNIVERSITY LAW DEPARTMENT

1st Year

Introduction to Law and Legal Institutions of Ghana
The Law of Contract
Introduction to Constitutional Law
Elective in Philosophy, Economics or Sociology

2nd Year

Law of Torts
Property Law I
Constitutional and Administrative Law
Criminal Law

3rd Year

Property Law II
Family Law
Commercial Law
Law of Evidence

4th Year

Four courses from—
Comparative Law
Public International Law
The Conflict of Laws
Company Law
African Customary Law
Jurisprudence

Plus participation in the Trial Practice program.

373

B. GHANA LAW SCHOOL

Part I

Introduction to The Law and Legal Institutions of Ghana

Law of Property I

Law of Contract

Law of Tort

Part II

Constitutional Law

Criminal Law

Property Law II

Family Law

Practical Course

Main courses to meet for 2 hours each week—

Civil Litigation and Advocacy

Conveyancing and Drafting

Commercial Law and Practice

Criminal Prosecutions and Appeals

Subsidiary courses to meet for 1 hour each week—

Evidence

Private International Law

Taxation

In addition to the formal instruction it is contemplated that students will make observational visits to the courts, lawyers' chambers and various law departments of the Government. General open lectures by leading judges and practitioners on professional etiquette, office management and account-keeping are also planned. In contrast to the part-time Diploma program, students in the Practical Course are expected to devote full time to their studies.

It should be pointed out that the present departmental syllabus in the University as well as individual course syllabi are regarded as most tentative. They were prepared during recent months without adequate staff, there being in some instances no current member of the staff teaching or having taught the course for which the syllabus was prepared. During the coming year, a re-thinking of curricular problems will have high priority with the Law Faculty. With the staff additions now provided for, these tasks can be begun with greater vigor. Certainly there is awareness of the hazards in continual revision of curriculum; yet inadequate or unsound programs must be revised as early as possible.

It is also of interest to note the extent to which University and Law School syllabi in their current development have departed from the recommendations of the International Advisory Committee. In the University's first year program, the syllabus does not include a course in Customary Law of Tropical Africa; in its place has been substituted a course in the Law of Contract. The change reflects the Department's belief that, in their first year, students should be taught at least one basic common law course, in large part for its methodological value. Further, it is believed that Customary Law should be taught on a broad comparative basis, thus requiring a much higher degree of sophistication than can be expected of first-year students. The nonlaw electives have also been somewhat restricted from the scope contemplated by the International Advisory Committee. Perhaps more important, it should be noted that the syllabus for the third and fourth years includes courses in Commercial Law, Company Law and Jurisprudence which the Committee had not proposed.

The Diploma syllabus in the Law School does not differ from that proposed by the Committee. In the "Practical Course," however, to the Committee's recommendations has been added some instruction in Civil Procedure, Criminal Prosecutions and Private International Law. The Committee also recommended a course in "Industrial Law" which the "Practical Course" does not now include.

The authorized staff of the University Law Department now includes a Professor, two Senior-Lecturers and six Lecturers. Of these posts, one Senior

Lectureship and two Lectureships remain unfilled. In addition to regular staff, the Department has part-time assistance from a Supreme Court Justice, a Senior Lecturer from the Law School, an English lawyer in Ghana primarily for graduate research and an American lawyer supported by a Fellowship from the Maxwell School of Syracuse University. Professor A. C. Kuma, the Presidential Professor of Law, is not participating in the instructional program of the Department. At the request of the Head of Department, Professor Kuma is investigating needs and plans for the development of a major institutional research program in law and related disciplines.

The staff of the Law School consists, in addition to the Director, of two Senior Lecturers and one Lecturer on a full-time basis and five part-time Lecturers. The Maxwell School Fellow also assists in the teaching program. Three members of the staff teach only 2 hours per week, two teach 1 hour each, two teach 4 hours, one 5 hours, and only one teaches 6 hours per week.

The status of the Law Department in the University is now being reconsidered. At present the Department is a division of the Faculty of Social Sciences. Under new University statutes which have been extensively discussed within the University and given tentative approval by the Interim University Council, Law will be given Faculty status under its own Dean.

The Law School operation in Accra is well housed in a building providing considerable room for expansion. The Law Department of the University is temporarily lodged in a wing of Balme Library. This space is urgently needed for Library expansion and it seems unlikely that it will be available long beyond the current academic year. Even if it were to continue to be available, however, it is inadequate for even the present needs of the Department. Office space cannot be provided for all members of the staff and room for expansion of the Law Library is urgently needed. A building program at Legon must be initiated soon.

PROBLEMS

Without doubt, the most serious problem to confront the development of legal education thus far has been the constant shortage of teaching staff and the serious obstacles in the way of effective recruitment. The three years of experience to date have been characterized by rapid turnover of full-time staff, teaching loads which in general are incompatible with much needed research, and a heavy reliance on part-time teachers. Efforts are being made to improve the staff situation. In the University there are three Ghanaians on long-term appointments. A highly experienced American lawyer will join the staff on January 1, 1963, for a four-year term. Efforts are being made to locate qualified Ghanaians here or abroad who may be interested in an academic career. Some promising prospects have been located.

One of the more serious obstacles to effective recruitment is the large disparity between the economic returns which can be offered by the University and those available to able young Ghanaians in private practice, some civil service posts and international agencies. Thus far, the University has not provided a professional differential of the kind universities in some countries have found necessary for the building of acceptable professional faculties. If the University is to secure its fair share of the outstanding talent of the country, it cannot rely too heavily on the altruism of those attracted to the tasks of education. The need for a professional differential will be encountered by the new Faculty of Medicine as well.

Another serious limitation of the present programs in both the University and Law School is that syllabi have been projected almost entirely in the flat plane of positive law. Primary emphasis has been placed on what the law *is*, with little attention given to the development of historical perspective, to the critical evaluation of positive institutions in the light of data provided by other social sciences or, for that matter, to the development of student capacities for careful reasoning and ability to communicate effectively. To a considerable extent, the latter deficiencies are functions of the dominant method of instruction—lecture by the instructor without enough painstaking preclass work on basic legal materials by the students. The teaching method reflects, of course, a chronic shortage of basic materials for student use. These comments are applicable much more fully to the Law School than to the University Law Department.

RECOMMENDATIONS

As the views expressed earlier indicate, we are in full agreement with the recommendation of the International Advisory Committee that the basic qualification for call to the bar should be a university education. The Director of Legal Education has already recommended to the General Legal Council the termination of the Diploma program in the Ghana Law School as early as possible, taking account of the equities of students already embarked on the program. For a brief transitional period the Council may deem it appropriate to regard a call to the English Bar as the equivalent of a Diploma in the Ghana Law School. The University should assume responsibility for those phases of the educational program now assigned to a so-called "Practical Course" during the fifth year. The Law Faculty of the University must be increased as rapidly as is consistent with quality in order to meet these expanded obligations, and an adequate physical plant should be constructed at Legon. The several recommendations thus summarized will now be discussed in detail.

(a) *Liquidation of the Ghana Law School*

The Director of Legal Education has reported to the General Legal Council as follows:

"In my judgment, the non-University route to the Ghana Bar, if ever justified by an urgent need for lawyers, is not now required. Even if a need existed, experience with the Diploma program to date strongly suggests that it is ill-equipped to meet the need. The only significant obstacle to immediate liquidation of the program is created by the students who have already invested time and energy in it. I would therefore recommend that all students in the Law School be advised immediately of the impending termination of the Diploma program and that only those successful on subsequent examinations will be permitted to continue. Repeat or partial examinations should not be permitted. With no further intake into the Diploma program, and with continuations so restricted, it should be possible to operate the liquidation phases fairly economically and to conclude all instruction in this program by July, 1964. I would also recommend that persons called to the English Bar by July, 1964, should be regarded as of comparable status with Diploma holders and thus permitted to continue into the final phase of their legal education in Ghana.

"Consideration must be given to the future of the 'Practical Course' in the Law School or, more accurately, how the educational objectives assigned to the fifth year are to be achieved. I must confess a profound skepticism of the dichotomy between an academic program of legal education and a so-called practical phase. Admittedly, as the premises initially stated indicate, I believe that instruction in law within a University has great utility for students having no professional objective. Also some law courses would have much less interest or benefit for such students than for the embryonic professional. Nevertheless, I think the 'academic or theoretical—practical' distinction invidious. As Mr. Justice O. W. Holmes once said: 'Theory is the most important part of the dogma of the law, as the architect is the most important man who takes part in the building of a house. . . . It is not to be feared as unpractical, for, to the competent, it simply means going to the bottom of the subject.' I too would respectfully urge that insofar as a sound theoretical grounding is the objective of University teaching of law, it is the most practical of all achievements. Further, the so-called practical, the 'is' and 'how' of the law, if not based on an acceptable theoretical underpinning, is either useless or pernicious. I would therefore urge that the distinction be down-graded or eliminated from our consideration of Ghana's emerging program of legal education.

"I would strongly recommend that instruction within the areas now assigned to the fifth year be brought within the University's instructional program. If the subject-matter to be dealt with can be taught at all, it will be better taught if organized by full-time, committed teachers and supported by the continuing research such persons would be expected to do.

"Work in the more strictly professional courses, which I do not think properly confined to the fifth year, would require special staff considerations. For example, from those with English educational backgrounds, it would be necessary to employ persons with solicitor's qualifications to teach course in procedure and drafting. Among techniques of instruction should be included the working out of problems and the drafting of documents by the students, to be criticised by the instructor and revised under his supervision. Organised courses involving student participation in such areas as trial and appellate practice are also needed. As parts of the instructional programs it should be entirely feasible to include regular visits to the courts with subsequent critiques. Among the several areas to be dealt with in these ways, I would include conveyancing and drafting, procedure and evidence. In the development of such courses, it should be expected that the instructors would enlist wherever possible the aid of leaders of the Bench and Bar, not only to expose the students to the expertise such men possess, but to begin during student days a close fraternal association with the distinguished men of the profession.

"If the University should assume responsibility for the full range of formal instruction, there would seem to be no reason for a separate 'practical' program in the Law School. Thus that program may be terminated at the end of the current year. It has always been contemplated that those doing the fifth year would be full-time students; no special problems of scheduling evening courses therefore arise. Students completing four years in the University would continue as University students through the fifth year. I will recommend that Diploma holders and those called to the English Bar during the transitional period be accepted by the University as special, non-degree and non-residential students for the necessary one year. Parenthetically, it should be noted that persons seeking admission in Ghana on the basis of call to the English Bar will doubtless require supplementary work here in special features of Ghanaian law. These too should be accommodated as special students within the University's program."

The Faculty of Law would add its endorsement to these recommendations.

(b) *University Degree Programs*

Aside from programs which have always been regarded as temporary, Ghana has already decided on an education program for lawyers covering five years. If liberal and professional education is to be provided adequately, this period should not be reduced. While more time might fruitfully be used, we would not recommend any extension, however.

As has been pointed out earlier, instruction in law should be regarded as useful for many persons who do not seek full professional qualification. For example, many persons who aspire to senior posts in the civil service, the diplomatic corps, or managerial roles in economic enterprise might find instruction in law the most desirable University program. Such persons would not need a number of the more strictly professional courses. Their University period should be fixed at the three- or four-year level and a wider range of courses in the social sciences and humanities opened to them than would be taken by those anticipating professional qualification. We would therefore recommend that the University recognize a sequence of law courses as an appropriate concentration for students working toward the General B.A. degree. Such courses should fit into the basic degree syllabus in the same manner as a sequence in History or Sociology. The professional course should be a five-year program, the ultimate degree objective being the LL.B.

Without commitment to all details but as a basis for our later discussion, we suggest the following outline syllabus for the professional degree program and the group of courses within the B.A. option.

LL.B.

First Year
> Introductory Political Theory and Practice and The Constitutional History of Ghana
> The Law of Contract and Contract Remedies
> English or French Language and Literature
> Option: Philosophy or Sociology

Second Year
> Constitutional Law (Comparative)
> Criminal Law
> Law of Tort
> Law of Immoveable Property

Third Year
> Jurisprudence
> Public International Law
> Comparative Law
> Administrative Law and Practice

Fourth Year
> Commercial Law
> Law of Evidence
> Civil Procedure—Trials and Appeals
> Company Law
> Equity and Succession

Fifth Year
    The Conflict of Laws
    Law of Taxation and Public Finance
    Conveyancing and Drafting

For the next few years, it seems wise to limit students to only four courses at a time. The fourth and fifth year programs are based on the assumption that not all courses would extend through the entire year. It would thus be possible to deal with more areas of the law. It is not the objective, however, to treat the entire *corpus juris*. The emphasis will be on the development of knowledge of fundamental legal institutions and the acquisition of basic intellectual and methodological skills.

It will be noted that a number of the more professional courses are concentrated in the fourth and fifth years, though obviously the understanding of basic institutions and the disciplined powers of reasoning developed in the first three years are essential to the professional. It seems to us clear, however, that the work of the first three years has an educational integrity and coherence which should entitle those completing it to recognition by the award of a degree. We therefore recommend that on their satisfactory completion of the syllabus for the first three years, persons be awarded a B.A. degree with honors in Law. A few students might interrupt or terminate their law studies at this point. We would anticipate, however, that most would continue with the fourth and fifth years, on the satisfactory completion of which they should be granted the LL.B. degree.

Law Option in General B.A. Program

The following courses in Law seem especially well adapted to general, liberal, educational purposes:

    Introductory Political Theory and Practice and The Constitutional History of Ghana
    The Law of Contract and Contract Remedies

Constitutional Law
Criminal Law
Law of Tort
Property Law I
Public International Law
Legislation
Comparative Law including Customary African
  Institutions
Jurisprudence

Various sequences could be developed from this group of courses. We recommend that a Law option be recognized within the General B.A. syllabus and that students electing it should take four courses from this group. In addition to the benefit to them from such study, we believe these non-professional students could contribute to a wider perspective for the LL.B. students.

(c) Staff Needs

The minimum staff required for the teaching of Law in the proposed programs is twelve, distributed over the several ranks as follows: 1 Professor, 4 Senior Lecturers and 7 Lecturers. The building of a qualified staff of this size will take time. One possible source of immediate supplementation of the University staff is the personnel of the Law School who will no longer be needed in a separate program. We do not believe block absorption of staff is wise, however. Members of the staff of the Law School who are interested in University appointment should be invited to submit their applications with appropriate supporting credentials, these to be considered on the same criteria as are generally applied within the University. We have no fixed views at this time as to how many of the Law School personnel could be given University appointment on this basis. We are, however, convinced that Ghana does not need to compromise a high standard of quality in University appointments. It is to be hoped that the majority of the members of the Law Faculty, including senior members, will soon be Ghanaian. This can, in our judgment, be accomplished over the next few years by building from the existing nucleus in the University while maintaining a standard of quality that treats Ghanaians and expatriates alike.

(d) *Physical Plant*

A physical plant adequate for the Law Faculty should be constructed at Legon without delay. We are aware that planning toward this end has already begun in the University. While a number of issues affecting the nature and size of the needed physical plant remain open, some preliminary comments on the building may be made.

The International Advisory Committee recommended planning for entry into the Law Department of at least 80 students per year. Present manpower allocations provide substantially less than this; the present allocation, however, is based almost exclusively on the assumed needs of the private, practicing bar. If legal education in Ghana is structured as here recommended, it becomes attractive to a wider range of students. Development of secondary education in Ghana will also increase the number available for University admission. Further, the higher educational requirement for admission to the Ghana Bar will doubtless reduce the number of students going to England for bar qualification; thus more students must be accommodated here. In the light of these factors, we would recommend that the Advisory Committee's minimum figure be increased to 100 and that planning of physical facilities proceed on this basis.

The new building should contain at least five large classrooms and several smaller seminar rooms. Office space should be provided for each member of the Faculty. If at all possible, the present office arrangement which provides enough room in an office to accommodate small tutorial groups should be preserved. One of the most complex sets of problems relates to the development of a law library. The legal collection is now part of Balme Library. Since the library is the working laboratory of the law student, teacher and research scholar, it is imperative that the library, staff offices and classrooms be housed together. For reasons of economy it is appropriate to keep some library functions such as ordering, cataloging, etc., on a unified basis. Substantive control of acquisition and of the rules relating to library use should be kept in the Law Faculty, however.

Consideration of library facilities immediately raises another major problem. In addition to the books needed by law students and the Faculty in the research they regularly do in connection with the instructional program, there is a pressing need for the development of a collection adequate for major inter-disciplinary research. No such research center exists in sub-Saharan Africa with the possible exception of the Rhodes-Livingstone Institute in Lusaka. If a center with facilities to meet the needs of resident researchers and visiting scholars is developed, it should be associated with a university community, since only there can the necessary qualified people in all relevant disciplines be assembled. We know of no more promising place in Africa for the development of such a center than Legon. We would therefore recommend that in the planning of facilities for the Law Faculty consideration be given to the provision of office space for institutional research staff and visiting scholars as well as library stack space easily expanded to accommodate at least 60,000 volumes.

In view of the recommended development at Legon, the question arises what use is to be made of the Law School building in Accra? This is, of course, a problem for the General Legal Council. Even now, the Law School does not fully utilize the building and part of it is rented. Some aspects of the University's instructional program might, by arrangement with the Council, be carried on in the building. The Council may also want to maintain a small working library there for the use of judges and practitioners. Doubtless, a wide range of uses will develop in time. The existence of the Law School building should not affect the desirability of the proposed development at Legon, however.

THE LEGAL FRAMEWORK

Consideration of the development of legal education in Ghana must take full account of the requirements laid down by the Legal Professional Act, 1960. The Act charges the General Legal Council with the duty to make arrangements for the establishment of a system of legal education, for selecting subjects in which those seeking to qualify as lawyers are to be examined, for establishing courses of instruction and opportunities for practical experience, for regulating admission of students to courses of instruction and for holding examinations. The statutory responsibility of the Council for legal education and admission to the Bar is thus plenary. There is no serious problem, however, of reconciling this responsibility with the assumption of functions by the University, as is here proposed. Parliament wisely provided that the Council might carry out its educational responsibilities either through a school set up by it or through any other educational institution.

Education is also the business of the University of Ghana which rests on its own statutory base, with its own system of government and with full power to provide instruction in law without reference to the powers articulated in the Legal Profession Act, 1960. The present problem is to relate these two agencies, both drawing their support from the Government of Ghana, so as to avoid wasteful duplication, establish sound educational programs and assure a reliable flow of qualified candidates to the Bar. The following recommendations are directly toward these ends.

While certain instrumental responsibilities may be delegated by the General Legal Council, the final responsibilities for determining eligibility for admission to the Bar cannot be. Lawyers are officers of the courts as well as private practitioners. Their admission and discipline must therefore remain the responsibility of that body whose membership is composed largely of the Justices of the Supreme Court. The Director of Legal Education has recommended that the Council, acting upon the recommendation of the statutory Board of Legal Education, specify the period of formal education required and the subjects in which candidates for admission to the bar must be examined. University examinations in the several subjects specified could also serve as Bar Examinations and the members of the staff of the University Law Faculty could be appointed by the Council to serve on a Committee of Bar Examiners. The Director has recommended further that the Council appoint to the Committee of Bar Examiners a number of distinguished members of the Bench and Bar who, in cooperation with the Examiners appointed from the University staff, would certify to the Council the names of those candidates who had successfully completed the required examinations. It should be noted that this Committee of Examiners, as such, would not determine the content of the University degree program nor the qualification of students for University degrees. The Committee would be an agency of the General Legal Council and in carrying out its functions would be fully responsible to that body. Under the system proposed it would be theoretically possible, though hardly probable, that a student might pass his University examinations while failing as a bar examinee or vice versa.

Thus far liaison between the educational program of the General Legal Council and that of the University has been maintained through the Director of Legal Education who has also held the Chair in Law in the University. This in our judgment is a good arrangement and should be preserved. We believe, however, that a further step should be taken to assure close, continuing cooperation between the Law Faculty and the General Legal Council. As a Faculty, Law has its own Faculty Board, composed of all of the teaching members of the staff, as well as representatives from related Faculties of the University. We recommend that the University statutes now being drafted provide that the Chief Justice and two other members of the General Legal Council (or three others if the Director of Legal Education is also Professor of Law) should be Adjunct Members of the Faculty Board, entitled to participate fully in the deliberations of the Board though without vote. In this way the University program of legal education can have the constant benefit of the counsel of professional leaders who in turn can effectively report and interpret the University's program to the Bench and Bar.

Under the plan proposed the University retains full control of its degree programs, just as the General Legal Council retains control of qualifications for admission to the bar. There is no reason to anticipate significant divergence in the aims and objectives of the two bodies. On the contrary, through the performance by each of its peculiar role, Ghana can be assured a stable supply of competent lawyers who are also educated citizens, ready to play their parts in individual counseling and private litigation, as well as the business of government and national development.

Accra
October 5, 1962

THE REPUBLICAN CONSTITUTION

OF GHANA

[The italicized provisions were added by the
Constitution (Amendment) Act, 1964, Act 224.]

WE THE PEOPLE OF GHANA, by our Representatives
gathered in this our Constituent Assembly,

IN EXERCISE of our undoubted right to appoint for ourselves the means whereby we shall be governed,

IN SYMPATHY with and loyalty to our fellow-countrymen
of Africa,

IN THE HOPE that we may by our actions this day help
to further the development of a Union of African States.
and

IN A SPIRIT of friendship and peace with all other peoples
of the World,

DO HEREBY ENACT and give to ourselves this Constitution.

This Constitution is enacted on this twenty-ninth day of
June, 1960 and shall come into operation on the first day
of July, 1960.

PART I

POWERS OF THE PEOPLE

Powers of the People.
1. The powers of the State derive from the people, *as the
source of power and the guardians of the State* by whom
certain of those powers are now conferred on the institutions
established by this Constitution and who shall have the right
to exercise the remainder of those powers, and to choose
their representatives in the Parliament now established, in
accordance with the following principle—

That, without distinction of sex, race, religion or political belief, every person who, being by law a citizen of
Ghana, has attained the age of twenty-one years and is
not disqualified by law on grounds of absence, infirmity of
mind or criminality, shall be entitled to one vote, to be
cast in freedom and secrecy.

National Party.
1A. (1) *In conformity with the interests, welfare and
aspirations of the People, and in order to develop the organi-*

sational initiative and the political activity of the People, there shall be one national party which shall be the vanguard of the People in their struggle to build a socialist society and which shall be the leading core of all organisations of the People.

(2) The national party shall be the "Convention People's Party."

2. In the confident expectation of an early surrender of sovereignty to a union of African states and territories, the people now confer on Parliament the power to provide for the surrender of the whole or any part of the sovereignty of Ghana. *Realisation of African Unity.*

Provided that the sovereignty of Ghana shall not be surrendered or diminished on any grounds other than the furtherance of African unity.

3. *With the exception of section (2) of Article 1A, the power to repeal or alter this Part of the Constitution is reserved to the People.* *Powers of the People Entrenched.*

PART II

THE REPUBLIC

4. (1) Ghana is a sovereign unitary Republic.

(2) Subject to the provisions of Article Two of the Constitution, the power to provide a form of government for Ghana other than that of a republic or for the form of the Republic to be other than unitary is reserved to the people. *Declaration of Republic.*

5. Until otherwise provided by law, the territories of Ghana shall consist of those territories which were comprised in Ghana immediately before the coming into operation of the Constitution, including the territorial waters. *Territories.*

6. Until otherwise provided by law, Ghana shall be divided into the following Regions, which shall respectively comprise such territories as may be provided for by law, that is to say, the Ashanti Region, the Brong-Ahafo Region, the Central Region, the Eastern Region, the Northern Region, the Upper Region, the Volta Region, and the Western Region. *Regions.*

7. *The Flag of Ghana shall consist of three equal horizontal stripes, the upper stripe being red, the middle stripe white and the lower stripe green, with a black star in the centre of the white stripe.* *National Flag.*

PART III

THE PRESIDENT AND HIS MINISTERS

Head of the State

Head of the State. 8. (1) There shall be a President of Ghana, who shall be the Head of the State and responsible to the people.

(2) Subject to the provisions of the Constitution, the executive power of the State is conferred upon the President.

(3) The President shall be the Commander-in-Chief of the Armed Forces and the Fount of Honour.

(4) Except as may be otherwise provided by law, in the exercise of his functions the President shall act in his own discretion and shall not be obliged to follow advice tendered by any other person.

(5) The power to repeal or alter this Article is reserved to the people.

Term of Office. 9. The term of office of the President shall begin with his assumption of office and end with the assumption of office of the person elected as President in the next following election, so however that the President may at any time resign his office by instrument under his hand addressed to the Chief Justice.

First President

First President. 10. KWAME NKRUMAH is hereby appointed first President of Ghana, having been chosen as such before the enactment of the Constitution in a Plebiscite conducted in accordance with the principle set out in Article One of the Constitution.

Election of President and Assumption of Office

Election of President. 11. (1) An election of a President shall be held whenever one of the following events occurs, that is to say—

    (a) the National Assembly is dissolved, or

    (b) the President dies, or

    (c) the President resigns his office.

(2) Provision shall be made by law for regulating the election of a President, and shall be so made in accordance with the following principles—

    (a) any citizen of Ghana shall be qualified for election as President if he has attained the age of thirty-five years;

    (b) the returning officer for the election shall be the Chief Justice;

    (c) if contested, an election held by reason of a dissolution of the National Assembly shall be decided by preferences given before the General Election by persons subsequently returned as Members of Parliament, or, if no candidate for election as President obtains more than one-half of the preferences so given, by secret ballot of the Members of the new Parliament;

(d) if contested, an election held by reason of the death or resignation of the President shall be decided by secret ballot of the Members of Parliament.

(3) If an election is to be decided by balloting among the Members of Parliament and a President has not been declared elected after five ballots the National Assembly shall be deemed to be dissolved at the conclusion of the fifth ballot.

(4) Where a person has been declared by the Chief Justice to be elected as President his election shall not be questioned in any court.

12. (1) The President shall assume office by taking an oath in the following form, which shall be administered before the people by the Chief Justice— *Assumption of Office.*

I .... do solemnly swear that I will well and truly exercise the functions of the high office of President of Ghana, that I will bear true faith and allegiance to Ghana, that I will preserve and defend the Constitution, and that I will do right to all manner of people according to law without fear or favour, affection or ill-will. So help me God.

(2) Instead of taking an oath the President may if he thinks fit make an affirmation, which shall be in the like form with the substitution of *affirm* for *swear* and the omission of the concluding sentence.

13. (1) Immediately after his assumption of office the President shall make the following solemn declaration before the people— *Declaration of Fundamental Principles.*

On accepting the call of the people to the high office of President of Ghana I .... solemnly declare my adherence to the following fundamental principles—

That the powers of Government spring from the will of the people and should be exercised in accordance therewith.

That freedom and justice should be honoured and maintained.

That the union of Africa should be striven for by every lawful means and, when attained, should be faithfully preserved.

393

That the Independence of Ghana should not be surrendered or diminished on any grounds other than the furtherance of African unity.

That no person should suffer discrimination on grounds of sex, race, tribe, religion or political belief.

That Chieftaincy in Ghana should be guaranteed and preserved.

That every citizen of Ghana should receive his fair share of the produce yielded by the development of the country.

That subject to such restrictions as may be necessary for preserving public order, morality or health, no person should be deprived of freedom of religion or speech, of the right to move and assemble without hindrance or of the right of access to courts of law.

That no person should be deprived of his property save where the public interest so requires and the law so provides.

(2) The power to repeal this Article, or to alter its provisions otherwise than by the addition of further paragraphs to the declaration, is reserved to the people.

Official Seals

Official Seals.

14. There shall be a Public Seal and a Presidential Seal, the use and custody of which shall be regulated by law.

Ministers and Cabinet

Appointment of Ministers.

15. (1) The President shall from time to time appoint by instrument under the Presidential Seal persons from among the Members of Parliament, who shall be styled Ministers of Ghana, to assist him in his exercise of the executive power and to take charge under his direction of such departments of State as he may assign to them.

(2) The power to repeal or alter this Article is reserved to the people.

The Cabinet.

16. (1) There shall be a Cabinet consisting of the President and not less than eight Ministers of Ghana appointed as members of the Cabinet by the President.

(2) Subject to the powers of the President, the Cabinet is charged with the general direction and control of the Government of Ghana.

(3) The appointment of a Minister as a member of the Cabinet may at any time be revoked by the President.

(4) The power to repeal or alter this Article is reserved to the people.

17. The office of a Minister of Ghana shall become vacant— *Tenure of Office of Ministers.*

 (*a*) if the President removes him from office by instrument under the Presidential Seal; or

 (*b*) if he ceases to be a Member of Parliament otherwise than by reason of a dissolution; or

 (*c*) on the acceptance by the President of his resignation from office; or

 (*d*) immediately before the assumption of office of a President.

Supplemental provisions as to President

18. (1) *There shall be a Presidential Commission consisting of three persons appointed by the President to execute the office of the President in accordance with advice tendered by the Cabinet in the event of—* *Presidential Commissions.*

 (*a*) *the death or resignation of the President before the assumption of office of his successor; or*

 (*b*) *the illness of the President or his absence from Ghana during which he cannot conveniently perform the functions of his office; or*

 (*c*) *the President being adjudged incapable of acting:*

Provided that nothing in this section shall be taken to prejudice the power of the President, at any time when he is not adjudged incapable of acting, to delegate any exercise of the executive power to some other person.

 (2) *A Presidential Commission may act by any two of its members.*

 (3) *The President may at any time revoke the appointment of any or all members of the Presidential Commission.*

 (4) *The President shall be deemed to be adjudged incapable of acting if the Speaker in pursuance of a resolution of the National Assembly—*

 (*a*) *has declared that, after considering medical evidence, the National Assembly is satisfied that the President is, by reason of physical or mental infirmity, unable to exercise the functions of his office, and*

 (*b*) *has not subsequently withdrawn the declaration on the ground that the President has recovered his capacity.*

19. (1) The President shall receive such salary and allowances, and on retirement such pension, gratuity and *Salary and Allowances of President.*

other allowance, as may be determined by the National Assembly.

(2) The salary and allowances of the President shall not be reduced during his period of office.

(3) Salaries and allowances payable under this Article are hereby charged on the Consolidated Fund.

PART IV

PARLIAMENT

The Sovereign Parlia- ment.

20. (1) There shall be a Parliament consisting of the President and the National Assembly.

(2) So much of the legislative power of the State as is not reserved by the Constitution to the people is conferred on Parliament *as the corporate representative of the People*; and any portion of the remainder of the legislative power of the State may be conferred on Parliament at any future time by the decision of a majority of the electors voting in a referendum ordered by the President and conducted in accordance with the principle set out in Article One of the Constitution:

Provided that the only power to alter the Constitution (whether expressly or by implication) which is or may as aforesaid be conferred on Parliament is a power to alter it by an Act expressed to be an Act to amend the Constitution and containing only provisions effecting the alteration thereof.

(3) Subject to the provisions of Article Two of the Constitution, Parliament cannot divest itself of any of its legislative powers:

Provided that if by any amendment to the Constitution the power to repeal or alter any existing or future provision of the Constitution is reserved to the people, section (2) of this Article shall apply in relation to that provision as if the power to repeal or alter it had originally been reserved to the people.

(4) No Act passed in exercise of a legislative power expressed by the Constitution to be reserved to the people shall take effect unless the Speaker has certified that power to pass the Act has been conferred on Parliament in the manner provided by section (2) of this Article; and a certificate so given shall be conclusive.

(5) No person or body other than Parliament shall have power to make provisions having the force of law except under authority conferred by Act of Parliament.

(6) Apart from the limitations referred to in the pre-

ceding provisions of this Article, the power of Parliament to make laws shall be under no limitation whatsoever.

(7) The power to repeal or alter this Article is reserved to the people.

21. (1) The National Assembly shall consist of the Speaker and not less than one hundred and four Members, to be known as Members of Parliament. *The National Assembly.*

(2) The Members shall be elected in the manner provided by a law framed in accordance with the principle set out in Article One of the Constitution, and the Speaker shall be elected by the Members.

(3) There shall be freedom of speech, debate and proceedings in the National Assembly and that freedom shall not be impeached or questioned in any court or place out of the Assembly.

(4) The President may attend any sitting of the National Assembly.

(5) The power to repeal or alter this Article is reserved to the people.

22. (1) There shall be a new session of the National Assembly once at least in every year, so that a period of twelve months shall not elapse between the last sitting of the Assembly in one session and the first sitting thereof in the next session. *Sessions of the Assembly.*

(2) The President may at any time by proclamation summon or prorogue the National Assembly.

(3) The power to repeal or alter this Article is reserved to the people.

23. (1) The President may at any time by proclamation dissolve the National Assembly. *Dissolution of the Assembly.*

(2) The President shall in any case dissolve the National Assembly on the expiration of the period of five years from the first sitting of the Assembly after the previous General Election.

(3) If an emergency arises or exists when the National Assembly stands dissolved, the President may by proclamation summon an assembly of the persons who were Members of Parliament immediately before the dissolution and, until the majority of results have been declared in the General Election following the dissolution, the assembly shall be deemed to be the National Assembly.

(4) The power to repeal or alter this Article is reserved to the people.

24. (1) Every Bill passed by the National Assembly shall be presented to the President who shall— *Legislation.*

(*a*) signify his assent to the Bill, or

(*b*) signify his assent to a part only of the Bill and his refusal of assent to the remainder, or

(*c*) signify his refusal of assent to the Bill.

(2) On the signifying by the President of his assent to a Bill passed by the National Assembly or to a part thereof, the Bill or that part thereof, as the case may be, shall become an Act of Parliament.

Presidential Addresses and Messages. 25. (1) At the beginning of each session of the National Assembly the President shall deliver to the Members of Parliament an address indicating the policies proposed to be followed by the Government during that session.

(2) At least seven days before each prorogation of the National Assembly the President shall deliver to the Members of Parliament an address indicating the manner and results of the application of the policies of the Government during the preceding period and otherwise setting forth the state of the Nation.

(3) If circumstances render it impracticable for the President himself to deliver any such address, he may instead send a message to the National Assembly embodying the address.

(4) In addition to delivering any address or sending any message under the preceding provisions of this Article, the President may at any time deliver an address to the Members of Parliament or send a message to the National Assembly.

(5) Every message sent by the President to the National Assembly shall be read to the Members of Parliament by a Minister.

PART V

PUBLIC REVENUE AND EXPENDITURE

Taxation

Restriction on Taxation. 26. (1) No taxation shall be imposed otherwise than under the authority of an Act of Parliament.

(2) The power to repeal or alter this Article is reserved to the people.

Custody of Public Money

Public Funds. 27. There shall be a Consolidated Fund and a Contingencies Fund, together with such other public funds as may be provided for by law.

Public Revenue. 28. (1) The produce of taxation, receipts of capital and interest in respect of public loans, and all other public revenue shall be paid into the Consolidated Fund unless required or permitted by law to be paid into any other fund or account.

(2) The President may, in relation to any department of State, direct that a separate public account be established for the department and that the revenue of the department be paid into that account.

29. (1) Expenditure shall not be met from any public fund or public account except under a warrant issued by authority of the President. *Payments out of Public Funds.*

(2) Whenever a sum becomes payable which is charged by law on a public fund or on the general revenues and assets of Ghana, the President or a person authorised by him in that behalf shall cause a warrant to be issued for the purpose of enabling that sum to be paid.

(3) A warrant may be issued by authority of the President for the purpose of enabling public money to be applied—

(*a*) as part of moneys granted for the public service by a vote of the National Assembly under this Part of the Constitution, or

(*b*) in defraying, in the manner provided by Article Thirty-four of the Constitution, urgent expenditure authorised under that Article, or

(*c*) in performance of an agreement to grant a loan made under Article Thirty-five of the Constitution.

30. Where— *Excess Expenditure.*

(*a*) money is drawn out of a public fund or public account for the purpose of being applied as part of moneys granted for a particular public service by a vote of the National Assembly, but

(*b*) the money so drawn proves to be in excess of the amount granted for that service.

particulars of the excess shall be laid before the National Assembly and, if the National Assembly so resolve, the amount originally granted for the service in question shall be treated for accounting purposes as increased to include the amount of the excess.

Moneys granted by Vote of the National Assembly

31. (1) The President shall cause to be prepared annually under heads for each public service estimates of expenditure, other than expenditure charged by law on a public fund or on the general revenues and assets of Ghana, which will *Moneys Granted on the Annual Estimates.*

be required to be incurred for the public services during the following financial year; and, when approved by the Cabinet, the estimates so prepared (which shall be known as "the annual estimates") shall be laid before the National Assembly.

(2) Each head of the annual estimates shall be submitted to the vote of the National Assembly but no amendment of the estimates shall be moved.

(3) A vote of the National Assembly approving a head of the annual estimates shall constitute a grant by the Assembly of moneys not exceeding the amount specified in that head to be applied within the financial year in question for the service to which the head relates.

Moneys Granted on Provisional and Supplementary Estimates. 32. (1) If it appears that the vote of the National Assembly on any heads of the annual estimates will not be taken before the commencement of the financial year to which they relate, the President shall cause to be prepared under those heads estimates of the expenditure which will be required for the continuance of the public services in question until the said vote is taken; and, when approved by the Cabinet, the estimates so prepared (which shall be known as "provisional estimates") shall be laid before the National Assembly.

(2) If, after the National Assembly has voted upon the annual estimates for any financial year, it appears that the moneys granted in respect of any heads thereof are likely to be insufficient or that expenditure is likely to be incurred in that year on a public service falling under a head not included in the annual estimates, the President shall cause to be prepared under the relevant heads estimates of the additional expenditure; and, when approved by the Cabinet, the estimates so prepared (which shall be known as "supplementary estimates") shall be laid before the National Assembly.

(3) Sections (2) and (3) of Article Thirty-one of the Constitution shall apply in relation to provisional and supplementary estimates as they apply in relation to the annual estimates:

Provided that, where an item of expenditure is included both in provisional estimates and in the annual estimates, a grant in respect of that item shall not by virtue of this section be taken to have been made more than once.

Extraordinary Grants. 33. In addition to granting moneys on estimates of expenditure the National Assembly may, if satisfied that it is necessary in the public interest to do so, make any extraordinary grant of money for the public service, including a grant on a vote of credit, that is a grant of money to be used for a purpose which, for reasons of national security or by reason of the indefinite character of the service in question, cannot be described in detailed estimates.

Expenditure out of Contingencies Fund

34. (1) Where in the opinion of the President—

    (a) money is urgently required to be expended for a public service, and

    (b) the payment thereof would exceed the amount granted by the National Assembly for that service or the service is one for which no amount has been so granted, and

    (c) it is not practicable to summon a meeting of the National Assembly in sufficient time to obtain the necessary grant,

Expenditure out of Contingencies Fund.

the President may by executive instrument authorise the money required to be drawn from the Contingencies Fund.

(2) An executive instrument made under this Article shall specify the head under which the expenditure in question would have been shown if it had been included in the annual estimates.

(3) As soon as is practicable after an executive instrument has been made under this Article—

    (a) the instrument shall be laid before the National Assembly, and

    (b) a resolution authorising the transfer to the Contingencies Fund from a public fund specified in the resolution of an amount equal to the amount of the expenditure to which the instrument relates shall be moved in the National Assembly by a Minister authorised in that behalf by the President.

(4) In addition to sums transferred under section (3) of this Article, the National Assembly may from time to time authorise the transfer from the Consolidated Fund to the Contingencies Fund of sums required to maintain an adequate balance therein.

Public Loans

35. (1) The President may on behalf of the Republic enter into an agreement for the granting of a loan out of any public fund or public account if he thinks it expedient in the public interest so to do.

Granting of Loans.

(2) If the National Assembly so resolve, agreements entered into under this Article for amounts exceeding the

amount specified in the Assembly's resolution shall not become operative unless ratified by the Assembly.

(3) As soon as is practicable after an agreement has been entered into under this Article, particulars of the agreement, and of the borrower and the purpose for which the loan is required, shall be laid before the National Assembly.

Raising
of Loans.
36. No loan shall be raised for the purposes of the Republic otherwise than under the authority of an Act of Parliament.

The
Public
Debt.
37. (1) The public debt, interest thereon, sinking fund payments in respect thereof, and the costs, charges and expenses incidental to the management thereof are hereby charged on the general revenues and assets of Ghana.

(2) The power to repeal or alter this Article is reserved to the people.

Audit of Public Accounts

The
Auditor-
General.
38. (1) There shall be an Auditor-General, who shall be appointed by the President and who shall not be removable except by the President in pursuance of a resolution of the National Assembly supported by the votes of at least two-thirds of the total number of Members of Parliament and passed on the ground of stated misbehaviour or of infirmity of body or mind.

(2) The Auditor-General shall retire from office on attaining the age of fifty-five years or such higher age as may be prescribed by law.

(3) The Auditor-General may resign his office by writing under his hand addressed to the President.

(4) The salary of the Auditor-General shall be determined by the National Assembly, is hereby charged on the Consolidated Fund and shall not be diminished during his term of office.

Duty to
Audit and
Report.
39. (1) The accounts of all departments of State shall be audited by the Auditor-General who, with his deputies, shall at all times be entitled to have access to all books, records, stores and other matters relating to such accounts.

(2) The Auditor-General shall report annually to the National Assembly on the exercise of his functions under section (1) of this Article, and shall in his report draw attention to irregularities in the accounts audited by him.

PART VI

LAW AND JUSTICE

Laws of Ghana

40. Except as may be otherwise provided by an enactment *Laws of* made after the coming into operation of the Constitution, *Ghana.* the laws of Ghana comprise the following—

(*a*) the Constitution,

(*b*) enactments made by or under the authority of the Parliament established by the Constitution,

(*c*) enactments other than the Constitution made by or under the authority of the Constituent Assembly,

(*d*) enactments in force immediately before the coming into operation of the Constitution,

(*e*) the common law, and

(*f*) customary law.

Superior and Inferior Courts

41. (1) There shall be a Supreme Court and a High *Superior* Court, which shall be the superior courts of Ghana. *and*
Inferior
(2) Subject to the provisions of the Constitution, the *Courts.* judicial power of the State is conferred on the Supreme Court and the High Court, and on such inferior courts as may be provided for by law.

(3) The power to repeal or alter this Article is reserved to the people.

Provisions as to Superior Courts

42. (1) The Supreme Court shall be the final court of *Jurisdic-* appeal, with such appellate and other jurisdiction as may be *tion.* provided for by law.

(2) The Supreme Court shall have original jurisdiction in all matters where a question arises whether an enactment was made in excess of the powers conferred on Parliament by or under the Constitution, and if any such question arises in the High Court or an inferior court, the hearing shall be adjourned and the question referred to the Supreme Court for decision.

(3) Subject to section (2) of this Article, the High Court shall have such original and appellate jurisdiction as may be provided for by law.

(4) The Supreme Court shall in principle be bound to follow its own previous decisions on questions of law, and the High Court shall be bound to follow previous decisions of the Supreme Court on such questions, but neither court

shall be otherwise bound to follow the previous decisions of any court on questions of law.

Composition of Courts.

43. Provision shall be made by law for the composition of superior courts in particular proceedings:

Provided that no appeal shall be decided by the Supreme Court unless the court hearing the appeal consists of at least three Judges, of whom at least one is a Judge of the Supreme Court; and no question whether an enactment was made in excess of the powers conferred on Parliament by or under the Constitution shall be decided by the Supreme Court unless the court considering the question comprises at least three Judges of the Supreme Court.

Judges of the Superior Courts

Chief Justice.

44. (1) The President shall by instrument under the Presidential Seal appoint one of the Judges of the Supreme Court to be Chief Justice of Ghana.

(2) The Chief Justice shall be President of the Supreme Court and Head of the Judicial Service.

(3) The appointment of a Judge as Chief Justice may at any time be revoked by the President by instrument under the Presidential Seal.

Judges.

45. (1) The Judges of the *Supreme Court and the Judges of the High Court* shall be appointed by the President by instrument under the Public Seal.

(2) Provision shall be made by law for the form and administration of the judicial oath, which shall be taken by every person appointed as Judge of the *Supreme Court, or as a Judge of the High Court* before the exercise by him of any judicial function.

(3) Subject to the following provisions of this Article, no person shall be removed from office as a Judge of the Supreme Court or a Judge of the High Court except by the President in pursuance of a resolution of the National Assembly supported by the votes of not less than two-thirds of the Members of Parliament and passed on the grounds of stated misbehaviour or infirmity of body or mind.

Provided that the President may at any time for reasons which to him appear sufficient remove from office a Judge of the Supreme Court or a Judge of the High Court.

(4) Unless the President by instrument under his hand extends the tenure of office of the Judge for a definite period specified in the instrument, a Judge of the Supreme Court shall retire from office on attaining the age of sixty-five years and a Judge of the High Court shall retire from office on attaining the age of sixty-two years.

(5) A Judge of a superior court may resign his office by writing under his hand addressed to the President.

(6) The power to repeal or alter this Article is reserved to the people.

46. (1) The salary of a Judge of a superior court shall be determined by the National Assembly and shall not be diminished while he remains in office.

[The original section 2 of Article 46 provided "The Chief Justice shall be entitled to such additional allowance as may be determined by the National Assembly." This section was repealed by the Constitution (Amendment) Act, 1964, Act 224.]

(2) All salaries and allowances paid under this Article and all pensions and other retiring allowances paid in respect of service as Chief Justice or other Judge of a superior court are hereby charged on the Consolidated Fund.

Salaries and Pensions.

Attorney-General

47. (1) There shall be an Attorney-General, who shall be a Minister of Ghana or other person appointed by the President.

Attorney-General.

(2) Subject to the directions of the President, there shall be vested in the Attorney-General responsibility for the initiation, conduct and discontinuance of civil proceedings by the Republic and prosecutions for criminal offences, and for the defence of civil proceedings brought against the Republic.

(3) The office of the Attorney-General shall become vacant—

> (a) if his appointment is revoked by the President; or
> (b) on the acceptance by the President of his resignation from office; or
> (c) immediately before the assumption of office of a President.

President's powers of mercy

48. (1) The President shall have power, in respect of any criminal offence—

President's Powers of Mercy.

> (a) to grant a pardon to the offender, or
> (b) to order a respite of the execution of any sentence passed on the offender, or
> (c) to remit any sentence so passed or any penalty or forfeiture incurred by reason of the offence.

(2) Where the President remits a sentence of death

he may order the offender to be imprisoned until such time as the President orders his release.

PART VII

HOUSES OF CHIEFS

Houses of Chiefs.   49. There shall be a House of Chiefs for each Region of Ghana.

Composition and Functions.   50. A House of Chiefs shall consist of such Chiefs, and shall have such functions relating to customary law and other matters, as may be provided by law.

PART VIII

THE PUBLIC SERVICES

The Public Services.   51. (1) The Public Services of Ghana shall consist of the Civil Service, the Judicial Service, the Police Service, the Local Government Service, and such other Public Services as may be provided for by law.

     (2) Subject to the provisions of the Constitution and save as is otherwise provided by law, the appointment, promotion, transfer, termination of appointment, dismissal and disciplinary control of members of the Public Services is vested in the President.

Retiring Allowances.   52. All pensions, gratuities and other allowances payable on retirement to members of the Civil Service, the Judicial Service and the Police Service are hereby charged on the Consolidated Fund.

PART IX

THE ARMED FORCES

Prohibition of Irregular Forces.   53. (1) Neither the President nor any other person shall raise any armed force except under the authority of an Act of Parliament.

     (2) The power to repeal or alter this Article is reserved to the people.

Powers of Commander-in-Chief.   54. (1) Subject to the provisions of any enactment for the time being in force, the powers of the President as Commander-in-Chief of the Armed Forces shall include the power to commission persons as officers in the said Forces and to order any of the said Forces to engage in operations for the defence of Ghana, for the preservation of public order, for relief in cases of emergency or for any other purpose appearing to the Commander-in-Chief to be expedient.

(2) The Commander-in-Chief shall have power, in a case where it appears to him expedient to do so for the security of the State, to dismiss a member of the Armed Forces or to order a member of the Armed Forces not to exercise any authority vested in him as a member thereof until the Commander-in-Chief otherwise directs; and a purported exercise of authority in contravention of such an order shall be ineffective.

PART X

SPECIAL POWERS FOR FIRST PRESIDENT

55. (1) Notwithstanding anything in Article Twenty of the Constitution, the person appointed as first President of Ghana shall have, during his initial period of office, the powers conferred on him by this Article. *Special Powers for First President.*

(2) The first President may, whenever he considers it to be in the national interest to do so, give directions by legislative instrument.

(3) An instrument made under this Article may alter (whether expressly or by implication) any enactment other than the Constitution.

(4) Section (2) of Article Forty-two of the Constitution shall apply in relation to the powers conferred by this Article as it applies in relation to the powers conferred on Parliament.

(5) For the purposes of this Article the first President's initial period of office shall be taken to continue until some other person assumes office as President.

(6) The power to repeal or alter this Article during the first President's initial period of office is reserved to the people.

GOVERNMENT PROPOSALS FOR
A REPUBLICAN CONSTITUTION

White Paper No. 1/60

The Government now presents for the consideration of the people of Ghana and the National Assembly (sitting as a Constituent Assembly) its proposals for a Republican Constitution. These proposals are set out in detail in the draft Constitution contained in an Appendix to this White Paper and are explained in general terms in the White Paper itself.

The draft Constitution recognises that ultimately all powers of the State come from the people, and it will be for the people and not primarily for the Constituent Assembly to determine the form of the Constitution. It is, however, the duty of the Government and of the elected representatives of the people in the Constituent Assembly to advise what is, in their view, the most suitable form for the Constitution of the Republic of Ghana. In order to enable the views of the Constituent Assembly to be expressed and made known the Government will immediately lay this White Paper before the Assembly and will ask the Assembly to endorse the draft Constitution before it is submitted to the people. If the Assembly does so the people will then be asked, in a Plebiscite to be held between the 19th and 26th April, 1960, whether they approve the main provisions of the draft Constitution. If this approval is given the Constituent Assembly will clearly be in duty bound to enact a Constitution along the lines of that approved by the people.

THE MAIN PRINCIPLES OF THE PROPOSED CONSTITUTION

In asking the people of Ghana to vote for the proposed Republican Constitution the Government ask them to adopt the principles upon which it is based and to endorse the draft Constitution contained in the Appendix to this White Paper.

ULTIMATE POWER TO RESIDE IN THE PEOPLE

The draft Constitution proclaims the principle that all power in the State, whether it be the power to run the Government, to make laws, or to sit in judgment in the courts, originates in the people. By adopting in outline the draft Constitution the people are asked to delegate their power of administering the Government to a President and to his Cabinet of Ministers. They are also asked to delegate most of their law-making powers to a popularly elected National Assembly, though certain important powers in regard to amending the basic provisions of the Constitution are expressly reserved by the draft Constitution to the people. By the draft Constitution the people are further asked to delegate to the President the power to appoint Judges to exercise the judicial powers of the people.

In essence, the draft Constitution makes the people of Ghana the ultimate sovereign authority but it provides for the exercise of their powers through various organs of Government.

In order that the people can be truly sovereign the draft Constitution provides that every citizen of Ghana over 21 who is not prohibited from voting because of absence, infirmity of mind or criminality shall have one vote. No one is to be prohibited from voting on account of sex, race, tribe, religion or political belief.

GHANA TO BE A UNITARY STATE

The Government ask the people, by voting for the draft Constitution, to show that they believe in the unity of Ghana and reject any form of federalism. The Government will consider a vote in favour of the draft Constitution as a mandate to maintain the unity of Ghana. The draft Constitution, however, is not based upon any form of nationalism. The Government realise that the present frontiers of Ghana, like so many other frontiers on the African continent, were drawn merely to suit the convenience of the Colonial Powers who divided Africa between them during the last century. The object of the draft Constitution is to provide firm, stable and popular Government in Ghana so that Ghana can assist in achieving a union of African states and territories. Apart from facilitating the entry of Ghana into a union of African states and territories, the draft Constitution is also designed to enable peoples who are at present outside Ghana but who are linked by racial, family and historical connections with Ghanaian peoples to join them in one integrated state.

THE ACHIEVEMENT OF AFRICAN UNITY

As a practical step towards the realisation of a union of African states and territories the Government ask the people to endorse the conception of African unity which is set out in the draft Constitution. By Article 2 of the draft Constitution the people are asked to entrust to Parliament the right to surrender the sovereignty of Ghana so that Ghana can, at any time when this becomes possible, be merged in a Union of African States.

THE PROPOSED REPUBLIC

The draft Constitution is not copied from the Constitution of any other country. It has been designed to meet the particular needs of Ghana and to express the realities of Ghana's constitutional position. It is therefore proposed that the actual Head of the Government should be the President of the Republic. In this respect the draft Constitution does not follow the traditional British model, where either a Monarch or a President (with only the same nominal powers as are exercised to-day by the Queen in the United Kingdom) is the technical Head of the State. Again, the Constitution of the Fifth Republic of France, which provides, in addition to a President, for a Prime Minister having little real authority, has not been followed. Nor is it proposed to copy the Presidential system as it exists in the United States and in other countries which have followed the United States type of government. Under the United States Constitution there is a division of authority between the executive part of the Government (the President and his Cabinet) and the legislative part of the Government (Congress, which consists of the Senate and the House of Representatives). Under the United States form of government Cabinet Ministers do not sit in Parliament and the Members of Parliament are elected quite separately from the President so that it is always possible that Parliament may be of one political complexion and the President of another. When there is a disagreement between the President and Parliament there is no machinery for an appeal to the people.

The proposed Republican Constitution for Ghana has been so devised as to provide as far as is possible that the person chosen as President will be the Leader of the majority party in the Assembly. It is the Government's view that it is essential in the interests of strong and efficient government that the President and the Assembly should work as one and that this can most effectively be secured by constitutional provisions which link the election of the President to the election of Members of the National Assembly and which provide that if the National Assembly and the President disagree the issue can be decided by a General Election.

THE PRESIDENT

The President, who will be eligible for re-election, must be a Ghanaian citizen of at least thirty-five years of age.

The President will exercise all the powers at present exercised by the Governor-General and by the Prime Minister. He will not be a member of the National Assembly but he will be entitled to address the Assembly and to send messages to Parliament when he so desires.

Unless he dies or resigns during the lifetime of a Parliament his term of office will be identical with that of the National Assembly.

THE FIRST PRESIDENT

The first President of the Republic will be named in the Constitution. At the same time as the people are asked to vote for or against the draft Constitution they will also be asked to decide who should be the first President if a Republican Constitution is approved. The arrangements for the election of the first President will be made by the Constituent Assembly. The Government will recommend to the Constituent Assembly that they provide that any Ghanaian citizen over thirty-five years of age may be nominated as a Presidential candidate by any ten Members of Parliament. If two or more candidates are nominated the election will be between these candidates. If, however, there is only one nomination the Government will propose that there should nevertheless be an election so that the people can express their approval or disapproval of the candidate nominated.

The Government will propose to the Constituent Assembly that voting for the Presidential candidates and for the draft Constitution shall be on a parliamentary constituency basis. This will enable the people of Ghana to know not only the total number of votes cast in the Plebiscite but also the state of opinion in each individual constituency.

ELECTION OF SUBSEQUENT PRESIDENTS

The method of election of the President, once the Constitution has been established, is dealt with in general terms in the draft Constitution itself and in much more detail in a Presidential Elections Bill which, if the Republic is established, the Government would hope should be among the first measures to be passed by the new Republican Parliament. The scheme proposed in the draft Constitution and the Bill is as follows.

An election for President will be held whenever the National Assembly is dissolved. At the General Election every parliamentary candidate can give notice that he supports a particular candidate for the Presidency. Before doing so, however, the parliamentary candidate must secure the permission of the Presidential candidate whom he seeks to support. The object of this is to avoid a situation where two or more candidates in any parliamentary constituency claim support for the same Presidential candidate, thus confusing the electors. No Presidential candidate can be nominated unless his nominators are prepared to make a declaration that they believe parliamentary candidates in at least half the constituencies in the country will pledge their vote to him if elected. The reason for this is to make it certain that the only persons who can stand for President are those who have a chance of commanding a majority in the National Assembly. Once a Parliamentary candidate has publicly declared his support for a Presidential candidate, and has obtained that Presidential candidate's permission to do so, his decision is irrevocable, and if he is elected as a Member of Parliament his vote is automatically cast in favour of the Presidential candidate for whom he declared his support. This enables the people to have a direct say in the election of the President and prevents a parliamentary candidate who has been elected on the strength of his pledge to support a particular Presidential candidate switching to another candidate without any mandate from those who have elected him.

Under the draft Constitution if any Presidential candidate has the declared support of more than half the Members of Parliament elected, then he is automatically declared elected as President. The draft Constitution, however, also provides for the situation which might arise if no one Presidential candidate obtained a clear majority of preferences. In these circumstances the election of President is entrusted to the Members of the National Assembly voting by secret ballot. The Members are released from their previous declaration of preference for a particular Presidential candidate and their duty is to choose a President who can command a majority in the Assembly. If, after five secret ballots, the Members of the Assembly cannot agree upon the choice of a President, then the National Assembly is automatically dissolved and another General Election is held.

Until his successor assumes office, the outgoing President (who may be a candidate for re-election) continues in office.

The draft Constitution provides that the President may, if he so desires, resign his office. If he does this, or if he dies during his term of office, the duty of choosing a President for the remainder of the term of the National Assembly is entrusted to the National Assembly, which will elect a new President to serve until such time as the Assembly is dissolved, when the normal form of presidential election will take place.

The draft Constitution provides that the President must have a Cabinet of at least eight Ministers who must all of them be Members of the National Assembly. The President will preside at Cabinet meetings and, subject to the general powers of the President, the Cabinet will have control over the government of the country in the same way as it has under the existing Constitution. The reason for this is to ensure that the Political Party which has won a majority of seats in the National Assembly is fully represented in the Government, and that the leading members of the Party which wins the election are closely associated with the President in the control of the administration. Normally each Cabinet Minister will be placed in control, under the President, of the functions of a particular Ministry.

MINISTERS OF GHANA

Under the draft Constitution, all Members of the Cabinet must be Ministers of Ghana chosen by the President from among the Members of Parliament; but not all Ministers need be appointed to the Cabinet. Normally Ministers not in the Cabinet would be entrusted by the President with the supervision of particular branches of Governmental activity.

PARLIAMENT

Except in so far as the draft Constitution reserves certain powers to the people to be exercised by them in a Referendum, the supreme legislative authority of the country is Parliament, which it is proposed shall consist of the President and the National Assembly. Subject to the limitations imposed by the draft Constitution, the power of Parliament to make laws is unlimited, and neither the President, the Cabinet, nor the Law Courts can change the law without the authority of Parliament.

No taxation can be imposed unless the tax has been first approved by the National Assembly and embodied in an Act of Parliament. In the case of Municipal and Local Councils, power to impose local rates or other taxes must derive from an Act of Parliament.

Under the existing Constitution a power is reserved to the Governor-General on behalf of the Queen to veto a Bill passed by the National Assembly. Under present conditions, if it were necessary to exercise this power, it would of course be exercised in the Governor-General's name by the Government. In the draft Constitution a similar power of veto is given to the President who is also entitled to veto a part of a Bill without vetoing the whole of it. These powers are inserted as a safeguard but the draft Constitution is based upon the theory that the system of election of President and National Assembly is such that they will always be in agreement.

The whole scheme of the draft Constitution is that the Government (that is to say the President and his Ministers) and the National Assembly should work as one. The President can at any time dissolve the National Assembly but by so doing he must either retire from office or submit himself for re-election. The effect of this is to ensure that if there is any dispute between the President and the National Assembly it will ultimately be resolved by the decision of the people.

The draft Constitution therefore provides that the National Assembly shall have the same opportunities of discussing Government policy as the National Assembly to-day possesses under the present Constitution. Sessions of Parliament will be opened by a statement by the President on Government policy, and before any Session of Parliament ends the President must make a report to the National Assembly on the way in which the Government has carried out the policy which was announced at the beginning of the Session. The National Assembly will be thus able to criticise and examine not only the Government's proposals for the future but the actual way in which those proposals have in fact been carried out.

FINANCE

Under the draft Constitution the National Assembly will have the same powers of control of the national finances as they possess at present. A considerable section of the draft Constitution is devoted to setting out in detail the method by which the Assembly will exercise its financial control. These provisions differ very considerably in wording from the financial provisions of the existing Constitution. They, however, in the main set out what in fact has been the past practice of the National Assembly in dealing with financial matters and the changes made are largely matters of detail.

THE DURATION OF PARLIAMENT

The draft Constitution provides that, as under the present Constitution, there shall be a General Election every five years and that this provision can only be changed by the people. The President will have the same power as the Governor-General at present possesses to dissolve Parliament at any time, even though the five year period has not elapsed.

The present National Assembly will, if the draft Constitution is adopted, become the first National Assembly of the Republic. Under the existing Constitution the present National Assembly is due to be dissolved by, at the latest, July, 1961. After the results of the Plebiscite are known the Government will consider whether to recommend to the Constituent Assembly that the life of the present National Assembly should be prolonged.

The forthcoming Plebiscite will correspond very nearly to a General Election. The method of nominating candidates is designed to provide that the contestants in the Presidential election will be the leaders of the Political Parties in the country. Since the results will be available for each individual constituency it should be possible to tell in which constituencies the Government or the Opposition Party have a majority. If the Presidential election shows that in fact there would be little change in the balance of Parties in the Assembly if a further election were held, the Government will consider that this gives them a mandate to recommend the extension of the life of the existing Assembly.

The cost of the Plebiscite may amount to as much as £G500,000, and it involves very considerable dislocation of Government service in providing for the technical organisation necessary. For these reasons alone, the Government consider a further country-wide election should be avoided unless it can be shown that it would result in an important shift in the balance of the Parties in the Assembly. Furthermore, it is essential that the energies of the country be concentrated upon development and that the new Republican Constitution be given a fair opportunity to work. This cannot be done under the shadow of an impending General Election.

THE COURTS AND THE LAW

The present law, amended to suit a Republican form of Government, will continue in force under the proposed Constitution.

The present system of a Supreme Court, divided into a Court of Appeal and a High Court, will continue in being. On the establishment of the Republic, however, all appeals from the Courts to the Judicial Committee of the Privy Council in the United Kingdom will be discontinued.

The Letters Patent under which Judges are at present appointed are issued in the name of the Queen and will automatically lapse on the establishment of the Republic. On the coming into force of the proposed Constitution the President will therefore reappoint Judges, who will derive their authority from the Constitution and will administer the law in accordance with its provisions.

CHIEFTAINCY

The draft Constitution is designed to preserve and guarantee Chieftaincy. In order to emphasise the importance which is attached to this institution the draft Constitution specifically provides for the continuance of Houses of Chiefs.

THE ARMED FORCES

Under the draft Constitution the President will become the Commander-in-Chief of the Armed Forces. This provision emphasises the fact that the Armed Forces, like the Civil Service, are the servants of the people and are ultimately under the command of the people's representative, the President. As Commander-in-Chief the President will not, of course, be concerned in the day-to-day administration of the Forces. Service conditions and discipline will be regulated by an Armed Forces Act which the new Republican Assembly will be invited to enact. Under the draft Constitution, however, there is reserved to the President the right, in the interests of national security, to dismiss or suspend any member of the Armed Forces whatever his rank or position. This provision is especially designed to deal with the situation which has unhappily arisen in a number of other countries where the Armed Forces have interfered in politics and have, on occasion, even usurped the people's right to choose the Government of the country.

THE CIVIL SERVICE

A Government White Paper explaining in detail Civil Service conditions under the proposed Republican Constitution is being issued at the same time as this White Paper. Broadly speaking, the Government proposals are that the Civil Service should be run on lines very similar to those governing the Civil Service in the United Kingdom and in many other Commonwealth countries.

In the same way as ultimate control of the Armed Forces is vested in the President as the representative of the people, so ultimately the final responsibility for the Civil Service must rest with the President. In fact, however, there will be a Civil Service Commission which will assist and advise the President in all matters of discipline, entry and promotion in the Service, and the position of civil servants will be regulated by a Civil Service Act based on the proposals set out in the White Paper on the Civil Service.

AMENDMENT OF THE CONSTITUTION

The draft Constitution contains a number of entrenched provisions regarded as of basic importance. These are as follows—

1. Provisions setting out the powers of the people and proclaiming the principle of One man—One vote (Article 1).
2. Powers conferred with a view to the realisation of African unity (Article 2).
3. Mode of exercise of powers reserved to the people (Article 3).
4. The status of Ghana as a unitary Republic (Article 5).
5. The office and powers of the President (Article 9).
6. The declaration of fundamental principles to be made by the President on assuming office (Article 14).
7. The appointment of Ministers and the existence and functions of the Cabinet (Articles 15 and 16).
8. The existence and legislative powers of Parliament, and the requirement to hold a session of the National Assembly annually (Articles 20 and 22).
9. The power of the President to dissolve Parliament at any time, and the provision that no Parliament shall last more than five years (Article 23).
10. The prohibition on the levying of taxes otherwise than under an Act of Parliament (Article 26).
11. The existence and judicial powers of the Supreme Court, and the tenure of office of Judges (Articles 40 and 45).
12. The prohibition on the raising of armed forces otherwise than under an Act of Parliament (Article 55).

The repeal or amendment of any of the entrenched provisions can only be effected after the people have given their consent. If the President considers that an entrenched provision should be altered he must ask the people, by way of Referendum, whether they approve the change or not. If approval is given it will be for Parliament to pass the necessary legislation. In this way the people will join with the President and the National Assembly in the responsible task of changing the basic provisions of the Constitution.

Apart from the entrenched provisions, the draft Constitution, if it is enacted, could be subsequently amended by an ordinary Act of Parliament. It is the Government's hope, however, that once the Constitution is adopted it will not be altered unless a pressing need arises. A Constitution should represent a system of Government upon which the people of

417

the country have agreed and it should not be changed unless experience very clearly shows that in some particular aspect it is inadequate.

FUNDAMENTAL PRINCIPLES

The proposed Constitution for Ghana is based upon Freedom and Justice and it is therefore desirable that these principles should be elaborated and protected by the Constitution.

The existing Constitution does make certain provisions in this regard. For example, there is a provision preventing the expropriation of property without compensation. Laws based on religious or racial discrimination are prohibited and the position of Chieftaincy is guaranteed.

In the draft Constitution these provisions, and a number of others, are set out in Article 14. This Article provides that whenever a President takes office he must make a solemn declaration of adherence to the following fundamental principles—

That the powers of Government spring from the will of the people and should be exercised in accordance therewith;

That freedom and justice should be honoured and maintained;

That the union of Africa should be striven for by every lawful means and, when attained, should be faithfully preserved;

That the Independence of Ghana should not be surrendered or diminished on any grounds other than the furtherance of African unity;

That no person should suffer discrimination on grounds of sex, race, tribe, religion or political belief;

That Chieftaincy in Ghana should be guaranteed and preserved;

That every citizen of Ghana should receive his fair share of the produce yielded by the development of the country;

That subject to such restrictions as may be necessary for preserving public order, morality or health, no person should be deprived of freedom of religion or speech, of the right to move and assemble without hindrance or of the right of access to courts of law; and

That no person should be deprived of his property save in accordance with law, and that no law should be made by which a person is deprived of his property without adequate compensation other than a law imposing taxation or prescribing penalties for offences or giving restitution for civil wrongs or protecting health or property.

418

MEMBERSHIP OF THE COMMONWEALTH

No provision is included in the draft Constitution in regard to Membership of the Commonwealth. It is, however, the intention of the Prime Minister to attend the Conference of Commonwealth Prime Ministers to be held in London on the 3rd May, 1960. On that occasion the Prime Minister will tell the other Commonwealth Prime Ministers of the result of the Plebiscite and, if the people vote in favour of the draft Constitution, will inform them that Ghana will become a Republic but would wish to remain within the Commonwealth.

THE ISSUE TO BE PUT BEFORE THE PEOPLE

At the proposed Plebiscite the people will be asked to endorse the draft Constitution printed as an Appendix to this White Paper. The Government will not consider itself bound to introduce into the Constituent Assembly a Constitution Bill which follows word for word the attached draft. Indeed, the time table for the enactment of the Constitution has been specially designed in order to give ample opportunity for the examination of the details of the Constitution, and it may well be that changes of detail, arrangement and emphasis will be found desirable. It will be the duty of the Constituent Assembly, after the people have given their verdict upon the Constitution, to consider each Article and see whether it adequately fulfils the purpose for which it is intended.

However, if there is a vote at the Plebiscite in favour of the proposed Constitution, the Government would urge upon the Constituent Assembly that the Constitution should be based upon the following fundamental principles contained in the draft Constitution. These are:—

1. That Ghana should be a sovereign unitary Republic with power to surrender any part of her sovereignty to a Union of African States.

2. That the Head of State and holder of the executive power should be an elected President responsible to the people.

3. That Parliament should be the Sovereign legislature and should consist of the President and the National Assembly, and that the President should have a power to veto legislation and to dissolve Parliament.

4. That a President should be elected whenever there is a general election by a method which insures that he will normally be the leader of the party which is successful in the General Election.

419

5. That there should be a Cabinet appointed by the President from among Members of Parliament to assist the President in the exercise of his executive functions.

6. That the system of Courts and the security of tenure of Judges should continue on present lines.

7. That the control of the armed forces and the civil service should be vested in the President.

THE INTERPRETATION ACT, 1960, C.A. 4

* * *

The Common Law and Customary Law

The common law.
17. (1) The common law, as comprised in the laws of Ghana, consists, in addition to the rules of law generally known as the common law, of the rules generally known as the doctrines of equity and of rules of customary law included in the common law under any enactment providing for the assimilation of such rules of customary law as are suitable for general application.

(2) In the case of inconsistency, an assimilated rule shall prevail over any other rule, and a rule of equity shall prevail over any rule other than an assimilated rule.

(3) While any of the statutes of general application continue to apply by virtue of the Courts Act, 1960 (C.A. 9), they shall be treated as if they formed part of the common law, as defined in subsection (1), prevailing over any rule thereof other than an assimilated rule.

(4) In deciding upon the existence or content of a rule of the common law, as so defined, the Court may have regard to any exposition of that rule by a court exercising jurisdiction in any country.

(5) A reference in an enactment to the common law shall be construed as a reference to it as affected by any enactment for the time being in force.

Customary law.
18. (1) Customary law, as comprised in the laws of Ghana, consists of rules of law which by custom are applicable to particular communities in Ghana, not being rules included in the common law under any enactment providing for the assimilation of such rules of customary law as are suitable for general application.

(2) A reference in an enactment to a customary law shall be construed as a reference to it as affected by any enactment for the time being in force.

* * *

THE COURTS ACT, 1960, C.A. 9

* * *

PART III—COMMON LAW AND CUSTOMARY LAW

66. (1) Subject to the provisions of any enactment other than this subsection, in deciding whether an issue arising in civil proceedings is to be determined according to the common law or customary law and, if the issue is to be determined according to customary law, in deciding which system of customary law is applicable, the court shall be guided by the following rules, in which references to the personal law of a person are references to the system of customary law to which he is subject or, if he is not shown to be subject to customary law, are references to the common law:— *Application of common law and customary law.*

Rule 1. Where two persons have the same personal law one of them cannot, by dealing in a manner regulated by some other law with property in which the other has a present or expectant interest, alter or affect that interest to an extent which would not in the circumstances be open to him under his personal law.

Rule 2. Subject to Rule 1, where an issue arises out of a transaction the parties to which have agreed, or may from the form or nature of the transaction be taken to have agreed, that such an issue should be determined according to the common law or any system of customary law effect should be given to the agreement.

In this rule "transaction" includes a marriage and an agreement or arrangement to marry.

Rule 3. Subject to Rule 1, where an issue arises out of any unilateral disposition and it appears from the form or nature of the disposition or otherwise that the person effecting the disposition intended that such an issue should be determined according to the common law or any system of customary law effect should be given to the intention.

Rule 4. Subject to the foregoing rules, where an issue relates to entitlement to land on the death of the owner or otherwise relates to title to land—

(a) if all the parties to the proceedings who claim to be entitled to the land or a right relating thereto trace their claims from one person who is subject to customary law, or from one family or other group of persons all subject to the same customary law, the issue should be determined according to that law;

(b) if the said parties trace their claims from

different persons, or families or other groups of persons, who are all subject to the same customary law, the issue should be determined according to that law;

(*c*) in any other case, the issue should be determined according to the law of the place in which the land is situated.

Rule 5. Subject to Rules 1 to 3, where an issue relates to the devolution of the property (other than land) of a person on his death it should be determined according to his personal law.

Rule 6. Subject to the foregoing rules, an issue should be determined according to the common law unless the plaintiff is subject to any system of customary law and claims to have the issue determined according to that system, when it should be so determined.

(2) [The original section 2 of Article 66 provided "Where under this section customary law is applicable in any proceedings but a relevant rule of customary law has been assimilated by the common law under any enactment such as is mentioned in section 18 (1) of the Interpretation Act, 1960, that rule shall nevertheless apply in those proceedings, but in the form in which it has been so assimilated." This section was repealed by Sec. 69 (1) of the Chieftaincy Act, 1961, Act 81.]

(3) Notwithstanding anything contained in the foregoing provisions of this section, but subject to the provisions of any other enactment,—

(*a*) the rules of the common law relating to private international law shall apply in any proceedings in which an issue concerning the application of law prevailing in any country outside Ghana is raised;

(*b*) the rules of estoppel and such other of the rules generally known as the common law and the rules generally known as the doctrines of equity as have heretofore been treated as applicable in all proceedings in Ghana shall continue to be so treated.

Ascertainment of customary law.

67. (1) Any question as to the existence or content of a rule of customary law is a question of law for the Court and not a question of fact.

(2) If the Court entertains any doubt as to the existence or content of a rule of customary law relevant in any proceedings after considering such submissions thereon as may be made by or on behalf of the parties and consult-

ing such reported cases, textbooks and other sources as may be appropriate, the court shall adjourn the proceedings to enable an inquiry to take place under the next subsection.

(3) The inquiry shall be held as part of the proceedings in such manner as the Court considers expedient, and the provisions of this Act relating to the attendance and testimony of witnesses shall apply for the purpose of the tendering of opinions to the Court at the inquiry, but shall apply subject to such modifications as may appear to the Court to be necessary:

Provided that—

(a) the decision as to the persons who are to be heard at the inquiry shall be one for the Court, after hearing such submissions thereon as may be made by or on behalf of the parties;

(b) the Court may request a House of Chiefs, State Council or other body possessing knowledge of the customary law in question to state its opinion, which may be laid before the inquiry in written form.

* * *

ACT 1

THE FIRST ACT
OF THE PARLIAMENT
OF THE REPUBLIC
OF GHANA

ENTITLED

THE PRESIDENTIAL ELECTIONS ACT, 1960

AN ACT to lay down the procedure
for the election of a President.

DATE OF ASSENT: 9th AUGUST, 1960

BE IT ENACTED by the President and the National Assembly
in this present Parliament assembled as follows:—

Preliminary

*Applica-
tion of
Act.*
1. The provisions of this Act shall apply in relation to the
election of a President whether—
> (*a*) the election falls to be held by reason of a
> dissolution of the National Assembly (in this
> Act referred to as "a dissolution election") or,
> (*b*) the election falls to be held by reason of the
> death or resignation of the President (in this
> Act referred to as "an interim election").

*Returning
officer.*
2. The returning officer for a dissolution election or an
interim election shall be the Chief Justice.

Nomination of Candidates

*Notices of
nomina-
tion.*
3. In the case of a dissolution election or an interim election the Chief Justice shall appoint—

(a) a place and a time or times, which shall be not less than seven days or more than twelve days after the event causing the election, for the receipt by him of nominations of candidates, and

(b) a place and time for the public scrutiny by him of notices of nomination.

4. (1) In the case of a dissolution election, a person shall be validly nominated as a candidate if, but only if— *Candidates for dissolution election.*

(a) he is a person (including a retiring or former President) who is a citizen of Ghana and has attained the age of thirty-five years; and

(b) he is nominated by a notice in writing delivered to the Chief Justice at the place and a time appointed by him under paragraph (a) of section 3 of this Act and signed by two or more persons who are citizens of Ghana; and

(c) the said notice includes a declaration in the following form:

"We the undersigned hereby declare that the person nominated by this notice has consented to the nomination and that we have reason to believe and do believe that at the forthcoming General Election candidates exceeding in number one half of the number of seats in the National Assembly will declare their preference for that person under section 7 of the Presidential Elections Act, 1960."

(2) A person who signs a notice delivered to the Chief Justice under this section knowing the declaration contained therein to be false in any material particular, or reckless as to its truth or falsity, shall be guilty of an offence and shall be liable to imprisonment for five years.

5. In the case of an interim election, a person shall be validly nominated as a candidate if, but only if,— *Candidates for interim election.*

(a) he is a person (including a retiring or former President) who is a citizen of Ghana and has attained the age of thirty-five years; and

(b) he is nominated by a notice in writing delivered to the Chief Justice at the place and a time appointed by him under paragraph (a) of section 3 of this Act and signed by ten or more Members of Parliament.

Uncontested Elections

6. If, at any time during the conduct of a dissolution elec- *Uncontested elections.*

tion or an interim election after the public scrutiny by him of notices of nomination, the Chief Justice is satisfied—

    (*a*) that no person validly nominated as a candidate in the said election has since died, and

    (*b*) that one person only was so nominated or remains so nominated after any withdrawal of candidates,

the Chief Justice shall declare that person elected as President, and none of the following provisions of this Act shall thereafter apply to the said election.

Dissolution Elections

Preferences.

7. (1) A person who, in a General Election, has been nominated as a candidate for the National Assembly may deliver to the Chief Justice during the period beginning twenty-eight days before the date fixed for the commencement of voting in the General Election and ending fourteen days before that date, a notice under his hand declaring his preference for a Presidential candidate specified in the notice:

Provided that a notice under this paragraph shall be invalid unless the Presidential candidate specified in the notice has consented to the inclusion of his name therein and the notice states that he has so consented.

(2) As soon as may be after he has received a notice given under the preceding subsection the Chief Justice shall cause to be published in the *Gazette* particulars showing the name of the person giving the notice, the electoral division for which he is a candidate and the name of the Presidential candidate specified in the notice.

(3) A notice given under subsection (1) of this section by a person returned as a Member of Parliament, shall, unless in the opinion of the Chief Justice it is invalid, be deemed to be a vote cast in the primary stage of the dissolution election for the Presidential candidate specified in the notice.

Primary stage.

8. (1) The counting of votes cast in the primary stage shall be carried out in public by the Chief Justice, at a place and time appointed by him, before the Members of Parliament and in the immediate view of such of the candidates as desire to witness the count.

(2) At the conclusion of the count the Chief Justice shall announce the number of votes obtained by each candidate, and—

    (*a*) if any candidate has obtained a number of votes exceeding one half of the number of persons returned as Members of Parliament, the Chief Justice shall declare that candidate elected as President, or

(b) if no candidate has obtained that number of votes, the Chief Justice shall adjourn the proceedings for such period as he thinks fit and then proceed to conduct the secondary stage of the election in accordance with the next following section.

9. (1) The Members of Parliament shall proceed to ballot for the election of a President in the manner following— *Secondary stage.*

(a) the Clerk of the Assembly shall display to the Members an empty ballot box in such a manner as to make plain that the box is empty and shall then place the box before the Chief Justice, who shall seal it;

(b) a blank ballot paper bearing a mark distinctive to the ballot about to take place shall then be handed by the Clerk to each Member present;

(c) the Chief Justice shall then read out the names of the candidates in alphabetical order and shall invite each Member to write on his ballot paper in legible characters the name of the candidate for whom he wishes to vote;

(d) the Clerk shall then take round the sealed ballot box, into which each Member who wishes to vote shall place his completed ballot paper;

(e) the Chief Justice shall then proceed to break the seal of the ballot box, to count the votes cast for each candidate in the immediate view of such of the candidates as desire to witness the count, and to announce the result.

(2) In a case where the votes cast for one of the candidates exceed the total votes cast for all other candidates the Chief Justice shall declare that candidate elected as President, but in any other case the Chief Justice shall declare that there is no result and adjourn the proceedings for such period as he thinks fit.

(3) If any question arises as to whether the vote of a Member has been cast for a particular candidate, the question shall be decided by the Chief Justice, whose decision shall be final.

(4) After the adjournment further balloting shall take place in accordance with the preceding provisions of this

section until either a President is elected or five ballots have been held without a President having been elected.

Interim Elections

10. An interim election shall be conducted in public by the Chief Justice at a place and time appointed by him, and in the like manner as the secondary stage of a dissolution election; and section 9 of this Act shall apply thereto accordingly.

11. If, after the death or resignation of the President, the National Assembly is dissolved before a new President has been declared elected in the interim election, no further proceedings shall be taken in the interim election.

Death, withdrawal and substitution of candidates

12. (1) If a candidate in a dissolution election dies before voting in the General Election has begun then—

    (*a*) the General Election shall be postponed by not more than two months to such date as the retiring President or the Presidential Commission, as the case may be, shall appoint;

    (*b*) all proceedings previously taken under this Act in relation to the dissolution election shall be void; and

    (*c*) section 3 of this Act shall apply as if for the reference therein to the event causing the election there were substituted a reference to the death of the candidate.

(2) If a candidate in a dissolution election dies after voting in the General Election has begun, sections 8 and 9 of this Act shall nevertheless apply with the substitution, for subsection (2) of section 8, of the following—

"(2) At the conclusion of the count the Chief Justice shall announce the number of votes obtained by each candidate, and—

    (*a*) if any candidate other than the deceased candidate has obtained a number of votes exceeding one half of the number of persons returned as Members of Parliament, the Chief Justice shall declare that person elected as President, or

    (*b*) if no such candidate has obtained that number of votes, the Chief Justice shall adjourn the proceedings for such period as he thinks fit and then proceed to conduct the secondary stage of the election in accordance with section 9 of this Act."

(3) If a candidate in an interim election dies—
- (a) all proceedings previously taken under this Act in relation to the election shall be void, and
- (b) section 3 of this Act shall apply as if for the reference therein to the event causing the election there were substituted a reference to the death of the candidate.

13. A candidate in a dissolution election or an interim election may withdraw his candidature by writing under his hand delivered to the Chief Justice at any time during the period beginning with his nomination and ending three days before the date appointed for the public scrutiny of notices of nomination, or— *Withdrawal of candidate.*

- (a) in the case of a dissolution election which proceeds to the secondary stage, during any adjournment of the proceedings immediately before or in the course of that stage;
- (b) in the case of an interim election, during any adjournment of the proceedings at the election.

14. (1) The persons who nominated a person (hereinafter referred to as "the original candidate") as a candidate in a dissolution election or an interim election, or a majority of those persons, may in the like manner nominate another person as a candidate in substitution for the original candidate if the original candidate withdraws his candidature, or— *Substitution of candidate.*

- (a) in the case of a dissolution election, if the original candidate dies after voting in the General Election has begun or if a President is not elected at the primary stage;
- (b) in the case of an interim election, if a President is not elected in the first ballot.

(2) Where the original candidate withdraws his candidature during the period beginning with his nomination and ending three days before the date appointed for the public scrutiny of notices of nomination, then, notwithstanding anything contained in section 4 or 5 of this Act, a notice of nomination under this section may be delivered to the Chief Justice at any time before the date appointed for the public scrutiny of notices of nomination.

(3) In any other case where a nomination may be made under this section, the notice of nomination may be delivered to the Chief Justice at any time at which, under paragraph (a) or (b) of section 13 of this Act, a notice of withdrawal could be so delivered.

429

THE EIGHTY-SIXTH ACT
OF THE PARLIAMENT
OF THE REPUBLIC OF GHANA

ENTITLED

THE NATIONAL ASSEMBLY ACT, 1961

AN ACT to consolidate the enactments relating to the National Assembly.

DATE OF ASSENT: 14th NOVEMBER, 1961

WHEREAS Article 20 of the Constitution established the Parliament of the Republic of Ghana, consisting of the President and the National Assembly:

AND WHEREAS it is expedient to enact provisions as to the National Assembly in addition to those contained in the Constitution.

Now THEREFORE be it enacted by the President and the National Assembly in this present Parliament assembled as follows:—

PART I—MEMBERSHIP

Persons qualified for membership.

1. (1) Subject to the provisions of this section, a person shall be qualified to be elected as a Member if, but only if,—

(a) he is a citizen of Ghana, and

(b) he has attained the age of twenty-five years, and

(c) he is able both to speak and read the English language with a degree of proficiency sufficient to enable him to take an active part in the proceedings of the Assembly:

Provided that a person who is unable to read by reason of blindness or other physical cause shall not for that reason only be treated as failing to satisfy the condition set out in paragraph (c) of this subsection.

(2) No person shall be qualified to be elected as a Member if he is at the time of the election a person such as is mentioned in the following Table.

TABLE

1. A person holding the office of President or Speaker, or being a public officer.

2. A person disqualified from practising his profession in Ghana by virtue of an order made in respect to him personally by a competent authority, not being an order made at his own request or more than five years previously.

3. A person adjudged to be of unsound mind or detained as a criminal lunatic.

4. A person who has been sentenced in Ghana for any offence to death or to imprisonment for a term exceeding twelve months, or for any offences to imprisonment for consecutive terms exceeding twelve months in all, not being a person—

  (a) who has been granted a free pardon in respect of the said offence or offences, or

  (b) whose said imprisonment terminated more than five years previously.

5. A person who has been convicted in Ghana of an offence which involved dishonesty, not being a person—

  (a) who has been granted a free pardon in respect of the said offence, or

  (b) whose imprisonment for the said offence terminated more than five years previously, or

  (c) who, not having been sentenced to imprisonment for the said offence, was convicted more than five years previously.

6. A person against whom an order under the Preventive Detention Act, 1958 (No. 17) is in force or has been in force at any time in the previous five years.

7. A person who is disqualified for membership of the Assembly under the provisions of section 256 of the Criminal Code, 1960 (Act 29) or section 16 of the Electoral Provisions Ordinance, 1953 (No. 33).

(3) If any question arises under this or the next following section as to whether an offence involved dishonesty it shall be determined by the Chief Justice, and a certificate signed by the Chief Justice setting out his determination shall be conclusive for all purposes.

Tenure of member-ship.

2. (1) Every Member shall cease to be a Member on the dissolution of the Assembly.

(2) A Member shall cease to be a Member if—

(a) an event occurs whereby he becomes a person such as is mentioned in the Table contained in the preceding section; or

(b) the Speaker receives a notice signed by him whereby he resigns his seat; or

(c) he is expelled from the Assembly under section 39 of this Act; or

(d) he is absent from twenty consecutive sittings of the Assembly in the same session (whether comprised in one or more meetings) without leave of absence having been given under the hand of the Speaker in respect of any one of those sittings before the termination of the sitting, and the Assembly does not, in any of the three sittings next following the last of those sittings, order that this paragraph shall not apply; or

(e) in the course of the proceedings of the Assembly he publicly declares his intention of systematically refraining from attending the proceedings of the Assembly, and the Speaker or other person presiding confirms that the Member made that declaration in his hearing.

Filling of vacancies.

3. (1) There shall be a general election at such time within two months after every dissolution of the Assembly as the President shall by proclamation appoint.

(2) As soon as may be after—

(a) the seat of a Member has become vacant by reason of his death or the operation of subsection (2) of the last preceding section, or

(b) it is established that the election of a person as a Member is invalid by reason that the person was disqualified for election or otherwise,

the Speaker shall order the holding of a by-election to fill the vacant seat.

Oaths.

4. Except for the purpose of enabling this section to be complied with, no Member shall sit or vote in the Assembly or a committee until he has taken and subscribed before the Assembly the Oath of Allegiance and the Oath of a Member of Parliament, or has made before the Assembly the appropriate affirmations in lieu thereof, as required by law:

Provided that if, between the time when a person becomes a Member and the time when the Assembly next meets thereafter, a meeting takes place of a committee of which that person is a member, he may, in order to enable him to attend the meeting and take part in the proceedings, take and subscribe the said Oaths or make the said affirmations before a Judge of the Supreme Court, who shall forthwith report to the Assembly through the Speaker that he has done so.

5. Subject to the provisions of this Act, there shall be paid to each Member a salary and allowances at such rates as may be fixed from time to time by the Assembly; and the payment thereof is hereby charged on the Consolidated Fund. *Salary and allowances.*

6. (1) A gratuity shall be payable in respect of service as a Member— *Right to gratuity.*

    (a) at the end of each period of five years' continuous service as a Member; and

    (b) on the death or retirement of a Member otherwise than at the end of any such period.

(2) Where a Member vacated his seat by reason of a dissolution and was returned as a Member in the following general election he shall be deemed for the purposes of this section to have continued to be a Member during the intervening period.

(3) For the purposes of the provisions of this Act relating to gratuities, a Member shall be deemed to retire if, but only if,—

    (a) he ceases to be a Member on resignation, or

    (b) he ceases to be a Member on becoming a person such as is mentioned in paragraph 1, 2 or 3 of the Table contained in section 1 of this Act; or

    (c) he ceases to be a Member by reason of a dissolution and is not returned as a Member in the following general election.

(4) In this section "Member" includes a Member of the former Legislative Assembly or the former National Assembly.

7. (1) Where a person who becomes entitled to a gratuity was a private Member throughout the qualifying period, the amount of the gratuity shall be equal to one-fifth (or in the case of a second or subsequent gratuity, one-tenth) of his total basic emoluments during that period. *Amount of gratuity.*

(2) Where a person who becomes entitled to a gratuity was a private Member for a part only of the qualifying

period, the amount of the gratuity shall be equal to the aggregate of—

    (*a*) one-fifth (or in the case of a second or subsequent gratuity, one-tenth) of his total basic emoluments during that part of the period, and

    (*b*) one-sixth of his total basic emoluments during the remainder of the period.

(3) Where a person who becomes entitled to a gratuity was not a private Member during any part of the qualifying period, the amount of the gratuity shall be equal to one-sixth of his total basic emoluments during that period.

(4) In this and the following section—

    "basic emoluments" means the aggregate of salary and basic allowance, that is an allowance not paid in respect of specific expenses;

    "designated office" means an office designated by the President as removing the holder from the status of a private Member;

    "private Member" means a Member not holding the office of Minister or Deputy Speaker, or any corresponding office or any designated office;

    "qualifying period" means the period of five years in respect of which the gratuity is payable or, where the gratuity is payable on death or retirement, means the period between the date on which the person in question became a Member, or became entitled to his previous gratuity, as the case may be, and the date of death or retirement;

    "salary" means the salary payable, as the case may require, in respect of service as Minister or Deputy Speaker or as the holder of a designated office or as Member,

and for the purposes of any reference in this section to a second or subsequent gratuity, account shall be taken of any gratuity paid under Part IX of the National Assembly Act, 1959 (No. 78).

Payment of gratuities.   8. (1) Subject to the provisions of this section, a gratuity payable under section 6 of this Act shall be paid to the Member in question.

(2) Where the Member has died—

    (*a*) the gratuity shall be paid to the person who was nominated by the Member as his beneficiary or, if two or more persons were so nominated, shall be divided in the proportions

434

indicated by the Member and paid accordingly, or

(*b*) if no such nomination was made, or if a person nominated has predeceased the Member, the payment or the proportion thereof allotted to the deceased nominee, as the case may be, shall be paid to the person in whom the Member's estate is vested under section 1 of the Administration of Estates Act, 1961 (Act 63).

A nomination for the purposes of this subsection shall be in writing signed by the Member and deposited with the Speaker, and may be revoked or varied by the Member at any time; and a person to whom a payment is made by virtue of the nomination shall be beneficially entitled to the amount received by him.

(3) When a gratuity becomes payable the Speaker shall notify the Accountant-General of the fact, and the notification shall include the following particulars—

(*a*) the name and address of the Member,

(*b*) the dates of the beginning and end of the qualifying period,

(*c*) the status and basic emoluments of the Member during the qualifying period,

(*d*) the amount of the gratuity, and

(*e*) in a case where the Member has died, the name and address of each person to whom a sum is payable under the preceding subsection, together with the amount of the sum payable to him.

(4) In making a payment in pursuance of a notification under the preceding subsection, the Accountant-General shall deduct the amount of any debt which to his knowledge is owed to the Government by the Member or his estate and, where the payment is made to a beneficiary nominated under subsection (2) of this section, shall also deduct the amount of any debt which to his knowledge is owed by the beneficiary to the Government.

(5) Payments falling to be made under this section are hereby charged on the Consolidated Fund.

(6) Neither a payment made under this section, nor, to the extent to which it represents the payment, any property in which the payment has been invested or which otherwise represents the same, shall be liable to be attached, sequestered or levied upon, whether by order of the court or upon insolvency or otherwise, in respect of any debt or other claim.

Part II—Speaker, Deputy Speaker and Officers

The Speaker.

9. (1) The Speaker shall be a person elected by the Members, not being a Minister or public officer.

(2) The election of the Speaker shall take place before the despatch of any other business at the first sitting of the Assembly after the office of the Speaker has become vacant.

(3) The office of the Speaker shall become vacant—

(*a*) immediately before the first sitting of the Assembly after a dissolution; or

(*b*) on the publication in the *Gazette* of a notice signed by the Speaker whereby he resigns his office; or

(*c*) if the Assembly resolves that it has no confidence in the Speaker and the resolution is supported by the votes of at least two-thirds of the total number of Members:

Provided that a resolution under paragraph (*c*) of this subsection shall be of no effect unless at least seven days' notice that it was to be moved was given in the manner required by Standing Orders for the giving of notices of motions.

Speaker's salary, allowances and gratuity.

10. (1) There shall be paid to the Speaker a salary and allowances at such rates as may be fixed from time to time by the Assembly; and the payment thereof is hereby charged on the Consolidated Fund.

(2) Service in the office of Speaker shall rank as qualifying service for the payment of a gratuity in the same way as service as a Member other than a private Member, and sections 6 to 8 of this Act shall apply accordingly.

The Deputy Speaker.

11. (1) The Deputy Speaker shall be a Member, not being a Minister, elected by the Members.

(2) The election of the Deputy Speaker shall take place at the first sitting of the Assembly after the office of Deputy Speaker has become vacant, or as soon thereafter as may be convenient.

(3) The office of the Deputy Speaker shall become vacant—

(*a*) immediately before the first sitting of the Assembly after a prorogation or dissolution; or

(*b*) if the Deputy Speaker ceases to be a Member otherwise than by reason of a dissolution, or becomes a Minister; or

(*c*) on the receipt by the Speaker, or, if the Speaker is absent or his office is vacant, by

436

the Clerk, of a notice signed by the Deputy Speaker whereby he resigns his office; or

(d) if the Assembly resolves that it has no confidence in the Deputy Speaker.

(4) There shall be paid to the Deputy Speaker, in lieu of any salary and allowances to which he would be entitled as a Member, a salary and allowances at such rate as may be fixed from time to time by the Assembly; and the payment thereof is hereby charged on the Consolidated Fund.

12. In the absence of any indication to the contrary in an enactment conferring functions on the Speaker, the Deputy Speaker shall have power, if authorised in that behalf by the Speaker or by Standing Orders, or if the office of the Speaker is vacant, to perform any of those functions, and, if the office of Speaker is vacant, shall in any case perform any of those functions which are obligatory; and references to the Speaker in any enactment shall be construed accordingly. *Powers of Deputy Speaker.*

13. (1) There shall be a Clerk of the National Assembly, who shall be a person who is a public officer. *Staff of Assembly.*

(2) The staff of the Clerk shall consist of persons who are public officers.

Part III—Proceedings of the Assembly

14. (1) Subject to the provisions of this Act, the Assembly may make Standing Orders for the regulation and orderly conduct of proceedings and the despatch of business. *Standing Orders.*

(2) Without prejudice to the generality of the preceding subsection, Standing Orders may empower the Speaker to issue a warrant of arrest for the purpose of securing the attendance of a person ordered by the Assembly or a committee to appear before it and may for that purpose apply, with such modifications as may be necessary, any enactment relating to the arrest of accused persons.

15. No business except that of adjournment shall be transacted in the Assembly if objection is taken by any Member present, not being a Member presiding, that there are less than twenty-five Members present, excluding any Member presiding. *Quorum.*

16. (1) Subject to the provisions of this or any other Act, all questions proposed for decision in the Assembly shall be determined by a majority of the votes of the Members present and voting; and if, upon any question before the As- *Voting.*

sembly, the votes of the Members are equally divided the motion shall be lost.

(2) The Speaker shall have neither an original nor a casting vote, but any other person presiding, including the Deputy Speaker, shall have an original vote but no casting vote.

Right to introduce Bills, etc.

17. Subject to the provisions of this Act and of Standing Orders, any Member may introduce any Bill or propose any motion for debate in, or may present any petition to, the Assembly, and the same shall be disposed of according to Standing Orders.

Restriction on financial business.

18. Except with the recommendation or consent of the President signified thereto, the Assembly shall not proceed upon any Bill, motion or petition which, in the opinion of the person presiding, would dispose of or charge the Consolidated Fund or other public funds of Ghana, or revoke or alter any disposition thereof or charge thereon, or impose, alter or repeal any rate, tax or duty.

Irregularities not to invalidate proceedings.

19. The Assembly or a committee shall not be disqualified for the transaction of business by reason of any vacancy among the Members, including any vacancy not filled at a general election; and any proceedings therein shall be valid notwithstanding that some person who was not entitled to do so sat or voted or otherwise took part in the proceedings.

Part IV—Privileges and Immunities

Freedom of speech and proceedings.

20. There shall be freedom of speech, debate and proceedings in the Assembly and that freedom shall not be impeached or questioned in any court or place out of the Assembly.

Immunity from proceedings for acts in the Assembly.

21. Without prejudice to the generality of the last preceding section, no civil or criminal proceedings shall be instituted against a Member in any court or place out of the Assembly by reason of anything said by him in the Assembly or any matter or thing brought by him before the Assembly by petition, Bill, motion or otherwise.

Immunity from service of process and arrest.

22. No civil or criminal process issuing from any court or place out of the Assembly shall—

   (*a*) be served on, or executed in relation to, the Speaker or a Member while he is on his way to, attending at or returning from any proceeding of the Assembly, or

   (*b*) be served or executed within the precincts of

438

the Assembly while the Assembly is sitting, or

(c) be served or executed through the Speaker, the Deputy Speaker or any officer:

Provided that the Speaker, on an application being made to him in that behalf, may direct that paragraph (a) of this section shall not apply to the service or execution of any criminal process specified in the direction.

23. (1) Neither the Speaker nor any Member or officer shall be required, while attending the Assembly, to appear as a witness in any court or place out of the Assembly.

(2) The certificate of the Speaker to that effect shall be conclusive evidence of attendance at the Assembly.

Immunity from witness summons while attending Assembly.

24. Neither the Speaker nor any Member or officer shall be required to serve on a jury or as an assessor in any court or place out of the Assembly.

Immunity from service as juryman or assessor.

25. (1) No person shall be under any civil or criminal liability in respect of an act ordered or authorised, in accordance with law, by the Assembly or by the Speaker, a Member or officer.

(2) The certificate of the Speaker to that effect shall be conclusive evidence that an act was in fact ordered or authorised by the Assembly or by such a person as aforesaid, as the case may be.

Immunity for acts authorised by Assembly.

26. Subject to the provisions of this Act, no person shall be under any civil or criminal liability in respect of the publication of the text or a summary of any report, paper, minutes, votes or proceedings of the Assembly unless it is shown that the publication was effected maliciously or otherwise in want of good faith.

Immunity for publication of proceedings.

27. (1) Every person summoned to attend to give evidence or to produce any paper, book, record or other document before the Assembly shall be entitled, in respect of his evidence, or the production of the said document, as the case may be, to the same privilege as if he were appearing before a court of law.

(2) Except with the consent of the President, no public officer shall be required—

(a) to produce before the Assembly any document, or

(b) to give before the Assembly evidence on any matter,

if the document or evidence is stated by the public officer to form part of or to relate to the unpublished official records

Privilege of witnesses.

439

of any naval, military, air force or civil department, or to relate to any affairs of State.

(3) An answer by a person to a question put by the Assembly shall not be admissible in evidence against him in any civil or criminal proceedings out of the Assembly, not being proceedings for perjury brought under section 210 of the Criminal Code, 1960 (Act 29).

PART V—CONTEMPT OF PARLIAMENT

General. 28. Any act which impedes or tends to impede the Assembly in the exercise of its functions, or affronts the dignity of the Assembly, is a contempt of Parliament, and the setting forth in the following provisions of this Part of this Act of particular contempts shall not be taken to affect the generality of this section.

Interference with Members and officers.

29. (1) It is a contempt of Parliament—
   (a) for any person to assault, obstruct, molest or insult the Speaker or a Member while he is within the precincts of the Assembly or is on his way to or returning from any proceedings of the Assembly;
   (b) for any person who knows or has reasonable grounds for believing that a person is an officer to assault, obstruct, molest or insult him while he is exercising his functions or is on his way to or returning from the exercise of his functions.

(2) It is a contempt of Parliament—
   (a) for any person to endeavour, by means of bribery, fraud or the infliction or threatened infliction of violence, restraint or spiritual or temporal injury, to influence a Member in the exercise of his functions;
   (b) for any person to inflict violence, restraint or spiritual or temporal injury on a Member by reason of anything done or omitted to be done by him in the exercise of his functions;
   (c) for a Member to accept, or procure for himself or any other person, any benefit in return for undertaking to exercise any of his functions in a particular manner or by reason of anything done or omitted to be done by him in the exercise of his functions.

Interference with proceedings.

30. It is a contempt of Parliament—
   (a) for any person to create or join in any disturbance which interrupts or is likely to

440

interrupt the proceedings of the Assembly;

(b) for a stranger to sit or vote in the Assembly;

(c) for a Member persistently to obstruct the proceedings of the Assembly, whether or not in contravention of Standing Orders.

31. It is a contempt of Parliament— *Inducing false or incomplete evidence.*

(a) for any person to give evidence to the Assembly, whether or not on oath, which is false or incomplete, or, with intent to deceive the Assembly, to produce before it any false document, or wilfully to conceal, destroy, mutilate or alter a document ordered by the Assembly to be produced to it;

(b) for any person wilfully to hinder the attendance of a witness before the Assembly or the giving of evidence or production of a document to the Assembly, or to suborn a witness or otherwise tamper with evidence, or to inflict violence, restraint or spiritual or temporal injury on a person by reason of evidence given by him to the Assembly.

32. It is a contempt of Parliament— *Disobedience by witnesses, etc.*

(a) for any person to disobey without reasonable excuse an order made by the Assembly to attend before it or to produce a document or answer a question, not being a document or question as to which the witness is entitled to claim privilege or which is ruled by the person presiding to be irrelevant;

(b) for any person to publish evidence taken by, or a document presented to, the Assembly in contravention of Standing Orders or any other order of the Assembly.

33. It is a contempt of Parliament for a Member to disobey *Disobedience by Members.* an order given in accordance with Standing Orders by the person presiding at any proceedings of the Assembly.

34. It is a contempt of Parliament— *Disobedience by strangers.*

(a) for a stranger to enter or remain within the precincts of the Assembly in disobedience of an order of the Assembly or of Standing Orders or an order given thereunder;

(b) for a stranger to behave within the precincts of the Assembly otherwise than in accordance with Standing Orders or an order given thereunder.

Defamation of Assembly. 35. It is a contempt of Parliament for any person to make a statement or otherwise publish any matter which falsely or scandalously defames the Assembly or the Speaker, a Member or officer in his capacity as such, or which contains a gross or scandalous misrepresentation of any proceedings of the Assembly.

PART VI—PUNISHMENT OF OFFENCES

Exclusion of disorderly Member. 36. If in the opinion of the person presiding over the Assembly or a committee the conduct of a Member is grossly disorderly, the person presiding may order the Member to withdraw from the precincts of the Assembly and the Member shall forthwith leave the precincts and shall not enter them again during the remainder of the day's sitting.

Reprimand of Member in contempt. 37. When a Member has been found by the Assembly to be guilty of contempt of Parliament the Assembly may direct that he be reprimanded in his place by the Speaker.

Suspension of Member in contempt. 38. (1) When a Member has been found by the Assembly to be guilty of contempt of Parliament the Assembly may suspend him from the service of the Assembly for a period not exceeding nine months, whether or not that period extends beyond the end of the session.

(2) Where a Member has been suspended from the service of the Assembly—

(*a*) he shall forthwith leave the precincts of the Assembly and shall not enter them again while the suspension continues;

(*b*) he shall forfeit the salary and allowances to which he would otherwise be entitled as a Member in respect of the period of suspension;

(*c*) if he is entitled to a salary and allowances as a Minister or as the Deputy Speaker there shall be deducted therefrom an amount equal to the amount which would be forfeited by him under paragraph (*b*) of this subsection if he were not so entitled.

Expulsion of Member. 39. (1) Where a Member has been found by the Assembly to have been guilty of conduct which, whether or not it amounts to contempt of Parliament, is so grossly improper as to indicate that he is unfit to remain a Member he may be expelled by the Assembly.

(2) A resolution for the expulsion of a Member under this section shall be of no effect unless—

442

(*a*) at least seven days' notice that it was to be moved was given in the manner required by Standing Orders for the giving of notices of motions, and

(*b*) it is supported by the votes of at least two-thirds of the total number of Members.

40. (1) When an officer has been found by the Assembly to be guilty of contempt of Parliament the Assembly may order the finding to be reported to the secretary of the Civil Service Commission with a view to disciplinary proceedings being taken against the officer, and may further order that, pending the conclusion of such proceedings, the officer be suspended from duty in the Assembly. *Punishment of officer in contempt.*

(2) A person suspended from duty under this section shall not enter the precincts of the Assembly while the suspension continues.

41. When a stranger has been found by the Assembly to be guilty of contempt of Parliament the Assembly may order him not to enter the precincts of the Assembly for a period not exceeding nine months, whether or not that period extends beyond the end of the session. *Exclusion of stranger in contempt.*

42. (1) An officer may arrest without warrant or order– *Detention of stranger causing disturbance, etc.*

(*a*) a stranger who commits in his presence a contempt under paragraph (*a*) or (*b*) of section 30 of this Act or under section 34 thereof; or

(*b*) a stranger within the precincts of the Assembly whom he reasonably suspects to have committed such a contempt.

(2) As soon as is reasonably practicable after the arrest of a person under this section, the Speaker shall be informed of the arrest and may order that the person arrested be detained in the custody of an officer for a period not extending beyond the end of the day's sitting, or otherwise dealt with according to law.

43. When a stranger has been found by the Assembly to be guilty of contempt of Parliament the Assembly may order him to appear at the bar of the Assembly at a time specified in the order to be reprimanded by the Speaker. *Reprimand of stranger in contempt.*

44. Any person who is within the precincts of the Assembly in contravention of this Act may be removed therefrom by an officer, who shall be entitled to use such force as is reasonably necessary. *Removal of trespassers.*

Criminal prosecution.

45. (1) A stranger who is guilty of contempt of Parliament shall be liable to a fine not exceeding one hundred pounds or imprisonment for one year or both.

(2) Proceedings taken in respect of any act under one or more of the preceding sections of this Part of this Act shall not affect the liability of any person to prosecution and punishment in respect thereof under this section or any other enactment.

(3) The Assembly may order the Attorney-General to prosecute a person whom it suspects to be guilty of a contempt of Parliament which constitutes an offence under this section or any other enactment.

Part VII—Supplemental

Interpretation.

46. In this Act, unless the context otherwise requires—

"the Assembly" means the National Assembly, and in Parts IV and V includes a committee;

"the Clerk" means the Clerk of the Assembly;

"committee" means a select committee or other committee of the Assembly;

"meeting" means any sitting or sittings of the Assembly commencing when the Assembly first meets after being summoned at any time and ending when the Assembly is adjourned *sine die* or at the conclusion of a session;

"Member" means a Member of Parliament;

"Minister" includes Parliamentary Secretary and Deputy Minister;

"officer" means the Clerk or any person acting within the precincts of the Assembly under the orders of the Speaker, and includes any police officer on duty within the precincts of the Assembly but does not include a person suspended from duty under section 40 of this Act;

"the precincts of the Assembly" means the offices of the Assembly and the galleries and places provided for the use or accommodation of strangers, and includes, while the Assembly is sitting and subject to any exceptions made by direction of the Speaker, the entire building in which the Assembly is situated and any forecourt, yard, garden, enclosure or open space adjoining or appertaining to that building and used or provided for the purposes of the Assembly;

"session" means the sittings of the Assembly commencing when the Assembly first meets after prorogation or dissolution and ending when the

Assembly is prorogued or is dissolved without being prorogued;

"sitting" means a period during which the Assembly is sitting continuously without adjournment, and includes any period during which the Assembly is in committee;

"Standing Orders" means orders for the time being in force under section 14 of this Act;

"stranger" means any person other than the President, the Speaker, a Member or an officer.

47. (1) The following enactments are hereby repealed— *Repeals.*
The National Assembly Act, 1959 (No. 78);

Section 3 of the Constitution (Consequential Provisions) Act, 1960 (C.A. 8);

The National Assembly (Amendment) Act, 1961 (Act 34).

(2) Without prejudice to the general effect of the Interpretation Act, 1960 (C.A. 4) as to repeals, nothing in this Act shall affect the continued payment of the pension payable under section 52 of the National Assembly Act, 1959 (No. 78).

(3) Standing Orders made under section 15 of the National Assembly Act, 1959 (No. 78) shall, subject to the Assembly's powers of revocation and amendment thereof, continue to have effect as if made under section 14 of this Act.

THE TWO HUNDRED AND FORTIETH ACT
OF THE PARLIAMENT OF
THE REPUBLIC OF GHANA

ENTITLED

THE PREVENTIVE DETENTION ACT, 1964

An act to consolidate with amendments the enactments relating to preventive detention.

DATE OF ASSENT: 22nd MAY, 1964

Be it enacted by the President and the National Assembly in this present Parliament assembled as follows:—

Detention order.   1. Subject to the provisions of this Act, the President may make an order (in this Act referred to as a "detention order") for the detention for a period not exceeding five years of any person who is a citizen of Ghana if the President is satisfied that the order is necessary to prevent that person from acting in a manner prejudicial to—

      (*a*) the defence of Ghana;
      (*b*) the relations of Ghana with other countries; or
      (*c*) the security of the State.

Restriction order.   2. (1) The President may, in lieu of making a detention order in respect of a person liable to be detained under section 1 of this Act, make an order (in this Act referred to as a "restriction order") restricting the movements of such person for a period not exceeding five years within such place or area as may be specified in the order if in the opinion of the President a detention order would not be

446

suitable on account of the age or health of the person or for any other reason.

(2) A restriction order made restricting the movements of any person may impose such conditions as may be specified in the order in respect of his employment or business, and in respect of his association or communication with other persons.

3. A detention order or a restriction order made in respect of any person may, at any time before the expiration of such order, be extended for a further period not exceeding five years if in the opinion of the President the release of the person detained or the removal of the restrictions imposed on the movements of the person, as the case may be, would be prejudicial to the matters specified in paragraphs (a), (b) or (c) of section 1 of this Act. *Extension of period of detention order or restriction order.*

4. Any person who is detained under a detention order or whose movements are restricted under a restriction order shall, not later than five days from the beginning of his detention or of the restriction of his movements, as the case may be, be informed of the grounds on which he is being detained or his movements are being restricted and shall be afforded an opportunity of making representations in writing to the President with respect to the detention order or the restriction order as the case may be. *Notification of grounds of detention order or restriction order.*

5. An order made in respect of any person under this Act shall constitute an authority to any police officer— *Power of police to arrest, etc.*

    (a) in the case of a detention order, to arrest the person in respect of whom the order is made to be detained at such place as may be specified by the President; and

    (b) in the case of a restriction order, to arrest the person in respect of whom the order is made in order to restrict his movements in accordance with the restriction order.

6. (1) If the President has reason to believe that a person in respect of whom a detention order or a restriction order has been made is attempting to evade arrest, he may by a notice in the *Gazette* direct that person to report to a police officer at such place and within such period as may be specified in the notice. *Attempted evasion of an order.*

(2) If any person in respect of whom a notice has been published under subsection (1) of this section fails to comply with the notice, he shall—

447

(*a*) in the case of a detention order, on being arrested, be detained, during the President's pleasure for a period not exceeding double the period specified in the order; and

(*b*) in the case of a restriction order, be guilty of an offence, and on conviction thereof, shall be liable to imprisonment for a term not exceeding five years.

Termination, variation and suspension of orders.

7. Notwithstanding the preceding provisions of this Act, the President may, by order, at any time before the expiration of a detention order or of a restriction order—

(*a*) terminate such order, or

(*b*) reduce the period of detention or restriction of movements specified therein, or

(*c*) suspend the application of such order to the person to whom it relates either unconditionally or subject to such conditions as the President may determine.

Substitution of a restriction order for a detention order.

8. If the President is satisfied in the case of any person detained in pursuance of a detention order that, in all the circumstances, the restrictions imposed by a restriction order would be more appropriate than such detention the President may in that case substitute a restriction order for the detention order under which such person is detained.

Repeals.

9. The following enactments are hereby repealed—

(*a*) The Preventive Detention Act, 1958 (No. 17);

(*b*) The Preventive Detention (Amendment) Act, 1962 (Act 132);

(*c*) The Preventive Detention (Amendment) Act, 1963 (Act 199).

Savings.

10. Any order made under any enactment repealed by section 9 of this Act and in force immediately before the commencement of this Act shall continue in force as if made under this Act.

INDEX

449